MUHAMMAD, THE WORLD-CHANGER

MUHAMMAD, THE WORLD-CHANGER

AN INTIMATE PORTRAIT

MOHAMAD JEBARA

ST. MARTIN'S
ESSENTIALS
NEW YORK

First published in the United States by St. Martin's Essentials, an imprint of
St. Martin's Publishing Group

MUHAMMAD, THE WORLD-CHANGER. Copyright © 2021 by Mohamad Jebara.
All rights reserved. Printed in the United States of America. For information, address
St. Martin's Publishing Group, 120 Broadway, New York, NY 10271.

www.stmartins.com

Design by Meryl Sussman Levavi

Illustrations by Mohamad Jebara

Library of Congress Cataloging-in-Publication data

Names: Jebara, Mohamad, author.
Title: Muhammad, the world-changer : an intimate portrait / Mohamad Jebara.
Description: First. | New York : St. Martin's Essentials, 2021. | Includes
  bibliographical references and index.
Identifiers: LCCN 2021016104 | ISBN 9781250239648 (hardcover) |
  ISBN 9781250239655 (ebook)
Subjects: LCSH: Muhammad, Prophet, -632—Biography.
Classification: LCC BP75 .J43 2021 | DDC 297.6/3092 [B] —dc23
LC record available at https://lccn.loc.gov/2021016104

Our books may be purchased in bulk for promotional, educational, or business
use. Please contact your local bookseller or the Macmillan Corporate and
Premium Sales Department at 1-800-221-7945, extension 5442, or by email at
MacmillanSpecialMarkets@macmillan.com.

First Edition: 2021

1 3 5 7 9 10 8 6 4 2

CONTENTS

✧

To the Infinite Mystery of Mysteries,
the Great Unseen Force behind all life,
the Illuminating Light of the cosmic
order, the Wise Mentor, and Wondrous
Inspiration of the world-changer

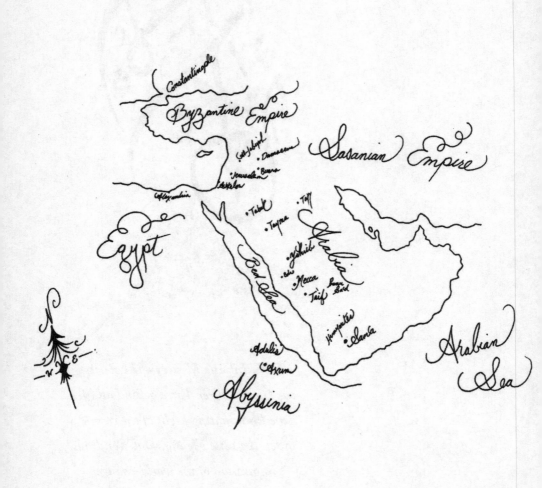

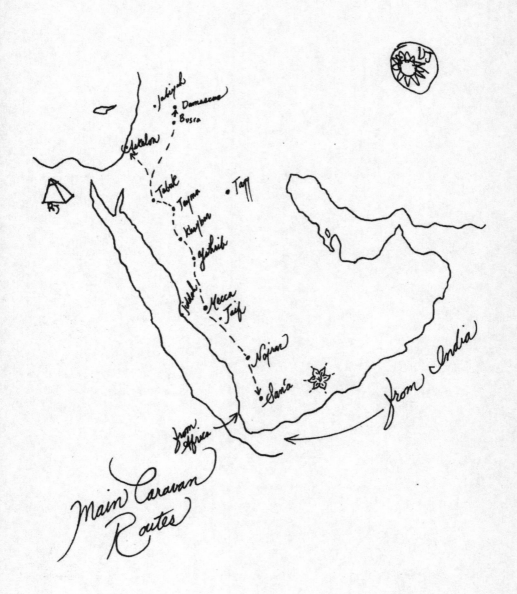

Main Caravan
Routes

AUTHOR'S NOTE

✧

Instructed in the methods of traditional Islamic scholarship yet writing for a popular audience, I had to balance a range of factors to make this biography both grounded in established Islamic sciences and accessible to readers of all backgrounds. My aim has been to harness the wisdom of the *'ulama* (traditional body of Islamic scholars and sages) to provide a humanized understanding of Muhammad and his world.

For ease of readability, I have not included the honorific "peace be upon him" customarily added after the mention of Muhammad's name. Similarly, rather than footnote each fact presented in the text, I have included source documentation at the end of the book.

Arabic transliterations of select consonants (*sirat*, not *zirat*) and vowels (*Musa*, not *Musé*; and *'alaihim*, not *'alaihum*) are based on the Kufic vernacular and *tajwid* (elocution) guidelines of Imam Hafs via 'Asim, which is the popular pronunciation of classical Arabic standardized by the Abbasids in the East (that is, the lands east of Egypt, including the former domains of the Ottomans, Safavids, and Mughals). For certain proper names, I use the standard English rendition: Mecca, not Makkah; Medina, not Madinah; Al-Zahiriya, not Ath-Thahiriyyah; Yemen, not Yaman. Also for ease of readability, I will not accentuate the long vowels or distinct Arabic sounds.

Translation from any ancient language into contemporary English has its challenges. My translations (including Qur'anic passages) draw on the Semitic root meanings of Arabic words, knowledge of what Arabic terms meant in Muhammad's era (many have evolved since then), and narrative context to identify the intended meaning among many potential homonyms. I have tried my best to convey the nuances of the original language without the doctrinal interpretations developed in subsequent centuries (which characterize many standard English translations of Qur'anic verses that try to compete with the King James Bible). Translations are based on combining the connotation of passages across Qur'anic variations, known as the *Qira'at* (expressions, vernaculars). As I explain later, I often use the terms *the Divine* or *Loving Divine* for the Arabic word *Allah*—and *Divine Mentor* or *Cosmic Mentor* for the Arabic *Rabb*.

I calculated the specific timing of key events outlined in the book by cross-referencing details from Islamic scholarship with other historical sources, as well as mapping the Islamic calendar onto the modern Gregorian calendar (with CE standing for Common Era). Certain Arabic words that convey nuances related to timing provided additional evidence. For example, diverse verbs pinpoint the moment of action, including: *asbaha* (at early dawn); *yaghdu* (at late dawn); *ashraqa* (at sunrise); *adh-ha* (in the morning); *zala* (at noon); *thalla* (in the afternoon); *amsa* (in the evening); *bata* (at night); *taraqa* (at midnight); and *raha* (late at night). Clues extracted from language can thus bring remarkable accuracy to events that happened centuries ago.

Finally, as I note in the introduction, Muhammad explicitly instructed that followers focus on his ideas rather than on his life and person. That request, however, was disregarded soon after his death, and the study of his life—*sirah*—emerged as a formal discipline of Islamic scholarship. While this book constitutes one small contribution to that field, I wrote it with mixed feelings, cognizant of the fact that I was invading Muhammad's privacy. Muhammad, the historical and spiritual icon, deserves to be better understood, and I hope he will pardon the intrusion.

MUHAMMAD, THE WORLD-CHANGER

Introduction

❖

MUHAMMAD
BEYOND
STEREOTYPES

Mecca: 10:00 a.m., Friday, March 20, 610 CE

The aroma of fresh spices and frankincense saturated the crisp morning air as a striking figure in red and white navigated Mecca's marketplace filled with shoppers preparing to celebrate the spring equinox.

The man in red and white stood out amid the crowd, his bold garments defying standard tribal classification in a society where clothing functioned as an identity card. Residents of Arabia declared their clan affiliations via the distinct styles, colors, and shapes of their apparel and the arrangement of their headdresses. Yet the man's color combination matched no established tribal look and suggested instead a fusion of identities, including styles from beyond Arabia.

Friday was supposed to be a time of heightened Arab pride. The Meccans called it *yawm-ul-'urubah* (day of Arab-ness). Its weekly observance reflected Arabia's obsession with tribal identity. The market crowd had no idea the man in red and white would one day convert Fridays to *yawm-ul-jumu'ah* (day of inclusion).

Though Arabs of that time lagged behind neighboring empires in literacy and development—Byzantium, Persia, and Abyssinia far outshone

Arabia—pride remained central to Arabs' sense of self. Their legendary code of honor yielded high standards of generosity and trust. In Mecca, no visitor went hungry, as clans fiercely competed to welcome guests, many of them merchants drawn to trade their wares in Mecca because of the locals' reputation for honesty in commercial affairs.

Rainfall had returned at winter's end, and the desert flora had begun to blossom. February's flash floods had subsided, clearing wilderness pathways for local merchants, who would soon depart on the seasonal caravan north to Syria.

Caravans carrying merchandise and pilgrims now converged on the capital city, heading down largely treeless streets past mud-brick buildings toward an asymmetrical cube construction at its center. Known as the Ka'bah (nexus), it housed Arabia's most prized objects: 360 devotional idols. The shrine, Mecca's sole stone building, was managed by priests who permitted only well-dressed wealthy elites inside. Poor pilgrims who could not afford the required fine clothing milled about the Ka'bah naked. Thanks to the man in red and white, the shrine would one day be transformed into an egalitarian gathering point without gatekeepers or idols—and without special clothing required.

Meccans produced no goods of their own for export. Instead, they were trusted middlemen connecting India and East Africa to Byzantium, which craved spices for cooking and frankincense (worth its weight in gold) for Christian rituals.

The man in red and white had many times made the monthlong caravan journey north toward Damascus, transporting his cargo through desolate sands. For most Arab traders, the caravan journey was a mundane business necessity. They passed through foreign cultures without truly expanding their minds. But the man in red and white had keenly observed the world beyond Arabia: speaking with locals, exploring their cultures, and examining how nature functioned in more verdant climates beyond the desert.

A contemplative analyst, he had come to understand that his people's intense pride had deprived them of dynamism. So committed were they to maintaining the ways of their forefathers that they feared any change. Their code of honor entailed not just blind reverence of ancestors but

also scapegoating others, prejudice against women, disdain for the destitute, distrust of foreigners, and a deep fear of innovation.

But Mecca's refusal to change was about to be tested.

Several hundred feet from the Ka'bah, the man in red and white
emerged from the crowd and began to ascend a small mount overlooking the marketplace. The outcropping had a distinct civic function and
a special name: Abu Qubais (short summary site). When pressing news
needed to be shared, it was delivered from this prominent location.

As the man in red and white climbed with confidence, a trail of aromatic myrrh lingered in the air behind him. The market crowd took notice and drew silent. Buyers and sellers paused their haggling to look up.

Six feet tall and broad shouldered, the forty-year-old looked fit. He
appeared youthful yet mature, with captivating dark eyes and bright
white teeth offset by clear olive skin. His hair was shiny, black with a tint
of red, combed into curled locks behind his ears.

Reaching the summit of Abu Qubais, the man took in the scene below: the Ka'bah and the desert, which stretched out beyond the town into
the distance. He paused, then broke his silence. One by one, he called
out to the fourteen great clans of Mecca, each by its name: "Oh Banu
Hashim! Oh Banu Umayyah! Oh most honorable among Quraish!"

Each of the clans recognized the man for his skillful diplomacy, which
less than five years earlier had averted a civil war in Mecca. The winter
flash floods had swept through the city and destroyed the Ka'bah. When
it came time to rebuild the shrine, each clan had sought the honor of
placing the new cornerstone. The heated debate grew to a fever pitch—
until the man took his emerald-green *burdah* (mantle) and placed it under
the would-be cornerstone. Elders from each clan grabbed the sides of the
man's mantle and collectively carried the stone to its intended spot.

Such clever civic mediation cemented the man's reputation as an up-
standing citizen in addition to being one of Mecca's most respected businessmen. Not only had he risen from abject poverty to amass a fortune
with his commercial acumen but he maintained the town's safe depository, keeping valuables secure for other residents when they traveled.

The man in red and white began by evoking his sterling reputation.
"Let me ask you—and you all know me well, for I have lived a lifetime
among you—how have you known me to be in manner and words?"

Responses rang out from the crowd: "*amin*" (trustworthy), "*rahum*" (compassionate), "*karim*" (generous),"*ibnu sayyidi qawmih*" (the descendant of a great chief), " *'athimun shanuka, sadiqul-lisanuk*" (honorable in your manner, truthful in your speech).

The stage set, the man in red and white launched into his *'ardh* (great pitch), chanting precisely articulated Arabic in a sonorous voice, each word rich in expressive meaning. In vivid, florid rhetoric evoking spring blossoming, he called on the people arrayed before him to break free from stagnation and open themselves up to new possibilities.

The marketplace crowd stared in quiet astonishment at his shocking appeal. After a minute of tense silence, a red-headed man with piercing green eyes finally barked, "Damn you oh Muhammad! Is this why you gathered us here?" The crowd, shaking their heads with looks of disdain, dispersed. Some laughed as they walked away, wondering if "Muhammad had lost his senses." A wealthy man like him secluding in a desolate cave on Mount Hira for years, only to return with a strange call to change their ways!

Muhammad was left standing alone on Abu Qubais. The great declaration heralding a new era had seemingly had no impact. What he and the crowd present that March morning could not know was that his declaration would actually change the course of world history, that the bold process of personal transformation extolled from the mount would galvanize millions of people, and that this solitary man on the mount would become one of the most influential people ever.

Over the next twenty-two years, Muhammad would recover from his unsuccessful pitch, repeatedly overcome nearly overwhelming obstacles, and lead a burst of innovation that laid the intellectual mindset for the modern world. He would ultimately return to Mecca, stand before a multitude of 120,000 people, and be heralded as a great world-changer. His bold call to blossom would in the end triumph, echoing down through history until today and inspiring people of all backgrounds to transform themselves and the world.

❖ ❖ ❖

I have lived with Muhammad my entire life: I was given his name the day I was born, yet for years knew nothing about him.

When I was a ten-year-old, growing up in Canada, I found school monotonous, as teachers required learning facts without analysis—just one right answer and no independent discernment. Regurgitating received information did not sit well with me, and I began questioning everything in a kind of preadolescent rebellion.

Meanwhile, the mystery of my Muslim identity loomed in the background. Aside from occasional visits to my city's only mosque and fasting during Ramadhan, I went through the motions of my family's religious traditions without understanding *why*. On the walls in people's homes I observed tapestries depicting a black cube surrounded by what looked like water (only later to find it was a mass of people circumambulating). I assumed it was a water-filtration plant.

During a school camping trip, counselors inquired if I had any special dietary restrictions. I was puzzled by their question. "Your name is Mohamad," they explained, trying to be sensitive. But I had never heard the word *halal* (unrestricted) and had no idea I might be expected to eat differently from other students. Still, I carried the name of Islam's prophet with me everywhere. One time at the park, someone learned my name and joked, "Hey, Mohamad, how's your mountain?" I didn't get it: I liked hiking, but there were no mountains in my city.

One Saturday I flipped to the French-language TV station, which ran a regular cartoon series depicting historical figures. The episode that morning featured a wild character named Mahomet who looked like a pirate. He wielded a sword and killed people in battles. I had no idea this was my namesake until I later found a 1952 edition of Funk & Wagnalls encyclopedia. The tome's "Islam" section included an image of a bearded man carrying a sword and a book. In the background was a black cube set amid evergreen trees (the Ka'bah in Scotland!?) surrounded by men with sabers aloft. Above it a caption read: "Mohammed, founder of Islam, with the sword and the Koran, symbols of his faith."

Could this be the man I was named after? This disturbing image could not be accurate, but I lacked access to any other description aside from elders in my community praising Muhammad to punctuate their Arabic conversations.

Just in time, I came across *The Message*, an English-language film (shot simultaneously in Arabic and released under the title *Al-Risalah*) that originally hit theaters at about the same time as *Star Wars*. Like the George Lucas classic, *The Message* was filmed in North Africa and portrayed an orphan in a strange land embarking on an identity quest and in the process saving the world.

My friends and I devoured the VHS tape of the film, binge-watching the desert epic dozens of times. We were thrilled to be watching a grand cinematic thriller that was part of our tradition. We knew little about our religion's roots, but here was an amazing introduction with stylish costumes, vivid sets, and sweeping panoramas. For the first time I felt a connection to a heritage I could be proud of. Even though Muhammad says nothing in the film and is in fact never depicted—the camera instead shows the world from his vantage point—at last I had an opportunity to see the world through his eyes.

Still, there were two clashing messages: the people of my Muslim culture revered Muhammad as a model of absolute perfection, and my Western popular culture presented him as a wild warrior. I had to resolve the contradiction.

At the suggestion of a neighbor, my quest began at the mosque with a lecture by a visiting scholar. The topic—Muhammad's teachings on hygiene—did not sound auspicious. But the lecturer grabbed my attention by decoding Arabic terms from sayings of the prophet (known as Hadith) and cross-referencing information from various accounts of Muhammad's life. The scholar seemed like a detective: digging through sources to piece together a puzzle, deciphering old words to unlock rich hidden meaning, and pausing throughout to ask the audience what we thought as a way to help guide us toward synthesizing our own conclusions.

I was hooked. Islamic studies became my hobby the way other neighborhood kids took up hockey. Just as they never really expected to play in the National Hockey League, I never expected to become a cleric. But I soon poured all my paper route earnings into bus tickets to after-school Qur'an classes, traveling on weekends to study with visiting scholars from the Middle East, and buying any Arabic grammar book I could find.

Diving down the rabbit hole into the fourteen-hundred-year-old world of Muslim sciences was not always easy. Mastering the correct elocution of Qur`anic Arabic (*tajwid*) proved daunting. I struggled to produce the correct pronunciation of an ancient language foreign to my native English. Once I had to recite a twenty-page Qur`anic segment (*juz`*) from memory as part of my lessons. A minor mistake on the nine-teenth page prompted my instructor to wordlessly tap his thigh, a signal that I had to start over from the beginning.

Finally, at age twelve, I managed to complete my memorization of the Qur`an. But to my surprise, Muhammad's name made only four appearances in his holy book. Learning the Qur`an literally word for word had revealed nothing about him. And while I had memorized the words and their precise pronunciation, I had no clue what they meant. I would devote the next three years to mastering the Arabic language and grammar, which uncovered new layers of meaning yet only raised more questions about the Qur`an's message.

Teachers urged me to be patient—"like a palm tree that may take seventy years to bear fruit." Because I had never seen a palm tree, their metaphor about the value of deferred intellectual gratification did not resonate. Still, I began to develop discipline: pay attention to instruc-tions, memorize accurately, stay organized, and remain prepared.

Finally, one evening, after five years of study, my teacher handed me a new book: Ibnu Hisham's *Siratu Rasulillah*, a ninth-century account of Muhammad's life written by a scholar in Egypt. I consumed the tome in three days while riding the bus, sitting by the local duck pond, and even navigating the hallways at high school. The narrative was fascinating and far more fantastic than I had expected. The author provided few con-crete details about the prophet himself, focusing instead on side stories from the world around him.

My teachers could tell the book had piqued my curiosity yet resolved nothing. They kindly offered another book: At-Tabari's *History of Proph-ets and Kings*, a review of world history by a historian writing in tenth-century Iraq that included a section on Muhammad. At-Tabari provided not only historical context but also different details from Ibnu Hisham. At-Tabari chronicled more detailed conversations Muhammad had with key figures, like his wife's cousin Waraqah, a Christian hermit. At-Tabari also provided background on the world Muhammad was born into, in-cluding, to my surprise, that the city of Medina possessed a large Jewish quarter (not depicted in the film *The Message*) and had been founded by Jewish refugees fleeing the destruction of the Temple in Jerusalem.

Scholars evidently knew a great deal about Muhammad's life and society, yet these details remained scattered across disparate sources. Moreover, the discrepancies between Ibnu Hisham's and At-Tabari's accounts meant that there was no definitive consensus on several details concerning Muhammad. How could this be? Unlike Moses or Jesus, Muhammad had lived in the relatively recent past. Hundreds of people known to historians spent extensive time with him. Surely they must have recorded the remarkable events they witnessed.

Trying to unravel this mysterious absence, I came across a Hadith where Muhammad declared, "Do not glorify me, do not magnify me, and do not praise me as the Christians had done with Jesus, son of Mary, for I am merely a simple mortal." When followers felt intimidated in his presence, he insisted, "I am a simple mortal just like you."

Muhammad, I realized, had purposefully obscured himself. In fact, as Muhammad's cousin 'Ali recounted twenty-five years after the prophet's death: "The messenger of God forbade us from writing anything about him or from him, aside from the Qur'an." Muhammad entreated his followers to focus on the message, not the messenger, so he would not become frozen like an idol. This solved the first part of the mystery: there were few primary sources because Muhammad had forbidden them.

Decades after Muhammad died, a new generation began embellishing the narrative about him. Zealous new converts attributed fabulous miracles to Islam's prophet. Some of Muhammad's closest followers realized it was time to set the record straight. Original associates like 'Urwah ibnuz-Zubair, Ibnu 'Abbas, and Ibnu Mas'ud all composed biographies, yet they soon became lost to history. By 700 CE these texts were already missing, many destroyed during a siege of Mecca and Medina by the Umayyad Empire.

Lacking any eyewitness testimony in written form, scholars had to rely on an oral tradition of vignettes that were not transcribed until a century after Muhammad's death. Identifying the historical Muhammad thus requires sifting through myriad accumulated sources (not all reliable) known as *sirah* (retracing footsteps). *Sirah* comprises hundreds of diverse narratives accumulated over centuries that exist in a kind of dialogue with one another. *Sirah* constitutes an evolving fusion of history and literature that seeks to make sense of Muhammad's life and relevance. The book you are now reading is another chapter in that unfolding discourse.

Each biographical narrative was crafted in a distinct social and political context. The first popular books of *sirah* were produced around 750 CE as distinctive schools of Islamic jurisprudence (*mathahib*) were forming and seeking sources to justify their principles. Biographies from that period recounted stories about Muhammad in a style reflecting specific schools of thought. As writers cannot easily prevent their worldview from naturally coloring their prose (a charge to which I plead guilty in this book), *sirah* writers typically present evidence in a way that makes sense to their contemporary audience.

Political pressures also deeply influence *sirah*. The oldest existing work of *sirah*, "The Chronicles of the Messenger of God," was commissioned by the caliph Al-Mansur as a collection of inspirational stories for his ten-year-old son, Al-Mahdi. A raconteur from Arabia named Ibnu Ishaq was tasked with providing a role model for the caliph's preteen heir. The caliph, who had recently helped lead a massacre of some thirty thousand Umayyads in a coup d'état, hoped to groom his son as a powerful successor. Not surprisingly, Ibnu Ishaq's Muhammad is a valiant conqueror and shrewd statesman. Prominent scholars at the time, such as Medina's Imam Malik, rejected the work as fiction, yet the book remains a founding classic in the field.

By contrast, take the classic *Ash-Shifa* (The Healing), a biographical work by a jurist living in the open multicultural society of twelfth-century Islamic Spain. The compiler, Qadhi (judge) 'Iyadh al-Yahsubi, was clearly a broad-minded soul known for his leniency from the bench. His Muhammad is more an empathetic humanist than a desert warrior. The prophet comes across as smart but not intimidating, welcoming to all, and a self-help exemplar of spiritual growth.

The traditional attitude of Islamic scholars over the centuries has been to prioritize conserving information—even if inconsistent—so that any merit in a text might be extracted by later analysts. Their metaphor for semiproblematic content was a cactus (*sabr*): though prickly and bitter it nonetheless might produce lifesaving water in dire conditions. *Sirah* is thus filled with occasional bizarre details that can make readers cringe. Ibnu Hisham, for instance, in his introduction to an anthology of earlier vignettes, admits to omitting details that "may cause certain people distress."

The books of *sirah* may have once been well organized as a coherent collection in the medieval libraries of Baghdad, Cordova, and beyond. But during the Mongol sack of Baghdad in 1258 CE, hundreds of thousands of manuscripts were tossed into the Tigris River. During the Inquisition, most of Cordova's books were burned in public squares; monks rescued only a few volumes from the inferno for their monastery libraries. Whatever material was salvaged remains scattered across libraries in Europe, Africa, Asia, and the Middle East.

Sirah is thus a shattered field that has never had its shards formally put back together. Once I made sense of this scholarly diaspora of dispersed works, the challenge of finding fragments in unlikely places became a passion. Searching for rare biographies was a bit like scouring used-record stores in the days before iTunes. Once, at a remote rest stop in Syria, I chanced upon a small bookstore with a rare volume by the twelfth-century scholar Ibnu 'Asakir about Muhammad's time in Damascus, including vivid accounts of his interactions with locals. Here was a hidden gem that provided fresh insights on previously obscured aspects of his life.

Under these circumstances, Muhammad's life emerges only as a fragmented mosaic that does not directly depict the main subject. Piecing together an accurate portrait becomes a complex archaeological puzzle. Clues are out there yet often buried under centuries of dust waiting to be rediscovered.

I began my detective work with forty open books scattered across my bedroom floor. One text would cross-reference another, which in turn yielded leads to additional books. I followed the trail across biographers, centuries, and dialects, seeking solid sources amid a swirl of prose. As I assessed raw data, I had no idea where the evidence would point and allowed the information to guide my quest without jumping to conclusions.

So how did I determine which information was credible while sifting through hundreds of accounts of events that transpired more than a millennium ago? Appropriately, Muhammad himself provided a clear three-stage methodology in a classic Hadith on the parable of a bee gathering pollen to process into honey:

✧ Start with a clean slate and gather information from diverse sources without prejudice.
✧ Analyze all the information to determine the parts that can be useful.
✧ Synthesize the remaining evidence in ways that can produce benefit.

I based my standards for assessing data on an analytical system. Arabic vocabulary and expressions not used in Muhammad's time were common red flags, along with references to technology and concepts that did not exist until long after his death. (Imagine a seventeenth-century Puritan speaking like a twenty-first-century California surfer and checking the news on a mobile phone.) When multiple independent sources provided the same detail, a vignette had more validity, unless the sources were copying each other. Archaeological evidence could also help bolster or invalidate narratives. Tracing a vignette to its original appearance helped determine the likelihood that it emerged from eyewitness testimony rather than hearsay.

A particularly egregious example of a specious story is the notorious "Medina Massacre" myth that alleges Muhammad ordered the execution of seven to nine hundred Jewish men on the charge of treason in Medina. Investigation reveals that the earliest source of this legend dates from more than a century after Muhammad's death. Moreover, reliable seventh-century sources relating to extensive construction work at the massacre's supposed mass grave site reveal that no human remains were uncovered, impossible after such a mass killing only a few years earlier. Eminent Islamic scholars (such as Al-Awza'i, Ibnu Hajar Al-'Asqalani, At-Tabari, and many others) rejected the story as a fabrication as it contradicted both the historical record and Muhammad's core values. Finally, it is well known that when Muhammad died five years after the alleged extermination of Medina's Jews, several of his close neighbors were Jewish.

This character assassination leveled against Muhammad reveals that the stakes can be quite high when navigating the uncertain terrain of *sirah*. If Muhammad indeed ordered the slaughter of hundreds of prisoners of war, the information necessarily taints his legacy. If, on the other hand, the vignette is a fabrication from a later political context (in fact, a misappropriation of the Masada story), then analysts must be on guard lest they issue a verdict based on false testimony. Bogus claims have consequences: extremists have invoked the Medina Massacre to justify atrocities, and critics of Islam have invoked it to impugn Muhammad's character.

I have therefore included in this book details of Muhammad's life that I subjected to an extensive analytical process. In fact, cross-referencing sources and researching the historical record is insufficient without also developing expertise in the particular nuances of Muhammad's cultural context. One cannot understand his world without appreciating the information he himself was sifting through on his life journey.

Of critical importance is language, as the Arabic of Muhammad's day differs significantly from today's modern standard Arabic. Take a classic Qur'anic command: "*Turhibuna.*" Modern Arabic would render this injunction: "You shall strike terror into the hearts." Yet the root word, *irhab* (which today does mean "terrorism"), in Muhammad's time was a term for earning respect. Thus, the quote more accurately translates as "You shall influence people by earning their respect." Indeed, the Qur'an speaks of Jews' and Christians' *rahbah* (reverence) for God. When the Qur'an discusses terror, it uses the traditional concept of *irjaf*, meaning "quaking," condemning *murjifun* (terrorizers) for causing people's hearts to quake in horror.

Arabic, like most languages, is filled with homonyms that hold multiple meanings within the same letters. English speakers have to determine, based on context, whether *bar* refers to a chocolate candy, a piece of soap, a pub, a weapon, or a lawyer's guild. Similarly, the Qur'an's first word, *iqra*, could mean "Read!" But given that the context was Muhammad addressing a crowd of mostly illiterate Arabs locked in a state of self-imposed stagnation, the word instead suggests his goal was to inspire purposeful growth. Thus, *iqra* renders as a distinctive homonym: "Blossom forth!"

Further complicating linguistic sleuthing are the many distinct dialects of Arabic spoken across Arabia in Muhammad's era. The same word could have different, sometimes opposite, meanings in different cities. Indeed, scholars have noted the linguistic style of the Qur'an changes after Muhammad moves from Mecca to Medina. Some critics cite this shift as a reflection of Muhammad's rising political fortunes, claiming that the Mecca portion features gentle language, whereas the tone in Medina becomes aggressive as he gains power. In reality, Muhammad astutely tailored his message to local dialects. Due to their ancient, shared heritage, Meccans preferred a few rich words—imbedded with layers of profound nuances—to express complex ideas. The more emotive and multicultural Medinians, conversely, favored a barrage of many explanatory words to express concepts. Trying to understand Meccan chapters via the prism of the Medina dialect—and vice versa—is a fruitless task.

Muhammad also traveled beyond Arabia's borders, carefully tracked news of the clashes between neighboring empires, and sought to learn whatever he could about other cultures from foreign visitors to Arabia. Making sense of the world beyond his local bubble was essential to his efforts to convey his message in a way that could resonate with as large an audience as possible. Delving into Muhammad's linguistic and sociopolitical context enables a richer appreciation of his life and work.

Shining the spotlight on a sacred figure like Muhammad can seem intimidating. Examination might lead to the desecration of a venerated relic, and exploring the unknown might shatter established beliefs. Considering a fresh perspective might provoke harsh reactions.

To those apprehensive about the journey ahead, consider a classic vignette from Muhammad's life. After the aborted pitch at Abu Qubais, the Meccan public continued to reject his message as violating Arabia's most sacred customs. One day Muhammad helped an old lady carry her heavy water jug home from Mecca's well. She did not recognize the man who came to her aid and thanked the seemingly anonymous stranger with a piece of advice: "As you can see, my son, I am a poor woman, so I cannot offer you anything to reward your kindness. But I will give you a word of advice. That man Muhammad has created so much harm, misguiding the youth. Avoid him."

Muhammad gently replied, "I regretfully decline your well-intentioned advice." As he walked away, he added, "Because I am Muhammad!" The next morning, the old lady heard a knock on her door and found a large food basket along with a pouch of silver coins.

The old lady told this story to explain the unusual way Muhammad had inspired her to change. Her testimony should inspire us today to overcome any fears about exploring a sacred figure as a human being.

❖ ❖ ❖

After searching out the human Muhammad in *sirah* books and scholarly discussions for several years, I realized my inquiry required visiting his old stomping grounds. I come from Canada and had never seen a desert in my life. Making the traditional Muslim pilgrimage at age twenty-one was my first exposure to Muhammad's heartland.

As the bus doors opened in Mecca, the smell of diesel and overripe fruits overwhelmed my senses. Welcome to hajj!

Beneath Arabia's pounding sun I learned that even the shade of a tree offered little protection when a gust of hot wind blasted my face as if from an open oven door. Then, during a sudden desert downpour, massive raindrops pelted me with such force that my skin hurt. In seconds, inches of water reached my ankles, and caused massive mudflows. Just as suddenly, the rains subsided, and the water sank into the dry ground as if sucked by a vacuum. Mecca, a city of extreme weather patterns, has a character that lives up to the Arabic meaning of its name, "the skull crusher."

As a North American, I had taken water and trees for granted, and the many Qur'anic references to them had previously gone over my head. On a nine-hour bus ride from Medina through the desert to the Jordanian border, I stared wide-eyed out the window for miles and observed nothing growing, not even a weed. From my air-conditioned luxury coach, I imagined Muhammad walking through the desolate landscape dozens of times on caravan journeys to and from Damascus.

At night, far from the artificial light of cities, the desert unveiled a brilliant sky studded with stars arrayed like diamonds. Not surprisingly, the Qur'an is filled with references to the heavens—including chapters titled *An-Najm* (The Stars), *Al-Buruj* (The Constellations), and *At-Tariq* (The Pulsar)—as well as numerous images of vast openness.

Clearly the environment of Arabia deeply informed both Muhammad's worldview and the language he used to popularize what he referred to as *fikr* (mindset)—a term mentioned eighteen times in the Qur`an. The curl of a wave in a pool of water, a spring bubbling forth, huge droplets making the earth shake—the Qur`an describes all these physical phenomena as reference points to convey abstract ideas for an illiterate people whose understanding of the world was formed in this desert crucible.

As I explored the desert outside Mecca, I observed ancient dried-up riverbeds, massive canyons dotted with fossils of shellfish once abundant in Arabia. These clearly caught the eye of Muhammad, who revealed his desire to see "Arabia green as it had once been before, with verdant meadows and flowing rivers." To Muhammad, the disappearance of waterways signaled untapped potential.

Recovering Arabia's latent natural and human potential required an entrepreneurial mindset—something Muhammad likely learned in his early caravan travels to Damascus. The city's Semitic name, Damashq (quickly built up), reflects its status as the world's first and oldest planned metropolis.

As a young adult, I decided to follow Muhammad to Damascus, even studying at the city's ancient Umayyad mosque. My instructors included Shaikh Muhammad Sukkar and Shaikh 'Abdur-Razzaq al-Halabi, senior Qur`anic scholars whose line of teachers stretched back directly to Muhammad via chains of eminent scholars.

Damascus, a place of transformation, is where Sha'ul (Saul) became Paul, influencing the spread of the Christian Church. The Umayyad mosque itself had at one time been shared for over eighty years by Muslims and Christians as a hybrid cathedral-mosque. The building had served as a temple for the Persians, Greeks, and Romans before becoming a church. As I sat in the courtyard, I noticed evidence of repeated transformations etched in the building's mélange of stones: Roman carvings on one block, Persian designs on another, and so on.

Muhammad had gazed upon this tapestry of reinvention using the building blocks of the past, a visual depiction of the city's age-old cycle of entrepreneurship. As he later declared, "I am but a single stone within a house where each previous prophet and sage contributed his own unique stone." Only in Damascus did I understand the nuance of this Hadith and its emphasis on a mosaic of unique individuals complementing one another.

I also discovered the medieval Al-Zahiriyah Library in the Old City. Filled with many ancient manuscripts, the library was a hidden treasure amid the cobblestone alleys. It captivated me with its old leather-bound books, austere wood shelves, and intimate reading spaces. The archives revealed numerous gems of long-buried information about the prophet's day-to-day interactions with people. These humanizing vignettes about Muhammad helped crystallize the portrait I had been refining in my mind.

In essence, I came to see Muhammad as a world-changing entrepreneur operating across a remarkably wide range of fields. He did this in spite of—or perhaps because of—a lifelong struggle to overcome daunting obstacles in a frozen society. These forced him to confront the pain of stagnation on a deeply personal level and compelled him to adopt a relentless commitment to dynamic flow.

The more I considered his unique story, the more Muhammad's life seemed relatable to people living in the twenty-first century. After making a fortune as a rags-to-riches serial entrepreneur, Muhammad devoted the second half of his life to popularizing knowledge and making it accessible to the masses. When his initial pitches failed (as at Abu Qubais), he had to pivot to new prototypes that might resonate better with resistant audiences. His efforts attracted a group of angel investors and early adopters, a rare mix of successful entrepreneurs unhappy with the status quo and society's most underprivileged, desperate for new opportunities.

Eventually, Muhammad found in Medina a pilot site for implementing his civic vision and became a prolific civic builder who transformed the city with irrigation canals, sanitation systems, community centers, and even a constitution for shared governance. His enormous success in Medina threatened Arabia's entrenched monopolies. At first the competition tried to buy him out, but Muhammad's refusal to retire drove them to seek his annihilation.

With his new movement suddenly under literal siege, Muhammad had to operate in an entirely new arena: military strategy. Though he and his cohorts were outnumbered, Muhammad quickly pioneered bold strategies that led to victories with minimal bloodshed and ultimately resulted in his becoming the unifier of Arabia's scattered tribes.

Indeed, the last two years of Muhammad's life saw his message spread widely, setting the stage for it to become a major world religion. At the same time, the humble founder eschewed the spotlight, appointing a talented teenage protégé to take the reins as Mecca's chief cleric and another teenager as Arabia's top general. Committed to his new meritocratic system, Muhammad chose not to appoint a successor—a principled yet fateful decision that would leave his legacy open to exploitation.

Key to his success was the mindset he championed. An optimist, Muhammad constantly sought new solutions to surmount obstacles and promote *yusr* (flow). He also insisted that people make the most of their limited time on earth, observing that "the beginning of time is serenity (*ridhwan*), the middle of time is optimism for a better future (*rahmah*), and the end of time is accountability (*'afw*)." The first mechanical clocks, produced in Syria in the eleventh century, prominently displayed this quotation in elaborate calligraphy.

Muhammad's innovative mindset produced key concepts that helped start the ninth-century Muslim renaissance and later the sixteenth-century European Renaissance. These include the precursor to the scientific method he pioneered to work through problems; a social order based on meritocracy, not bloodlines; a commitment to conserving the natural environment; a free market, which encouraged the flow of wealth and avoided stagnant hoarding; a code of ethics in war; and, of course, unbridled monotheism as inspiration for self-improvement.

Muhammad's key insight was that what we today call "modernity"—innovative meritocracy with open inquiry, individuality, and opportunity—derives primarily from mentality, not superior technology or natural resources. This book chronicles the evolution of his thinking.

While the market crowd at Abu Qubais laughed off Muhammad's pitch and retreated to their stagnant safe spaces, he persevered and ultimately pioneered innovative thinking that has indelibly shaped the modern world. The epilogue assesses that legacy and briefly explores how individuals might harness it in their own lives.

Let the journey begin.

PART I

⬦

ROOTS
OF THE
MINDSET

1

A UNIQUE NAME

Burdened with a Bold Mission

Mecca: Dawn, Monday,
April 21, 570 CE

Without fresh dates the woman in labor could bleed to death.

As soon as 'Abdul-'Uzza received word after midnight that his sister-in-law was in labor, he had sent a horseman rushing to the nearby town of Ta`if to fetch fresh dates from the local groves. The dates had to be picked at once to maintain the potency of their juicy nectar. The midwives of Mecca relied on an elixir of fresh unrefined date juice to stimulate uterine contractions, helping to push the baby through the birth canal quickly and protect the mother from excessive bleeding.

Now 'Abdul-'Uzza was frantic, as the birth could come at any moment. The next hour would determine whether mother and child would survive the precarious delivery. Pacing in the courtyard doorway, he anxiously surveyed the horizon. As dawn broke, a cloud of dust arose in the distance. Then, a veiled horseman emerged, galloping through Mecca's southern pass to deliver his emergency package: twenty succulent dates known as *rutab* (luscious).

Thuwaibah, a young enslaved Greek woman, stood by the door with an earthen clay platter. 'Abdul-'Uzza grabbed the package from the horseman and quickly poured its contents onto the plate. Thuwaibah, known for her speed and agility, sprinted out of her master's courtyard with the date platter.

Zigzagging through narrow alleyways, Thuwaibah dodged pecking hens and young shepherds and their sheep on their way to grazing grounds outside the city. She dashed past women carrying cloth-covered dough, as the aroma of freshly baking barley bread blended with the fragrance of acacia wood crackling in Mecca's ovens.

Living up to her name (bearer of gifts), Thuwaibah tightly clutched the plate as she wove between women balancing clay water jars on their heads outside the Zamzam Well, Mecca's main freshwater source. In the Ka'bah shrine beside the well, white-clad priests with shaven heads and emerald-encrusted gold amulets lit frankincense. Burning the precious spice marked a new-day thanksgiving offering to the city's 360 crudely carved idols.

Thuwaibah's master had much at stake. If the lady in labor did not birth a son, he—as the brother of her recently deceased husband—could be expected to sire a male heir on his brother's behalf. If her labor failed, it would mark yet another tragedy for a family still reeling from a terrible loss.

As she passed the Ka'bah, Thuwaibah descended the Marwah hill, running faster down the incline toward the simple three-room mud-brick house. Inside, a frail baby made his own tenuous journey through the darkness of his mother's birth canal toward the early morning light. Awaiting him was a world laden with challenges and obstacles—a world he would soon be tasked with changing.

❖ ❖ ❖

Throughout his life, Muhammad remained deeply conscious that he had nearly never been born.

Every Monday, he would refrain from eating and drinking during daylight hours. When asked why he fasted, Muhammad replied, "That was the day on which I was born." In sixth-century Arabia, many people did not even know the year of their birth, let alone the day of the week. Yet Muhammad not only held on to this fact, he reminded himself of it every week.

The details of Muhammad's unlikely birth were well known to him, thanks to the eyewitness testimony of his lifelong foster mother, Barakah. When Thuwaibah burst through the door of the delivery room at dawn on that Monday morning, it was Barakah who took the date platter from her and passed it to the midwife.

Like Thuwaibah, Barakah was a slave. She had been abducted as a child in Abyssinia, ripped from her elite family and sold into bondage thousands of miles from home. Muhammad's grandfather 'Abdul-Muttalib purchased her as a gift for his beloved son 'Abdullah. But 'Abdullah had died just two months earlier, leaving Barakah to take care of her widowed mistress, Aminah.

In the lantern-lit delivery room, Aminah lay on the floor atop a palm-fiber mattress. The frail twenty-year-old struggled to push the baby out. At her side, an experienced midwife named Ash-Shifa (healing) took the fresh dates and squeezed their juices into Aminah's mouth, smearing her lips and urging her to swallow. From the other side, Barakah poured water from a flask into Aminah's mouth to help wash down the date juice as the woman struggled to drink amid painful contractions.

No one expected Aminah to live. Tension filled the room as the three attendants braced for what they expected would be the last moments of this poor woman's life and hoped at least to avoid a stillbirth. Lingering unspoken was the misfortune Aminah had endured over the past few weeks.

Less than a year after marrying her childhood sweetheart, Aminah had bid 'Abdullah farewell as he departed on his trading trip to the Mediterranean port of Ashkelon, hundreds of miles to the northwest. Every morning Aminah stood with Barakah on the outskirts of Mecca awaiting the return of 'Abdullah's caravan while a growing baby kicked inside her. At last, on February 15, the women sighted a lone rider advancing on the horizon wearing 'Abdullah's distinctive indigo cloak—another gift from his father. Drawing near, the horseman uncovered his face; he was Aminah's cousin Sa'ad.

"Where is 'Abdullah?!" Aminah cried. Barakah watched as Sa'ad broke the news of 'Abdullah's unexpected death from the plague during the caravan trip. Aminah's knees buckled as she fainted.

For two weeks, a heartbroken Aminah cried on Barakah's shoulder. Fearing that the trauma would induce a miscarriage, Barakah tried to sooth her mistress, who struggled to eat. As the two young women huddled at dusk in a dimly lit room, Aminah's brother-in-law Al-'Abbas dashed into the room to warn them that an Abyssinian general was marching up from Yemen to besiege Mecca with a massive army headed by thirteen colossal war elephants. Barakah had to escort her feeble mistress through treacherous terrain to a refuge on a mountaintop outside the city. When the siege subsided several weeks later, the beleaguered Aminah returned to her bedroom even frailer than before.

In her weakened condition, Aminah could sense mounting pressure from 'Abdullah's family, who expected her to deliver a male heir. Her in-laws were no ordinary Meccan family. 'Abdul-Muttalib was the city's chief elder, and 'Abdullah had been his favorite among seventeen children. The entire city awaited the outcome of her pregnancy.

Amid all this stress, Aminah was without the support of her own family. She was an only child and not a Meccan native but rather a recent transplant from the distant oasis of Yathrib. Her parents remained several hundred miles away, oblivious of their daughter's tragic condition.

Aminah pushed with every ounce of her remaining strength. Against all odds, she suddenly heard the cries of a baby, delivered into the capable hands of Ash-Shifa. The baby was frail, but he had made it. 'Abdullah had a male heir!

Barakah immediately took the boy and bathed him in a basin of warm water she had prepared with myrrh and sage. She patted him dry with a cotton cloth, then wrapped him in an emerald-green silk shawl, a gift from his grandfather, who had ordered it from Persia to serve as an omen that the baby might lead a comfortable life. Barakah handed the infant to Aminah, who cradled the boy with tears in her eyes.

Thuwaibah rushed out of the room to herald the news. She sprinted through the alleyways to Mecca's main square and rushed up to 'Abdul-Muttalib, who was sitting outside the Ka'bah with a group of city elders. "It's a boy!" she gushed, before dashing off again to her master's house.

Overjoyed at the great news, a beaming 'Abdul-'Uzza declared, "Thu-waibah, you are now a free woman!"

Meanwhile, 'Abdul-Muttalib had immediately set off to meet his new grandson. In the home of his late son, he approached his daughter-in-law, who was still lying on the mattress. Aminah struggled to raise the baby toward his grandfather. Barakah stepped in to pass the infant to him. 'Abdul-Muttalib lifted the boy and gazed at him silently. 'Abdul-Muttalib, as Mecca's leading elder, had named hundreds of the city's newborns over the years, but now it was time to name the surviving grandson who would carry on the lineage of his beloved 'Abdullah.

After a long pause, 'Abdul-Muttalib looked into the boy's eyes and declared, "I name him 'Muhammad'!"

The midwives turned in shock. They had never heard this name before. The women were confused by an archaic Semitic root, H-M-D, not commonly used in Mecca, and asked, "Why did you choose a new name?"

'Abdul-Muttalib explained, "I named him 'the exemplary role model' so that his example would be exulted in the highest places and his name would come to be known among the nations."

The women responded with joyful ululations welcoming little Muhammad into the world.

The midwives did not ask 'Abdul-Muttalib to elaborate on the meaning and origins of his unusual choice. The root H-M-D describes someone standing on an elevated platform who demonstrates actions to be emulated by onlookers. The quality of his example is so impressive that it inspires other people, such as a master carpenter modeling how to shape wood into beautiful designs for eager apprentices.

In naming his grandson, 'Abdul-Muttalib not only revived this archaic term but placed it in a grammatical form with an M at the beginning. The prefix transformed the root action described from something finite to something timeless. Rather than a onetime action, Muhammad describes a constant state of doing, perpetually inspiring desire in others to emulate his example.

The name did not come out of thin air. As the Qur'an would later explain about Muhammad, "they can find him written in the Jewish Scriptures." The Old Testament uses the root H-M-D sixty-five times, with the plural form, *Mahamadim*, appearing in the Song of Songs (5:16) and "*M'hamudeha*" in the Book of Lamentations (1:7)—not to mention *tehmod* (covet, or desire) in the Ten Commandments. 'Abdul-Muttalib had fashioned a new biblical name for his grandson—reflecting his own maternal roots in the city of Yathrib, where he had spent the first eight years of his life with his mother's Jewish family.

'Abdul-Muttalib created the moniker not to honor but to challenge his grandson: be great to help others be great. His name would serve as a reminder—both to others and to himself—of his lifelong mission. The name had action built into it, a dynamic of perpetual striving.

'Abdul-Muttalib returned his grandson to Aminah's arms. He grabbed a moist date from the platter and squeezed its juicy contents onto Muhammad's lips, a ritual called *tahnik* (consecration, initiation). Then he let mother and baby rest for an hour.

Later, with the morning sun shining, 'Abdul-Muttalib stepped out of the house with his new grandson wrapped in the shawl. As the chief walked through Mecca's streets toward the Ka'bah, the crowds parted and looked on with concern: Was there a live or dead baby in the shawl? Rumor had spread that both mother and child had died. The citizens of Mecca had come to offer their condolences.

'Abdul-Muttalib ascended the seven stairs leading up to the only entrance to the black cube. At the top, he slowly turned, raising his hands and the baby toward the sky. Beaming at the child's face, he declared, "This is my son, a gift from heaven, born in honor, a source of coolness to my liver and soothing to my eyes." The Meccan crowd understood the liver as the symbolic container of intense emotions. 'Abdul-Muttalib was acknowledging that beneath his stoic exterior he had been devastated by the loss of his beloved son. The grandfather's rare moment of public candor only heightened the joy shining from his face.

Then, 'Abdul-Muttalib added, "I have named him Muhammad!" Murmurs of confusion arose. What was that name? It sounded foreign. 'Abdul-Muttalib could see their puzzled looks, so he repeated his earlier explanation to the midwives.

Sixty years later, the newborn he now held would return as an adult to Mecca after years in exile and stand on the same top step of the

Ka'bah. In the crowd would be some of the same people who had witnessed the first public declaration of his name—only now the name was
known among nations. Closing a circle, Muhammad would declare, "I
am the son of 'Abdul-Muttalib!"

✦ ✦ ✦

All of Mecca's elite families with male babies stood in a line in the city's
main square beside the Ka'bah. Each mother clutched her child, with
each father standing behind, a hand on his wife's shoulder. The babies
were all freshly bathed, rubbed with aromatic spices to enhance their
appeal, and decked out in their finest clothing. A parade of women from
the Banu Sa'd clan passed along the line of families, inspecting each
child's face and assessing each father's wealth.

This was a semiannual matchmaking ritual that was centuries old.
Mecca's elite wanted to strengthen their children's cultural identity by
entrusting them to the Bedouins, one of Arabia's few remaining nomadic clans, for several years of an immersive desert survival experience.
The children would also learn a pure form of Arabic from the clan, one
of the few that spoke it. For the Banu Sa'd nomads, temporarily adopting a city child offered the promise of a hefty honorarium. Breastfeeding
the infants also solidified symbolic family ties to Arabia's elite clans, a
valuable form of protection and insurance in the event of famine.

Twenty families stood in a line, each hoping the strongest women
would choose their child for the desert surrogacy. Aminah stood among
them, clutching her son with mixed emotions.

Muhammad had struggled to grow in the first months of life. His
best chance of survival would be to spend time with a hearty Bedouin
wet nurse in the healthy desert air, away from the diseases brought to
Mecca by foreign traders. But that meant Aminah would have to give up
her precious only child after just a few months together.

The Banu Sa'd women did not know what to make of this single
mother and her feeble infant. 'Abdul-Muttalib stood behind Aminah as
her sponsor. The nomads noted the absence of a father and assumed a
grandfather would be a less generous benefactor. One by one, nineteen
Bedouin women passed by Muhammad, shaking their heads and hands

in a gesture of rejection. Barakah, standing to the side, watched with concern as each child was quickly paired with a foster mother, who took the baby in her arms and rode off with him into the desert.

Aminah, Muhammad, and 'Abdul-Muttalib were soon left standing in the square alone as all the other boys headed off. Barakah approached Aminah and embraced her in consolation. Suddenly, 'Abdul-Muttalib exclaimed, "Ah, look! One more woman is approaching." In the distance, a Bedouin woman on a bedraggled she-donkey (*atan*) trudged toward the Ka'bah with her husband struggling to pull the beast forward. Aminah and Barakah exchanged worried glances.

Halimah—whose name means "repressed temper"—was accompanied by her husband, Al-Harith (the harvester of souls, which was also used as a nickname for fierce lions). Halimah inspected the infant and frowned. "The weak boy will be a burden," she argued. "Besides, we won't get much money for all the extra trouble of caring for him." She turned to catch up with the caravan of departing women.

"We've come all this way already," Al-Harith interjected. "How often have we seen barren deserts bloom after rainfall? Perhaps our family may be the very drops that can rejuvenate the boy. Who knows, he may bear us great fruit one day."

Slightly embarrassed to go back on her initial decision, Halimah nonetheless turned around and silently took the baby from Aminah's arms. Aminah bent over to kiss Muhammad's forehead as a tear rolled down her cheek and dripped onto her son's face. She wept as she watched Muhammad disappear over the horizon with his new foster family.

Baby Muhammad stared out at the unfolding scene, his first trip beyond the confines of Mecca. The entourage of Banu Sa'd women descended into a desolate valley east of the city that was dotted with hundreds of black goat-hair tents. The stench of goats, manure, bitter herbs, and weeks-old sweat permeated the air. Women, men, and children sporting distinctive tribal tattoos, their hair styled to resemble horns, wandered among the tents. The sound of amulets rattling to ward off evil spirits rung from the camp amid the distant occasional hiss of snakes and scorpions.

The Banu Sa'd represented a rare vestige of the ancient Semitic nomadic life. The clan was constantly on the move, never resting in one spot for more than a few months at a time.

Like most ancient nomadic cultures, the Banu Sa'd functioned like a matriarchy. While men provided protection against external threats, women ran the clan's internal affairs: managing livestock, supervising children, weaving tent fabric, preparing meals, gathering wood and water, and handling the clan's communal coffers. As he descended into the camp, little Muhammad might have noticed, amid the sea of black tents, a solitary bright red tent in the center. Here the Banu Sa'd women's council gathered in formal session. Muhammad spent many days sitting on Halimah's lap as she participated in the council's deliberations.

In his first months with the Banu Sa'd, Muhammad went everywhere with Halimah. She tied him to her back with a linen strap dyed red with the juices of desert berries. The crimson carrier stood out against the tan desert landscape, enabling Halimah to find him quickly when she set him down while she worked. Once he was strong enough to walk, he toddled behind her carrying a water pitcher that he would fill at local wells and drag back to the campsite as she carried a jug on her head.

Halimah nursed Muhammad until he turned two. He was now a robust child, thanks to a regular diet of fresh camel milk, dried dates, wild bananas, honey, berries, and bitter herbs paired with fresh air. In a formal weaning ceremony, Halimah repeated 'Abdul-Muttalib's *tahnik* ritual, rubbing Muhammad's lips with date juice to symbolize his transition to a child with responsibilities and chores.

His first task was literally a cliff-hanger: he was suspended over a 150-foot drop to harvest honey from bees' nests nestled in cliffside crevices. The bees built their nests along the sheer cliffs precisely to protect them from predators. Young boys with small hands were lowered down to stick their fingers inside to extract the honeycombs.

Two-year-old Muhammad was strapped to palm fiber ropes secured around his legs and arms. With a clay pitcher in one hand and a burning piece of acacia wood in the other, he was cantilevered over the cliff top. If the rope broke, he was done for. The men slowly released the rope, lowering Muhammad along the rock face until he reached the nests.

Muhammad then blew out the flame and inserted the smoking stick into the nest. After the smoke tranquilized the bees, Muhammad tossed away the acacia wood, watching its slow fall into the valley below. He then reached his bare hand into the hole and slowly pulled out sections of honeycomb, placing each piece gingerly in the clay pitcher in his other hand. He purposely left behind part of the honeycombs. Once the pitcher was filled, he signaled to the men above and was gradually raised back to the top.

The bees gave him an early education: They gathered pollen from diverse sources and refined it in their honeycombs to produce a sweet liquid that the nomads used for healing wounds and enhancing their cuisine. The honey's hue and taste differed in each location, reflecting the unique pollen of local wildflowers. The bee, moreover, was peaceful, fighting off threatening invaders only in self-defense and as a last resort.

In addition to learning by observing nature up close, Muhammad first began to speak under Halimah's tutelage. She would take Muhammad in the evening to the campfire, setting him alongside her daughter Huthafah (the eradicator), his foster sister and a primary source of information about this early formational period of his life. They would sit beneath a canopy of stars listening to the clan's elders tell stories of their ancestors and share age-old wisdoms. These nighttime gatherings captivated Muhammad's imagination, and he would later use vivid parables to teach lessons to groups sitting in a *halaqah* (circle).

The nomadic culture left the young boy in awe. He would later observe that the nomads' only constant was change, and he marveled at their remarkable adaptability. Every time the wind blew, the desert landscape shifted. Every night the stars rotated in the sky. In an environment of absolute freedom, the nomads had to both improvise and rely on collective cooperation to navigate through the wilderness.

Yet Muhammad was also troubled by the Banu Sa'd's lack of destination. They rarely formed lasting loyalties to any land or people. That was why settled Arabs would often ask the Banu Sa'd to serve as neutral arbitrators and mediators.

After three years in the desert, Muhammad had grown into a hearty boy. The clan marked his maturation by entrusting him with shepherding their greatest asset: the vast herd of goats. Each morning, Muhammad and a group of thirty other boys (ranging in age between three and thirteen) would take hundreds of goats to graze several miles from the camp. They split into pairs to cover the perimeter of the herd, which was spread out over several acres. Accompanied by trained dogs, the boys protected the goats from predators with sticks and slingshots.

One morning, when Muhammad was paired with his foster brother 'Abdullah, he noticed a stray goat wandering away over a nearby hill. He called out that he would pursue the goat, and 'Abdullah watched as Muhammad disappeared. But it soon became clear that something was amiss. Muhammad did not return. 'Abdullah scampered up the hill. As he reached the top, he saw two men dressed in Himyarite garb struggling with Muhammad. The little boy was fighting back valiantly.

'Abdullah called to the older boys for help. They followed him, their daggers raised and glinting in the sun. Seeing the group of boys in hot pursuit, the men tossed the now-unconscious Muhammad to the ground and sprinted off. The shepherd boys carried Muhammad back to the encampment. His chest was bleeding where the men had struck him; he would bear a permanent scar.

That evening, Halimah and Al-Harith listened in horror as 'Abdullah described the encounter. They had originally promised Aminah that they would keep Muhammad until he turned five but could not entertain the thought of losing a child entrusted to their care. Muhammad, they decided, must be returned the next day to his family in Mecca. His nomadic childhood was over.

❖ ❖ ❖

Compared with flimsy desert tents, the stone Ka'bah was massive. Luxurious tapestries from Persia, Egypt, and Yemen hung from its roof. Mecca's only stone structure seemed to soar, a monument to its grandeur as the Arabs' ancestral capital. According to tradition, it was the patriarch Abraham who had built it thousands of years earlier. Muhammad stared at it as he rode into Mecca seated behind Al-Harith on a donkey.

Outside the Ka'bah's northwestern wall, Mecca's elders sat in a semicircle reserved for them. Called Hijr-Isma'il (Sanctum of Ishmael), it marked the burial spot of Abraham's firstborn. A low horseshoe-shaped wall cordoned off the elders' traditional meeting spot. Twenty elders sat with their backs against the wall, while Muhammad's grandfather, as chief elder, sat on a red cushion against the Ka'bah.

'Abdul-Muttalib leapt up when he saw his grandson and Al-Harith. "Why the sudden visit?" he asked, before catching himself. Meccan code required upholding Abraham's legendary hospitality. "I'm forgetting my manners," he apologized. He ordered servants to prepare a great feast of precious camel meat for his honored guests and called for the city's premier poets to entertain them with epic tales of Arabian ancestors and long-lost empires. Over dinner, Al-Harith explained Muhammad's sudden return, and 'Abdul-Muttalib compensated him generously with a large purse of gold coins.

Aminah was ecstatic when 'Abdul-Muttalib knocked on her door that evening to reunite mother and child. She embraced Muhammad as the four-year-old wiped away her tears of joy. Barakah had not seen her smile so radiantly since before her husband's death. The next morning, Aminah and Barakah drew a hot bath for Muhammad, scrubbing away years of desert dirt with olive oil soaps imported from Syria. They gently applied honey to his chest wound.

Then Aminah took her son out for a walk to acquaint him with the city of his birth. After years among the nomads, Muhammad observed Mecca with the critical distance of an outsider. Whereas the Banu Sa'd were constantly moving and adapting, the Meccans emphasized permanence and stability. Families he encountered had lived in the same home for generations, with each clan living in its own designated neighborhood. The city's market square was similarly divided into specific plots based on ancestral claims.

The phrase "It's always been like this" constantly popped up in conversation as a source of pride. Meccans, Muhammad quickly realized, did not like change.

Freed from the chores of nomadic life, Muhammad used his newfound leisure to make friends and play, which he had never done before. He liked to roam the streets with his friend 'Umair, making shapes with twigs and pebbles. One day they went to the market with 'Umair's father, who, like most Meccan men, carried a six-inch idol fashioned out of mashed dates.

'Umair's father instructed his son, "Guard our deity while I shop." Yet the boy soon grew hungry and could not resist the dates, quickly gobbling up the idol. Fearing his father's wrath, 'Umair ran home to grab dates from the family storage shed and quickly fashioned a new idol. He returned to the market and presented the idol to his proud father, who promptly placed it on a ledge and prostrated himself before it. "Thank you for protecting my son!"

Muhammad had witnessed some casual idol veneration among the Banu Sa'd, but the Meccans' devotion struck him as comical and illogical. Everyone in Mecca revered their ancestor Abraham and knew he had worshipped one God called Allah, the same God their cousins the Jews worshipped. What young Muhammad could not understand was how the Arabs had lost their connection to that heritage and replaced it with idolatry.

A thousand years before Muhammad was born, the Arabs had begun to sense that their connection to Abraham was eroding. A Meccan elder, 'Amr ibn Luhayy, traveled to Mesopotamia—Abraham's birthplace—and returned with an idol, Hubal (gateway to the great spirit), declaring the statue represented Abraham's wisdom. Hubal—a human figurine carved of red agate with two pearls for eyes and a solid gold right arm—was, ironically, the same deity Abraham had spared when he smashed the idols at his father's shop. Priests from Mesopotamia soon followed, promoting a cult of venerating statues as representatives of tribal ancestors who could serve as intermediaries with Abraham's God. Allah by this time had become obscure and distant, a mere name devoid of meaning or intimacy.

If Allah was like a far-off uninterested king, the ancestor idols served as local governors who could manage the Arabs' affairs. The Ka'bah, which had originally been a bare shrine dedicated to monotheistic worship and accessible to all people, was filled with idols and open only to powerful elites. Tribes from across Arabia had once made an annual pilgrimage to Abraham's shrine to reconnect with the Divine and with people of other lands. In the new system, pilgrimage became superficial and commercialized tourism: rubbing one's tribal idol, buying souvenir idol amulets and talismans.

The Meccans had seen flourishing Arabian kingdoms rise to prominence only to attract foreign invasion and annihilation. The magnificent but abandoned temples carved out of solid rock by Nabateans in northern Arabia testified to this fate. Their once grand and boastful city called

Raqmu (deep impression) became the abandoned Petra (annihilated—from al-Batra, those who are cut off). No male descendants survived to carry on the Nabateans' name and remember the ancestors.

With no concept of an afterlife, the Arabs needed to be remembered by their descendants in order to have a legacy. The Arabic word for male, *thakar*, means "one who remembers," while *untha* (female) means "bearer of praiseworthy heritage."

Afraid of being wiped out and forgotten, Arabia's elders had centuries earlier convened at Mecca during the pilgrimage season to adopt a policy of *taqlim* (pruning). Poets of the time preserved their reasoning: "Allowing a tree to grow uncontrollably will make it noticeable and thus a target. Limiting society's growth will keep it healthier and safer." They decided to protect their capital by restricting Mecca's growth. Indeed, in Muhammad's childhood only six thousand people lived permanently in the compact city.

To mislead would-be invaders, the Arabs gave inverted names to their most prized cities. They rationalized that no king would be tempted to invade Makkah (skull-crusher) or its second name, Bakkah (eye-gouger). They called fertile lands Hadhramawt (place of imminent death) and Ma`rib (ripper of orifices)—while they named barren landscapes 'Adn (garden of delight) and Riyadh (lush gardens with cool flowing rivers).

Similarly, they gave their sons terrifying names to ward off both evil spirits and potential enemies. Popular names included 'Umar (life-taker), Mus'ab (inflictor of agonizing suffering), Mu'awiyah (fierce bitch), 'Uthman (viper), Hatim (calamity), Hashim (pulverizer), Sufyan (double-edged sword), Hafs (hyena), Khalid (invincible), Hamzah (stalking lion), Hydar (attacking lion), Asad (guarding lion), Layth (roaring lion), Fahd (panther), and Kilab (hounds of hell).

In addition to scaring off foreign invaders, the Arabs scared themselves from innovating or risk taking, construing both as mortal threats to Arab identity.

Insulated by fear, people put their faith in superstition. They called ravens "bearers of bad omens." In the streets of Mecca, young Muhammad constantly heard people exclaiming "*Tiyarah!*" (bad omen—literally, It's the bird's fault!) to explain their misfortune. Muhammad once observed a merchant call off his expedition after a raven landed atop merchandise already packed on the back of a camel. The bird's mere appearance was sufficient warning.

In a way, the Arabs' system worked: no foreigners invaded Mecca to force taxes or new languages on them. As once-mighty empires crumbled around them, the Meccans remained untouched. "Better illiterate and free than a literate slave," the elders rationalized. Preserving themselves at all costs required consciously choosing to stagnate. Sensitive young Muhammad quickly noted this contradiction: A people who presented themselves as magnificent heirs had instead squandered their ancestral heritage; it was a grand edifice with a rotting core.

As an adult, Muhammad would name Arabia's willfully stagnant state *Jahiliyyah*. Connoting "ignorance," the word's root, *J-H-L*, describes a potter reusing an old mold—even after it had worn down—simply to avoid having to create a new one.

Jahiliyyah conveys a mindset of accepting inherited traditions without question. The Qur'an describes *Jahiliyyah* as confining. It cautions against "reverting to the stagnant ways of the past by acting with a haughty air of superiority, as if defensively isolated in a secluded fortress."

Mecca, of course, was only metaphorically walled off. Merchants from Africa, Persia, Byzantium, Egypt, and beyond flowed through the city's markets. There was religious tolerance, and some Arabs even converted to Christianity and Judaism (as long as you did not defy Arabian social order or belittle the ancestors, your religion did not matter). Yet some Meccan parents so feared foreign traders might corrupt their children's Arabic that they stuffed cotton in the ears of their offspring—though Aminah never did this to Muhammad. As people who made a living by exchanging goods, Meccans embodied the mercantile mentality of middlemen, which only exacerbated *Jahiliyyah* attitudes. Meccans produced nothing and feared that any changes to the goods they transported could reduce their value. They lived off *ex*change, not change. The Qur'an describes Mecca as a "valley devoid of any growth."

The Meccans' one product was their children, whose primary value was as memory maintainers. If offspring were perceived as handicapped or a liability, they could be discarded like damaged goods. Muhammad noticed that girls from his neighborhood would occasionally disappear. As a young man he learned they had been buried alive by their fathers, who considered having too many daughters a sign of weakness. In fact, femicide (*wa`d*) would be one of the first societal ills the Qur'an addressed, asking rhetorically: "For which crime was she killed?" These burials occurred outside Mecca without public spectacle yet with tacit public approval.

Accepting infanticide despite a code of chivalry was just one of *Jahiliyyah*'s contradictions. Muhammad witnessed another episode, when two clans in Mecca fought over who had sales rights for particular souvenirs marketed to pilgrimage tourists. One angry tribe suddenly declared that the newly begun sacred month of pilgrimage, Burak (a time when all forms of violence were forbidden under tribal code), was over, allowing them to attack their rival, Muhammad's Quraish tribe. These wars were called *harb-ul-fijar* (sacrilegious war—literally, defiling the sacred) because they were violating the pilgrimage's required calm. The two tribes promptly faced off on the plains outside Mecca, shooting arrows at one another. Five-year-old Muhammad joined other children from his tribe, running to pick up fallen arrows for reuse. The incident—Muhammad's only exposure to warfare for the next five decades—was absurd. Even a five-year-old could see that. *Jahiliyyah* was a rigid and confining mindset without adaptability or moral purpose.

The following year, six-year-old Muhammad first comprehended the painful reality of slavery, a particularly stark and brutal form of forced stagnation. One day he asked a friend where his parents were. The boy revealed that he was a slave and his master had sold him, thus separating him from his parents.

With tears in his eyes, Muhammad sprinted home to Aminah with a burning question: "Where is my father?" Until this point, he had been told nothing about 'Abdullah. Unable to contain herself, Aminah began to cry and left the room. Barakah hurried to comfort Muhammad and reassure him he had done nothing wrong.

A little later Aminah returned to the room, where Barakah sat cradling Muhammad on her lap. Aminah sat down beside them, put her hand on Muhammad's head, and began to tell him about his father. He had been a great man. After he contracted an illness in the port of Ashkelon while on a caravan trip, he made it as far as Yathrib. Sadly, he could not be saved, and he was buried there.

Aminah had been waiting to reveal the full story to her son when he was old enough to understand, but since he had now broached the topic, it was time to visit his father's grave.

Thankfully, the annual caravan—coordinated with the coming of the full moon—was leaving the next day for Damascus. And so Aminah made the impromptu decision that she, Barakah, and Muhammad would join the caravan for first leg of the trip up to Yathrib.

Muhammad would at last get to unlock part of his hidden heritage.

✤ ✤ ✤

A trumpet blast signaled that the caravan of over a thousand camels was leaving Mecca. The camels began to rise one by one. On one of them sat Muhammad, cradled between Aminah and Barakah.

For two weeks, the caravan traversed barren landscapes, resting during the hottest parts of the day and making up ground by moonlight, winding along like a slithering serpent. The travelers used specially made earthen jars to catch the early morning desert dew for drinking water.

As the caravan approached Yathrib from the south, Muhammad stared out at vast stretches of lava rock formations that surrounded the oasis from three sides like an irregular horseshoe. It would take another day to reach the city's main entrance in the north. As the sun rose the following morning, Muhammad beheld an island of green amid the vast ocean of sand. Thousands of palm trees dotted the city's fertile volcanic soil, as streams carved through its many orchards and gardens filled with birdsong.

The moist air and cool refreshing breeze overwhelmed Muhammad's senses. He had not breathed such pleasant fresh air before and as an adult would describe it as a "source of blissful healing." He had also never seen an agricultural settlement before, with vineyards, palm groves, barley fields, and rows of vegetables—interspersed with watering holes.

Shimmering in the morning sun were hundreds of two-story mud-brick homes with decorative lattice brickwork attesting to the artisanal skill of the city's carpenters and builders. With over fifteen thousand inhabitants, Yathrib dwarfed Mecca in size and grandeur. Amid the homes arose several large forts, each serving as a clan's vault and produce storage.

Muhammad had never experienced so much green (which would become his favorite color), so many people, so many buildings—and so many Jews.

In fact, Jews had founded Yathrib more than one thousand years earlier. The first wave came as exiles from the destruction of the First Temple in Jerusalem in about 585 BCE. For destitute refugees, the low wall of spiky volcanic rocks surrounding a lush oasis offered a secure place to put down roots without having to construct defensive walls. Additional waves of Jewish migrants from Jerusalem arrived after the Romans' destruction of the Second Temple (70 CE) and a failed revolt against Roman rule (132 CE). Pagan farmers fleeing drought in Yemen had settled among the Jews after 400 CE.

Unlike their Arab neighbors who gave their towns forbidding names, the founders of Yathrib saluted a higher being: "God (*Yah*) makes fertile (*tharib*)"—a construct of two Aramaic words, reflecting the founders' roots. Indeed, the Yathribites fused their Aramaic language with Hejazi Arabic, forming a dialect distinct from the "purer" Meccan vernacular.

Relatives from the Banu Najjar clan greeted Aminah and her son upon arrival. Her cousins led the visitors from Mecca south from the camel depot down to their clan's lands.

Passing through the center of Yathrib, Muhammad observed a new culture. Many of the men wore white and blue-violet tassels on the exterior of their long linen shirts and covered their heads with distinctive turbans wrapped around skullcaps. Whereas Meccans had lost a direct connection to the God of Abraham, the Jews of Yathrib connected to God with their everyday dress and daily rituals. A small box called a mezuzah (literally, doorjamb) contained scrolls with biblical passages and dotted the doorposts of every home. Everywhere Muhammad looked were reminders of the Divine Presence (Shekhinah) without any physical idols or pagan shrines.

When Aminah and Muhammad arrived in the Banu Najjar quarter, their family embraced them. She had not seen her parents since her wedding seven years earlier. Her father, Wahb (an Aramaic version of the Hebrew name Natan, "gift of God"), and her mother, Barrah (benevolence), were overjoyed to be reunited with their only child and meet their first and only grandchild. The details of their encounter are vague, but Wahb by tradition would have greeted his grandson by placing his hands over Muhammad's forehead and reciting a blessing. Aminah found comfort among her relatives, who prepared a welcome feast. Muhammad watched as his relatives washed their hands and face before eating—a custom unknown in Mecca—and then for the first time he tasted garlic, onions, leeks, lentils, squash, and other root vegetables (all later mentioned in the Qur`an). Due to the barren landscape of Mecca, its cuisine consisted mainly of meat, barley, breads, and dried foods. Unlike the Meccans who loved camel meat, constituting a large part of their diet, the Yathribites avoided it entirely due to religious dietary restrictions.

The next morning, a Friday, was a busy time of cleaning and cooking as the Banu Najjar made preparations for the Sabbath. Muhammad, like the other members of the family, bathed and dressed in his finest clothes. At dusk, the women of the clan recited blessings as they lit small lanterns to mark the beginning of the Sabbath, a ceremony repeated in every home throughout the Banu Najjar quarter. Imagery of lamps casting away darkness and beautifying the world pervades the Qur`an, which dedicates a chapter (Surah An-Nur, "The Illumination") to the enlightening energy of the Divine.

That evening at services, the males chanted the Song of Songs, which included a Hebrew version of Muhammad's name: Kullo Mahamadim, "he is altogether lovely" or "he embodies everything people desire to emulate" (5:16). Whereas in Mecca, Muhammad's name sounded foreign, among the Yathribites it evoked a familiar concept. For the first time, the young boy heard an assortment of biblical names: Abraham (no one in Mecca was named Abraham although Meccans revered the patriarch), Joseph (Yusuf), Moses (Musa), Jonah (Yunus), and Job (Ayyub).

On Saturday morning, Yathrib was still. No one traded in the market, rode horses, or worked the fields. For the first time, Muhammad experienced a day of rest—what the Qur`an refers to repeatedly as *yawm as-sabt* (the day of repose, or day of eternity). While the men went to synagogue, Aminah took Muhammad for a walk through the family orchards. As they strolled hand in hand, accompanied by Barakah, Aminah shared childhood memories. Barakah noted how Aminah's demeanor had brightened. She played with Muhammad in the date palm groves, laughing in ways she hadn't in years. Suddenly, Aminah pointed to a section of the garden and explained it was the spot where, as a child, she had first seen his father, 'Abdullah. It was, Aminah recalled, love at first sight. "This is where your story began," she informed Muhammad.

Once the workweek resumed, Muhammad had his first chance to observe the profession of his relatives. The Banu Najjar lived up to their family name: "clan of carpenters." They were skilled artisans. They constructed molds for bricks, door frames and doors, plates, cups and bowls, tables, benches, and roof beams. They also carved the wooden mezuzahs Muhammad had seen on the doorposts of homes, as well as the wooden pegs used to roll Torah scrolls. They braided palm fibers, making the kind of rope that had held Muhammad during his desert honey harvesting and was used to draw buckets of water up from wells.

Yathrib's farmers cultivated several species of crops in accordance with natural agricultural cycles.

On the edge of the Banu Najjar quarter, Muhammad came upon a date-processing factory consisting of a rectangular plaza covered by a canopy of nets to keep out birds; it provided space where workers laid dates out to dry on straw mats. Like bees in a hive, the workers busily transformed the dried dates into syrup, cakes, even a fermented drink called *nabith*. The plant was a creative enterprise; forty-seven years later, Muhammad would select it as the site of his first mosque.

Amid the date palm groves Muhammad also learned a new way to play. In a watering hole owned by a Jewish man named Aris (agriculturalist), Muhammad learned to swim and spent hours splashing about with newfound relatives and friends. As an adult, Muhammad would not only make a point of urging parents to teach their children to swim, but he would also often gather his closest followers around this particular well for deep discussions. In fact, he was inspired with the Qur'an's second-to-last passage at the well during such a session. The well of Aris clearly evoked positive memories for Muhammad, who would often return there in times of stress to recall the pure childhood joy of being with his mother when she was happy.

On July 23, the Jews of Yathrib gathered at the northern entrance to the city, an area they called *thaniyyat al-wada'* (gateway hills of lamentation). Staring longingly north toward Jerusalem, the site of their twice-destroyed Temple, the Jews marked a day of mourning known as Tishʿah Bʾav (the ninth of Av) by putting ashes on their heads, sitting on the ground, and wailing for their loss. It was a communal day of fasting, when everyone abstained from food, drink, and marital relations.

The Temple in Jerusalem had been built on the spot where Jews believed Abraham had bound his son and received a covenant from God. While the Yathribites had established a thriving oasis in exile, they nonetheless yearned for a lost shrine and a city the Byzantine Empire had barred them from entering. Unlike the Meccans, the Jews of Yathrib had lost their physical link to Abraham yet maintained a strong connection to his spiritual legacy. That evening, they recited the Book of Lamentations (with the cognate of Muhammad, *Mahamudeha*, appearing in its seventh verse)—a reminder that despite their displacement, the Yathribites were bound together by a formal scripture and a common longing for a better future.

The problem was that the Yathribites were deeply divided. They were waiting for divine deliverance. In the meantime, their community lacked effective leadership. Unlike Mecca, Yathrib had no citywide central council of elders. Each clan ran its own rabbinic council, on which sat a mix of genuine scholars and corrupt politicos.

The Yathribites' incessant squabbling would eventually become paralyzing, leading city elders decades later to approach Muhammad to serve as a mediating leader.

But for the moment, Muhammad was just a young boy gathering impressions. In Yathrib, though, he had discovered powerful rituals and acquired an inspiring sense of mission that would shape the rest of his life.

❖ ❖ ❖

Three months later, on the eve of the full moon, a herald on horseback burst into Yathrib to announce the imminent arrival of the caravan returning from Damascus to Mecca. For their entire visit, Aminah had delayed taking Muhammad to his father's grave, the ostensible reason for their trip. But the caravan was their only ride back to Mecca, so she could delay no longer.

The next morning, after Barakah helped pack up their belongings to be loaded on a caravan camel, Aminah took her son by the hand and headed for the Banu Najjar's cemetery.

Her cousin Sa'ad, who six years earlier had delivered the news of 'Abdullah's death, guided the small entourage to the grave. 'Abdullah's burial site—a simple earthen mound rising a foot above the ground—was marked on four sides by dried palm leaves and mud bricks.

Seeing the grave, Aminah broke down. For six years, she had lived in denial about her beloved's death.

Barakah and Sa'ad carried the frail young woman back to her parents' home, placing her on a mattress in a bedroom on the second floor. Her mother and other female relatives gathered around her with worried expressions, as Barakah daubed her feverish forehead with a wet cloth. When Aminah refused to eat, Barakah realized that—unlike at Muhammad's birth—this medical episode would not have a happy outcome. She escorted Muhammad from the room so he would not have to see his mother suffering.

At sunset, Aminah whispered for Muhammad. When Barakah brought him into the room, the six-year-old was unable to contain his distress and broke out in tears. Barakah propped Aminah up against a pillow so she could draw Muhammad to her chest, embracing him as her tears moistened his black hair. He gently wiped away her tears and held her chin as he told her he loved her. Muhammad, who had just that morning confronted the reality of his father's death, could not imagine also losing his mother.

At first, Aminah said nothing. She kissed Muhammad and tried to hug him with her little remaining strength. Then, looking hazily into his large black eyes, she struggled to articulate her final words. In a weak voice, she uttered: *"Ya Muhammadu kun rajula !"* (Oh Muhammad, be a world-changer!).

Then she closed her eyes. The sun had set, and the full moon had risen, casting its light on the somber bedroom scene as the now-orphaned boy cried hysterically over his mother's lifeless body.

Everyone in the room wondered why Aminah had used her last breath to burden her six-year-old son with such a weighty life mission. She had chosen her last few words carefully. *"Kun rajula,"* she had repeated twice. The root word, *rajala*, refers to someone with the rare ability to make an impact on the world. It originally described an expert with the specialized talent for transforming unrefined stones into exquisite jewelry. The form *kun rajula* grammatically turned this process into a timeless, constant state of being.

Aminah had harnessed her last energy to plant a seed in her son. No doubt inspired by her example, Muhammad would later counsel his followers: "If the world were ending before your eyes but you held a sapling in your hands, plant it! Don't be concerned with its fate. Your task is to plant."

With her final words, Aminah turned Muhammad into someone special, telling him he already had the ability to transform the world. He just had to unlock that potential inside himself. It was a heavy but profound lesson for an impressionable six-year-old who had just become an orphan in a society built upon family ties. Muhammad would spend decades making sense of her parting gift.

2

✤

THE ORPHAN

Yathrib: 4:30 a.m., Thursday, August 20, 576 CE

Muhammad spent the night clinging to his mother.

At dawn, three men wielding hoes and shovels labored in the Banu Najjar cemetery, carving out a niche at the foot of Aminah's tomb. The nocturnal symphony of crickets began to give way to the chirping of birds as dew carpeted the landscape in a pale wet blanket. In the city's deserted streets, a solitary group of women from the clan's burial society carried white linens, incense, and clay jars filled with fresh water toward the house in mourning.

With Muhammad in her arms, Barakah ushered the women in. She directed them to the second-floor room where Aminah lay. In the tradition of their people, the women removed Aminah's garments and gently washed her before anointing her with perfumes. They quietly chanted melancholic litanies as they wrapped her with three layers of delicate linen to form a white burial shroud.

Crowing roosters woke city residents and signaled the start of the funeral procession. While some relatives carried Aminah's corpse through the streets, others surrounded the body as they held palm leaves aloft, enveloping it in a green cocoon. Muhammad joined the procession in stunned silence. He would utter not a word that day. In the cemetery, he looked on in disbelief as the white shroud was lowered into the grave, gently placed within the niche at its foot, and sealed with baked bricks. Then the burial soil was shoveled atop the grave, forming a physical barrier separating Muhammad from his mother.

In the eyes of his tribal society, Muhammad was now *yatim* (orphaned)—literally, "incomplete." With no parents to nurture him and no network of siblings to support him, he lacked vital assets in a social order in which family ties determined standing. How could he fulfill his mother's dying wish to change the world?

It was a seemingly impossible task.

❖ ❖ ❖

The caravan had left as Aminah lay on her deathbed. By the morning of her burial it had already progressed a day southward. Muhammad would have no time to mourn with his grandparents. In accordance with Arabian custom, the now orphaned Muhammad would mourn in the care of his grandfather in Mecca. Relatives from the Banu Najjar clan placed him and Barakah on horses to race toward the camel caravan, catching its tail end during a rest stop by the wells of Badr (full moon).

Muhammad spent most of the two-week journey to Mecca crying and struggling to sleep. Barakah comforted him, assuming the role of foster mother—even though the six-year-old in her care was technically her owner (a fact of which the boy remained oblivious).

As the caravan wound through the barren desert landscape, Barakah's challenge was to help restore Muhammad's will to survive. The two rode atop their camel in a howdah—a wooden frame enclosed in beige linen with a leather canopy. The linen sides allowed air to circulate while blocking blowing sand, and the leather cover shielded them from the intense sun. As the camel plodded forward, Barakah would lift the compartment's side flaps to show Muhammad the passing landscape. From time to time, she pointed out solitary trees growing in the middle of the barren desert, a symbol of life persisting despite the odds.

At one of the rest stops by a desert watering hole, Barakah spotted a butterfly emerging from a cocoon dangling on a nearby bush. What looked like a funeral shroud, Barakah noted to Muhammad, was actually an incubator of life, helping a dull caterpillar transform into a beautiful winged insect soaring in the sky. Barakah hailed from a Christian family that had instilled in her a strong belief in life after death and resurrection. Citing all the natural examples of life's resilience in the face of seeming death, Barakah urged her young charge not to give up.

The caravan's last rest stop before Mecca was at the wells of Hudaibiyyah (back bender). Barakah pointed out to Muhammad that wherever water splashed to the ground around the well, little patches of green plants emerged from the dry desert. All it took to transform the sand was something as simple as water. Muhammad, she suggested, should look for the metaphoric drops of water around him that could nurture his growth despite his sense of hopelessness. These drops could be people like her and inspiring examples like the desert butterfly. Sources of hope and nurturing were everywhere; Muhammad just had to recognize them.

As the midday sun blazed, panic suddenly ripped through the camp. A *qidam* (east wind), a massive sandstorm, was rapidly approaching, a desert tsunami that swallows everything in its path. Within minutes, the camp was engulfed by the scorching dry sands while fierce winds howled, shrieking against the fragile tents. Barakah threw her body over Muhammad, shielding him in case the wind snatched the tent.

Meanwhile, in nearby Mecca, an advance herald from the caravan brought news of Aminah's death to 'Abdul-Muttalib, who braced himself to meet his heartbroken grandson. His own wife had passed away only two weeks earlier. Grandfather and grandson would be reunited in grief.

When the caravan arrived, 'Abdul-Muttalib warmly embraced Muhammad and brought him and Barakah to live in his home. With an open courtyard and ten whitewashed rooms decorated with red geometric designs and latticed windows, the house was one of Mecca's largest.

Muhammad was not the only child living there. His eighty-one-year-old grandfather still had two teenage sons at home: Hamzah and Az-Zubair. Hamzah adored wine, women, and hunting. At sixteen, he had already earned renown for fearlessly wrestling lions with his bare hands before unsheathing his dagger to slay them. His older brother,

Az-Zubair, was living up to his name, "invincible rock," and served as his father's chief supporter. Dependable and meticulous, Az-Zubair ran the household after his mother's death, organizing banquets and hosting dignitaries.

But 'Abdul-Muttalib focused his energies on the grandson on whom he had bestowed a unique name. The morning after the caravan arrived, 'Abdul-Muttalib took Muhammad with him on his civic rounds. That Friday morning at the elder's council next to the Ka'bah, Muhammad sat on 'Abdul-Muttalib's lap before the semicircle of twenty elders. The chief elder's cushion was placed beneath the Ka'bah's only rain spout, symbolizing life and rejuvenation.

Following the council meeting, 'Abdul-Muttalib led his grandson to the market at 'Ukath (pride place), so named for its annual competition for poets to declaim odes to their clans. Located in a large plaza, the market featured over a hundred raised stalls. Merchants sold all manner of goods: spices, dates, vegetables, textiles, goats, horses, tools, and more. Muhammad looked around the market with interest, observing its dynamics. One stall in particular caught his attention: the goods being sold were human beings, even children his age.

Perplexed, he asked his grandfather why boys and girls were being sold like animals. 'Abdul-Muttalib explained that these were children whose parents could not afford to pay off their debts. Other children had been abducted, similar to what had nearly occured to Muhammad while tending goats with the Banu Sa'd nomads. 'Abdul-Muttalib suggested that Muhammad ask Barakah about slavery if he wanted to learn more.

After dinner, Muhammad went to find Barakah and told her what he had seen at the marketplace. He explained that his grandfather had suggested he ask her about slavery. Placing him on her lap, Barakah responded, "Here is my story."

Barakah hailed from a noble Abyssinian family in a town at the foot of the Semien Mountains. One day, while picnicking with her mother and servants among the fig and olive trees on the mountain's slope, rebels opposed to the king abducted her, tied her up, concealed her in a merchant caravan, and transported her to the Nile, where they placed her on a barge; she subsequently was sold in Egypt. A Midianite slave trader purchased her at auction and brought her to Ashkelon, where 'Abdul-Muttalib had bought her at the portside market as a gift for his son 'Abdullah. When Barakah finally reached Mecca, she was eight years old.

Muhammad leapt up and ran to 'Abdul-Muttalib with a pressing question: "Grandfather, how can an enslaved person be emancipated?" The chief elder understood what his grandson was asking and responded, "Since Barakah legally belongs to you, in order to liberate her, you must publicly declare her emancipation, at the Ka'bah." Technically, this was not true: he could make the declaration anywhere. But 'Abdul-Muttalib evidently wanted his grandson to make a public declaration—a chance to prove to skeptics in Mecca that his grandson was his rightful protégé.

The next morning, Muhammad took Barakah by the hand and hastened toward the Ka'bah. Joined by his grandfather, Muhammad stood on the steps of the temple and declared, "This is Barakah. I, Muhammad, the son of 'Abdullah, with the support of my grandfather, hereby declare Barakah from this moment forward to be free like the wind, no longer weighted down by the yoke of bondage. Oh people, bear witness and let those present inform those who are absent."

Some in the crowd started to snicker but contained themselves out of respect for the chief elder. Barakah was overjoyed. Tears filled her eyes as she embraced Muhammad. Though free to return to her homeland and her family ('Abdul-Muttalib offered to arrange an escort for her) twenty-two-year-old Barakah chose to remain with Muhammad. If this young man was going to be a world-changer, she wanted to be at his side.

❖ ❖ ❖

The wise men of Mecca—known as the Majlis ash-Shuyukh (congress of elders)—had no formal political power but rather served as respected mediators, helping people from Mecca and its surrounding areas resolve disputes. These retirees gathered almost daily to receive petitioners, who would stand waiting their turn at the entrance to the elders' special enclosure.

On this particular morning, two men approached the council. 'Abdul-Muttalib motioned for each to state his case.

The first began: "My neighbor and I decided to combine our flock to share the same pastures and goatherds. One of my bucks impregnated my neighbor's doe and she gave birth. I feel entitled to the offspring, as they are my flocks' lineage."

The other man disagreed, arguing: "The doe is mine. I cared for her, fed her, and spent money to keep her healthy and safe. Therefore, the kids she bore [does usually bear twins or triplets] while I was caring for her should be mine, as my neighbor played no part in her care."

The elders motioned for the men to depart while they discussed the case. Most elders were inclined to the patriarchic interpretation that the man whose buck impregnated the doe had right to the young goats, as the buck's seed had made the offspring possible. After listening to their arguments, 'Abdul-Muttalib offered a different view. Because the doe's master fed and cared for her during the entire pregnancy, the kids belong to him—but he should pay his neighbor appropriate compensation for his buck's services.

The unorthodox ruling swayed the council and satisfied both parties to the dispute. Decades later, Muhammad would be asked to resolve a parallel situation: a man suspected his wife had given birth to another man's son. In this case of unclear paternity, Muhammad ruled that the child belonged to the husband, declaring, *"Al-waladu lil-firash"* (The child owes its obligations to the one who cared for the pregnant mother).

After the council session ended, 'Abdul-Muttalib had a rare treat for his grandson. Rising from the chief elder's red cushion, grandfather and grandson ascended the steps of the Ka'bah. The onlookers were astonished: aside from a privileged few elders and priests, no one was allowed inside the shrine, certainly not an orphaned six-year-old. Ignoring the scandalized expressions of the spectators and the dismay of the shrine's priestly custodians, 'Abdul-Muttalib pulled aside the massive embroidered curtains draping the doorway, allowing a shaft of light into the gloomy interior. He took his grandson's hand and led the boy across the threshold.

The curtain closed behind them. As Muhammad's eyes adjusted to the darkness, he beheld a rectangular hall filled with crudely carved statues secured to the walls by lead pegs. A few miniature oil lanterns illuminated the idols from below. Hazy smoke drifted out of incense burners suspended from the ceiling, while ghostly white-clad priests chanted ancient Mesopotamian incantations (the first priests were Mesopotamian), their voices echoing in the gloom. Muhammad grasped his grandfather's hand tightly.

Then, out of the corner of his eye, he noticed a striking portrait. At the center of the shrine's interior northern wall hung a rectangular wood icon featuring the image of a veiled woman embracing her young son. It was a Byzantine depiction of Mary and Christ that someone had transported from Damascus. Muhammad stared at the mother and child, who were depicted cheek to cheek. The mother looked sad; the boy seemed to comfort her as he gently touched her chin.

Presumably the icon sparked memories of events in Yathrib only three weeks earlier. The young boy let go of his grandfather's hand and approached the painting. After some time, Muhammad felt a hand on his left shoulder. "It's time to continue our rounds," said his grandfather. As they exited the shrine, Muhammad stared back at the image.

The midday sun blinded Muhammad as the pair left the shrine. In the haze, Muhammad noticed a couple with an infant approaching a pair of idols situated opposite the Ka'bah's door. They bowed before the statues—which depicted the ancient Arabian lovers Isaf and Na`ilah—and then handed their child over to a priest, who placed the baby on a small altar set between the two statues. The priest took two wooden arrows, marking the first with a cross using blood taken from the baby's big toe and marking the second with a white circle using chalk. In a rhythmic trance, the priest shook the arrows and then cast them on the ground before the idols. (If the blood-cross arrow fell on top of the white-chalk one, the baby would be sacrificed.)

Noticing the astonishment on his grandson's face, 'Abdul-Muttalib remarked, "I had to undergo that test as well, with your father." As the pair continued across the plaza toward the Zamzam Well, he continued. "See that well, my son? It was I who uncovered it."

The chief elder noted his grandson's confusion at these two seemingly unrelated and surprising facts. He motioned for Muhammad to sit with him in the shade of the well's canopy, where local women were filling clay jugs with water. Then he began to recount a remarkable story.

At twenty-one, 'Abdul-Muttalib was not yet a member of the elders' council. Because he had spent his early years in Yathrib, many Meccans regarded him as an outsider. One day in the market, he struck up a conversation with an elderly stranger who told him about the legend of an ancient well called Zamzam that had been in the heart of Mecca, not far from the Ka'bah. The Jurhumites—Mecca's ancient kings—had concealed its opening centuries earlier, when they were overthrown from power and exiled. Over time people forgot about the well and its location. Other merchants overheard the old man's tale and dismissed it as a legend. But 'Abdul-Muttalib was intrigued. Mecca must have had a water source in its center or no one would have established a city there.

How could he find this missing well? 'Abdul-Muttalib spent days pondering the challenge while sitting near the Ka'bah. One day he noticed a raven digging in the ground. Perhaps 'Abdul-Muttalib could dig up the well. He began to interview old people to gather clues about the Zamzam story. Piecing together fragments of information, he deduced the approximate location of the buried well. As Mecca slept, he dug small holes to look for moisture beneath the surface. In three weeks, he sampled soil across the entire area where Zamzam should have been, yet he came up empty-handed.

About to give up, 'Abdul-Muttalib watched a magpie (*al-ghurab al-a'sam*) land in the plaza and push aside a rock to dig beneath it. It was a eureka moment: the one place he had neglected to dig was under the idol of the two lovers. That night, he pushed the altar to the side and began digging. Lo and behold, the earth was moist. He dug until the sun rose. When city elders saw his excavation, they rushed to stop the desecration of the love idols. Just then 'Abdul-Muttalib's pickax hit a stone with a loud clang. As the angry elders surrounded him, he cleaned off the stone and lifted it to the side. Cool fresh water gushed out, soaking him. The source of life-giving waters had been concealed for centuries beneath an altar upon which children were sacrificed.

The statues were soon relocated a few meters away, and a new wall built to protect the well. Delighted to have a water source in the city's center, the elders demanded authority to regulate use of the well. 'Abdul-Muttalib was offended; he felt it rightly belonged to him as the one who had uncovered it. While the dispute raged, some elders mocked 'Abdul-Muttalib as a half-breed son of a Jewish woman, an orphan with no recollection of his father, and himself the father of just one son. In the tribal code of Meccan society, the number of a man's male offspring increased his honor.

Feeling powerless and humiliated, 'Abdul-Muttalib suddenly swore out an oath in front of all the elders. *"Allahumma,"* he cried, invoking Abraham's God. "If you reinforce me with ten sons, I will sacrifice one of them to you as a thanksgiving offering." Decades later, with the birth of his youngest and tenth son, Hamzah, 'Abdul-Muttalib faced a quandary. He had to make good on his vow, especially as he had made it not to the idols but directly to the Divine.

Like the parents Muhammad had observed at the lover idols (Al-'Ashiqan), 'Abdul-Muttalib began to cast lots. The sacrificial burden fell on his son 'Abdullah. Was there any way he could avoid sacrificing his most beloved son? 'Abdul-Muttalib consulted the high priestess of the Banu Sa'd nomads, who told him to make two arrows: one with 'Abdullah's name, the other with the word *camel*. 'Abdul-Muttalib tossed the arrows at the ground, ultimately obtaining a favorable compromise: he could sacrifice one hundred of his camels in lieu of losing the then ten-year-old 'Abdullah. (Not surprisingly, Muhammad would later set the value of blood money—called *diyah*—to one hundred camels).

For Muhammad, the story offered another reminder that he had nearly never been born. But his grandfather's creativity also impressed him. There had been a source of life buried underneath Mecca without anyone's knowing it. His grandfather invested the time and energy to uncover it. What other powerful forces might lie unseen in the world around him?

❖ ❖ ❖

The grand white villa shimmered in the midday sun.

After the elders' session ended, 'Abdul-Muttalib and his grandson had headed north from the Ka'bah up Mecca's only straight boulevard toward the white mansion. While city residents stopped the chief elder en route to convey their regards, Muhammad stared straight ahead at by far the largest house in Mecca. Most of the city's buildings were lackluster brown and just one story. This gleaming edifice was more than three times their size and twice as tall. A latticed wooden veranda jutted out from the second floor, shaded by a thick tapestry canopy.

'Abdul-Muttalib noticed his grandson's fascination with the building, which functioned as Mecca's formal town hall. He told Muhammad his ancestor, 'Abdul-Muttalib's great-grandfather Qusai, had built it. Qusai had been born Zaid ibn Kilab, a Meccan citizen whose family had produced the first rulers of Mecca but had not held power for several generations. Kilab died when his only child was just a few months old. A visiting Christian merchant then proposed to Zaid's widowed mother and brought the two of them back to Damascus. Raised as a Christian, speaking Aramaic and Greek, the little boy had no recollection of his hometown and limited knowledge of its culture, religion, and language. But his mother reminded him that he was descended from Ishmael and his Jurhumite wife, and urged him to one day return to Mecca to reclaim the throne of his ancestors.

From a young age, Zaid trained hard to be a leader. He learned to read and write in several languages and excelled in the art of diplomacy. But despite Zaid's best efforts, his stepfather's family never accepted him, and Damascus's elite made him feel like an outsider who could never succeed. He joined the Roman Auxilia at age sixteen, quickly rising through the ranks and earning the right to Roman citizenship. In the army, he traveled throughout the Roman Empire, observing the diverse peoples, languages, and cultures all united under Pax Romana. Zaid mastered archery and renamed himself Qusai (far-reaching master archer). By discarding the name bestowed upon him by his father, Qusai was reinventing himself for his return to Mecca.

At twenty-one, he returned to the city of his birth for the first time in over two decades. Disguised as a Syrian merchant, he surveyed Mecca's political and social scene. He dressed extravagantly, hoping to catch the attention of Mecca's elders by creating the impression that he was fabulously wealthy. The chief elder, Hulail, soon heard the buzz about this striking young man and held a banquet in his honor. At the dinner, the stylish Qusai captivated his audience with eloquence in both the Meccan Arabic dialect and foreign languages. Impressed, Hulail then and there offered his coveted daughter, Hubbah, in marriage.

By marrying the chief's daughter, Qusai positioned himself as the city's crown prince, for Hulail had no sons and had anointed Qusai as his successor. Within a few months, Qusai had consolidated power and revealed his true identity as the heir to Mecca's original ruling clan. In effect, he had cleverly worked within the system to change it—and achieved a result that the city's elders could not overturn.

At this time, Mecca had no central leadership council. The city's ruler functioned as a de facto autocrat while each tribe operated its own informal council to resolve small disputes. Inspired by his experiences in the Roman Empire, Qusai envisioned a strong Mecca powered by a united tribal council that included the heads of all the city's clans. An organized system of civic order would enhance the city's unity and make it possible to gain wide acceptance for major changes.

Qusai understood the importance of both order and symbolism, no doubt influenced by his Roman experiences. Mecca needed an impressive building to house the council in order to establish its prestige. He purchased a plot that overlooked the Ka'bah and set about building a miniature replica of the Roman Senate. While stationed in Greece during his army training, Qusai had become enamored of its whitewashed homes. He imported Greek artisans to whitewash the new parliament's plaster walls, adding decorative designs in red paint. Carpenters from Yathrib's Banu Najjar clan were hired to build a grand ceiling, design lattice windows, and construct the expansive veranda from which members could look south toward the Ka'bah.

Qusai called this edifice Dar-un-Nadwah (the House of Assembly). The bottom floor included twelve guest rooms to host prominent dignitaries. The upper story contained a great hall with twelve large windows, their frames made of imported cedar. Decorating the hall's main pillars were twelve circles of red paint that had been mixed with blood taken from the right arms of Mecca's chieftains as a sign of their joint commitment to the new civic order. In the main hall, twelve red cushions were laid out, with the banners of the clans anchored behind them.

The repetition of the number twelve was no accident. To the Semites, the number symbolized completeness: twelve tribes of Israel, twelve disciples of Christ, twelve signs of the zodiac, and twelve months of the year. Dar-un-Nadwah welcomed the chiefs of Mecca's twelve main clans. The clan leaders, who had to be at least forty years old to join, received access to a luxurious club featuring private events and the city's best food and entertainment. Qusai in turn gained a centralized court of nobles through which he could keep a close eye on the city's top elites.

As he stared at Dar-un-Nadwah, Muhammad marveled at this monument to his ancestor. The building stood as a testament to Qusai's ability to overcome his outsider-orphan status and live up to his mother's grand expectations. And Qusai had worked within the logic of the established order to change it.

'Abdul-Muttalib directed Muhammad's gaze to an exquisitely carved wooden post in front of Dar-un-Nadwah. His grandfather noted that the post marked the departure point for the annual caravan to Damascus. Smiling, 'Abdul-Muttalib revealed another remarkable family story. It was Qusai's grandson Hashim—'Abdul-Muttalib's father—who secured for Mecca the safe trading routes that these caravans now take. It was he who decreed that all camels embarking for Damascus should unite as one to form a great caravan and that they should first convene at his grandfather's hall.

The centralized caravan system had put Mecca on the map, drawing merchants from all across the region. Before then, Mecca's claim to prominence was simply as Arabia's premier pilgrimage destination. As the convener and organizer of the great caravan—with its guaranteed safe passage and tax-free trading rights—Muhammad's ancestor Hashim had transformed his hometown into an economic powerhouse.

Hashim's innovation had not come easily. After Qusai died, his children lost their position of prominence in a clash of Mecca's clans. His grandson Hashim grew up in Mecca as a political outsider. Born as 'Amr (immortal), after his father's death, he renamed himself Hashim (pulverizer) to burnish his reputation as Qusai's heir. Tall and muscular with long wavy black hair, Hashim was known for his brilliant smile. An extrovert and go-getter, Hashim knew he had to create his own opportunities.

One day, as he sat in the shade of the Ka'bah, he heard a Syrian merchant complain about the strife between the Byzantines and Sasanians that threatened to cut off trade along the ancient Silk Road. Hashim decided to leverage that rivalry to his advantage. With an introduction from the Syrian merchant, Hashim traveled to Al-Jabiyah, the hillside capital of the Ghassanide kingdom, to meet King Al-Harith IV, who ruled as vassal of Byzantium in southern Syria through which much of the caravan trade passed. Hashim, now twenty-seven, procured a contract that granted him exclusive rights to import goods from India and Africa via Mecca.

King Al-Harith also agreed to provide a letter of introduction for Hashim to Emperor Anastasius I in Constantinople. Hashim leveraged his grandfather Qusai's outstanding military record to help secure a meeting with Anastasius, who did not normally grant audiences to random young men from Arabia. Hashim's impressive diplomatic skills charmed the emperor, who granted him exclusive import rights and provided a signed letter formally exempting Meccans from taxes and tariffs. Empowered by this diplomatic coup, Hashim approached Arabia's other neighboring empires and personally negotiated similar trade treaties with Persia, Abyssinia, Egypt, and even India.

Four years later, Hashim returned to Arabia, having transformed it into an essential trading thoroughfare. Elders representing Arabia's main tribes gathered in Mecca for a ceremony to establish the Hilf-ul-Mutayyabun (Pact of the Perfumed). The elders all placed their hands in a cauldron with an amalgam of rich spices—nutmeg, cinnamon, cardamom, and cloves from India mixed with frankincense, musk, and myrrh from Africa—signifying the trade routes Hashim had secured for them. To seal the pact, they smeared their hands over the Ka'bah's walls, wiping their faces and placing their right hands over their hearts.

Hashim had earned the right to recognition as an elder. Though he was now only thirty-one, the council granted him membership as a clan leader in Dar-un-Nadwah—a special exemption from the age limits established by his own grandfather.

The innovative Hashim struggled to find a wife who would match his pioneering spirit. He had his eye on one remarkable woman from Yathrib. She was a self-made independent businesswoman from the Banu Najjar clan named Salma (complete), a noble Jewish woman descended from King David. To the dismay of Yathrib's rabbinic council, she had married and divorced several times of her own volition, and she was not eager to remarry. Hashim and Salma often did business together, and he repeatedly and unsuccessfully proposed marriage.

Salma at last agreed to marriage after Hashim proved himself by earning membership as a Meccan elder. In addition to requiring Hashim's conversion to Judasim, Salma insisted on setting her own terms for the marriage, specifically that she retained the right to divorce, that she would maintain her home in Yathrib, and that any children would live with her there until age thirteen—enough time to complete the bar mitzvah ceremony. Even by Yathrib's standards, these were exceptional demands. Hashim happily accepted, and the couple soon produced a son, Muhammad's grandfather.

The boy was given the name Shaibah (wise sage, literally, silverish-white) and lived with his mother in Yathrib. When he was two, messengers from Gaza delivered the news that his father had died there while on a business trip. This broke the boy's link to his Meccan ancestry. Shaibah remained in Yathrib with his mother until she died six years later, rendering him a *yatim*.

Hashim's brother Al-Muttalib came up from Mecca to retrieve his nephew. When they returned together, Shaibah's tanned skin confused his relatives, who were meeting him for the first time. They assumed he was Al-Muttalib's new apprentice and dubbed him 'Abdul-Muttalib (Al-Muttalib's apprentice). The moniker stuck.

'Abdul-Muttalib was of course unfamiliar with Mecca's dialect and customs. Local boys teased him because of his foreign accent and strange cultural references. As a *yatim*, he had no obvious path to influence in the city, despite his father's and great-grandfather's legendary status. 'Abdul-Muttalib quickly learned that he would wield influence only if he mastered the one tool available to all people: the Arabic language.

❖ ❖ ❖

Finding the Zamzam Well had not earned 'Abdul-Muttalib leadership status. Although he had some success in business, he had not become chief elder because of his wealth. Rather, the outsider had risen to the top ranks of Meccan society primarily due to his linguistic abilities.

When clashing tribes were at one another's throats, his diplomatic skills—particularly the ability to speak to each clan using their own dialect and persuasive idioms—averted conflict. When the Abyssinian general Abraha besieged Mecca with plans to level the city and enslave its inhabitants, 'Abdul-Muttalib managed to secure a meeting with him and convinced Abraha to turn back. Preventing war and carnage with words alone marked 'Abdul-Muttalib as a unique talent and propelled him to the honored position of Mecca's chief elder.

'Abdul-Muttalib recounted many of his own diplomatic interventions while sitting with his grandson on Abu Qubais overlooking the center of Mecca. As the sun set, he impressed upon the boy the importance of effective communication. Language was the basis of leadership. Because Arabs lacked standing armies, power came from persuasion. To be a leader, one had to be eloquent, adept in nuance, and able to speak to people of different backgrounds in a way they could appreciate.

'Abdul-Muttalib taught his grandson that the sign of true eloquence is when you can make the blind see, help the person who cannot smell experience fragrance, enable the person who cannot taste experience flavors; when you can awaken the senses and stir the emotions. The Arabic word for eloquence—*fus-hah*—described a process of revealing internal dimensions not visible from the exterior. An eloquent Arabic speaker could evoke vivid scenes that moved listeners to experience ideas with their senses.

'Abdul-Muttalib knew that Muhammad would have to develop outstanding Arabic to make a lasting impact, so he set about equipping the eight-year-old with such mastery. 'Abdul-Muttalib began by explaining the fundamental building blocks of Arabic and the social context in which the language had been formed. He pointed to three key stages. Arabic as a Semitic language emerged among nomads who developed words related to movement, adaptability, and freedom. Then, when nomads began to form agricultural settlements, Arabic incorporated a new set of words related to planting, natural cycles, and growth. Finally, when small towns grew into urban centers, the people required new words related to structure, cooperation, and established standards.

Each stage enriched the language. 'Abdul-Muttalib noted that Muhammad had already lived among the nomads and then experienced the agricultural climate at Yathrib. Now it was time for him to master the most developed linguistic context: elite urban communication that drew on the earlier two stages while taking expression to a new level of sophistication. Nomads and farmers did not need to persuade others on a large scale; their communication was primarily with family members. But to be a leader in a city required the ability to influence thousands of diverse people.

The Semitic language had begun with alphabetic forms, created during the transition from the nomadic life to agricultural settlement. For the first time, individuals who were not related by blood lived together. They needed a way to create a new united identity beyond lineage. Recording words gave them a common reference point.

Each letter began as an image representing common physical objects in the daily life of these newly settled communities: an ox (for plowing), a house (unlike the nomad's tent), and a pitchfork (for harvesting). These complemented preexisting concepts represented by other letters: body parts (hand, palm, head, eye, mouth, tooth, molar, back, chest), tools (fishhook, ink holder, pitchfork, bow, needle), and animals (camel, fish).

The Semites' innovation was to use these physical images to represent abstract concepts: The *alif* (A), based on an ox, came to connote mastery. The *bayt* (B), based on a house, evoked belonging. The *mim* (M), based on water, represented life flow and fertility.

Arabic words were constructed by combining three letters into core roots. The three letters together fused separate concepts into something new and evocative. *A-L-H*—the word for the Divine—combined the concepts of mastery, guidance, and praise. Arabic used its twenty-eight letters to form thousands of roots, each with different, nuanced meanings based on grammatical structure. As Arabic had developed numerous grammatical forms, each with a unique meaning, the language contained myriad possibilities for expressing ideas.

The Arabic term for these three-letter combinations was *juthr* (root). Indeed, language was understood to be like a tree, with roots that nurtured a trunk supporting many branches, each with its own subbranches and buds that blossomed to eventually become fruit. While the root words were concrete physical objects, their fruits developed into highly abstract concepts. The link between the physical and the metaphoric gave the language its power.

Since the Arabs lacked written books, most elders did not see any necessity to be literate. Muhammad noticed that they instead possessed a massive mental store of information. Members of the elders' council were familiar with at least sixty thousand Arabic roots and thousands of grammatical forms. Because Arabic was based on Semitic roots, elders were also able to decipher other languages like Ethiopic, Syriac, and Aramaic in the region—allowing them to navigate markets in other cities like Damascus.

'Abdul-Muttalib stressed to his grandson the importance of appreciating the context in which particular words developed. Most farmers and city residents would not be aware, for example, that the root *Sh-M-R*—used to convey safeguarding—originally referred to a ring of acacia thorns that protected sleeping nomads from wild animals during the night.

The root *Q-R-A* developed among farmers to describe the blossoming of fruit trees. This was in contrast to the root *Z-H-R*, used for all forms of blossoming, including fruitless flowers. The root image of blossoming evolved to become associated with the opening of the mouth to utter a command. Again, nomads or urban dwellers used the word constantly while remaining oblivious to the underlying physical concept.

The root *S-L-M* had developed to describe repairing cracks in city walls and urban buildings (distinct from the root *S-L-H*, used to describe repairing orchard walls). With time, the concept *salam* came to mean the safety of being surrounded by solid walls and then further evolved to mean peace (the absence of insecurity). Urban dwellers understood that *S-L-M* required scaffolding, cooperation, and regulations—concepts largely lost on nomads and farmers.

The same word could have different meanings in different communities, even if they spoke the same language. The root *D-F-A* described helping someone become warm by building a fire for them or covering them in blankets. In western Arabia, it became associated with making sure someone special was comfortable. In eastern Arabia, it became associated with putting a suffering animal out of its misery. In one classic story, a leader from western Arabia ordered that an elite prisoner be accorded every comfort, yet his soldier from eastern Arabia understood it as a beheading order. The result was not pretty.

Going back to the core physical roots of words could unlock special meaning. *Taqwa* and *amal* both could be used to convey the concept of hope. While *amal* was built on the underlying concept of reveries, *taqwa* referred to a rope used to draw water up from a well. One connoted passive daydreaming and wishing, the other taking action. Rather than simply hoping water would arrive at one's mouth, one could weave a rope to pull water up from a well.

Thanks to his grandfather, Muhammad came to possess the most powerful persuasive tool set of anyone in Arabia. Indeed, the basis for Muhammad's prophethood in Muslim tradition is the Qur'an: divine insights revealed via Muhammad. In traditional understanding, the miracle of the Qur'an is its language as much as its content. In a way, the Qur'an offers a window into the lost world of the elders' creative eloquence. It employs their artisanal approach to language, fashioning words into images, smells, tastes, and emotions—only to forge a striking new message. It shifts among nomadic, agricultural, and urban modes, strategically referencing concepts and situations familiar to diverse audiences.

In the short term, the language talents bequeathed by his grandfather gave Muhammad the ability to connect with much older people. In just a few years he would be able to hold his own when speaking with elders and quickly earn their respect.

❖ ❖ ❖

As sunset gradually draped Mecca in darkness, trumpets resounded from the city's hills proclaiming 'Abdul-Muttalib's imminent death. Two weeks earlier the eighty-three-year-old chief elder had unexpectedly taken ill. All Mecca entered into a formal state of civic mourning, as the city's women began to wail. Meccans believed a dying elder deserved to hear the lamentation of his people before he succumbed.

The old man lay prostrate in a white Egyptian tunic; he was in his bedroom, which was illuminated only by small lanterns. His daughters had gathered around him, cooling his feverish forehead with damp cloths and reciting flowery poetry about his life. In pagan Arabia, which lacked the concept of an afterlife, friends and relatives delivered eulogies before someone died so that the dying person might pass away in a happy state.

Because society expected men to remain stoic, 'Abdul-Muttalib's sons watched their dying father silently. Muhammad, however, could not hold back his tears. He lay at his grandfather's side, hugging the old man. For two years they had slept beside each other on the same mattress. By day they had also been inseparable. Yet now a final separation loomed.

'Abdul-Muttalib motioned to his son Abu Talib to draw near. "Take care of this son of mine," he said in a weak voice while caressing Muhammad's head. "Be a father to him as though he is yours or even greater." Abu Talib bowed in acceptance, declaring, "I shall fulfill your bequest to the best of my abilities. I will keep him safe as though he is my own body, flesh of my flesh, blood of my blood."

The dying grandfather then tucked his hand under Muhammad's chin, raising the crying boy's face so he could look him in the eyes. With this last breath, 'Abdul-Muttalib declared, "Oh Muhammad, let your name be eternal—become an exemplary role model!" Then his eyes closed.

The women in the room wailed, striking their faces in despair. The men watched silently, tears rolling down their cheeks. Muhammad clung to his grandfather for the next hour. No one dared to pry him loose, until at last Barakah intervened and led him away.

The next morning, the elder's funeral procession headed north toward Mecca's main cemetery, Jannat-ul-Mu'allah (the elevated forest). Muhammad and his uncle Abu Talib walked at the front of the procession while the remaining eight brothers carried the bier. The symbolism of Muhammad—alone among the grandchildren—leading the procession marked him as 'Abdul-Muttalib's protégé and spiritual heir. Abu Talib's presence at the front marked him as Muhammad's new guardian. Following the three-day funeral rites, the young boy moved into his uncle's home, along with Barakah.

'Abdul-Muttalib had carefully selected Abu Talib to be Muhammad's new guardian. He might have chosen his wealthiest son, yet 'Abdul-'Uzza (the provider of fresh dates during Aminah's labor) lacked his brother's compassion and sensitivity. Abu Talib's easygoing and accepting nature made him the ideal candidate to take care of a traumatized boy afflicted with the loss of yet another dear relative. Moreover, Abu Talib's devoted wife, Fatimah Bint Asad, possessed sophisticated social and emotional intelligence. Women struggling with marital crises and parenting challenges regularly turned to Fatimah for counseling.

Fatimah had to muster the full power of her therapeutic skills to care for the newest member of her household. Muhammad had withdrawn in a repeat of the mourning process he had experienced two years earlier when his mother died. In a state of shock, he hardly spoke, and when he did, it was with a feeble voice. For the family meals, Fatimah would prepare a large platter for the entire household, yet Muhammad sat silently to the side as his cousins gobbled down all the food. Fatimah began setting aside a plate for her nephew in advance, and she made a point to dine alongside him to ensure he actually ate.

Fatimah took a sunrise walk every morning in the hills surrounding Mecca. The exercise was precious alone time before her large household awoke, yet she began to invite Muhammad to join her. She would rouse him before dawn and hold his hand as they traversed rocks glowing soft violet and orange beneath the rising sun. Their breath would condense in the cool morning air, as oryxes and jerboas bustled in the distance and falcons swooped overhead, scanning the terrain for their breakfast.

Muhammad mostly remained quiet, but Fatimah made conversation the whole way, pointing out the different creatures stirring around them and recounting stories from the previous day. Following the lead of her late father-in-law, Fatimah sensed that Muhammad had enormous potential, yet she worried that in his traumatized state he might withdraw into complete silence.

One day, the duo's path brought them to a bridge traversing a small ravine outside Mecca. Because Mecca lacked any trees, bridges were constructed of palm fiber ropes. As Fatimah and Muhammad crossed the rickety rope bridge, she seized the moment to share a therapeutic insight. A natural process that split the earth had formed the ravine below. Rather than remain stuck on one side, feeling helpless, someone had woven this structure to make traversing the gulf possible, and others benefitted from that person's hard work. The ropes, though formed from dead material, had become a vital connecting force.

Using the metaphor of the rope bridge, Fatimah encouraged Muhammad not to withdraw, despite being split from his grandfather; she advised him to recognize how something that is usually discarded can have immense value. *Salah*, the word for these bridges, had come to mean "connection." Guiding Muhammad across the bridge, Fatimah urged him to repair the connections in his life. She pointed out that the rope bridge required constant maintenance, as its fragile fibers withered with age; tying new knots preserved the bridge's strength.

Under Fatimah's guidance, Muhammad began to emerge from isolation. Though he still held back from forging deep relationships with others, Muhammad soon became known in Mecca as an affable and friendly young man with many acquaintances. He remained forever grateful to Fatimah for drawing him out when no one else knew how. When she died decades later, Muhammad buried her himself after wrapping her body in his trademark green tunic. "She stepped in to serve as my mother after I lost my mother," he declared in tribute at her graveside. "She believed in me and helped me through my grief."

Fatimah's mentorship enabled Muhammad's other foster mother, the newly liberated Barakah, to move out. She married and had a son of her own. Muhammad saw her regularly but continued to live with his aunt and uncle and developed relationships with their children. Muhammad spent much of his day shadowing his uncle Abu Talib and assisting with deliveries of merchandise and performing other errands.

One day, Abu Talib and Muhammad were walking through the market when a nomad with amulets dangling from his crude leather garments glared at them and started screaming. His piercing black eyes—encircled with kohl to reduce the sun's glare—locked on Muhammad, and the nomad's braided white beard shook.

The old man was an expert in the ancient art of *firasah* (literally, unveiling the hidden)—a divination skill Arabs used to reveal an individual's character and destiny. He had come to the city from his desert encampment to read the faces, hands, and other physical characteristics of Mecca's children, charging parents for the examination. When his gaze fell on young Muhammad, however, the *firasah* specialist was captivated. "Bring the boy to me!" he shouted in a raspy voice, as Abu Talib drew Muhammad away. "He will one day become master of great empires!"

The market crowd laughed at the nomad's dramatic performance and dismissed the aging master as a senile old man. Yet one twelve-year-old girl amid the mocking swarm suspected there might be something more to the old man's hysteria. Her name was Khadijah.

Abu Talib was shaken by the incident. He had yanked Muhammad out of the market before the situation escalated and reported the details to his wife when they returned home. Fatimah wondered whether the *firasah* expert had perceived the same unique qualities in Muhammad that 'Abdul-Muttalib had recognized. She urged her husband to nurture the young boy in order to develop his full potential. Maybe it was time for Muhammad to accompany Abu Talib on the caravan journey to Damascus, she suggested.

Abu Talib rejected the idea out of hand. He had made a pledge to safeguard Muhammad; staying in Mecca was safer. For two years, Fatimah kept after her husband, challenging him to stop confining the boy. Finally, when Muhammad was ten years old, Abu Talib relented.

The evening before the caravan was set to depart, Fatimah and Abu Talib informed Muhammad that he would be accompanying his uncle. Excited and nervous, Muhammad rushed off to share the news with Barakah. As the two sat beneath the stars, Barakah recalled details of the northern Arabian landscape, which she had last seen as a child.

The next morning, the dew seemed to dance as it evaporated, whirling above hundreds of camels laden with goods. Merchants from all over the region had gathered to join the Meccan caravan, both for the safety it afforded and the advantage of Meccan's tax-exempt status in Byzantine territory. Wives bid their husbands farewell, handing them four pebbles as charms to ward off evil from all four directions.

Influenced by his monotheistic mother, Muhammad had no interest in charms, so Fatimah handed him a different gift for the journey: a small goatskin water pouch. As scores of trumpets thundered, camels rose like plants sprouting from the barren landscape. Muhammad had briefly joined the caravan four years earlier for the trip to Yathrib, but this time he was setting out on the full journey to Damascus—and riding without the company of Aminah and Barakah.

Driving his own camel was a big deal. As he mounted the beast, someone handed Muhammad its *'aql*—an adjustable securing rope. When the camel was in a seated position, the *'aql* was tied around its right knee to keep it from standing. Indeed, the Qur'an uses the word *'aql* (intellect) forty-one times, applying it figuratively to evoke leveraging mind and logic to unlock flow and flexibility.

As Mecca receded, Muhammad held tight to the camel's reins. The sensitive ten-year-old sorrowfully recalled the last time he had joined the caravan, then with his mother by his side. Abu Talib saw tears rolling down his nephew's cheeks as their entourage headed out into the desert.

3

THE APPRENTICE

The Red Sea Coast: 6:30 p.m., Tuesday, May 21, 580 CE

The mass of blue water seemed to swallow the setting sun, its vibrant red hues dissolving on the horizon. Titanic waves pounded the sandstone coast.

Muhammad stared out, awestruck, from atop his camel as the caravan descended the vast west Arabian dunes toward the Red Sea. The aquamarine waters dwarfed Yathrib's small ponds and the short-lived puddles of Mecca's rainy season. For the first time, he heard the soothing sound of the sea's waves.

A massive sandstorm had made the usual inland route impassable, so the lead desert tracker diverted the caravan along the coast. The Bedouin wilderness guide, called a *hadi* (literally, recall expert), was a master navigator. While the Meccans could follow the well-worn trade routes by reading the evening stars, they hired a *hadi* for help when alternate routes were neessary. The nomad had the skills to adapt to fluctuating weather conditions and quickly shift course, with a flexibility Muhammad greatly admired.

The navigator relied, in part, on his ability to analyze the tracks of wild animals, particularly the oryx, whose heightened sense of smell and deep knowledge of terrain enabled them to stay on safe paths. The oryx knew how to avoid danger (lions, hyenas, and leopards) and stay near water sources. The *hadi* treated the oryx as trailblazers for the caravan camels: where they went, the camels could follow.

Muhammad witnessed how the tracker could re-create a scene just by analyzing the traces the oryx left behind. The size of an animal's hoofprints reflected its height and age. The depth and proximity of the prints' impressions specified weight, agility, and speed. The pattern of steps yielded clues to the animal's general health and anatomic structure.

On the shores of the Red Sea, the entourage paused to rest and take in the salty air. Camels relaxed or wandered in the wet sand. Muhammad sat on the beach in the twilight and watched as the camels etched patterns with their footsteps, adorning the tracks with dung. Years later he would remark, "The dung is a proof of the camel's existence, and the impressions in the sand prove this creature can walk and reveal its characteristics—even if it cannot be seen. An earth that is so vast and full of wandering, beautiful paths and a heaven full of majestic constellations and guiding stars, are they not a proof of unseen genius behind it all?" If evidence of the camel's existence and characteristics remained after its departure, human beings might similarly understand the Divine by observing the universe.

The ten-year-old boy on the beach was still decades from becoming a prophet. But he was developing important tools of deduction, able to extract valuable insights about larger phenomena from small and seemingly trivial pieces of information.

As Muhammad enjoyed roasted fresh fish for the first time in his life, he looked out over a darkening sea illuminated by the last rays of the setting sun. The flowing waves offered a mirror to the vast desert dunes behind him that seemed to have no end.

❖ ❖ ❖

The following day the caravan moved on, traversing a surreal landscape. Muhammad admired beautiful rocks rising like majestic roses from the sand, each uniquely sculpted over millennia by swirling winds. Deep alcoves in the sides of these outcroppings made ideal resting places for travelers during the hottest hours of the day. When dust storms suddenly roared across the massive dunes and enveloped the encampment, people crouched while gripping long lances painted red at the top—markers for rescuers in case the sandstorm buried them alive.

Mounted archers flanked the caravan, keeping a watchful eye out for marauding bandits and wild beasts. At the head of the caravan, a group of horsemen scouted the ever-changing landscape for concealed subterranean caverns. By day, the *hadi* thrust rods into the ground to determine the time based on the shadows they cast in the shifting sun. By night, constellations illuminated the path forward. To keep the camels moving in sync, nomadic musicians played flutes to lull the otherwise obstinate beasts into a swaying hypnotic march.

Muhammad beheld the extended caravan flowing like a stream, adjusting to disruptions and seizing unexpected opportunities. The concept of *yusr* appears repeatedly in the Qur'an, evoking the image of water flowing around obstacles. Muhammad would later preach, "The foundations of faith lie in flow and ease; anyone inflexible will be overcome and ruined by their rigidity."

Two weeks after departing Mecca, the caravan made its first major stop at Yathrib to let the camels rest and to restock supplies. It had been four years since Muhammad's first and only visit to the city. Mindful that his mother's deathbed wish remained unfulfilled, Muhammad refrained from visiting her grave. Banu Najjar relatives shared the sad news that his grandparents Wahb and Barrah had died. Muhammad's entire immediate family was now gone.

As the caravan continued northward, it passed all sorts of communities and cultures. Accents, buildings, clothing styles, and cuisines changed along with the landscape. At the oasis of Tayma, Muhammad found a vibrant city ruled by a dynasty of Jewish kings and inhabitants who spoke a fusion of Arabic and Aramaic. At Tabuk, a town in the ancient lands of Midian, Muhammad explored the first stone homes he had ever seen while the caravan replenished water supplies from centuries-old wells. At Mada`in Saleh, the caravan passed abandoned Nabatean burial chambers with grand facades hewn out of massive rocks.

At last the caravan traversed the northern tip of Arabia and entered the ancient city of Bosra, which featured a grand entrance archway and the first paved streets Muhammad had ever walked on. Groups of trees shaded the paths, and lush grasses grew between buildings. The caravan passed a massive Roman amphitheater, headed down a central boulevard surrounded by columns, and paused to rest outside a two-hundred-year-old monastery built of large grey stones. The monastery featured an elegant arch, vaulted ceilings, and images of grapevines engraved in its smooth stone exterior—a masterwork of architecture compared with the Ka'bah's flimsy stone structure that often buckled in flash floods.

For weary travelers, arriving at the monastery marked the end of the desert portion of their journey and a chance to enjoy fresh local cuisine: chickpeas, beans, and other legumes unavailable in Mecca. The monks earned a steady stream of revenue by feeding the passing caravans. As Muhammad's traveling companions rushed to devour the lunch meal, the ten-year-old paused to wash his hands. Muhammad, the youngest member of the group by several years, walked slowly to the back of the serving line, observing the frenzied diners with composure. When it was at last his turn, Muhammad politely thanked the monk who ladled his serving into a wooden bowl.

Bahira, the monastery's abbot, gazed at the boy. The old man normally remained aloof from the pack of caravan participants, whom he warily regarded as boorish. But Muhammad's unusual maturity and eloquence impressed the cleric. Bahira was reed thin from long fasts, with chiseled cheeks and a long white beard. His coarse brown woolen garments riddled with holes conveyed an aura of piety. Of mixed Assyrian and Armenian heritage, the abbot had spent years traveling across Asia and Africa, seeking knowledge and collecting rare manuscripts before retreating to a life of seclusion in this monastery at the edge of the desert.

Bahira asked to be introduced to the boy, and caravan members pointed the cleric to Abu Talib, who informed Bahira that Muhammad was his orphaned nephew. Abu Talib permitted Bahira to converse with Muhammad and shadowed the pair as they sat in the shade of an ancient olive tree. The old man and the young boy spoke in soft voices, so Abu Talib could make out only the general tone of their intense conversation.

Muhammad never revealed the precise details of their conversation, but the two immediately bonded. Aside from the *firasah* face reader,

Bahira was the first nonrelative who saw potential in Muhammad. The young boy, who had never before seen a Christian religious site or met a Christian cleric, intuitively saw the monk as a mentor. Moved by their conversation, Bahira impulsively broke with monastery policy—which generally prevented Arab caravan travelers from entering the abbey—and invited Muhammad inside. Abu Talib followed a few paces behind.

Bahira, living up to his name (which means "profoundly learned"), knew multiple languages, and his monastery library housed dozens of remarkable manuscripts and scrolls. He allowed Muhammad to explore the library's contents. At Yathrib as a six-year-old, Muhammad had seen rabbis reading from scrolls, but in Bahira's library he held and opened a bound book for the first time. Muhammad admired the enchanting shapes of the letters in Bahira's Syriac Bible and explored other books decorated with illuminated images. The Arabs produced no written books, certainly not illustrated ones or bound volumes containing divine guidance.

On the library wall, Muhammad noticed the same icon of Mary embracing baby Jesus that had captivated him inside the Ka'bah—the image, it seemed, was displayed throughout the region. Bahira was the first expert on Christianity whom Muhammad could ask about the striking picture. He learned about a boy born without an earthly father and raised by a single mother and called to address the woes of his society.

Bahira described the Orthodox Christian tradition of the nativity of Mary, a captivating narrative echoed in the Qur'an: While Mary's mother, Anne, was pregnant, she pledged her future child, who she assumed would be a boy, to serve at the Temple in Jerusalem. But Mary insisted on fulfilling her mother's vow. At age six, Mary lived up to her name (Maryam in Hebrew means "rebellion") by marching into the Temple in Jerusalem. She strode past all the priests and went straight to the holy of holies—a sacred place only the high priest was allowed to enter once a year (on Yom Kippur).

Mary refused to be bound by her society's restrictions and was not afraid to take risks to change the world around her. She instilled that same commitment in her son, who also rebelled against his society's elite. Jesus ministered to the blind and lepers, hailed the positive example of the Samaritan enemy, and went to Galilee to teach the fishermen.

He delivered his greatest sermon not in a temple but on a mountain, in nature where everyone could attend.

While Muhammad gained insights from Bahira, he was not drawn to the monastic life, which required retreating from the world rather than trying to change it. The Qur'an nonetheless would declare that "Christian monks in solitude are sincere in their words and actions—their demeanor is one of humility." It would contrast corrupt clergy who abuse their leadership with humble monks who exercise no power over others in their sincere devotion. Further, when Muhammad later developed a code of war, he specifically cited monasteries and monks as institutions and individuals who cannot be harmed or disturbed. (Bahira's monastery still stands today, as do many other ancient monasteries in Muslim lands.)

After their initial discussion inside the monastery, Bahira returned Muhammad to the caravan. Turning privately to Abu Talib, the monk declared, "This boy is unique. Guard his talents well because he will make an impact upon the world. He will face much opposition, and many will try to assassinate him." Abu Talib expressed surprise that such a young boy could inspire such animosity. Bahira clarified: "He will shake the very foundations of their faith and will refuse to conform to their world."

❖ ❖ ❖

The caravan had to reach Damascus before the city gates closed on Sunday. As the train of camels approached its destination after six weeks en route, Muhammad stared wide-eyed at the largest city he had ever seen. Its silhouette loomed in the distance with massive walls capped by fluttering banners and a skyline of church bell towers.

Damascus, one of the oldest cities in the world, was the gateway to Europe from Asia. Bordered by high mountains on three sides, the city was constructed on a plateau that made it appear imposing when approached from below. The Barada River, which flowed along Damascus's northern edge, connected the city with the fertile agricultural lands to the northeast.

While most urban centers had evolved from fledgling agricultural settlements, Damascus, a bustling metropolis of over one hundred thousand people, had been established thousands of years earlier as a planned city, favorably situated on the commercial nexus of the Silk Road. Damascus was a hub of refinement and entrepreneurialism, a place to incubate new products and ideas. As skilled craftsmen and innovators, Damascenes prided themselves on quality. Raw materials streamed into the city and streamed out as refined goods primarily bound for European markets.

Mecca's annual caravan brought a variety of products unavailable in the Levant and Europe. In the winter, the Meccans made a caravan trip south to stock up on goods delivered by ship to Yemen: spices like cinnamon, cardamom, and black pepper, as well as uncut rubies and emeralds. They also loaded up African imports like ivory, leather, and frankincense. Stored in Mecca for several months until winter ended in Damascus, the goods then headed north with the early summer caravan, which also carried ostriches, cheetahs, hunting dogs, and falcons to market.

As the caravan approached Damascus early on Sunday morning, the rising sun illuminated mountains to the west capped in snow—a new sight for Muhammad. Most of the winter snow at lower altitudes had melted, yielding flowing rivers and a green countryside stretching in all directions. Lush pastures lined the main road, and on the surrounding hills shepherds steered their flocks through verdant meadows.

People in the towns south of Damascus stared as the entourage of hundreds of camels lumbered toward the city accompanied by the men of the desert. Unlike the bearded, long-haired Arabs, Damascenes were clean shaven, with close-cropped hair and lighter skin; they also were shorter than the Arabs. Muhammad observed other caravans approaching from the west, bringing European buyers via the port city of Caesarea and North Africans from Egypt. While direct trade from the east was largely cut off by the Byzantines' ongoing war with the Sasanians, some Indian merchants still managed to reach Damascus, and prized Persian products like silk and spikenard (treasured by Damascene women for its exotic fragrance) were smuggled out of Persia.

Each approaching caravan raised banners to identify its origin, and each was greeted in return by the imposing red and gold standards of the Byzantine Empire that flanked the road into Damascus. Muhammad's caravan flew the Meccan flag, featuring five rectangular embroidered red tapestries connected together atop a long pole. Beads on leather cords adorned its shaft, along with ostrich and falcon feathers to ward off evil.

The caravans made a point of arriving in Damascus on Sunday, when the city's market closed for the Christian Sabbath, enabling merchants to more easily unload and prepare their products for sale the next day. The city's main entrance was its massive western gate, Bab al-Jabiyah, which opened from sunrise to sunset before clanging shut in the evening. Muhammad stared at the arched gate, which was nestled between two huge watchtowers and guarded by armored sentries wielding short swords and circular bronze shields decorated with a red cross. Arabia had no army, but in Damascus hundreds of Byzantine soldiers patrolled the streets. They defended against attacks from the Sasanians and kept out the riffraff, ensuring that Damascus remained an urban oasis predominantly for the middle and upper classes.

Visitors to Damascus had to pay a toll to enter the city, as well as a tax on their goods. But the Meccans were equipped with the letter that Hashim (Muhammad's great-grandfather) had secured years earlier from the Byzantine emperor that exempted them from all tariffs. Two worlds met as the Meccans presented that letter to the customs officials, communicating in a combination of Greek, Arabic, and Aramaic. Once matters were resolved, the caravan paused outside the city walls by the banks of the Barada River. The camels would camp there for the remainder of the visit, while the precious goods they had transported on their backs were carted into rented storehouses beside the city's main market.

Damascus was a sensory overload for young Muhammad. Entering through the Bab al-Jabiyah gate was like passing from a monochrome world into a vibrant explosion of color. People of diverse backgrounds wearing a variety of clothing swirled around him. Egyptians, Greeks, Armenians, Slavs, Kurds, Spaniards, Indians, and others formed a melting pot of cultures and languages. The people of Damascus had several thousand years of experience living together and had developed a genteel politeness and polished manners. Damascenes always bowed when greeting each other.

The aroma of freshly ground spices and rosewater infused the crisp morning air. Braids of garlic, a staple of Damascene cuisine, hung to dry everywhere. Known as the City of Jasmine, Damascus was filled with the delicate flowers (whose oils were distilled into perfumes), as well as rosebushes, grapevines, and cedar trees. It was a far cry from the stench of the Banu Sa'd encampment.

Chaperoned by a vigilant Abu Talib, young Muhammad walked down Damascus's main street, Via Recta, a boulevard flanked by massive columns stretching west to east. Large rectangular paving stones, fitted perfectly together, magnified the avenue's grandeur. Reminders of civilizations from the city's previous ten thousand years were layered on one another, a kind of living history. Impressive three-story homes were mostly built of skillfully shaped stone and fine baked brick. Exquisitely carved statues adorned the city.

The melodious ringing of bells from the city's many churches called the faithful to Sunday worship—a reminder that Damascus was an overwhelmingly Christian city. Pilgrims came from afar to visit shrines dedicated to Jesus's early followers (who had made Damascus one of their centers), including the house where Saint Ananias converted Paul. Indeed, it was on the road to Damascus where Paul had a blinding vision of Jesus, transforming Paul from a persecutor of Christ's followers into one of his greatest disciples. Paul effectively expanded Jesus's Jewish reformation movement into a religion with its own rites and theology targeting a universal audience. By 325 CE, Damascus was a majority Christian city, one of the world's first.

Wealthy pilgrims and other visitors to Damascus rented rooms at inns and guesthouses. Most of the caravan members, however, lodged in hostels that surrounded the main marketplace. The two-story halls—used as reserve army barracks during war—slept one hundred people on thin straw-filled mattresses on each floor. Abu Talib and Muhammad were assigned side-by-side mattresses on the second floor. From the roof of the building, Muhammad gazed up at the towering Cathedral of John the Baptist and down at the market-side docks along the Barada River. Small reed and wood barges delivered lumber, fresh vegetables, and grains from farmlands in the north. Massive waterwheels transported water from the river to a large aqueduct that supplied the city's public baths and fountains.

Abu Talib showed him the public lavatories, where more than thirty people could sit in a chamber lined with many holes carved out of long stone slabs. It was an uncomfortable experience for the shy boy—as were the public baths, where Muhammad insisted on wearing a loin-cloth as he washed himself amid a crowd of naked men. The bathhouse had several rooms: a frigidarium with cold water, a caldarium with hot steam, and a tepidarium with a warm pool where men ladled water over themselves and scrubbed their skin with olive-oil soaps. Muhammad noticed that enslaved boys, some younger than he, were carrying wood to heat the water.

On Monday morning, the market burst to life. Meccan merchants began circulating in the crowd, seeking out buyers for their wholesale goods and inviting the interested to sample their wares in the nearby storehouses. Muhammad headed into the throng with Abu Talib, grip-ping his uncle's hand as they wandered among hundreds of stalls. The market was generally divided by product: grains in one place, textiles in another, and so on.

Almonds, pistachios, walnuts, figs, raisins, apricots, and oranges were sold along with fresh mulberries that had been squeezed into a sweet syrupy drink. Street vendors offered licorice and tamarind beverages, and carts hauling snow from the nearby mountains sold an expensive dessert of mulberry syrup over the snow. The market also had an entire section dedicated to Damascus's world-renowned delights, such as halva (*halwah*), candied fruits, and assorted nuts. It was a bounty of exciting new tastes for Muhammad.

He took an instant liking to olives. (Bread dipped in olive oil would become one of his favorite meals.) In the olive market, he watched olives being pressed between large stone cylinders to extract their green golden oil, which was then processed with lye and aromatic herbs into square bars of soap.

Muhammad was intrigued as he watched master craftsmen refine raw materials into finished consumer products. Jewelers in the market cut the rough stones from India, also delivered by the Meccan caravan, into polished gems. Blacksmiths forged swords, sending sparks flying into the road. A spark once singed Muhammad's tunic, burning a hole in it.

Muhammad had a more appealing experience as he watched per-fume makers extract oils from flowers and herbs. As the experts mixed oils into perfumes and bottled them in elegantly sculpted containers, some ointment splashed on Muhammad's garments, leaving a pleasant fragrance that lingered for hours.

Toward the end of their trip, Muhammad asked Abu Talib if they could visit the childhood home of their ancestor Qusai, who 150 years earlier had forged a new identity for himself in Damascus before returning to Mecca. They tracked down their distant cousins, descendants of Qusai's half siblings, and Muhammad enjoyed seeing their large home with its beautiful enclosed courtyard with trees and roses.

After six weeks in Damascus, the caravan's preset departure date arrived. Abu Talib wrapped the gold coins from his sales in a long cloth (*nitaq*) that he tied around his waist.

As the entourage departed, young Muhammad looked out at the camels, which now were carrying little or nothing, and wondered why the Meccan merchants returned largely empty-handed, aside from their personal purchases of swords, silks for their wives, dried raisins, nuts, olive oil, and, of course, enslaved people of Slavic origin.

❖ ❖ ❖

After the dynamism of cosmopolitan Damascus, home felt oppressive. Mecca's physical confinement—geographically squeezed by four mountains that trapped extreme heat and stunted plant growth—mirrored the backwater town's stultifying dreariness. (Muhammad would later liken Mecca's inertia to a rib cage crushed by external weight.)

A few months later, Muhammad asked his uncle if he could join the annual winter caravan south to Yemen to purchase goods that the caravan would transport to Damascus in the summer. Abu Talib agreed.

The Yemenites differed from their central Arabian cousins in one significant way: paganism had mostly given way to monotheism. Though Muhammad found the language and culture generally familiar, he found a land with a large Jewish population and a significant Christian minority. The people, as he would later praise them, were sincere, sophisticated, dependable, and good-hearted.

By the time he returned to Mecca, Muhammad had lost patience with the pagan rites that dominated the city; of Mecca's fourteen major clans, only one, the Banul Harith, was Jewish. To be sure, Meccans were hardly fanatics: their devotion to maintaining the system of idol-atry was driven more by the desire to preserve traditions than by deep commitment. Religious practice remained mostly casual, with no for-mal pressure to participate in worship. Nonetheless, Muhammad's con-temporaries noticed that he never took part, later remarking, "We never saw Muhammad offer sacrifices at altars, participate in religious rituals, consult a priest, or wear an amulet."

Muhammad also eschewed alcohol, noting how intoxication led to ridiculous behavior. As a twelve-year-old, he was shocked to learn that the curator of Dar-un-Nadwah had sold the building entrusted to his care for a mere flask of wine while in a drunken stupor. Compared with most Meccans, Muhammad was modest. After flash floods damaged the Ka'bah, he assisted with repair efforts. Most of the workmen removed their loincloths and placed them on their shoulders to transport bricks without scraping their skin. When Abu Talib suggested he do the same, Muhammad fainted.

As a child, Muhammad mostly did odd jobs to help contribute to his uncle's household. Finances were often tight, and Muhammad con-stituted an extra mouth to feed. In the fall and spring, between caravan seasons, Muhammad worked as a shepherd. He awoke before dawn to take his employer's herd out to pasture. Trained by his uncle Hamzah, Muhammad soon became a skilled archer—a necessity when wolves, lions, hyenas, eagles, and other predators regularly attempted to attack his flock. The cost of any lost animal would be deducted from his wages.

As a shepherd, Muhammad led the flock from hill to hill, scouting for the best grazing grounds. He kept an eye out for plants and herbs harmful to his sheep and collected those that made good brews and medicines. And he learned how to anticipate the behavior of predatory animals and birds of prey. He carried a staff (with his lunch tied to the top) to guide the flock and ward off wolves. Several sheepdogs accom-panied him, and he admired them as loyal guardians—reflected in a Qur'anic verse (18:22) that honors a particular dog by mentioning it three times to underline its value as a devoted companion.

While camel guides had to be tough with their stubborn beasts, shep-herding taught Muhammad how to lead with gentleness. According to

Muslim tradition, all prophets needed to serve as shepherds. Herding sheep taught prophets-to-be patience, responsibility, safeguarding, and how to guide with action rather than words. Muhammad would later tell his followers, *"Kullukum ra'i"*—"You are each shepherds in your own way"—and observed that "gentle conduct yields positive outcomes; harsh conduct the opposite."

Before returning to town at dusk, Muhammad took his flock to the nearby wells of Hudaibiyyah. Like most of Arabia's wells, access to the water was regulated by a pact called an *ummah*—an Arabic term that described a force attracting elements like a magnet drawing in metallic objects. A watering hole's *ummah* agreement stipulated when different herders could bring their animals to drink, avoiding chaos and delineating a shared understanding for how to divide a collective resource. A well guardian, called a *warid* (water manager), with a carved staff directed access to the water in an orderly manner. As Muhammad waited for his turn, he observed that people embraced the *ummah* system because it yielded a beneficial outcome.

Muhammad added carpentry to his repertoire at age fourteen. He likely acquired tools and basic know-how from his cousins in Yathrib when the caravan passed through the city.

Young men in Mecca observed what they considered a rite of passage into manhood at fifteen. One day, some youths invited Muhammad to join them for a visit to Al-Hanut (the shop), a windowless tavern on the outskirts of town. Muhammad innocently assumed the establishment was, as its name suggested, a store. He arrived to find two thuggish men guarding a wooden door covered by a dark blue curtain. After looking the boys over, the bouncers pulled the drape aside and ushered them in. Small olive-oil lanterns provided minimal mood lighting, while shepherd boys played sensual melodies on their flutes. The room had no chairs, and servers, passing among the standing patrons, poured wine from amphorae. In the corners of the room, teenage girls with styled hair, heavy makeup, and cheap jewelry lined up to be ogled, some dancing to the beat of drummers playing animal-skin cylinders.

The only product sold at Al-Hanut, Muhammad suddenly realized, was girls, some as young as twelve. When their pimp saw an interested client engage one of his charges, he would approach and negotiate a price. The client would take the girl outside to a nearby sand dune and returned once business was concluded.

Repulsed by the scene, Muhammad dashed out of the tavern, never to return. He understood that the young women were victims, many orphans like himself. Their exploitation angered him, and he determined to oppose the practice. In no uncertain terms, the Qur`an declares: "You shall not force your slave girls into prostitution" (24:33). At the same time, Muhammad recognized that these girls had great potential. One of his most famous sayings would describe such a prostitute, whose pure heart transcended her outcast state.

In spite of his abrupt departure from Al-Hanut, his peers continued to invite Muhammad to parties. In keeping with his nonconfrontational nature, he politely declined, citing work responsibilities. When his friends invited him to a wedding party, he took on extra shepherding duties so that he could not attend, just in case *wedding* was a euphemism for carousing at Al-Hanut. Alone among his peers, Muhammad chose to remain a virgin, saving himself for the right woman.

Muhammad began working for one of the Dar-un-Nadwah elders, Ibnu Jud'an, who hired him to repair his rooftop terrace. Ibnu Jud'an soon noticed the young worker's maturity and invited him to chat. The two sat on the roof, watching the setting sun cast its final rays upon Mount Hira, which loomed over Mecca. In a reflective mood, Ibnu Jud'an began to relate how he had grown up poor and became embittered about his family's marginalized status. He had turned to crime, only to have his relatives disown him, after which he found himself sinking into depression.

In the depths of his despair, Ibnu Jud'an fled into the wilderness at dawn, determined to end his life by jumping off a cliff. He climbed a mountain outside Mecca and noticed a cave well hidden by a cairn and guarded by a cobra. Overcome with panic, Ibnu Jud'an suddenly realized he really did not want to die. Then the rising sun's rays reflected off his amulet and illuminated the cobra—it was a statue made of solid gold with two rubies for eyes. The cave was a tomb of Jurhumite kings. Inside, precious jewels and treasures surrounded mummified bodies. Inspired by the fortune he had stumbled upon en route to committing suicide, Ibnu Jud'an resolved to use his newfound riches to help others who saw no hope.

Ibnu Jud'an returned to Mecca a transformed man. He stopped drinking alcohol. To atone for his years of crime, he sent bags of money to the families of the men he had murdered and/or stolen from. These expiations and many munificent acts of charity ultimately exhausted the entire fortune. Meanwhile, Ibnu Jud'an became a successful business-man and charismatic leader, rising to represent the same clan that had once disowned him in the Dar-un-Nadwah assembly.

Muhammad listened in awe. Ibnu Jud'an's example reinforced the young man's growing conviction that choosing wisely—even in chal-lenging circumstances—was vital. No longer a child, he recognized the importance of taking responsibility for his conduct, including whom he chose to befriend. He would later declare, "A healthy friend is like a perfume seller: either you acquire perfumes from him or at least leave his presence smelling better. But a toxic friend is like a blacksmith who will either singe your clothes or leave you smelling awful."

Ibnu Jud'an, meanwhile, looked at the young man sitting across from him and saw he had potential far beyond carpentry repairs and shep-herding. He had shared the story of his life's defining moment to en-courage Muhammad to seize his own opportunities—and he would continue to encourage the young man's maturation in the coming years. Muhammad had gained a new mentor.

❖ ❖ ❖

On his next caravan trip, the monks at the monastery in Bosra greeted Muhammad with sad faces: Bahira had died.

Nineteen-year-old Muhammad was on his ninth caravan trip to Da-mascus, and he now walked alone beside the camels without his uncle's constant supervision. Over the past year he had grown muscular from shepherding and carpentry.

The caravan continued on to Damascus, arriving just before the Feast of Saint John the Baptist, one of the city's greatest holidays. Like Bahira, John the Baptist was a hermit. He had emerged, disheveled, from the wilderness to meet Jesus, later baptizing him in the Jordan River. King Herod later had John decapitated, his head buried in Damascus beneath a pillar in an imposing cathedral that bore the saint's name. In preparation for the feast, Damascenes draped red ribbons from roofs and along pillars lining the main road, and they hung garlands of flowers in many colors on doors and windows.

As Muhammad entered Damascus, the Sunday church bells rang out. A procession wound through the city streets toward the cathedral. Men in long white robes waved incense burners filled with frankincense brought from Yemen by earlier Meccan caravans. The city's bishop—wearing a golden miter and embroidered robes featuring rubies the Meccans had imported—carried a staff in his left hand and a gilded cross in his right. Two boys in white robes prevented his cape from dragging on the ground, and rows of men carrying painted icons of saints chanted as they paraded past the crowds lining the cobbled streets. The procession eventually reached the cathedral, where the multitudes streamed into the sanctuary behind the clergy.

Taller than the average Damascene, Muhammad took in the ceremonies from behind a row of spectators. He was intrigued by the locals' devotion. After the service ended and the worshippers departed, he decided to explore the ancient shrine, which had for several thousand years served Persian, Greek, and Roman rites before being converted to a cathedral in 395.

As the seat of the bishop of Damascus, the cathedral was built to impress. Towering over the city, the imposing building was ornately decorated, its ceiling made of Lebanese cedar trunks featuring a colossal image of Christ Pantocrator painted at its center. Beautiful frescos depicting the signs of the zodiac and stylized biblical scenes decorated its floors. Muhammad beheld the same icon of Mary and Jesus he had seen hanging in the Ka'bah thirteen years earlier, only this one was much finer. Colossal wooden doors, built by craftsmen far more skilled than the Banu Najjar, were held together with beautiful metallic hinges. Muhammad observed stones with inscriptions in various languages on the walls. The murmur of people in prayer resonated in the large hall. As the interior had no pews, men stood on one side and women—their heads covered for the prayer service—on the other.

Muhammad stepped out of the cathedral's dark, serene sanctuary into the bright light, taking in the square that every day but Sunday housed a bustling vibrant market. The cathedral's location near the main market was emblemic of the city's willingness to juxtapose the sacred and the commercial.

Muhammad rejoined his compatriots as they loaded their merchandise into the storehouses adjacent to the market. The next morning, the city awoke with a formal changing-of-the-guard ceremony at the city's entrance, where an army official gave the command to open the main gate and people streamed in for the Monday market. The Meccans manned their stalls or wandered the marketplace seeking potential customers.

While his uncle tended their stall, Muhammad made his rounds to find customers. He noticed a middle-aged merchant dressed in elegant robes inside a store with intricate carved-wood finishing. Evidently wealthy, the merchant sat in a large chair as he directed his workers. Muhammad overheard an elderly customer, with back bent and a crude olive-stalk cane, awkwardly explain that he was unable to repay a debt on time. The merchant, in a magnanimous gesture, motioned to his foreman to forgive the debt. Impressed, Muhammad introduced himself to the merchant and arranged to meet the following afternoon to present the merchandise he had brought from Mecca.

The next day, Muhammad arrived on time at the appointed meeting spot, yet the merchant did not appear. For two more days, Muhammad returned at the same time and hour. Finally, on the third day, the merchant—who had forgotten about the meeting—happened to pass by on the street and saw Muhammad waiting. The merchant realized what had happened and was deeply impressed with Muhammad's persistence. The two struck up a friendly conversation, and the merchant (whose name remains unknown) purchased all of Abu Talib's stock that week and soon became Muhammad's primary eyes and ears (to keep up with the trends) in Damascus.

Freed of being chaperoned by his uncle, Muhammad explored the city with the keen eyes of an adult. The other Meccans preferred to squander their free time in the city's many taverns and brothels, teasing the celibate Muhammad. He had no interest in their fetish for imported Slavic prostitutes, though he had noticed that Damascus's slave market featured a much broader array of ethnicities and types than Mecca's.

Slave traders here specialized: some sold intellectuals, like tutors and private secretaries, or scribes and clerks. Some sold nobles, such as elite Persians captured in battle; others sold domestic servants. The Meccans mostly purchased young female entertainers, who would sing and dance for them on the return journey and were forced into prostitution.

A month into his stay in Damascus, as Muhammad was exploring the city one day, a forlorn-looking older man in a beige Coptic tunic caught his attention. Muhammad complimented his tunic as a way to strike up conversation. The man, who turned out to be Egyptian, invited Muhammad to join him for a meal. As they dined at a nearby restaurant, Muhammad sensed the man's distress and asked whether something was wrong. The old man revealed the source of his misfortune: he had purchased a large load of sorghum and millet in the Nile Delta and brought his goods to Damascus, only to learn that the locals preferred wheat and barley. The return caravan to Egypt departed in just three days, and he had failed to sell any of his merchandise.

Muhammad wanted to help the man and still had ten days left in Damascus. He decided to seek the counsel of his new mentor, the Damascene merchant who had purchased his uncle's entire stock. That evening Muhammad visited the merchant, who was hosting a group of friends who had just arrived from Mesopotamia. The men spoke of reports of swarms of locusts converging from the east. Muhammad deduced that the locusts would arrive in the vicinity of Damascus within a week. He had a eureka moment: the incoming locusts were the solution to the Egyptian merchant's unwanted grains!

Rising with excitement, Muhammad excused himself and ran to meet his uncle. He somehow convinced Abu Talib to entrust him with all his uncle's gold coins and rushed back to the Egyptian merchant to purchase his entire grain stock. The long-suffering man was so overjoyed to have found a buyer in time that he sold his stock at a discounted price. News of Muhammad's purchase quickly spread among the bewildered Meccans. Was he mad? How could Abu Talib allow his nephew to talk him into something so ludicrous?

Muhammad went every day to the city's outer walls and looked toward the horizon. His clansmen laughed. "What are you looking for, Muhammad—a customer to appear on the horizon to purchase your lemons?" The young man responded with a confident smile. A week passed. The caravan to Mecca was due to depart in three days. Abu Talib began to panic, yet his nephew's eyes sparkled with quiet confidence.

Then it came. Horsemen burst into the city heralding an emergency. The great horde of locusts was fast approaching. Merchants rushed from the market to the city walls and beheld a huge black cloud surging from the east, darkening the sky. The terrifying cloud was a swarm of millions of locusts, capable of devastating acres of crops in minutes. The merchants dashed back to the market in a frenzied stampede to purchase replacement grains. At Abu Talib's storage depot, Muhammad stood atop a wooden box as merchants shouted out desperate bids. Soon Muhammad's entire stock was sold, returning a high profit.

It was Muhammad's first good deed to literally pay dividends. He had helped a stranger in dire need—and provided a remarkable profit for his uncle. Those who had mocked him just hours earlier now congratulated him. The young man had taken a bold yet calculated risk and reaped the rewards.

Abu Talib, however, quickly squandered the returns by hosting a grand banquet for the caravan. His generosity kept him financially unstable.

❖ ❖ ❖

As was the Meccans' habit, the caravan returning from Damascus rested for the night in the middle of the Arabian desert. Camels tied down by their right front knee snoozed, their breath condensing in the cool night air as they snorted and grumbled in their sleep. Crickets chirped, owls hooted, and bats fluttered about. The howls of wolves and hyenas occasionally echoed in the distance.

The men huddled around dozens of small campfires to keep warm and unwind after traveling twenty miles that day. Jerboas scavenged uneaten scraps from the men's dinners as flutes played over the murmur of conversation from each campfire. The caravaners had spent most of the day walking alongside the camels in silence, as talking too much could lead to dehydration. The evening campfire was an opportunity to catch up with others on the caravan, reuniting after weeks apart to swap stories from their time in Damascus.

Muhammad had wandered among the campfires, looking for his former employer and mentor Ibnu Jud'an. He found the elder in front of his tent. Ibnu Jud'an warmly embraced his protégé and congratulated him. Word had quickly spread of Muhammad's exploits, and the elder proudly saluted the young man for holding his ground against the naysayers.

Muhammad smiled but seemed distracted, glancing to the side, drawn by the conversations at the nearby campfire. A seventeen-year-old was politely but firmly criticizing the men for wasting their time carousing in the whorehouses and taverns of Damascus instead of learning new ideas from the locals and improving themselves. The men roared with laughter. "You're missing out on all the fun. You don't drink and you don't join us at the brothels. A trip like this is a complete waste on people like you!"

Muhammad noticed that the young man did not back down. Muhammad had learned from Bahira to always be on the lookout for talent—and for the first time he sensed potential in a young fellow Meccan.

Ibnu Jud'an observed Muhammad's curiosity and said, "I see you are impressed with my cousin's son. Come, let me introduce you to 'Atiq." The young man's name—which means "freethinker"—was unusual for a Meccan. With Ibnu Jud'an's introduction, Muhammad joined the campfire, sitting next to 'Atiq and listening quietly as he continued his banter with the older men.

The next morning, Ibnu Jud'an sat astride his camel with a proud smile on his face. As flutes played in the distance, he looked down on Muhammad and 'Atiq walking together and engrossed in animated conversation. The two celibate teetotalers had hit it off. Ibnu Jud'an chuckled to himself, glad to have seized the opportunity to introduce them. Little did he know the revolution this duo would spark.

The two spent the entire caravan journey home immersed in deep conversation, exchanging ideas and revealing their personal stories. For the first time, Muhammad had a peer to connect with—'Atiq was two years younger—someone of Muhammad's generation who shared his outlook that *Jahiliyyah* society needed to change.

'Atiq hailed from a wealthy family; his father had hired a tutor to

teach the young man to read and write. He carried himself with a digni-
fied refinement that reflected his noble upbringing. With a knack for
poetry, he was soft-spoken yet eloquent and sought to excel within the
best aspects of Arabian culture while rejecting its excesses. As an adolescent he had already demonstrated both business acumen and generosity,
making profits that he gave away to benefit the poor. At a young age he
had also become a master genealogist, able to recall and discuss tribal
ancestors and complex family connections.

As the pair walked, 'Atiq recounted something that had happened to
him when he was twelve. Early one morning he was running errands for
his father and came upon a drunken man collapsed on the side of the
road. The man was smearing fresh dung from passing sheep on his face.
Disgusted by the sight, 'Atiq resolved then and there never to drink.
He began to question other aspects of Meccan society. He had become
aware that a free woman could never be a prostitute in Arabian society,
that only enslaved women were exploited. In turn, he rejected slavery
and the repression of women. As a child, he watched a fox urinate on the
side of an idol as his father was prostrate before the statue—an absurdity
that turned the boy into an agnostic. If idolatry was illogical, what other
sacred elements of his ancestral tradition might also be flawed? he wondered. Remarkably, his father respected his son's independent thinking.

'Atiq could easily identify problems and adjust his behavior accord-
ingly, yet he struggled to articulate any profound systemic solutions. His
reaction to widespread poverty was to be charitable, and he countered
slavery by freeing his own enslaved people—yet he had done little more
to agitate for change. He was motivated by noble intentions but pursued
small, short-term solutions within societal norms and never pushed his
views on others. His lack of ego was remarkable; he never promoted
himself and performed charitable acts anonymously.

Listening to 'Atiq's stories, Muhammad realized he was not the only
one who found flaws in Meccan society. The two young men were on the
same wavelength and would largely remain so for the rest of their lives.
No record exists of their ever being in conflict or doubting each other. On
occasion, 'Atiq would politely make small corrections, for example, by
editing Muhammad's less-than-stellar poetic compositions. 'Atiq was an
active listener, respectfully suggesting different approaches if necessary. He

complemented Muhammad, contributing wealth, knowledge, persuasive skills, and a network of discontented young Meccan elites.

By the time the caravan arrived in Mecca, Muhammad had made his first true friend. Theirs was a companionship of ideas. The duo often met after work and headed out for late afternoon walks on Mecca's outskirts, frequently sitting atop Abu Qubais to watch the sunset over the city. Shortly after they returned from Damascus, in a gesture of intimacy, Muhammad gave his friend a new nickname: 'Abdullah, after Muhammad's late father.

Two years later, Muhammad and 'Atiq confronted the first test of their shared commitment to challenge Mecca's harmful stagnation. A Yemenite merchant had arrived to sell his wares: fabrics, furs, and leathers imported from Africa. A member of the Dar-un-Nadwah assembly had purchased his entire stock yet delayed in making the promised payment. The winter caravan was about to depart for Yemen, and the merchant was still without his money.

Desperate for help, he stood by the Ka'bah and publicly aired his grievances. Most passersby ignored him because the man was not a local and lacked any tribal support in Mecca. But word reached Muhammad, who resolved to act. He asked 'Atiq, Az-Zubair, and Hamzah to meet him that evening at the home of Ibnu Jud'an. As they sat on the roof terrace, Muhammad urged that the five of them go together to the council member's home to rectify the situation—the honor of their city was at stake.

The next morning, the group set out for the home of the offending elder, 'Amr ibn Hisham. 'Amr was a brilliant and ambitious businessman whose accomplishments had earned him the epithet Abul-Hakam (the wise) and a seat in Dar-un-Nadwah at the unheard-of age of thirty, only the second person after Muhammad's ancestor Hashim to earn an exemption from the usual age limit. The man was literate, poetic, handsome, accomplished—and deeply insecure, with an insatiable need to prove himself at the expense of others.

'Amr ibn Hisham always charged ahead, indifferent to the suffering he caused in others. He overloaded his camels on the caravan, overworked his slaves, and trapped vulnerable people in debt so he could demand their daughters in payment. With his cold self-centered cynicism,

'Amr ibn Hisham did not care about the suffering Yemenite merchant. Day after day he strung the man along, preferring to delay payment so he could use the money to make other investments in the meantime.

Ibn Hisham's home, located east of the Ka'bah, was one of the town's finest. People passing by turned in curiosity to look at Muhammad and his small band of supporters. Muhammad grasped the elaborate brass knocker—an import from Egypt—and firmly pounded it against the door. A servant soon appeared and invited the men inside. They declined, requesting that 'Amr ibn Hisham come outside to meet them—a strategic decision to avoid becoming guests obligated to their host.

'Amr ibn Hisham emerged to greet them. "How can I serve you, gentlemen?" he asked, nodding at fellow elder Ibnu Jud'an and staring at the younger men quizzically. "We have come together to ask you for justice for someone you have worked with," began Ibnu Jud'an. Then Muhammad stepped forward. "A Yemenite merchant has spoken near the Ka'bah of a grievance with you concerning your purchase without payment, and he claims that you have continued to delay paying him. He must return home with the winter caravan in a few days and cannot do so without his money. What do you say to his accusations?"

'Amr ibn Hisham laughed in embarrassment: "Yes, of course, I have every intention of paying the merchant, but I need more time to get my finances in order." Muhammad would not be swayed by another delaying tactic, declaring, "We will not move from here without the man's money."

Muhammad was putting 'Amr ibn Hisham on the spot, as a crowd had gathered to watch the confrontation. The vain merchant cared deeply about his public image and would never forgive Muhammad for making him look bad. Yet he had no choice but to save face. "Fine, wait here," he said with a grunt, angrily returning a minute later with a sack of coins. He silently handed the bag to Ibnu Jud'an, then slammed the door in their faces.

Twenty-one-year-old Muhammad remained oblivious to the challenge his new nemesis would pose. For the moment, he and his allies hurried to the market to hand the sack of coins to the overjoyed Yemeni merchant, enabling him to return home at last. The group then headed to Ibnu Jud'an's home to celebrate their achievement.

As they sat on the roof terrace beneath a canopy, the men drank camel milk and enjoyed their lunch, cooled by the midday breeze. They recounted the look on 'Amr ibn Hisham's face and applauded their un-likely breakthrough. Muhammad, however, sat quietly. "Wouldn't it be much greater if we took what we did today and helped more people?" he asked the group. "What if we united to support all who are wronged in the city yet lack someone to help them?"

"That's a brilliant idea!" said Ibnu Jud'an. Later that afternoon, just before sunset, the five headed to the Ka'bah. Exercising his privilege as an elder, Ibnu Jud'an stood at the top step and declared, "Today we have made a pact to enhance our society's honor. We will stand to uphold the right of anyone who is wronged. This pledge shall stand so long as the sea wets wool and the mounts of Hira and Thabir remain standing." The name of their agreement was Hilf-ul-Fudhul, "the Pact to Enhance Society's Honor."

Three days later, the men met with the assembly at Dar-un-Nadwah to secure backing for their pact. As an assembly member, Ibnu Jud'an could not present the idea himself, but he arranged for the others to be admitted for the weekly Friday council session. Muhammad recruited his cousin Al-Fadhl as the group's spokesperson. Muhammad was not accustomed to public speaking and recognized that his cousin would do a better job. Neither Muhammad nor 'Atiq strove for acclaim; they wanted the council to adopt the initiative on its own merit.

Al-Fadhl addressed the assembly, invoking the prestige of Mecca and its ancestors' legendary chivalry. "We have joined together to make this pact in order to raise the honor of our society by upholding a principle of our ancestors: the principle of good conduct." The elders looked over at 'Amr ibn Hisham, as word had spread throughout the city about the incident. To maintain appearances, the elder cleverly responded, "That's very noble of you." Inside, however, he burned with wounded rage. The other council members nodded silently, indicating they would not op-pose the pact.

Word of the pledge quickly spread—and it soon became popular in Mecca. A month later, a visiting merchant learned that a rich Meccan called Nubaih had abducted the visitor's beautiful daughter. The for-eigner went to the Ka'bah begging for help, wailing, "Where are the nobles of Hilf-ul-Fudhul?" Muhammad and his companions went to Nubaih's home and demanded that he return the young woman, declaring at his doorway, "You know who we are and what we pledged to do!" Nubaih asked to keep the woman for the night—to which Muhammad exclaimed from the back of the group, "No, by God, not even the tip of her fingernail will you keep, and not even for the blink of an eye!" Seeing their determination, Nubaih reluctantly returned the woman to her father.

At last, Muhammad had developed the self-confidence to live by his values. The seeds of his world-changing mindset had begun to sprout.

PART II

✧

FORMING
THE MINDSET

4

✧

THE IMPRESARIO

Becoming a Man
Who Makes an Impact

Mecca: 9:30 a.m., Friday, May 8, 593 CE

A well-dressed figure in a gold-embroidered silk tunic zigzagged among the stalls in Mecca's market while furtively observing Muhammad from afar. As the man pretended to inspect merchandise, he kept an eye on the twenty-three-year-old helping his uncle at their family stall. A source had told the man that Muhammad was special, but he needed to see for himself.

The surreptitious talent scout was Hakim ibn Hizam, the nephew of a wealthy Meccan widow named Khadijah. She needed a new financial manager for her business. The search had to be surreptitious so Hakim could assess the prospective hire without his knowledge.

Mecca's *Jahiliyyah* code did not permit a woman to own wealth, let alone manage it openly in the city's markets. No respectable woman sold goods in public. Yet Khadijah had a brilliant commercial mind and led a successful business enterprise—from behind the scenes. Publicly, her late husband had managed the family's financial affairs, but she wielded the true power, making bold strategic decisions and negotiating trade deals.

At twenty-six, Khadijah had already married, and been widowed, twice. She needed a new front man for her business: someone secure enough to respect a woman's ability to lead.

To manage his aunt's financial affairs Hakim sought a man willing to think unconventionally. By now, news of the business ethics pact had spread throughout Mecca. The young man who had initiated this audacious effort could be just the person Khadijah needed for her business. Hakim asked Ibnu Jud'an for an introduction and assumed the person he wanted to meet was Al-Fadhl, Muhammad's cousin. After all, he was the one who had eloquently persuaded the elders' assembly to bless the pact.

To Hakim's surprise, Ibnu Jud'an revealed that the real force behind the pact was an even younger man named Muhammad. "I know him well," explained Ibnu Jud'an. "He worked for me in his youth, and we became close." Then the elder recounted Muhammad's accomplishments.

Hakim was convinced, yet he could not suggest Muhammad to Khadijah without vetting him. So, the next morning, Hakim was intrigued as he watched Muhammad handle his merchandise with care, neatly organizing products by type, shape, and color. Most Meccan merchants simply heaped their wares in a pile at their stall. Muhammad's method, inspired by examples he had observed in Damascus's market, made his merchandise more visible and thus more desirable.

As Hakim drew near, he could smell Muhammad's pleasantly perfumed garments. The young man took care of his merchandise and of himself. But how did he carry himself in conversation?

"Good morning. Are you Muhammad?" asked Hakim.

Muhammad turned to him respectfully and responded, "Good morning! Yes, I am Muhammad." Hakim peppered the young man with questions about his views on business ethics and trading techniques. A bit surprised by the unusual inquiries, Muhammad nonetheless responded politely and engaged his customer, who bought a few items before disappearing.

That evening, Hakim told Khadijah that he had found the man for the job—the initiator of the Hilf-ul-Fudhul pact. She was intrigued. "You mean Al-Fadhl?"

"No, his cousin Muhammad." Hakim explained how Muhammad had masterminded the famous pact.

"Muhammad?!" she said with surprise. She had not heard that name since she was twelve, when the *firasah* master made a scene in the market by reading greatness in the face of the nine-year-old orphan. As memory of that strange incident flooded back, Khadijah listened to Hakim relay Ibnu Jud'an's recommendation and what Hakim had observed in the market.

Khadijah was impressed but needed to be sure. "Bring him to me tomorrow," she requested. "I would like to assess him myself."

❖ ❖ ❖

Vetting Muhammad was urgent. The caravan was leaving for Damascus in less than two weeks. If the wealthy widow did not find a financial manager in time, her storehouse of merchandise could sit in Mecca for another year.

Late in the afternoon, Hakim returned to the market, only this time he was not incognito. One servant shaded him with an exquisite Indian umbrella—red wool embroidered with white cotton with purple silk fringes on a gold-colored pole, the kind of imported luxury only Mecca's wealthiest could afford. Another servant cooled his master with an ostrich feather fan, while a third used a horsetail whisk to shoo away flies.

Merchants had begun packing up their stalls and stared quizzically at Hakim's entourage. Muhammad was loading his merchandise onto mules for transport to the storeroom in his late grandfather's home. Gusts of wind blew the stall canopy against the booth's wooden frame, emitting a cracking sound amid the clanging of chimes hanging from nearby stalls, devices used by many Meccan merchants to ward off evil.

Muhammad suddenly looked up to see Hakim's entourage approaching. Muhammad handed the textiles in his arms to his uncle and went to greet the merchant. Hakim revealed his identity, explaining that Ibnu Jud'an had recommended they meet. He informed Muhammad of the job opportunity with Khadijah and asked if he would come meet her at once. Surprised and intrigued, Muhammad left the stall.

Khadijah lived in a large mud-brick home with ornate latticed windows and whitewashed stuccoed brick walls. To the left of the main entrance, a *mastabah*, or stone terrace, functioned as a front porch where maids were churning butter and grinding barley in stone mills in preparation for dinner. A servant named Maysarah was roasting a goat over red glowing acacia wood coals. Maysarah rushed to greet the group, then addressed Muhammad by saying: "Welcome to the young master! My mistress awaits you inside."

Maysarah led Hakim and Muhammad to the front door, which was made of intricately carved olive wood and had a beautiful bronze door knocker. The sweet scent of burning incense inside invigorated Muhammad's senses. Zaid, an enslaved thirteen-year-old, led the men through a square foyer into a spectacular rectangular hall. Latticed windows capped the room's fifteen-foot ceiling; fine silken Egyptian tapestries and Syrian carpets draped its walls.

The home's grandeur proclaimed the wealth of Khadijah, who lived up to her epithet, Amiratu Quraish (Empress of Mecca). She entered the room clad in Chinese embroidered silk robes. She sat down on a red cushion and asserted her authority as chief of the household. A servant cooled her with a peacock feather fan attached to an indigo pole imported from Alexandria.

Like Hakim with his entourage, Khadijah was taking great care to make an impression on Muhammad. Her red cushion evoked the elders' seats in Dar-un-Nadwah; the peacock fan signified royalty; and the raised platform ensured she was looking down at six-foot-tall Muhammad. She motioned for him to sit on the carpeted floor before her, while her nephew sat on a cushion to the right of the platform.

Khadijah was slender, with wavy black hair braided with golden thread and studded with emeralds. Dangling golden earrings framed her brilliant smile. Her lighter complexion proclaimed a life of luxury and comfort out of the sun's glare, and kohl-adorned lids strikingly set off her large hazel eyes. Her long thin fingers matched her slim feet, and she wore Persian-style sandals of the highest quality. Her elegant gold necklace was inlaid with mother-of-pearl, jade, and rubies.

Zaid entered carrying a silver salver with sculpted crystal glasses containing fruit juices and ice, a rare luxury only the wealthiest Meccans could afford. But the boy tripped and dropped one of the crystal chalices, which shattered. Muhammad observed Khadijah's reaction carefully. Her face remained calm, yet she became concerned when she noticed Zaid's finger bleeding from a small cut. Khadijah's compassion for the boy greatly impressed Muhammad.

Silence hung over the hall as Muhammad and Khadijah sized each other up. Khadijah spoke first, thanking Muhammad for making the time to meet and explaining that she sought someone with vision to help make her business more profitable. As she spoke, servants laid out a large leather spread and began to bring in food.

Khadijah said she was aware of Muhammad's brilliant ideas. She noted that his bold deals in Damascus had made a lot of money for his uncle, yet Muhammad lacked substantial capital to work with, as all his earnings went to supporting his uncle's large family. She revealed that she was prepared to put her extensive resources at his disposal. He would earn a salary and have the added advantage of commission and bonuses if he performed well.

Muhammad asked for three days to think it over. He did not want to seem too eager by leaping at the remarkable opportunity. Khadijah agreed and bade him farewell. After the meal, Zaid showed Muhammad out and, as a sign of respect for an honored guest, walked him to the end of the street.

The next evening, Zaid came to Abu Talib's door with a basket of fresh figs from Khadijah as a symbolic gesture of partnership. Zaid was surprised to find Muhammad helping his aunt Fatimah prepare dinner; Arabian men generally did not help with domestic work. Abu Talib invited the boy to stay for dinner, during which Zaid and Muhammad quickly engaged in a deep conversation. Zaid's precocious maturity impressed Muhammad, who sensed from the teenager's refinement that he had an unusual story. In response to Muhammad's prodding, Zaid revealed a painful account:

"I was born to a noble of the Tayy tribe [in north-central Arabia]. My father, Harithah, was a wealthy and powerful man. I was loved and honored by him and my mother. My parents made special effort to educate me well, bringing me a tutor to teach me how to read and write.

A devout Christian, my mother took special care to teach me her faith. When I was seven, she took me on a pilgrimage to visit a saint's shrine in Damascus.

"On our return, we passed through the terrain of the Qayn clan. As I slept beside my mother, I was startled by rough hands over my mouth and hands. Two masked men yanked me out of the tent. I was gagged, tied up, and flung over the side of a horse. I tried to squirm loose but to no avail. I cried as we rode away. A few days later, I was sold in the slave market at Yathrib, where Hakim ibn Hizam purchased me for four hundred drachmas [three times the typical price for slaves]. He brought me back to Mecca and presented me as a gift to his aunt Khadijah, who has afforded me every comfort, even continuing my education."

Zaid's story moved Muhammad greatly. His ordeal echoed Barakah's and reminded Muhammad that he had nearly suffered the same fate as a four-year-old shepherd. It also revealed more about Khadijah, the mysterious woman who might soon become his boss. She had nurtured Zaid, providing him lessons in literature and mathematics and treating him like a son.

After Zaid left, Muhammad discussed Khadijah's unusual job offer with Abu Talib and Fatimah. Accepting the position would entail ending his work for his uncle, but Abu Talib encouraged him to seize the opportunity. Fatimah was delighted that an outsider had seen potential in the young man.

Before making his final decision, Muhammad insisted on seeking the blessing of Barakah. She had now been married for over a decade and was raising a young son named Ayman (fortunate). Still, she followed her foster son's exploits and watched his growth with pride. Pleased to hear about his new professional opportunity, Barakah smiled as she observed: "Khadijah evidently likes you." Muhammad sensed that there was something more to her smile, but she did not say more.

Three days after their first meeting, Muhammad returned to Khadijah's house to formalize the partnership. Abu Talib accompanied him as a witness; Hakim served as Khadijah's witness. Over an extravagant meal followed by dates and raisins from both Yemen and Damascus—symbols of the caravan's two destinations—they entered into a verbal agreement.

Muhammad pledged to honorably manage Khadijah's wealth, and she pledged to honor him as a partner with appropriate compensation.

Following the ceremony, Khadijah brought Muhammad to a large warehouse linked to the rear of her house and introduced him to the workers and slaves who lived in her storehouse and managed her merchandise. The great caravan to Damascus was departing in just a few days. Muhammad had to quickly get up to speed on his new job.

❖ ❖ ❖

For the first time someone outside Muhammad's immediate family was ready to invest in him financially. His new employer offered access to massive sums of money and a team of workers. While working for Abu Talib, Muhammad had both devised strategy and then executed it with limited capital. With Khadijah, Muhammad could focus on planning and training others to execute.

In the limited time he spent in her presence, Muhammad had tried to size up his unusual boss, who exuded great self-confidence. She was literate yet could not execute any financial deals without a male representative. She was an independent thinker yet could not trade openly in Mecca's market. She lived surrounded by comfort yet carried the pain of losing two husbands in quick succession. Khadijah, in a sense, was trapped in an opulent prison. Her life was a giant subterfuge: running an international business empire behind the scenes. Her home, Muhammad noted, had no idols. As a child Khadijah had rejected idolatry, though not in a way that might offend her parents.

As he rushed to prepare for the caravan's departure, Muhammad made his first priority establishing trust with his new boss. When he surveyed the large warehouse at the back of her home, he found the inventory in shambles. Muhammad directed Khadijah's enslaved workers to empty the warehouse and assigned Zaid to catalog each item. As they conducted the inventory, Muhammad used his carpentry skills to construct new shelves and storage niches. Khadijah could finally see what she owned and where each item was stored, a commercial transparency that enabled her to track Muhammad's sales.

Once the merchandise was organized, Muhammad had Khadijah's

workers load up the camels. For twenty-three-year-old Muhammad, this trip to Damascus would be his first as the head of his segment of the caravan. Unlike other merchants, who overloaded their camels, Muhammad made sure to slightly underload his desert train and planned to rest the animals periodically. Caring for the comfort of his herd was not only humane but efficient: Muhammad's camels remained fresh longer than overladen camels, which often collapsed from exhaustion.

Before the caravan departed, Khadijah took Zaid aside and instructed him to keep a close eye on Muhammad during the three-month trip, particularly how he treated her workers and merchandise. And then, they were off.

Muhammad and Zaid walked together, engrossed in conversation. The young man was not only literate and educated but capable of holding his own in discussion of profound topics. Muhammad began calling him Al-Habib (the adored, beloved) and even sought his feedback on potential business ideas.

In Damascus, Muhammad took Zaid to meet his merchant friend, the mentor who had helped facilitate much of Muhammad's previous commercial success. The older gentleman introduced Muhammad to an Armenian merchant who sought the very products Muhammad had just transported. The next day, Muhammad and Zaid met the Armenian for lunch at a local restaurant and sealed a deal to sell their entire stock. Zaid was amazed at how Muhammad's connections had enabled him to be so efficient.

With their main work completed and weeks left before the caravan's scheduled departure for Mecca, Muhammad and Zaid toured Damascus, taking daily swims in the Barada River and often venturing into the countryside to ride horses. Each day, Muhammad chatted with local merchants, which Zaid soon realized served more than a social function. Muhammad was collecting information and learning how to discern the quality of fine goods. Shortly before their return to Mecca, Muhammad did something highly unusual: he took most of the profits from his grand sale a month earlier and purchased a large supply of jewelry, fabrics, and other expensive items.

No one had ever loaded up their camels with a variety of merchandise for the journey home. But Khadijah had given Muhammad the opportunity to fulfill his dream of maximizing both ends of the caravan trade. He returned to Mecca and quickly sold his entire stock of in-demand yet rare luxury items. With no other merchant offering similar wares, people rushed to buy Muhammad's merchandise, often bidding up the price. In the process, Muhammad doubled the profits he had already made in Damascus. Impressed by her employee's bold risk-taking and the massive profit boost, Khadijah gave him a large bonus. Muhammad rushed to share the funds with Barakah and his uncle in gratitude for the years of tutelage.

Khadijah realized that her new hire, who had effectively doubled her wealth in just a few months, was a rare talent. Rather than attempting to dominate her or steal from her, this young man had instead elevated her.

After a year of work together, she no longer insisted on sitting above him when they met in her home's main hall. One day, as they sat beside each other for a review of business strategy, Khadijah informed Muhammad that she was elevating him to the role of partner in their joint enterprise. Muhammad had earned it.

A year later, shortly after Muhammad turned twenty-five, Khadijah (now twenty-eight) began to notice that her interest in Muhammad went beyond the professional. Yet as a fiercely independent woman, she could not allow herself to impulsively yield to emotions. She needed empirical evidence that her business partner could be trusted at an even higher level: as a loyal spouse. With the annual caravan set to depart for Damascus, Khadijah hatched a plan. Her household manager, Maysarah, would accompany Muhammad to Damascus. The two had not worked together before and had no particular friendship. Maysarah would ostensibly assist Muhammad in his work while in reality spying for Khadijah. She provided clear instructions not to let Muhammad out of his sight and to report his behavior. Did her partner frequent the legendary brothels of Damascus and spend his free time carousing?

Unbeknown to Maysarah, Khadijah made a similar arrangement with two undercover informants on the caravan. That year, as the train of camels departed Mecca, three men were independently monitoring Muhammad. The three investigators watched as Muhammad arrived in Damascus and visited his mentor, who immediately connected him with an eager merchant from Cyprus. Within a day, Muhammad had sold his entire stock.

The three emissaries then followed Muhammad as he spent the next five weeks exploring Damascus and gleaning information from other merchants. Maysarah joined Muhammad on his daily rounds, while the two undercover spies each surreptitiously followed the pair through the bazaar and into restaurants. They watched as Muhammad learned from a visiting Iraqi merchant about a pestilence ravaging wheat near the Euphrates two weeks earlier. Muhammad calculated that same plague would take about two weeks to reach Damascus. Equipped with this vital piece of intelligence, he set out to determine what pesticide would protect the harvest.

Muhammad himself went undercover, disguising himself as a farmer and inquiring of local chemists which compound could best protect wheat from pestilence. Meanwhile, he remained oblivious to his three shadows. As this layered espionage played out, Muhammad set about capitalizing on his two vital pieces of information. The next morning, accompanied by Maysarah, Muhammad went around Damascus purchasing all the red sulfur (*kibrit-ul-ahmar*) he could find, exhausting most of his funds. Merchants offered bargain wholesale prices to get rid of their sulfur, and the other merchants laughed at his folly. "Muhammad has purchased a big stink," they mocked.

Two weeks passed with no news, and the merchants increased their ridicule. Then, two days before the caravan's scheduled departure, the pestilence broke out, threatening the fertile breadbasket that surrounded Damascus. Demand for red sulfur exploded. Within a few hours, Muhammad sold his entire stock at double what he paid for it. Though Maysarah begged him not to, Muhammad promptly purchased goods to take back to Mecca—where he sold the merchandise for a great profit. This time, he had tripled Khadijah's wealth.

Back in Mecca, Khadijah met one by one with her three spies, each of whom recounted the same story. They noted Muhammad's kind treatment of strangers, his integrity in dealing with servants, his quiet endurance of the Meccan merchants' ridicule, his steadfastness on the sulfur deal, and his eschewing brothels and bars. Khadijah had found her man.

She called Muhammad to her home the evening of his return from

Damascus. Escorted by Zaid, Muhammad entered the house to find Khadijah sitting beside her elder brother, Hizam (the father of Hakim ibn Hizam). The scene was similar to when Muhammad first met her two years earlier, only this time Khadijah wore her finest jewelry and garments. She invited him to sit next to her on a cushion and proceeded to reveal that she had hired two undercover investigators to monitor his conduct on the caravan. She wanted to show Muhammad how much thought and scrutiny she had invested in the decision to make her proposal: "With the support of my brother, I offer you myself in marriage."

Muhammad paused in silence for a moment and then replied, "I would be honored." He asked for three days to speak to his family before returning for an official proposal. He then dashed to Barakah's home and breathlessly declared, "Dear Mother, I bring delightful news!" Barakah was overjoyed and embraced him.

Three days later, Muhammad returned to Khadijah's home with a group of his uncles along with Barakah, Aunt Fatimah, and his best friend, 'Atiq. Muhammad introduced Barakah to Khadijah's family, who never expected that a formerly enslaved and unrelated foreign female would join an engagement entourage. "This is Barakah, my mother after my mother," Muhammad explained to the astonished group. "She is the last remnant of my immediate family."

During the few weeks leading up to the wedding ceremony, Muhammad dedicated himself to a critical project: building a new master bedroom on the roof of Khadijah's house. He designed the layout, built molds for bricks, constructed scaffolding and wooden beams, and elaborate latticed windows. He stretched a canopy of woven palm leaves and mud over the roof beams and whitewashed the walls.

The elevated bedroom—for which Muhammad also built a new marital bed—reflected his desire for a symbolic fresh start for him and Khadijah. It would become a small sanctuary for the new couple as they set out on a journey together.

❖ ❖ ❖

Under a late October full moon, hundreds of guests gathered for a wedding unlike any Mecca had seen. The moonlight provided natural illumination for the festivities, which took place in a courtyard out-side Hizam's estate. The affair was fit for royalty. But unlike most elite Meccan weddings—to which only other wealthy elites were invited—Muhammad had opened the celebration to anyone. Beggars in rags packed into the courtyard alongside Dar-un-Nadwah elders attired in the finest fashion.

Muhammad wanted his bride to have a day she would never for-get. Barakah had assumed the traditional role of Muhammad's mother and had gone that morning to Khadijah's home to prepare her future daughter-in-law for the wedding. She brought rare gifts Muhammad had imported from Yemen, delivered by a messenger on a fast horse. Agarwood from India burned as an incense to perfume Khadijah's embroidered Egyptian tunic. Silver earrings from Yemen adorned the bride's ears, as Barakah wove gold threads into her hair and anointed her eyelids with Indian kohl. Topping off Khadijah's clothing was a green silk veil embroidered with gold thread. She was a radiant bride.

Muhammad and Khadijah agreed that their wedding should be a sec-ular ceremony. The couple exchanged vows without priests or religious rituals. They did so in each other's presence, unlike traditional Meccan ceremonies where bride and groom sat in different rooms. Another atyp-ical feature was the festive meal's lack of wine. The feast included thirty roasted camels, their sizzling meat served on wild banana (*talh*) leaves by Banu Sa'd nomad cooks. Bedouin musicians entertained the crowd.

Joining the Banu Sa'd contingent at the wedding was Muhammad's "desert mother," Halimah, whom he had not seen in years. In a rare ges-ture of deep respect, Muhammad had invited her, along with Barakah and his aunt Fatimah, to sit next to him at dinner. Meccan men almost never surrounded themselves with women. But Muhammad chose to celebrate this landmark moment with his three foster mothers, a sym-bolic link from the orphan's original support family to the new family he was building with Khadijah.

A few days after their wedding, Muhammad and Khadijah went for a holiday to the resort town of Ta'if, on a plateau known for its mild weather, beautiful scenery, and natural springs. It was the couple's first opportunity to be truly alone. Muhammad was a virgin when he married. Though a private man who would conceal most aspects of his personal life, including his intimate relations with Khadijah, he did later give advice to his followers about the importance of intimacy between husband and wife. He observed: "Some men, like camels, are harsh and abuse their partners all day, only to expect them to be submissively intimate with them at night. Before approaching your partner, first precede it with messengers: kisses, hugs, caresses, and flowery words of affection." (An entire branch of Islamic scholarship would later focus on marital relations, one that recognized intimacy as a spiritual act of devotion just as blessed as prayer.)

The couple returned to Mecca with a foster child. Khadijah's bridal gift to Muhammad was the now sixteen-year-old Zaid, whom Muhammad immediately freed. Muhammad encouraged the young man to return home to his biological family, but Zaid insisted on remaining. Standing on the steps of the Ka'bah, Muhammad raised Zaid's right hand and declared, "This is Zaid. From this day forth, he is my son, all that is mine is his." Muhammad was now a foster father, and his new son became known as Zaid ibn Muhammad (son of Muhammad). He was the only one of Muhammad's followers who later would be mentioned by name in the Qur'an.

In the crowd that day was a distant cousin of Zaid's. The cousin hastened home to inform Zaid's father that his long-lost son was alive and living in Mecca with a man named Muhammad. Zaid's father quickly journeyed to Mecca, arriving late in the evening. The entire household was asleep, but Muhammad welcomed the stranger, offering the hungry traveler a platter of food. Muhammad sat beside him as he ate and asked, "How can I serve you?"

"I am Harithah ibn Sharahil from the tribe of Tayy," the man said. "My son Zaid was abducted six years ago and I have frantically searched for him. News has reached me that he is with you. I am willing to pay you double what you paid for him, for his return."

Muhammad smiled. "Zaid is not for sale, not for any price." The father looked crestfallen. Muhammad explained, "Zaid is a free man." Muhammad then went to wake up Zaid and bring him to the main hall. Harithah leapt up to embrace his son, noting with surprise that he was anointed with expensive perfumes, dressed in a fine Egyptian tunic, his skin clean, and his nails smooth.

Awakened by the weeping reunion of father and son, Khadijah had come down the staircase from their rooftop bedroom. She watched silently from the side as Zaid looked to Muhammad and declared, "I choose you!" before adding, "If you permit me, Father?" Harithah nodded. His son was in good hands, afforded every comfort and opportunity. After spending the night sleeping beside Zaid, he returned home the following day.

Zaid thus became Muhammad's first mentee and a crucial eyewitness to his life with Khadijah. Zaid observed how Muhammad often warmly embraced Khadijah, kissing her forehead and nose when greeting her. In a society that frowned on public displays of affection between husband and wife, Muhammad strolled hand in hand with Khadijah, taking daily sunset walks. Many Meccans snickered at what they saw as a ridiculous spectacle, and some even complained to Khadijah's brother Hizam. The smitten couple paid them no mind.

Like all married couples, Muhammad and Khadijah had their occasional disagreements. Yet Zaid observed how they always talked through their problems, often while sitting on the rooftop terrace. These talks would end in a passionate embrace.

The newly married Muhammad returned to work. Every morning he packed his merchandise on mules and set up a stall in Mecca's market next to his best friend. 'Atiq had also married and was already the father of three young children. The friends spent the time between sales engrossed in deep conversation. Then they returned home during the midday heat for a lunch break. Muhammad joined Khadijah on their rooftop terrace, eating from the same plate and drinking from the same cup. When Khadijah handed Muhammad the cup of yogurt drink, he placed his lips where her lips had been. After eating, they slept for an hour, before Muhammad returned to the market.

A few months into their marriage, after Muhammad returned from the winter caravan trip to Yemen, Khadijah had a special surprise: she was pregnant. Seven months later, she gave birth to a boy, delivered into the capable hands of Barakah. Barakah wrapped the baby in the same silk shawl Muhammad was wrapped in as a newborn twenty-six years earlier.

An orphan who had never known his own father, Muhammad gazed

in wonder at his firstborn. He had the solemn responsibility of naming the little boy. Continuing the tradition of his grandfather 'Abdul-
Muttalib, Muhammad invented a new name: Al-Qasim (the gap-filler).
The image came from Muhammad's carpentry experience; the word
qasam described a fragment of wood that carpenters fashioned to fill
natural gaps in a slab of lumber. With the new name, Muhammad acknowledged himself as an incomplete mortal and expressed his joy at
receiving a son to help fill a gaping hole in his life.

As the little boy grew, Muhammad carried Al-Qasim atop his shoulders, taking him along to the market and for walks in the wilderness
and playing with him. Unlike most Meccan men, Muhammad was a
hands-on father: changing his son's clothes, bathing him in a small tub
of rosemary-infused water, and cleaning soiled cloth diapers. Even the
most mundane aspects of fatherhood seemed to delight Muhammad,
whose own father had never enjoyed the same privilege.

When Al-Qasim turned two, he was ready to be weaned. With delight, Muhammad performed the toddler's *tahnik* ceremony, smearing
the syrup of fresh *rutab* dates on his son's lips. The celebration was a
reminder of the remarkable transformation Muhammad's life had made
over the previous three years. Only twenty-eight, he was now one of
Mecca's wealthiest men, with a grand home and a beautiful, intelligent
wife who had given him a handsome and healthy son.

❖ ❖ ❖

Upon marrying Khadijah and joining her household, Muhammad technically became a co-owner of slaves. As his liberation of Barakah and
Zaid demonstrated, Muhammad reviled the institution of slavery, which
represented to him the ultimate example of forced stagnation. In Meccan society, the enslaved were visually distinguished from the free. Male
slaves had their heads shaven, and most walked around naked or wore
only a small loincloth. Female slaves could not cover their hair, and
most went topless. Owners had little concern for their comfort or needs,
often forcing them to work even when they fell ill.

Khadijah's slaves, of course, belonged to her—and could be freed
only with her consent. When Muhammad became her business partner,
he began to subtly sow the seeds of liberation in her mind. He treated

enslaved members of her household with a consideration unheard of in Meccan society. He helped them load camels, gave them rest breaks and time off to recover from illness, dressed them in fine linens, shared his perfumes with them, and paid them for doing exceptional work.

One day on his way to work, Muhammad saw a master ruthlessly whipping his enslaved servant. On the spot, he offered the owner double the man's worth and purchased his freedom. With Khadijah's slaves, Muhammad took an alternative approach. He chose to sit on the ground and eat with them from the same serving platter. He learned that most had been abducted as young children and hailed from noble families. They not only knew what it was like to be free but had endured the trauma of abduction and dehumanization.

Recognizing that Khadijah's enslaved workers had free minds inside their bonded bodies, Muhammad encouraged them to voice their opinions and, in the process, restored their sense of dignity. And as a result of their income and time off, their production at work soared. When treated like human beings, they performed their labor with greater enthusiasm and energy.

Muhammad began to demonstrate to his wife that they did not need forced labor. He took on many chores completely foreign to Meccan men. He swept the house, cooked meals, and gathered kindling in the nearby hills—all tasks reserved for slaves. Khadijah, though unaccustomed to Muhammad's unorthodox behavior, was inspired by his example. While she had grown up with servants attending to her every need, she began to help the slaves in the kitchen and found domestic labor empowering, as she learned for the first time how to do things for herself.

After Al-Qasim's birth, Muhammad felt the time had come to ask his wife to liberate her household. Khadijah did not need much convincing. Yet she and Muhammad recognized that publicly freeing over a dozen domestic slaves in front of the Ka'bah would spark an uproar. Because slavery was such a widespread practice, Muhammad understood that trying to eradicate it at once would infuriate masters who relied on slave labor for their livelihood. Instead, Khadijah organized a private ceremony in her warehouse with Ibnu Jud'an, 'Atiq, and Barakah as witnesses. The enslaved listened with astonishment as Khadijah officially liberated them with the declaration: "You are now all free, like the birds of the sky and like the wind to wander where you please."

In addition to a salary, Muhammad offered the newly free workers the possibility of promotions and raises. The formerly enslaved worked harder and soon production doubled, bringing in more profits for all.

Muhammad's pioneering civic efforts were not limited to freeing the enslaved; he also found opportunities to provide valuable services to elites. After some of Khadijah's formerly enslaved servants moved out to start their own households, Muhammad transformed their former quarters into Mecca's first vault. He constructed a solid new door as well as shelves to keep valuables organized. Zaid created a ledger to track the items brought for safekeeping.

As Mecca had no banks, the city's elites appreciated a trusted space that would safeguard their precious items—even more so because Muhammad offered the service for free. While they could have stored family heirlooms and prized jewelry in their own homes, Mecca's elites evidently trusted Muhammad more than their own relatives or servants. In fact, after establishing his safety deposit system, Muhammad became known as Al-Amin (the trustworthy) among the Meccans, with the items in his depository called *al-amanah* (the trust). Fidelity and honor defined the emerging leader.

Muhammad's prestige grew with the birth of his second son. The proud father named the boy 'Abdullah, in homage to his own father. With two sons born in quick succession, Muhammad seemed to be following in his grandfather's footsteps, building a large clan of male heirs.

But then tragedy struck. One night Muhammad tucked Al-Qasim in to sleep and was looking forward to taking his toddler on a hiking trip the next day. In the morning, when Muhammad went to his son's room to awaken him, he found Al-Qasim had died during the night.

Barakah comforted the distraught Khadijah as Muhammad prepared their son's body for burial. As tears flowed down his face, Muhammad wrapped Al-Qasim in the same emerald-green shawl both the little boy and Muhammad had been wrapped in as newborns. In the evening, Muhammad carried the lifeless child to Mecca's cemetery, accompanied by close family and friends, 'Atiq and Ibnu Jud'an. They buried Al-Qasim next to his great-grandfather 'Abdul-Muttalib in the family plot. The graveside ceremony was private, and Muhammad wept by the grave.

The boy whose birth had filled a gaping void in Muhammad's life was now gone. 'Atiq and Barakah did not leave Muhammad and Khadijah's side during this traumatic time. Barakah helped with baby 'Abdullah, while Khadijah—once again pregnant—grieved for Al-Qasim. Compounding the pain, Ibnu Jud'an died a few weeks later, leaving Muhammad without his mentor at a particularly vulnerable time.

Shortly after Ibnu Jud'an's death, Muhammad ran into a former employee of Ibnu Jud'an's named Suhaib. The son of a Persian-Arabian governor and a European mother, the blond-haired blue-eyed Suhaib had been abducted in a Byzantine raid at age five. He was soon sold at the slave market in Constantinople to a Greek family, who trained the young boy to be a scribe and a jeweler. After two decades in slavery, Suhaib met Ibnu Jud'an in Damascus, and the kindly elder helped smuggle him to freedom on the caravan back to Mecca.

Muhammad had met Suhaib occasionally at Ibnu Jud'an's home, as he often performed paid labor for the old man who had helped liberate him. With the death of his patron, however, Suhaib was stuck. He had skills but little capital and could therefore not compete with the established merchants of Mecca. "How can I overcome these obstacles?" Suhaib asked as he sat in the shade of Muhammad's market stall.

After pausing for a moment, Muhammad picked up some pebbles and assembled them into a heap. "Like this!" he declared to the young man. "If you and others pool your wealth together, your individual small capital can become a great sum, which you can use to compete with the wealthy."

The next morning, Muhammad invited a group of fourteen impoverished residents of Mecca, many of them former slaves like Suhaib, to his home. Each brought whatever limited capital he had. Muhammad's idea was to launch Arabia's first corporation. On his rooftop terrace, Muhammad asked Zaid to catalog the money and valuables each person brought (including funds Muhammad provided on Barakah's behalf). Each individual's ownership stake in the new corporation was based on their investment. Fifty percent of all profits would be divided proportionally among the investors and the other half reinvested.

As Suhaib had contributed the largest sum and had unique skills as a jeweler, Muhammad suggested he lead the enterprise. The group used its pooled funds to purchase uncut emeralds, rubies, and diamonds, which Suhaib fashioned into beautiful jewelry. He also trained several other former slaves. The wealthy women of Mecca quickly became Suhaib's regular customers. Thanks to him, they could order custom jewelry without having to ask their husbands to place orders with jewelers in Damascus. The corporation's profits boomed.

Muhammad encouraged the group to think creatively, concentrating their efforts on developing businesses previously nonexistent in Mecca, like fine jewelry. Finding a niche market with no competition gave them an advantage over the entrenched elite.

Shortly after the corporation's founding, Khadijah gave birth to a beautiful girl, whom the couple named Zainab (a sweet-smelling flowering bush that grows in the midst of decay). Her name suggested that Zainab would restore the void left by Al-Qasim. Muhammad gave her a white silk tunic, as well as an exquisitely carved wooden doll from Damascus. For a few months, Zainab's birth brought her parents some happiness. But then, just like his older brother, 'Abdullah died suddenly overnight.

Losing a second child, and his only surviving son, was another devastating blow to Muhammad. In response, he and Khadijah continued to grow their family. When Muhammad was thirty, Ruqayyah, later known for her remarkable beauty, was born. Two years later came Um Kulthum. With three young daughters at home, Muhammad decided to stop joining the annual caravan to Damascus. Increased strife between the Byzantines and the Sasanians created greater peril along the route, and Muhammad could not risk leaving his wife and daughters without an immediate male relative. If Muhammad died, his daughters would be viewed as unmarriageable in Meccan society.

Around the same time, Muhammad adopted a new foster son, his young cousin 'Ali (heavenly). To ease the burden on his uncle and aunt, who were struggling to feed their many children, Muhammad offered to raise 'Ali. He saw potential in the boy and wanted to mentor him. Khadijah taught 'Ali to read and write, and he would later become a master of Arabic poetry, grammar, and calligraphy—and a pioneer of advanced Islamic education. In fact, Muhammad would declare, "'Ali is the gate to the institution of profound knowledge and learning." 'Ali lived in Muhammad's home for years, and the two became close, as Muhammad had with Zaid. 'Ali would play a critical role in Muhammad's life: many of the most revealing personal stories about Muhammad are known because he shared them with 'Ali.

By the time Muhammad turned thirty-five, Khadijah was pregnant once again. When the midwives attending to her alerted Muhammad that Khadijah might soon go into labor, he rushed to the market to purchase fresh pomegranates. Pomegranates contain high levels of folate, iron, and other essential nutrients extremely beneficial for pregnant women.

As Muhammad headed home from the market and passed the Ka'bah, he heard loud shouts. A group of elders were grabbing each other's tunics, their fists raised and voices rising in anger. A bucket of sheeps' blood from a nearby butcher was sitting on a rock pile marking the spot where, according to tradition, Abraham had stood while designing the shrine. The elders rolled up their right sleeves and plunged their hands in the bucket, signifying their intent to shed blood.

Muhammad rushed over and implored the men: "Oh esteemed elders of Mecca, oh wise and respected as mediators in all disputes. Surely every dispute can be averted with understanding."

The elders responded, "This is an honor that only one man can carry."

"To what are you referring?" Muhammad asked. They explained that the dispute was about the cornerstone of the Ka'bah. Flash floods had recently damaged the building's foundation. After the Ka'bah was rebuilt, the only thing that remained out of place was the shrine's original black cornerstone, reputedly placed by Abraham himself at the eastern corner, to the right of the main door.

With tempers flaring, Mecca's elders prepared to fight, and no one from Dar-un-Nadwah had the power to stop the impending bloodshed. But Muhammad removed his striped emerald-green mantle, or *burdah*. The elders watched in sudden silence as he took Abraham's cornerstone and placed it in the center of the cloak. Muhammad asked each of the twelve elders to grab a piece of the mantle. They lifted the cornerstone in the sling, walked slowly toward the cavity and dropped the stone in place.

With his spontaneous action, Muhammad had cemented his reputation as a wise peacemaker who had earned the trust of all of Mecca's tribes. As Muhammad dashed home clutching the pomegranates for his wife, the elders gazed after him. Surely, they murmured, this wealthy and diplomatic young man had a bright future ahead of him in the Dar-un-Nadwah assembly.

❖ ❖ ❖

As Muhammad burst through the front door, Barakah met him and delivered the wonderful news: Khadijah had just given birth to a healthy baby girl. Cradling his fourth daughter, Muhammad knew what to name her: Fatimah (self-reliant). It was both an homage to the aunt who had nurtured him in some of his darkest days and a hope that the little girl might follow in her parents' independent footsteps.

Fatimah would indeed grow up to resemble her father in behavior and mannerisms, earning the nickname Ummu Abiha (her father's epitome). She developed the same confident stride and eloquent speaking style as his, even mimicking him by tapping her right index finger over her open left palm when making a point. Fatimah was also the only one of Muhammad's offspring whose children survived to adulthood, producing his sole line of descendants.

Though Muhammad could not know just how fragile his future lineage would be, Fatimah's birth did signal that he would be viewed in *Jahiliyyah* society as a man cut off with no male heirs. For the Arabs, only sons counted as preservers of memory. Daughters got absorbed into their husbands' clans, while adopted sons like Zaid and 'Ali did not count. With two biological sons dead and Khadijah turning thirty-eight, the birth of Fatimah had been Muhammad's last chance for a male heir. Khadijah never again became pregnant.

Muhammad's path to leadership was blocked by his lack of sons. Al-'As Ibn Wa`il, a prominent member of the Dar-un-Nadwah assembly, began to refer to Muhammad as an *abtar*, a metaphorically castrated man, cut off from memory and leadership. "He must be cursed," nattered another elder.

A sensitive man, Muhammad was perhaps hurt by such gossip. Try as he might to overcome obstacles through hard work and determination, thirty-six-year-old Muhammad once again confronted the harsh reality that key aspects of life remained beyond his control. Coming to terms with his status meant facing the limits of self-reliance—the very quality he had evoked in naming Fatimah. Rather than rally once again, Muhammad sank into an extended midlife crisis.

From within his melancholy, he drew his daughters closer. He knew of his great-grandmother Salma, who had earned acclaim as a master merchant in the Yathrib market; he had been reared by Halimah, a member of the Banu Sa'd women's leadership council; and he had married his boss, Khadijah. Now it was his turn to raise a new generation of independent women, nurturing his daughters as well as supporting 'Atiq in empowering his spirited daughters, Asma and 'Aishah.

While Muhammad made sure his daughters were well dressed in beautiful tunics from distant lands, Khadijah taught the girls to read and write. Muhammad observed, "To educate a man is to empower an individual, but to educate a woman is to empower an entire nation." Years later, when a man came to Muhammad seeking to bequeath his wealth to the community because he had no sons, Muhammad insisted that the father invest it to benefit his daughters. To make the point clear, Muhammad proclaimed, "Let anyone who has a daughter honor her and not prefer his sons over her."

In turning inward to focus on his family, Muhammad was in effect recognizing that his main sphere of influence was now his household, not the larger world around him. He had amassed a fortune—one his family could live on for the rest of their lives without working—but he had found no deeper purpose. Wealth had not bought happiness nor enabled him to be a world-changer. Muhammad needed a call to action to inspire the rest of his days. But where could he find that?

As she accompanied her husband on one of their late afternoon strolls, Khadijah noticed that Muhammad was preoccupied. They paused on the Abu Qubais outcropping to watch the sun set over the market below, and Khadijah gently remarked, "My beloved, I have for some time sensed a great burden weighing you down. I will not pressure you to reveal it, but please know that I will support you always and stand by you with all my might."

Muhammad turned to Khadijah with an expression of deep love. His remarkable wife had invested in him, given him a family, respected his unique character, and supported his ideals even when they clashed with societal norms. With tears in his eyes, he embraced her and kissed her forehead. "I need to reflect," he admitted quietly. "I need time to look deep into my soul. There has to be a greater purpose to my existence than these menial accomplishments."

Khadijah suggested the storage room in the front section of their home become Muhammad's meditation space. After putting the girls to bed, he could withdraw to this private area and enjoy some time to himself. Muhammad seized on the idea, clearing out the eight-by-eight-foot room and furnishing it with a clay olive-oil lamp, a small Persian carpet, and a modest mattress. From the room's simple window, he looked out toward the tallest mountain on Mecca's horizon, known as Hira (place to resolve confusion).

Every evening, Muhammad would retreat into the meditation room, often staying until late at night while everyone else slept. After midnight one evening, 'Ali awoke to relieve himself. From the hallway, he heard Muhammad moaning, "Oh Great Force behind all life, Oh Wondrous Architect of creation, Oh Wise Creator of all things, guide me to you. Show me the way to you!" Peeking into the room, 'Ali noticed tears streaming down Muhammad's face.

Until his midlife crisis, Muhammad had lived a relatively nonspiritual life, observing many religions with interest but abstaining from any religious practice. Influenced by the monotheism of his mother, Barakah, and of Bahira, Muhammad believed in a higher being yet had found faith uninspiring. Pagans worshipped idols as intercessors, Jews awaited a messiah, and Christians had turned a human being into an expiating savior. While Muhammad had rejected the idea of needing an intermediary to the Divine, he had not proactively sought out God.

Amid his sadness, Muhammad for the first time expressed the desire for such a relationship. The yearning that 'Ali overheard reflected Muhammad's attempt to bring about a substantive connection. In addressing God directly, Muhammad sought inspiration for his own life, a calling. But he also admitted he was lost and confused about how to find a path forward. Muhammad's plaintive cry revealed a man desperately searching for a new mindset powerful enough to overcome his stagnation.

After several months of reflection, Muhammad had made no progress and struggled to focus. The bustle of a household filled with little girls and noises from the street outside were constant distractions from his meditation. But one day, as he sat on his mattress, Muhammad looked out the window beyond the commotion of Mecca's streets, his eyes drawn to Mount Hira. As the sun set, its dark red rays illuminated the mountain.

That was it! Muhammad needed to get away, to go somewhere quieter and more remote, an elevated spot where he could have a greater perspective. If by society's rules he was irreparably broken, he would leave society for a place closer to the heavens, the peak of Mecca's tallest mountain. Like his mentor Bahira, he would retreat from society and its restrictions. Like his mentor Ibnu Jud'an, he would, in a moment of anguish, climb a mountain in the hope of finding a hidden treasure that might transform his life.

When Muhammad shared his plans with Khadijah, she gave her support—but insisted he not go alone. Hira was far off and isolated. In case he hurt himself or got bitten by a snake, he needed companions. Muhammad chose his adopted sons Zaid (age twenty-six) and 'Ali (age six) to accompany him. Quiet and mature, neither would infringe on his meditation on the mountain.

On a cool spring morning, Muhammad headed out at dawn with his two adopted sons. He had dressed modestly, eschewing his usual elegant clothes for a simple white linen tunic, a black outer garment, and a black turban. Khadijah had packed dried dates, water, bread, and a flask of olive oil to sustain the trio on their planned three-day excursion.

As roosters crowed in the fresh morning air, Khadijah stood at the doorway of their home, holding baby Fatimah in a cotton shawl. She watched the three figures disappearing over the crest of a hill.

During the next three years, Muhammad would make the same trek many times, leaving his wife and young daughters behind to search for meaning on the mountaintop accompanied by his adopted sons. Day after day, month after month, he would head out . . . yet return empty-handed.

5

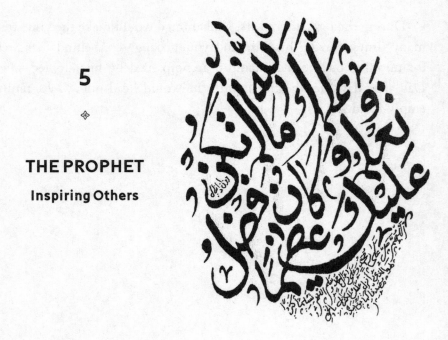

THE PROPHET

Inspiring Others

Mount Hira: 3:00 a.m., Friday, March 13, 610 CE

The tightness in his chest came out of nowhere, just as the first ray of light peeked over the horizon. Muhammad felt a profound energy transpire from the depths of his body. As it pulsated through his limbs, it seemed to unfold and echo across the mountains. With it, a word emerged, mysterious and numinous, as if the cosmos—*malakut*—were suddenly calling to him: *Iqra`!* The term describes the moment a bud unfurls and opens to the world around it. Delivered in the form of a command, *Iqra`!* meant "Allow yourself to blossom!"

Then complete silence.

Muhammad trembled from the shock of hearing the word revealed from the depth of his soul. His gasping breaths were condensing in the cool predawn air as he sat atop Mount Hira at the mouth of a cave burrowed out of its peak. Far below him, Mecca lay blanketed by a misty cloud of premorning dew. All night, Muhammad had gazed out over the city as he meditated, closing his eyes in concentration and then opening them to explore the infinite horizon.

Over the past four years, he had spent more than a hundred nights on the summit in this pose: seated with legs crossed on bare ground, back straight, hands on thighs. His foster sons, Zaid and 'Ali, had slept inside the cave behind him to respect the silence Muhammad maintained on their excursions. At first, the trio's treks to Hira were monthly, but for the past six months their frequency had intensified. With his fortieth birthday rapidly approaching, Muhammad spent three nights each weekend meditating on the mountaintop, desperately seeking something substantial to fill the painful emptiness lingering inside him.

Now, while his foster sons slept, Muhammad maintained his watch. Brilliant stars sparkled above. To his right, the moon descended past the horizon. To his left, a thin white line appeared from the east, slicing the darkness. Arabs called this predawn period *sahar* (mystical), the moment the night sky is at its darkest and then an initial sliver of refracted sunlight, called *al-falaq* (the cleft), breaks over the horizon.

In anguish, Muhammad finally opened his mouth. *"Ma aqra`!"* he exclaimed in confusion. ("I do not know how to blossom forth!") Muhammad repeated it twice more, each time slightly shifting the meaning. "What is blossoming forth?—How can I blossom forth?"

As if in answer, Muhammad suddenly heard five short sentences echoing through his entire being, flowing out of his depths like a hidden spring bursting from the ground:

Iqra`!
Blossom forth!

Bismi-rabbikal-lathi khalaq,
Inspired by your rejuvenating Cosmic Mentor,

Khalaqal-insana min 'alaq,
Who revives the dormant to forge empowering connections,

Iqra`!
Dare to blossom!

Wa rabbukal-akram
As your Cosmic Mentor provides spiritual comfort.

Al-lathi 'allama bil-qalam,
The Visionary One, who guides the unlocking of layers of
   learning,

'Allamal-insana ma lam ya'lam.
Elevates the stagnant to once inconceivable heights.

Nothing like this had ever happened to Muhammad. Though respected in Mecca for his character, he was not known for his rhythmic
style. His few attempts at poetry had resulted in clunky verse. Yet from
out of nowhere he had uttered several lines of deep insight, each word
layered with profound meaning, the phrases painting a vivid call to action for human beings, urging them to emerge from their cocoons to
unleash their dormant potential.

Muslim tradition ascribes this monumental event to the first divine
revelation through the medium of the Archangel Gabriel. For Muhammad, this sudden out-of-body experience was terrifying. He had originally planned to spend two more nights atop Hira, but his instinct told
him to flee. He spun around to rouse his foster sons. Ten-year-old 'Ali
looked up from his makeshift mattress and stared into Muhammad's fright-
ened eyes. "We must leave at once!" Muhammad whispered anxiously, as
Zaid shook himself awake.

Yawning and confused, the two grabbed their packs and hurriedly
followed Muhammad down the mountain. On the way, he suddenly
paused to look up at the sky and take a deep breath.

As the trio approached a still-slumbering Mecca, Muhammad kept
murmuring the mountaintop mantra under his breath: *"Iqra'! Iqra'!
Iqra'!"* He would never again return to Hira.

❖ ❖ ❖

In the predawn hours Khadijah experienced her own frightful awakening. A sudden pang of female intuition that her husband was in distress
sent her bolt upright in bed. She rushed to rouse Maysarah with urgent
instructions to ride out to Hira to check on Muhammad. As Maysarah
mounted a black stallion, Khadijah went outside to scan the horizon.
She spotted three figures approaching.

Muhammad ran toward her and she to him. He had taken his foster sons on a roundabout route home, winding through wilderness paths and back alleys to avoid bumping into anyone. As his wife embraced him, Muhammad struggled to speak, still shivering in fear. Calm as always, Khadijah quietly guided her husband inside to the room where they had first met seventeen years earlier.

Muhammad collapsed, his head resting on Khadijah's lap and his arms embracing her. "Cover me! Cover me! Cover me!" he begged finally. The morning was warm, but Muhammad trembled with intense cold. He had gone to Hira to escape Mecca's restrictive social rules and found on the remote mountaintop a truth inspired by nature. But while the metaphor of springtime blossoming should have been an uplifting inspiration—precisely the kind of call to action he had sought fruitlessly for years—the insight had come in a most unusual way.

Muhammad's cries of distress roused the household. Barakah had slept over that night, as she often did to help watch the girls while Muhammad was off meditating. Awakened by the pained voice of her foster son, she came running with a woolen blanket. The couple's sleepy daughters—twelve-year-old Zainab, ten-year-old Ruqayyah, eight-year-old Um Kulthum, and five-year-old Fatimah—also rushed into the salon. The older three curled up at their father's feet, hugging his legs, while little Fatimah draped herself over his back to help him feel safe.

As his anxiety began to wear off slightly in the presence of his family, Muhammad at last mustered the strength to explain himself. "I had a very strange experience," he said in a strained voice. "As I sat at the entrance of the cave, I felt these words echo, vibrating through my entire being. I felt my chest compressed and then cleft open with each word. I can't make sense of it. I fear I may be losing my senses."

Khadijah gently soothed her husband. "The Divine will never abandon you," she counseled. "You are an honorable man: kind to the weak, generous with the stranger. You help the downtrodden, the widow, and the orphan. You are honest in your words and trustworthy in your deeds. You are a noble father and a magnificent husband. These are not the characteristics of someone who is insane. What were the words that you received?"

Muhammad sat up and slowly repeated the revelation he had heard up on Hira just a few hours earlier. Everyone listened attentively as he proclaimed the brief layered phrases. They had never heard anything like the cadence or content of his words. 'Ali immediately committed them to memory and dashed to his room. Using a parchment from his writing lessons with Khadijah, he jotted down the phrases. Without knowing it, he was beginning a collection of Qur'anic manuscripts to which he would add over the next twenty-two years, cataloging each revelation in chronological order and storing the parchments in a wooden trunk.

As Muhammad recited his revelation, Khadijah recalled the prophesy of the *firasah* reader at the market three decades earlier, that young Muhammad would become a great man. She had long sensed her husband's latent potential and at last it had emerged. But the clarifying moment for Khadijah remained a terrifying one for her husband. Repeating the words from Mount Hira only reminded him of the trauma of their initial revelation. Muhammad lay on the couch all day, unable to eat as his stomach churned with the fear he was descending into insanity. At Barakah's insistence, he drank some warm milk yet still shivered under the blankets.

That evening, the whole family brought their mattresses to the salon to sleep alongside a still-quivering Muhammad. Meccan men never allowed themselves to appear vulnerable, yet Muhammad had admitted his fears in front of his wife and children. His family responded in turn by trying to ease his anxiety and help him feel protected. Muhammad slept fitfully, though, constantly waking up in a cold sweat while Khadijah and Fatimah snuggled beside him to keep him warm.

As the sun rose, light broke into the salon through the latticed windows above. Muhammad opened his eyes and sat up, waking Khadijah. She was relieved that her husband's pale face had regained its color and the beads of anxious perspiration had dissipated. More than twenty-four hours had passed since the mountaintop revelation, and Muhammad had turned the words over in his mind ever since. As the sun rose that day, he began to see the message in a new light. Casting off his blankets in a symbolic jettisoning of psychological burdens, Muhammad stood up and felt another revelation emerge. Waking his family, he began to chant:

Ya ayyuhal-muddaththir
Oh you who are covered up, shivering in fear

Qum fa anthir!
Get up and go out to proclaim the message of self-deliverance!

Wa rabbaka fa kabbir
Empower people to rebuild themselves inspired by the Cosmic
  Mentor

Wa-thiyabaka fa tahhir!
But bring clarity to yourself before you try to change others!

War-rujza fahjur!
Cast off the constellation of obstacles weighing you down!

Wa la tamnun tastakthir!
Help others out of sincerity without expecting any personal
  benefit!

Wa li-rabbika fasbir!
Trust in your Cosmic Mentor and persevere through the difficult
  process ahead!

His household stared in shock. Over the years they had grown accustomed to Muhammad's quirky manner—doing domestic work, changing diapers, freeing the enslaved—as well as Khadijah's calm support of her unusual husband. For the past three years they had watched him retreat into depression. Now, in an instant, his confidence had returned and along with it a new kind of philosophical declamation—and in rhyming Arabic phrases.

Once again, 'Ali memorized the revelation and rushed to his room to write it down. The few verses would become a part of the Qur'an known as Surah Al-Muddaththir (Chapter of the Shivering One Covered in Blankets). Like the initial *iqra hamza* revelation, Muhammad once again invoked *rabb*, a guiding mentor. He did not explicitly explain who this unseen mentor was. He did not seem to know exactly, even as he was buoyed by recognizing the mentor's presence.

Khadijah again recognized the divine call in her husband's revelations. "My cousin Waraqah is a man of learning and knows scriptures that are unknown to us," she informed her husband. "He has searched into the mysteries of the universe. Let us go consult him." While Muhammad had invoked a cosmic mentor, it might help for him to get some advice from a human mentor, too.

Waraqah, who had adopted Judaism, then Christianity, was a desert hermit who lived on a remote hill beyond Mecca's outskirts. His isolated hut—constructed from unbaked bricks with a roof of branches—was a far cry from the luxurious mansion in which he had lived as a member of one of Mecca's wealthiest families. Waraqah had cast aside exquisite silk garments and now wore ripped rags and had taken a vow of poverty and chastity. He spent his days in prayer and fasting. An ascetic, the recluse had renamed himself Waraqah (leaf), symbolic of his solitary existence amid the elements.

That Sunday afternoon, Waraqah, leaning on a wooden staff, slowly came out to greet Khadijah and her husband. Because his eyesight was feeble, the monk felt Muhammad's face with his hands as the three sat outside in the shade. Muhammad then shared his experience atop Hira as Waraqah listened attentively. The hermit remained silent for a few minutes before placing his hand upon Muhammad's shoulder and declaring, "You have been chosen as a prophet of God. The spirit that inspired you is the same one that touched Moses."

Muhammad was astonished. Waraqah had used the Arabic word *nabi*, which Arabs used to describe a spring bubbling forth in a barren desert and which Jews used to describe a prophet. The core concept of prophethood in the monotheistic tradition, Waraqah explained, revolved around divine revelations emerging from an unexpected source. Prophets were not brilliant scholars or devout clerics but rather unlikely and sudden bearers of a transcendent message. Moses, with his speech impediment and propensity to flee into the desert, was neither religious nor an intellectual—and he resisted the divine call to prophecy before reluctantly accepting the mission imposed upon him. Yet he ultimately came down from Mount Sinai with a revolutionary scripture that changed the world, inspiring people with a compelling call to lead a life of purpose and meaning.

As Muhammad struggled to wrap his mind around the concept, Waraqah explained that while his identity as a *nabi* might seem unexpected, prophets had always been destined for the role. "When the Creator chooses a person for a purpose, they are selected in the womb even before they are born," Waraqah said. "While the person is still a fetus, the plan of their life is already written, including all their experiences until the moment they are revealed to the world. Everything they do has been molded by the Creator for a particular purpose."

Waraqah was asking Muhammad to see his life until that moment as one of deliberate preparation rather than random fate. In that light, all the brokenness in his past had actually prepared him to unleash his potential as a world-changer. The message to "blossom forth" that Muhammad heard on Hira was a call to embrace the clefts in his life. Had his sons not died, he might have been content with society's limitation and thus blinded to his true mission. The hole made by nature had forced him to blossom forth despite himself.

Revelation, Waraqah reminded him, was not part of the Arabs' tradition. Prophecy was a Jewish experience expressed in Hebrew or Aramaic. But Muhammad's revelation on Hira had been delivered in Arabic. That Muhammad did not hail from a prophetic family yet could reveal such dazzling scriptures fit the prophetic requirements of unlikely revelation.

Yet Waraqah warned Muhammad that prophets had also often been persecuted, as their unexpected revelation by definition challenged the status quo. He declared, "I desire to live long enough to defend you when your people drive you out and try to kill you in order to silence you."

Muhammad could not believe this prognostication. He enjoyed a sterling reputation in Mecca. "Why would they drive me out and kill me?" he asked in confusion.

Waraqah explained, "Anyone who comes with a message like yours has always been persecuted."

Prophethood was not about prestige or authority, Waraqah tried to explain, but rather was an uncomfortable responsibility. The call to "blossom forth" expressed a mindset that required individuals to step outside their comfort zone. Meccans, who clung to the old ways, might not easily receive the message. Nor might they believe that the distant Divine would deign to speak to them, let alone in Arabic.

As Muhammad walked back to Mecca with Khadijah, Waraqah's words echoed in his mind. He was intimidated by the new role Waraqah had described yet also inspired to share the powerful message that had emerged from inside him. Surely the old hermit's warnings were overblown, he mused, and the people of Mecca would respond enthusiastically. Waraqah would not live long enough to see his prediction fulfilled. He died ten days later.

❖ ❖ ❖

The couple returned home with Waraqah's pronouncement of Muhammad's prophethood lingering in their thoughts. Though some details of this day remain lost to history, several aspects are recorded: Khadijah, quickly followed by 'Ali and Zaid, pledged allegiance to Muhammad's spiritual leadership. After dining with his daughters, Muhammad retreated to meditate on the rooftop terrace, and 'Ali, who came up occasionally to refill Muhammad's water flask, observed that his expression slowly evolved from deep worry to resolute calm.

The days of ruminating passively were over, Muhammad decided. Instead, it was time to heed the revelation's call and take action. He was not setting out to start a new religion but rather to revive the ancient call of biblical prophets to empower his community. As Moses had brought a message of liberation to Israelites in bondage, Muhammad was tasked to help the Meccans liberate themselves from self-imposed *Jahiliyyah*. What he needed to do was create a new civic movement of Meccans committed to progress.

The first step was to gather a core group of followers, and for that he needed the assistance of both his wife and his best friend. Late that evening, under the light of a full moon, Muhammad made his way to the home of 'Atiq. His friend's sixteen-year-old daughter, 'Aishah, opened the door. Muhammad had named her when she was born, the first name he had ever given. The young woman lived up to the moniker (vivacious). Her first betrothal had recently been broken off because her fiancé's family found her too independent and freethinking.

'Aishah observed how her father warmly welcomed his friend. As the two men sat in the living room facing each other on a mattress covered with an exquisite Yemenite rug, she tried to eavesdrop on their hushed conversation. 'Atiq listened attentively, then embraced his friend and declared, "I will sacrifice everything to support you." After Muhammad left, 'Atiq went to a wooden trunk and pulled out a hooded cloak, telling his daughter that he needed to go out.

The following morning 'Aishah prepared her father's bath. He had been out late for what seemed to be a mysterious series of meetings, yet he dashed to the market early with great enthusiasm. Intrigued, 'Aishah donned a white-hooded mantle and followed her father at a distance. At the market, she watched as he went from stall to stall, engaging in deep conversations with three renowned merchants: 'Uthman ibn 'Affan, 'Abdu-'Amru ibn 'Awf, and Mus'ab ibn 'Umair.

'Uthman was a sensitive young businessman who had shared his frustrations with *Jahiliyyah* with 'Atiq. While his relatives, the Banu Umayyah, dominated the Dar-un-Nadwah assembly, 'Uthman bucked the stereotype of Meccan elite males by being gallant and caring toward the poor. More thinker than doer, he was well educated. 'Abdu-'Amru was an economic genius who hailed from a wealthy family. His mother, Ash-Shifa, was the expert midwife who had delivered Muhammad four decades earlier, and his father had hired tutors to ensure 'Abdu-'Amru was learned in poetry and mathematics. His discontentment with *Jahiliyyah* was shared by Mus'ab, another well-educated young man who felt like a prisoner in a gilded cage: smothered by a domineering mother who showered him with material objects but starved him of emotional affection. Mus'ab's late father, 'Umair, was a childhood friend of Muhammad's.

That evening, the young men made their way one by one to Muhammad's home, part of a stream of surreptitious nocturnal visitors. They wore hoods and walked in the shadows on moonlit streets to avoid being recognized. Zaid waited by the front door to lead them into the house's main salon, where Muhammad and Khadijah sat together at the center of the room, with Barakah at Muhammad's side. The group of about a dozen visitors formed a circle around them. Like 'Atiq, Khadijah had also recruited several of the evening's participants.

Muhammad chanted his first revelation for the astonished group and advised them to keep it secret, to share it with only carefully chosen residents of Mecca who might be open to the message. There was electricity in the room as the small group formed a new community of purpose around the prophet in their midst.

Muhammad added to the energy by bestowing upon 'Atiq the new name Abu Bakr (the first one) in recognition of his being the first outside Muhammad's family to accept the call to blossom. Muhammad then revealed that he intended to make a public declaration of the revelation on Friday morning in front of the whole city. Abu Bakr and several other influential businessmen wanted to join him, but Muhammad refused to endanger his followers in case Waraqah's warning came true.

On Friday morning, Muhammad awoke ready to seize the day. He bathed and donned a white tunic, a red waistband, and a red-striped outer mantle. He wrapped a white turban around his head, anointed his eyes with kohl to protect them from the sun's glare, and perfumed his clothes with myrrh. Muhammad insisted that Khadijah, Barakah, and his daughters stay home, in case his speech did not go as planned. He asked 'Ali to wait by Dar-un-Nadwah to alert him when the council meeting ended so that the city's elders could hear his message.

Abu Bakr (né 'Atiq), 'Uthman, 'Abdu-'Amru, and Mus'ab all tended to their stalls while waiting excitedly for Muhammad to appear. They watched as Muhammad walked into the market, his confident stride and elegant robes turning heads as he passed through the crowd. Everyone watched as he advanced toward Abu Qubais. Head high, he stepped up to the civic podium, fulfilling the root meaning of the name his grandfather had bestowed on him forty years before: to stand on a platform and model behavior to inspire action in others.

The Meccans streamed toward him, and when a crowd had assembled, Muhammad asked, "If I were to tell you that a great army was advancing from the distance to annihilate you, would you believe me?"

The crowd answered, "Yes, for you are truthful and trustworthy."

The Meccans knew Muhammad was honest; after all, he was the one person they trusted to maintain the city's only safety depository. But they also knew he had withdrawn from civic affairs. Why had he disappeared, and why, just as suddenly, had he reappeared?

As Muhammad's garments reflected the morning sun and rippled in the gentle breeze, he repeated the words revealed to him exactly one week earlier.

Packed into each word of the revelation were evocative images and intricate connotations. The passage began with a message of hope: during the winter, plants appear to be dead, yet the return of spring reveals that they have instead been waiting for the right moment to unfurl themselves and begin flourishing again. He invoked the word *rabb*—the term for *mentor*—someone gently bestowing drops of water at the base of a new plant and then providing wooden supports to guide the plant's growth.

He reminded his audience that they were not alone. True blossoming required engagement with other livings things. The word *'alaq* evoked a vine clinging to a tree as a natural example of symbiotic growth. The vine elevates itself without harming the tree. To pursue their potential, people need to connect and cooperate, learning from one another and combining existing ideas to forge new ones.

To ease the fears of his audience, Muhammad issued the revelation as a source of comfort. The passage repeated the words *iqra hamza* to emphasize the centrality of blossoming and then used the word *akram* to evoke a vineyard. For Arabs, vineyards symbolized tranquil places to find peace and safety. Drawing on the previous verse's reference to vines, this verse described a place where the fruit of vines is transformed into something pleasant and nourishing.

The activities of a vineyard constituted a nice segue into the next verse's emphasis on process. The term *'allama* evoked a grand mountain (*'alam*), symbolizing both the stamina required to reach the summit and the durable memory Meccans sought to secure for themselves. Careful, focused effort was also embedded in *qalam*, the Arabic term describing the art of whittling down a reed to create a pen. Delicately peeling back layers could finally yield a core of profound understanding—and provide a tool for sharing insights with the world.

The passage ended by evoking the ultimate objective: transforming stagnation into previously unimaginable possibility. The word *insan* (used figuratively for human being) had multiple connotations for his audience. On the one hand, it meant one who forgets and procrastinates—and thus stagnates. But the term can also imply one who stands out. By making the conscious decision to unleash dormant potential, a once-stagnating person can become outstanding. If Meccans could embrace the example of spring rejuvenation visible all around them, they could achieve great things.

He delivered the call to blossom forth with the passion of a man who had achieved liberating clarity after more than three years of painful struggle. The verses had awakened Muhammad's own soul, and now he sought to awaken his neighbors to unlock their potential, to dare to open themselves up to new ideas.

Yet in the passion of his newfound clarity, Muhammad had neglected to acknowledge his community's understandable fear of change. Surrounding the Meccans was intense warfare between the Byzantines and the Sasanians that threatened the safety of the annual caravans and might even end the Meccans' prized tax-exempt status in Damascus. In a dangerous world, most Meccans saw no reason to abandon the successful policies of their ancestors. Nothing in Muhammad's declaration recognized those concerns. His message jumped straight to a bold new solution, one so abruptly shocking that few Meccans were prepared to even consider it.

After allowing the final chanted verse to linger in the air, Muhammad looked down. The crowd below was silent. Many wore puzzled expressions. Then Muhammad's uncle 'Abdul-'Uzza—the man who had rushed for fresh dates when Muhammad's mother was in labor—broke the silence. He barked, *"Tabban laka ya Muhammad!* (Damn you, Muhammad!) Is this why you have gathered us here? Taking us away from our work during the busiest time of day, just to tell us this?" The crowd broke into laughter and began to disperse.

Abu Bakr felt his heart break as he silently observed the humiliation of the new prophet. He wished he could embrace his friend, but Muhammad had warned his followers not to publicly associate with him. Abu Bakr glanced over at 'Amr ibn Hisham, the abusive elder

Muhammad had challenged with the Hilf-ul-Fudhul pact. The man wore a sardonic smirk as he watched Muhammad descend the hill with his head bowed.

It had taken Muhammad four decades to achieve his epiphany and less than four minutes for the Meccans to reject all of it.

❖ ❖ ❖

For Mecca's elders, Muhammad's message posed a threat not because it invoked the Divine; indeed, several Meccans (like Waraqah) had converted to Christianity, and one of the city's clans (Banul Harith) was Jewish. The call to blossom, rather, defied the long-established Arabian social order that venerated ancestors had put in place. By pointing to "potential in what appears hopelessly broken," Muhammad implicitly suggested that everyone in society had value and that even the hopelessly broken, such as women and slaves, could achieve "seemingly impossible heights."

Meccan society responded to the speech as Waraqah predicted. Though Meccans continued to trust Muhammad as a businessman—no one withdrew their deposits from his care—they openly belittled his ideas. People laughed at him as he walked in the streets, with some mothers even stuffing cotton in their children's ears to prevent the strange man from bewitching their offspring. Others hurled a slur at Muhammad: *muthammam* (one worthy of disgrace, rather than emulation).

In Mecca's tribal society, Muhammad's family felt enormous pressure to contribute to his social ostracism. Abu Talib stood by his nephew even though he did not initially embrace his message. Khadijah had recruited Lubabah, Khadijah's best friend and the wife of Muhammad's uncle Al-'Abbas, to secretly join Muhammad's core followers. But Muhammad's dear uncle 'Abdul-'Uzza harshly turned on his nephew. To maintain their honor among Mecca's elite, 'Abdul-'Uzza and his wife, Arwa, publicly disowned Muhammad. Every evening, Arwa instructed their servants to place garbage mixed with thorns at Muhammad's front door.

Muhammad's famous encounter with an elderly woman struggling to carry heavy water jugs occurred a few days after the Abu Qubais pitch, as Muhammad walked alone to gather his thoughts. He picked up the jugs and escorted her home. She thanked her mysterious helper, telling him, "As you can see, my son, I am a poor woman, so I cannot offer you anything to reward your kindness. But I will give you a word of advice. That man Muhammad has created so much harm, misguiding the youth. Avoid him."

Muhammad gently replied, "I regretfully decline your well-intentioned advice." As he walked away, he added, "Because I am Muhammad." The next morning, she found a large food basket and a pouch of silver coins at her door.

That evening, as he adjusted to his new status as a social outcast, Muhammad experienced his third revelation:

> *Al-hamdu-lillahi rabb-il-'alamin,*
> Emulate the ultimate source of unconditional love (*Allah*), who
>   gently nourishes growth in all things,
>
> *Ar-rahman-ir-rahim,*
> Who optimistically empowers even the most fragile and comforts
>   in moments of vulnerability,
>
> *Maliki yawm-id-din.*
> Who provides fresh energy for each unfolding phase in the
>   journey of life.
>
> *Iyyaka na'budu wa iyyaka nasta'in.*
> We strive to reflect the way you rejuvenate and trust in your
>   support to shield our weaknesses.
>
> *Ihdinas-sirat-al-mustaqim.*
> Guide us to navigate a safe path with flexibility.
>
> *Sirat-al-lathina an'amta 'alaihim.*
> A path previously forged by the foresighted, who steadily restore
>   brokenness to reach a state of serenity.

Ghayr-il-maghdubi 'alaihim wa la-dh-dhallin.
(A path) unconstrained by a stagnant reality of willful
   manipulation and blind acceptance.

The spurned prophet's revelation expressed a heartfelt resolve to stay focused and to never give up on others, despite their animosity. The opening verse also featured the first invocation of *Allah*, which evokes the image of a mother embracing her crying child. While his initial revelations had configured the Divine as *Rabb*, in this moment of pain and rejection, Muhammad was comforted by an embracing presence, an image reinforced by the second verse's invocation of a new name for God derived from the Semitic word for womb (*rahim*). Though Muhammad did not yet know it, these seven verses would become the Qur'an's most iconic chapter, Al-Fatihah (The Unlocking, or The Gateway).

Determined to put these words into action, Muhammad convened his small group of followers for a secret meeting at his home. That night, they decided to keep their movement underground and to focus their meetings on education. Abu Bakr argued the movement needed a place to study but that Muhammad's home was too conspicuous. He suggested recruiting another businessman, Al-Arqam, whose home was centrally located at the end of a small alleyway with a private interior hall buffered by surrounding rooms. Muhammad liked the suggestion because Al-Arqam was the first cousin of his nemesis 'Amr ibn Hisham. According to the tribal code, no one from Al-Arqam's clan could barge into his home or harm his guests.

Abu Bakr persuaded this merchant to offer his home. At the first learning session a few nights later, Muhammad arranged the group of about a dozen in a circle, just like the elders' council—only here the enslaved and women sat alongside elite male merchants. Mecca had never seen this before. Some slaves had sneaked out to attend, and some elites had not told their spouses. What united the unlikely cross section of Meccan society was intellectual curiosity. They were intrigued by Muhammad's bold call to action despite the risk of being ostracized socially (or, for the enslaved, subjected to physical punishment).

Dar-ul-Arqam (Al-Arqam's home, literally, the abode of leaving a lasting impact) became the dissident movement's secret academy, a democratic alternative to the Dar-un-Nadwah assembly. Muhammad, who had never taught before, used a pedagogic approach that fused those of his various mentors. After precisely reciting his revelations so the group could memorize the verses, Muhammad led an analytical discussion for the next hour, posing questions and encouraging all participants to share their ideas. The goal was to help the group train their minds to think outside tradition, restrictions, and conformity.

The brief yet intense secret learning sessions quickly became a regular occurrence. While Muhammad served as primary educator, others shared their expertise. Abu Bakr taught poetry and genealogy; 'Abdu-'Amru (now renamed 'Abdur-Rahman by Muhammad) discussed business strategy; and Mus'ab tutored in etiquette and culture. Zinnirah Ar-Rumiyyah, a Greek Christian whom Abu Bakr had liberated from forced prostitution, taught reading and writing. She became one of Muhammad's first scribes, formally recording his revelations.

A diligent student had to be disciplined, Muhammad believed, and discipline began with cleanliness. Muhammad taught proper hygiene, including the safety protocols for defecation and urination as well as principles for respecting the body as a sacred trust from God. He promoted the practice of handwashing after waking from sleep, before and after eating, and after reliving oneself—and even taught his followers how to brush their teeth and tongues. At Dar-ul-Arqam, Muhammad began molding a new generation of refined, health-conscious students.

Mecca's elders caught wind of Muhammad's clandestine network yet dismissed the idealistic cadre as *sabi'un* (silly rebellious youth—literally, unstable lids dancing atop boiling pots). Muhammad, however, offered his followers a more inspiring moniker for their fledging movement. A few months into their learning sessions, he shared a new revelation, which recounted the story of Abraham as a twelve-year-old dissatisfied with his people's idolatry and stagnation. Young Abraham established a new identity for himself and his movement. As Muhammad chanted, "This is the way of your patriarch Abraham; it was he who originally named you Muslims, and now you continue that legacy."

A person who strove for self-liberation from stagnation was a *muslim*—literally, someone making an effort to repair cracks in city walls—and, spiritually, someone constantly striving to achieve a state of wholeness (without ever fully achieving it). The life mission of Muslims was the unending pursuit of completion, described with the Arabic word *Islam*. The embryonic secret movement in Mecca had a new name—although Muhammad taught that Islam was simply the ancient core message of every monotheistic prophet. All that evolved was its application to respond to changing social contexts.

For Muhammad's followers, the connection to Abraham, Mecca's founding patriarch, was thrilling. Rather than rebelling against tradition, they were upholding it and infusing its core values with contemporary relevance. As Muslims they embraced the brokenness in all human beings while simultaneously inspiring them to strive to emulate the only perfect being in the universe, God. Islam at this point functioned not as a doctrinal religion with rituals but as an ideological civic movement.

Though Muhammad clearly instructed his followers to keep these bold ideas confidential for their own safety, one woman was so enthusiastic she could not keep quiet. Sumayyah (lofty and elegant) was a Himyarite who had been brought to Mecca from Yemen as a slave, along with her enslaved husband, Yasir (easy flowing), and son, 'Ammar (builder), after the fall of the Jewish Himyarite kingdom. While their master eventually emancipated the family, they lacked any tribal protection within Mecca's clan system. Sumayyah responded deeply to Muhammad's call to end constraints on human potential.

For several months, she kept her participation in Muhammad's movement secret even from her husband. But after mustering the courage to tell Yasir and then 'Ammar, who quickly decided to join the meetings, she began openly approaching people about the call to blossom, becoming the first person after Muhammad to advocate in public. She encouraged women not to accept female infanticide, and she urged the enslaved to think for themselves. Her message challenged the status quo and began to awaken a sense of defiance among the enslaved.

The elders decided that they needed to stop Sumayyah. Because her former master had died, prominent members of his clan were responsible for delivering the ultimatum. The brutal 'Amr ibn Hisham, a cousin of Sumayyah's late master, gladly took up the task along with his nephew

'Umar, a giant young man whose frightful temper intimidated all of Mecca. When she refused to heed 'Amr's warning to stop her street outreach, the elder had Sumayyah, Yasir, and 'Ammar tied to wooden stakes in the intense heat of the summer sun. Children hurled pebbles at them, and 'Umar beat the parents—though with clear instructions to keep them alive. To dissuade others, the Meccans wanted the family to confess that Muhammad's words had bewitched them.

For Muhammad, the torture of Sumayyah's family marked a nadir. The rules of *Jahiliyyah* blocked him from interfering in an intraclan dispute, and his nascent movement was too weak to mount any challenge. All Muhammad could do was extend his compassion to Sumayyah. He could easily have condemned her for defying his order to keep the message confidential. Instead, he visited her in captivity and saluted her independent thinking, even when it went against his own judgment. "Persevere and remain strong in spirit," he encouraged Sumayyah, "for yours is a lasting legacy." She needed to think for herself, his words implied; he was not her master.

In contrast, 'Amr ibn Hisham insisted on dominating Sumayyah. When he stood facing her bound body, verbally berating her, she responded with Muhammad's message that all human beings had to think for themselves: "You cannot control my mind and my heart, which belong to me and my Creator, as does my body." In a fit of rage at hearing a formerly enslaved woman address him this way, 'Amr grabbed a spear and plunged it through Sumayyah's womb, thrusting it with such force that he pierced her heart. Then with one stroke, he beheaded her husband. Islam had its first martyrs.

Their traumatized son, 'Ammar, shrieked that he recanted, frantically insulting Muhammad. 'Amr ibn Hisham unbound 'Ammar, gave him water and food, and sent him home. Grieving, the young man soon felt ashamed of his weakness. Muhammad met with him privately and reassured him: *"In 'adu fa'ud!"* (If they return to persecute you, insult me again!)

With Meccan persecution turning deadly, Muhammad's movement went even further underground. In three years, his followers grew to just forty people. Only the truly dedicated would join, mostly young elites chafing at the restrictions of *Jahiliyyah* and the enslaved seeking liberation. Anyone interested in Muhammad's message had to reckon with Sumayyah's murder.

But then Muhammad experienced a new revelation, one that questioned the commonly held understanding that death was the end of human experience: "Do not think that those killed while on the path toward the Divine are dead. Rather they are fully alive, unceasingly nourished and still growing under the gentle care of their Mentor, the Creator."

With these words, Muhammad introduced the concept of *akhirah* (afterlife), referencing an Arabic agricultural term that signified the period after planting seeds yet before initial sprouts. Invoking the *akhirah* suggested that, though people like Sumayyah might die, their initial investment would still yield a valuable return: the true benefit of one's deeds might emerge only many years later, or even after death. Muhammad's message to his underground followers was revolutionary: though you might face grave hostility, think, plan, and act for the long term.

❖ ❖ ❖

Hidden amid the sheets of textiles that 'Uthman and Mus'ab carried to their market stalls each morning was dangerous contraband: scrolls featuring transcriptions of Muhammad's revelations. Literate members of the underground movement recorded the revelations on parchment, and the sheets then circulated secretly among followers so each could memorize the words. By the time of Sumayyah's martyrdom, over twenty revelations had emerged, a growing corpus of material that was clandestinely exchanged at the stalls of Muhammad's merchant followers.

On the first anniversary of the *iqra hamza* revelation atop Hira, Muhammad had an epic revelation that gave these disparate passages a unifying identity. All revelations were part of a larger work called the *Qur'an* (the Blossoming), a title that conveyed both a perpetual process and a thematic goal. The word *Qur'an* appeared for the first time in the epic revelation's opening lines:

Ma anzalna 'alaikal-Qur'ana li tashqa
We did not reveal the Qur'an to weigh you down

Il-la tathkiratal-limay-yakhsha.
but rather to liberate and elevate for a lasting legacy anyone
   willing to listen.

Each Arabic word in the two brief verses was dense with imagery and multifaceted meaning. The term for *reveal* (*anzal*) evoked constellations (*manazil,* a cognate of the Hebrew *mazal*) that wilderness guides used to navigate the desert. Like starlight in darkness, the revelations aimed to provide hope amid despair and practical guidance to anyone seeking direction in life. The term for being weighed down (*shaqa*) described the sweaty and muddied face of an enslaved worker struggling to carry a heavy load. The Divine was not a master looking to abuse a slave for personal benefit but rather a mentor looking to help human beings persevere through life's challenges.

The term for liberating and elevating (*tathkirah*) described being free to stand up and stand out in a way that makes a lasting impression on others, to be remembered by the ramifications of one's actions. Finally, the word *yakhsha* literally meant to cut back a cocoon's sheath, suggesting breaking through a self-imposed obstacle blocking comprehension. It asked listeners to let down their mental defenses and engage in sincere, active listening: to open their minds to ideas powerful enough to liberate and elevate their legacy.

Packing layered meaning into just a few words, these verses were preceded by two Arabic letters—*ta* and *ha*—that gave the chapter its name: "*Taha*" (Stand Firm). The imperative command urged listeners not to waver. The letters themselves had meaning as well. The *ta* symbolized aiming for an objective and the *ha* alluded to a praiseworthy exemplar. Taken together, the letters asked listeners to steadfastly pursue the objective of liberating their dormant potential by learning from the example of others.

Surah Taha, unlike previous revelations, which were filled with intricate intellectual meditations, presented practical examples to learn from—content much more accessible for ordinary Meccans than the abstract musings of the past year. The new revelation was full-fledged narrative, stretching for over a hundred verses and filled with human stories of imperfect, broken people. Recounting the stories of Moses,

Aaron, and Adam, the *surah* introduced biblical figures who, aside from Mecca's founder, Abraham, were unknown to Arabian audiences.

The revelation's narrative begins with Moses traveling in the wilderness with his family and noticing a distant fire. He assumes it is an encampment of fellow travelers but soon comes upon a brilliant bush from within which God imposes upon him a mission: "I am the Loving Divine (Allah) . . . who knows the seen and the unseen . . . what is beyond the universe and beneath the earth. . . . Go to Pharaoh . . . [and] tell him to liberate the children of Israel."

Overwhelmed by this sudden demand from a divine presence that has never communicated with him before, Moses retreats. Yet God, alternating between the singular and plural first person pronouns to convey affection, insists, "I had chosen you for my service even before you were born, so listen and open your heart to what has been revealed." The Divine (now using the first-person plural, *we*) reminds Moses that he killed an abusive Egyptian taskmaster in a moment of rage: "You killed a soul, yet we saved you from the depth of guilt and depression, and we caused you to reflect and reconsider your life purpose."

Moses reluctantly returns to Egypt to confront its ruler. Pharaoh retorts, "Did we not raise you as an infant among us and for many years, treating you as one of our own—only for you to repay our graciousness by killing one of us in a deep display of ingratitude?"

Moses answers by accepting responsibility—both for his mistake and his new mission: "Yes, I confess that I did it in a state of loss and confusion. Then I escaped, fearing your wrath. But my Cosmic Mentor chose me and sent me as a messenger to liberate my people."

When Muhammad shared this revelation with his followers, they listened, riveted. The compelling drama brought Moses to life as a broken yet chosen world-changer. It reassured the small Dar-ul-Arqam group, which was still reeling from the murder of Sumayyah. The revelation's call to stand firm resonated, and, over time, more and more Meccans began to subtly change their behavior. Though only a handful became formal followers of Muhammad, many were inspired to perform their own small acts of rebellion. Many Meccan women no longer blindly submitted to their husbands' commands, and some children began questioning their parents' orders.

After two years of passively watching the situation erode, Mecca's elders decided to intervene. They sent the city's top poet, Al-Walid ibn al-Mughirah, to sway Muhammad with his eloquence. As the two men sat together, Al-Walid examined Muhammad's scrolls. The poet was stunned by the revelations' captivating language and compelling call to blossom—in which he perceived a hazardous intensity. "This message has an evocative sweetness that penetrates the depth of the heart and stirs the mind," declared Al-Walid, praising the material even as he condemned it. "Its deeply rooted call to blossom can bear fruit and overturn the social order. With its eloquence surpassing all others, it will surely shake the foundations of our established order, which is inferior to its powerful message."

When Muhammad politely declined Al-Walid's request to stop promoting his message, other elders tried to intervene, without success. Word of Muhammad's resistance spread among the tribes of Arabia, who began to question the Meccan elders' custodianship of the Ka'bah, due to their inability to contain a small protest movement. The elders called an emergency session at Dar-un-Nadwah to address the growing crisis. While the elders sat around debating next steps, in barged the largest man in Mecca.

'Umar, who was nearly seven feet tall, had heard about the emergency meeting the night before from his maternal uncle 'Amr ibn Hisham. "You are incompetently letting things get out of hand!" 'Umar thundered. "This man Muhammad is a menace. If you won't deal with him, I'll handle him myself—and I don't care what happens." 'Umar unsheathed his sword, pushed away several elders who tried to restrain him, and rushed out into the street with a murderous look in his eyes.

Hot-tempered yet sensitive, 'Umar towered over everyone in Mecca. Even as a child, he had been oversized. At age four, he had the body of a ten-year-old. His father, who did not recognize the large toddler's immaturity, had 'Umar ride behind him on a horse. One day 'Umar slipped off the back. He suffered a hard blow to his head that likely caused his lifelong, histrionic mood swings. His father's violent temper and unrealistic expectations further traumatized him, as did his parents' lack of affection.

Bald-headed and heavyset, 'Umar was known for his wrestling

skills. Beyond his physical prowess, he was highly intelligent and well educated—though he struggled to make sense of his outsize talents and temperamental personality. At age sixteen, he had a daughter, yet his machismo made him feel ashamed at having no sons. When his daughter turned five, 'Umar took her out into the desert and buried her alive. He later recounted how his daughter had reached up while he shoveled to gently wipe dust off his beard with her little hands. A few minutes after suffocating his daughter to death, he began to weep uncontrollably.

As 'Umar dashed through the streets of Mecca to murder Muhammad, rage surged through his body. One of Muhammad's secret followers, a Chaldean Christian named Khabbab, caught wind of the emergency and tried to intercept the angry giant by bumping into him in the street. "Where are you going?" Khabbab inquired.

'Umar seethed. "I'm going to rid society of this pestilence, sever this cancerous disease once and for all."

Seeking to buy time to get Muhammad to safety, Khabbab improvised: "Don't you think you should be fixing the problem in your own house before you go out tackling other people's problems?"

"What do you mean?" 'Umar roared.

Khabbab explained, "You want to kill Muhammad yet are oblivious to the fact that your own sister and her husband are his followers?" 'Umar was shocked: his own sister and brother-in-law had fallen under Muhammad's sway! He charged off toward their home. Khabbab had not lied: Fatimah bint al-Khattab and her husband were secret followers; the literate Fatimah served as one of Muhammad's scribes. When the couple heard 'Umar bellowing outside their front door, they quickly hid one of her scrolls—a transcription of Surah Taha—under a cushion.

When she welcomed her younger brother, Fatimah saw the anger in his eyes as he demanded, "What is this I hear: You two are followers of Muhammad?" Then he noticed a cushion out of place and strode over to see what might be hidden beneath. The couple dove to grab the scroll first, but 'Umar hurled his brother-in-law against the wall. As Fatimah ran at her brother screaming, 'Umar snatched the scroll with his left hand and with his right-hand slapped Fatimah across the face, flinging her to the ground and slicing her lip in the process.

Seeing his sister crying on the floor with blood dripping from her face, 'Umar melted—his rage converted instantaneously to regret. He meekly begged his sister to forgive him, as she dragged herself over to her unconscious husband to try to revive him. In a daze, 'Umar unrolled the scroll in his hand and began to read it, the parchment slowly unraveling toward the floor as he pored over every word.

'Umar was captivated. Just as the elder Al-Walid had predicted, the revelation's eloquent language and bold message penetrated straight to the heart and stirred the mind. 'Umar had been at the market three years earlier when Muhammad made his failed pitch from Abu Qubais, and the call to blossom had bounced off his ears with no effect. With his sister sobbing and bleeding beside him, however, 'Umar's defenses were down. The *surah* declared that the Qur'an could help "anyone willing to listen"—and 'Umar was suddenly all ears.

The *surah* depicted Moses as strong and temperamental, a man who killed another human being in a fit of rage and then fled into the wilderness. A man who violently grabbed his own brother by the beard in anger over a seeming betrayal. A man with a temper who threw God's tablets to the ground in fury—yet was forgiven. For the first time in his life, 'Umar understood that flawed people like himself had a chance at renewal.

In a moment of epiphany, 'Umar turned to his sister and demanded, "Take me to Muhammad."

Fatimah adamantly replied, "No, if you want to kill someone, kill me!" Seeing his sister's distress, 'Umar began sobbing and hugging her. She realized his anger had subsided and hugged back. 'Umar helped revive his brother-in-law, and then all three headed to Al-Arqam's house.

As they arrived, Khabbab discreetly exited the door of the underground school. Assuming the worst, he stretched his body across the entrance. "You'll have to kill me first!" he declared.

Fatimah reassured him: "No, he's not come for that purpose. He wants to be one of us now." Khabbab slowly dropped his arms in shock. The man he had seen beat Sumayyah and Yasir within an inch of death, the man he had seen only thirty minutes earlier in a murderous rage with sword drawn, had come to pledge allegiance.

Al-Arqam brought 'Umar into his courtyard, and Muhammad stood to greet him. "Come and sit beside me and let me hear what you have on your mind," said Muhammad gently. "What gave you this change of heart?"

"I loved the words in Surah Taha," 'Umar explained passionately. "The images penetrated my conscience. They moved me. It is the most beautiful thing I have ever read. I want to be part of what you have. I want to be like you."

Muhammad replied, "You are one of us." The twenty-five people present each welcomed 'Umar with a hug.

It was a remarkable scene. Muhammad had won over an oversize exemplar of *Jahiliyyah* mentality—a man who had murdered his own daughter and tortured Sumayyah. The call to blossom and self-liberate could penetrate even the most stubborn Meccan.

Basking in the embrace of his compatriots, 'Umar asked innocently, "This is amazing. If what we have is so good, why are we in hiding? Should we not proclaim it openly to the world? These classes need to be taught publicly beside the Ka'bah! Why is everyone sneaking into and out of the school?"

Muhammad gently placed his hand upon 'Umar's shoulder and smiled, as if to say, Because of people like you.

Proudly owning his new identity, 'Umar ran out of Dar-ul-Arqam and straight to the Ka'bah. As he stood before the shrine's front door, he bellowed, "Today, I am one of Muhammad's followers. Anyone who impedes them will have to deal with me!"

❖ ❖ ❖

From the balcony of Dar-un-Nadwah, Mecca's elders watched in disbelief as 'Umar proclaimed his allegiance to Muhammad.

Only a few weeks earlier, they had tried yet again to dissuade Muhammad from his mission, this time inviting him to join them at their weekly Friday council meeting. As Muhammad sat politely before the council, a leading elder named Umayyah ibn Khalaf attempted to outreason his guest. "You say that all men are created equal?" asked Umayyah.

Muhammad replied, "Yes, like the teeth of a comb."

Umayyah pointed to one of his enslaved servants offering drinks to the elders. "Is Bilal here, whom I bought with my own money and whose life I hold in my hands, equal to me?"

Muhammad responded candidly, "Yes, and he even has the ability to surpass you, if he aspires to."

Umayyah had recoiled in stunned silence. Yet for Bilal (moistening dew), Muhammad's words resonated deeply. Though born to enslaved parents in Mecca, Bilal knew his maternal ancestors had been Abyssinian courtiers. His mother had been born into a noble family and lived at the royal court in Yemen before being captured by Sasanian conquerors and sold into slavery. A devout Christian, she instilled her faith in her son. Bilal, who was known for his deep resonant voice, was tall and muscular, with curly hair and a small goatee.

When he heard Muhammad confront Umayyah, Bilal decided to seize the moment and join Muhammad's movement. Later that day, Bilal defiantly told his master that they were equals, just as Muhammad had argued that morning. Umayyah could not believe his ears, nor could he convince Bilal to recant his declaration. To help the young man "come to his senses," Umayyah had him whipped and tied down in the hot sun. When Bilal nonetheless persisted, Umayyah had him stripped naked and a large stone placed on his chest. Then members of Umayyah's clan dragged Bilal through the scorching sand, shredding his skin.

In his deep voice, Bilal screamed out *"Ahadun ahad!"* (The Creator is unique, and I too am unique!) On the brink of death, Bilal insisted on his inherent right to be his own person. Just then Abu Bakr appeared and blocked the path of the clansmen dragging Bilal through the sand. He calmly offered to purchase Bilal on the spot for several times his market value.

"He is worth nothing to me," spat Umayyah, accepting the offer. "You can have him."

Abu Bakr helped Bilal to his feet and brought him to his home to be nursed back to health. Bilal soon joined the small group of the formerly enslaved led by Suhaib and also began studying at Dar-ul-Arqam. Until he could get established on his own, he slept at Abu Bakr's home or in Khadijah's old warehouse.

Bilal's rebellion only further confounded the elders. Unable to convince Muhammad to renounce his message, they hatched a scheme to bribe his uncle Abu Talib to formally renounce guardianship (*ijarah*) of his nephew. Since Arabian society was tribal, all who lived in Arabia needed a guardian (*mujir*) to protect them and give them legitimacy. A delegation of elders visited Abu Talib (who never achieved great wealth) and dangled the promise of significant riches if he would abandon Muhammad. The normally easygoing Abu Talib became furious, clenching his fist as he declared, "So long as a breath passes through my lips, I will stand between you and him, protecting him with the last drop of my blood."

After the confrontation, however, Abu Talib went to see his nephew privately. "There is only so much I can do to protect you," he said, pleading with Muhammad to calm the situation. Muhammad promised to do so and began taking extra measures to restrain his followers. After 'Umar publicly declared his allegiance, Muhammad insisted his new follower devote himself to learning. The young man needed to train himself to control his behavior and to study the mindset of blossoming before rushing to take any action. 'Umar acquiesced and did not in any way disrupt the fragile status quo. In return, Muhammad offered 'Umar the attention and care he desperately craved yet had never received as a child.

Tensions nonetheless occasionally bubbled to the surface. One day, Muhammad's uncle Hamzah returned from hunting outside Mecca and passed by the Ka'bah on his way home. He overheard 'Amr ibn Hisham openly insulting Muhammad while conversing with other elders. Hamzah, a man who regularly wrestled with lions, was incensed to hear his nephew's honor brazenly impugned. With his leather hunting glove, he slapped 'Amr across the face, cutting his lip. "How dare you insult my nephew when I am one of his followers!" bellowed Hamzah. In fact, he had no particular affinity for Muhammad's message. But family pride won out, and Hamzah had to remain true to his impromptu declaration.

For four years, Muhammad and the elders maintained an unspoken truce. But that arrangement was shattered by one of the sons of Mecca's chief elder, 'Utbah (he who turns others' faces red in humiliation). The young man—named Abu Huthaifah (one who severs his enemies' roots)—had been groomed to succeed his father as leader of their clan, the Banu Umayyah. Yet for several years he had been a secret follower of Muhammad's, privately adopting the message of blossoming.

Eventually, Abu Huthaifah could no longer maintain his double life. To clear his conscience and at last be open with his family, Abu Huthaifah entered Dar-un-Nadwah one Friday during the weekly assembly meeting. Standing before the council, the young man declared, "Oh respected elders of Mecca, how long will you resist what is best for you and your people? All people are created equal: women and the enslaved have the same rights as we privileged men. Muhammad's message exalts the human spirit and brings out the best in all people."

His father, 'Utbah, grew flushed with anger. As a prominent owner of slaves and a trader, the chief elder had just heard his chosen heir directly attack the source of their family's wealth. Abu Huthaifah had embarrassed his father, his clan, and their ancestors. Though humiliated, the chief elder remained stoic in front of his peers. The elders, for their part, were distressed to witness how Muhammad's message had surreptitiously penetrated the upper echelons of their elite inner circle. Even the son of a top leader was not immune.

Drastic measures were needed. The elders demanded that Muhammad appear at the next Friday council meeting. There, one of the elders, Al-Mut'im ibn 'Adi, made a remarkable pitch: "We have resolved to make you an offer to end dissension and return stability to our land. We will each contribute a considerable portion of our wealth to you. The combined worth will make you the wealthiest in Arabia. Choose any woman you desire, and we shall seek her hand for you. The keys of the Ka'bah we shall hand over to you, and in this council, we will make you our chieftain, just as your grandfather once was."

The elders were clearly desperate. They were ready to forsake wealth, power, and prestige to preserve the traditional social order—even if that meant allowing a man with no sons to serve as chief elder. The council assumed that the main impetus driving Muhammad was restoring his family's lost honor by becoming the leader of Mecca. But Muhammad's quest was not self-aggrandizement or domination. He had repeatedly demonstrated that he wanted Meccans to think for themselves. To accept the elders' offer would violate the essence of the mindset he had promoted for the past seven years.

Smiling gently, Muhammad replied, "Even if you were to place the sun in my right hand and the moon in my left, I would not divert from my mission. Either I succeed, or I perish trying." He invoked the sun and moon as symbolic references to his father and mother, suggesting that even if the council revived his long-lost parents, he would not desist. With that extraordinary statement, Muhammad departed the assembly, leaving the elders dumbfounded.

The council called an emergency meeting for the following day, even though Saturday sessions were generally avoided out of respect for the Sabbath observance of the Banul Harith, the assembly's sole Jewish clan. The elders spent a sleepless night and arrived agitated at Dar-un-Nadwah on Saturday morning, as enslaved servants offered fresh camel milk and dates on silver platters.

First to speak was Al-Walid, the poet whose attempted intervention with Muhammad four years earlier had failed. He wailed, "The threat posed by Muhammad can no longer be ignored. If we kill Muhammad, his family will be required to avenge his death, leading to civil war. I am at my wit's end as to what we can do. Yesterday, we offered him what no sane man could refuse, yet Muhammad refused it. Noble elders, what do you advise?"

An awkward silence filled the room. Then 'Amr ibn Hisham declared that he had a foolproof solution. He had been biding his time, waiting for over twenty-six years to settle his score with Muhammad over the embarrassment of the Hilf-ul-Fudhul incident, when Muhammad demanded 'Amr pay what he owed the visiting Yemenite merchant. The time had come to deploy his diplomatic talents to move the assembly to formally act against Muhammad.

"I have an idea that can save us all this annoyance," he announced. "We can boycott the Hashemites [Muhammad's clan]. We would not need to kill Muhammad. We will spread word among the tribes and make it official by nailing it to the door of the Ka'bah. We will expel them from Mecca. Isolate them on their barren pasturelands outside the city. With time, the Hashemites will lose patience and force sense into him."

The elders agreed to make the economic and social boycott official. Even Muhammad's uncle 'Abdul-'Uzza signaled his assent, effectively disowning his nephew. The elders tasked one member to draft the official announcement, which they planned to unveil publicly the following Friday. Yet unbeknown to them, one of the enslaved servants overheard the heated conversation while preparing drinks outside the meeting hall. Lubainah was a secret follower of Muhammad, and she quickly leaked the news to Bilal, who conveyed it to Muhammad.

Now it was Muhammad's turn to call an emergency meeting. His closest followers assembled that evening at Dar-ul-Arqam: Khadijah, Barakah, Abu Bakr, 'Uthman, 'Abdur-Rahman, and Fatimah bint Al-Khattab ('Umar's sister). Joining the group was Muhammad's twenty-seven-year-old cousin Ja'far, one of Abu Talib's sons. An excellent archer and swordsman, Ja'far often hunted with his uncle Hamzah. When Muhammad adopted 'Ali, Ja'far's brother, their uncle Al-'Abbas and aunt Lubabah took in Ja'far.

With almost no time to prepare, Muhammad proposed that most of his followers leave Mecca for somewhere safe, while he would stay behind to bear the brunt of the boycott. Muhammad saw that the boycott could force his movement to adapt and evolve. After seven years of studying and analyzing in secret, his followers now needed to persevere and apply the mindset of blossoming without his direct guidance.

They would either succeed or perish trying.

6

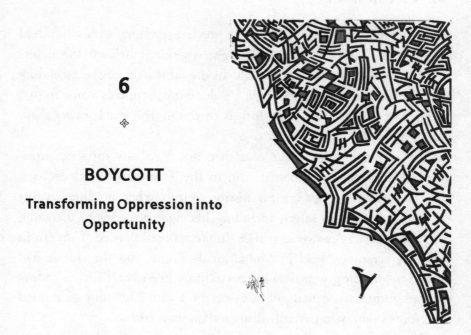

BOYCOTT

Transforming Oppression into Opportunity

Red Sea coast outside Jeddah: Thursday afternoon, January 6, 617 CE

Barakah stood on a ridge overlooking the sea and faced a stark reality: Muhammad had remained behind in Mecca to confront his fate, entrusting her to guide his followers to safety across the water. The west wind lifted humid, salty air off the sea, while the east wind carried dry heat from the desert sands. The combined breeze whirled her veil and garments.

To the southwest, across the waves, lay the land of her birth. During the emergency meeting two nights earlier, Barakah had proposed her native Abyssinia as the best hope for refuge. The king was an Abrahamic monotheist with a reputation for being just. He would be more likely to give a sympathetic ear to Muhammad's followers than the Sasanians currently encircling Arabia with a rapid series of conquests. And while she had been abducted from her homeland at age eight, Barakah remained fluent in Ethiopic and could serve as interpreter-emissary. Muhammad had agreed to the plan.

As she contemplated returning to her native land for the first time in over fifty years, Barakah glanced nervously back toward the east. The Meccans would surely be sending an armed party to look for

Muhammad's missing followers. The previous evening, over a hundred of them had slipped out at midnight, trekking through the desert toward the Red Sea port of Jeddah. In the faint light of the ascending crescent moon, they walked single file along the shepherds' route so that animals would cover their footprints in the morning and make them harder to track.

The fifty-mile hike to the coast had not been easy for sixty-three-year-old Barakah, the oldest person in the group by several decades. But the matriarch had a critical mission to inspire her: guiding her foster son's followers to safety, including his eighteen-year-old daughter, Ruqayyah. Just a few weeks earlier Ruqayyah had married 'Uthman in a private ceremony held in Muhammad's home, and the couple had chosen to join the group escaping persecution in Mecca. (Their wedding marked 'Uthman's formal public association with Muhammad and led the groom's family to partially disown their wayward son.)

Shortly after noon, Barakah had led the ragtag band of followers into a quiet fishing village just north of Jeddah. Avoiding Jeddah reduced the chances that someone in the city might alert the Meccans to where her group was headed. A few small mud huts with straw roofs dotted the coast; salted fish drying on wooden frames in the sun surrounded each of them. The dried fish was a luxury delicacy sold in inland cities like Mecca.

From the ridge overlooking the village, Barakah gazed down at the refugees sitting in small groups on the beach. She saw Sumayyah's son, 'Ammar, looking out toward the sea, his parents' murder a lingering reminder of the risks Muhammad's followers faced.

The impending boycott in Mecca could prove a devastating blow to their underground movement, and Muhammad had insisted that his followers flee to help ensure that they and their message would live on. As the boycott's primary target, Muhammad understood that he had to stay in Mecca as a distraction to allow his followers time to escape Arabia unnoticed.

While Barakah worried about her foster son's fate, she had to focus her attention on the hundred followers in her care. They included people newly liberated from enslavement like Lubainah, whom 'Amr ibn Hisham had brutally tortured after learning she was the mole who had leaked the elders' boycott to Muhammad through Bilal. Abu Bakr had rushed to purchase her freedom, paying five times her market value. A few days later, Lubainah, who was Abyssinian like Barakah, joined Barakah's group of refugees.

Sitting on the Red Sea beach alongside the formerly enslaved were sons of Mecca's wealthy elite, including Abu Huthaifah, whose father was Mecca's leading elder. Though disowned by their families, these young men remained resolute. Forced to cast off fine robes for simple linen, they appeared indistinguishable from their less fortunate compatriots.

To shepherd her unusual group, Barakah had assistance from Muhammad's cousin Ja'far. The twenty-seven-year old son of Abu Talib had been raised in the home of his uncle Al-'Abbas, one of Mecca's main moneylenders. Ja'far was literate, knew how to manage financial accounts, and was a skilled negotiator—all qualities vital to helping the refugees in their new home. He had already put his talents to use by negotiating with a captain in the fishing village to transport the group on his large whaling vessel to the African port of Adulis. Ja'far paid the captain handsomely with gold coins from a purse given to him by Muhammad.

As the sun descended toward the sea, the group boarded the large ship. The night stars would help the captain navigate, while the crescent moon's limited light helped the boat avoid detection by Byzantine and Sasanian navies. The lack of a full moon also meant the seas would be gentler, increasing the group's chances of surviving the long voyage.

After making sure everyone had safely boarded, Barakah walked across the plank and Ja'far followed. Crew members hoisted the mainsail to catch the east wind, as others plied the oars to guide the ship southward. The vessel pushed back from the Arabian coast and headed toward Africa. More than 90 percent of Muhammad's followers were huddled on the deck, watching the desert coast disappear over the horizon. If the whaling ship sank, most of his followers would be gone—and with them the best chance for his message to live on.

For seven years, Muhammad had been training his followers to blossom and think for themselves. With just a few days' notice, most had now fled their homes to seek refuge in a far-off land. The journey to Abyssinia would be a critical test: Could they apply their revolutionary mindset in a new environment while cut off from their prophetic leader?

❖ ❖ ❖

The next morning, oblivious to the nocturnal escape of Muhammad's followers, 'Amr ibn Hisham strode confidently toward the Ka'bah in full regalia, his fine silk robe dragging behind him over the hot sands. The top of his long red turban was bejeweled with a silver amulet that glittered in the morning light and ostentatiously proclaimed his piety to ancestral deities. In his left hand, he clutched a scroll that represented the culmination of his scheming to sideline Muhammad in Meccan society: an official declaration signed that morning by the elders' assembly declaring a formal boycott of Muhammad's entire Hashemite clan.

Mecca's elders had never before declared a boycott. Formally prohibiting commerce with a particular group went against Mecca's core identity as a hub of open trade. The concept of a boycott was not even part of Arabian culture, which regarded such passive-aggressive behavior as cowardly. To repress Muhammad's burgeoning movement, though, 'Amr ibn Hisham had ironically been forced to apply a new meaning to an ancient word, *muqata'ah*. Used by farmers to "set apart" infected crops, the word symbolically marked the Hashemite clan as damaged goods to be quarantined. The term was a jab at Muhammad's propensity for employing agricultural metaphors, countering the supposed blossoming of all living things with the need to trim back unwanted growth.

In composing his boycott declaration, 'Amr ibn Hisham also sought to co-opt Muhammad's invocation of the Divine. Once again parting with Meccan custom, the boycott proclamation began not with the standard invocation of the city's chief deity, Hubal, but rather cited *Allahumma*, the creator God of the Arabs' founding ancestor, Abraham. 'Amr ibn Hisham sought to present himself as a defender of tradition and Muhammad as a disrespectful upstart who was claiming a personal relationship with the great divinity. By appealing to Allah, the elders aimed to demonstrate that they were persecuting Muhammad not because he called them to Abraham's God but rather because he had stubbornly chosen to split society. Because Muhammad was a social plague, they needed to isolate and expunge him.

An entourage of elders and Muhammad's fiercest opponents followed

'Amr ibn Hisham through the streets of Mecca. A large crowd gathered as he ascended to the top step of the Ka'bah. He unfurled the boycott declaration and read it aloud to the shock of the assembled throng. "In your name, Creator God, we boycott the Hashemites! All are forbidden to buy from them, sell to them, marry them, or interact with them, so long as this parchment remains hung on the sacred door." He then nailed the parchment to the Ka'bah's cedar door, giving the boycott official status that, by tradition, all of Arabia's tribes must uphold.

The Hashemites, who had learned through Lubainah that the elders' boycott would entail the clan's expulsion from Mecca's city limits, had already packed their most essential belongings that morning. Armed warriors from the city's other clans soon descended on each Hashemite home, systematically rounding up families for deportation. The warriors placed a yellow bracelet around the right wrist of each Hashemite. Farmers and shepherds traditionally used such turmeric-dyed bands to mark plants and animals as diseased or contagious. For the first time, the elders were applying *muqata'ah* to human beings.

Muhammad, Khadijah, and their household were not exempt. The warriors tied yellow bands around their wrists and defaced the door to their home with a bloodred *X*. Neighbors observed this humiliation from the roofs of their homes; many were disturbed by the unprecedented boycott yet cowed into silence lest they become outcasts themselves. Even as Muhammad's family was driven from their home, the vault inside remained.

Officials brandishing swords forced the entire Hashemite clan outside Mecca and into the barren valley of Shi'b Abu Talib. Once a pasture, the land had mostly dried up and was dotted by thornbushes and wild banana trees. The warriors herded the Hashemites inside a barricade made of acacia thorns tied together with palm-fiber ropes. Armed sentries prevented anyone from leaving or receiving unauthorized visitors. It was, in effect, Arabia's first-ever concentration camp. Wealthier members of the clan set up large tents traditionally used for shelter during caravan trips. Poorer families created makeshift tents. The Hashemites had to survive on whatever meager goods they had brought with them.

While Muhammad silently accepted his fate along with the rest of his clan, one prominent Hashemite remained free inside Mecca: his uncle 'Abdul-'Uzza, who officially disowned the Hashemites and joined the elders' boycott. In an extraordinary move, he joined his wife's Banu Umayyah clan, which dominated Mecca. Standing on the steps of the Ka'bah between his wife's uncle 'Utbah (the chief elder) and his brother-in-law Sakhr (a rising young leader in the clan known as Abu Sufyan), 'Abdul-'Uzza declared his new allegiance, abandoning his siblings and cousins, who had been led off to their desert prison.

The defection of 'Abdul-'Uzza offered Mecca's elders a symbolic victory in their public relations battle with Muhammad. They understood the need to burnish their image and simultaneously degrade Muhammad's. They hoped for another victory when Khadijah's nephew Hakim ibn Hizam went to the camp to appeal to his aunt. A rising member of the Dar-un-Nadwah assembly and close friend of 'Amr ibn Hisham's, Hakim arrived at the enclosure dressed in splendid attire with a retinue of servants—a sharp contrast to the beleaguered Hashemites. The guards allowed Hakim to enter the camp to speak with Khadijah. He urged her to save herself by divorcing Muhammad and marrying 'Amr. Khadijah immediately turned her back and declared firmly, "So long as a breath passes through my lips, I will stand with Muhammad."

Hakim responded, "Then I am powerless to assist you." He left the camp and would never see his aunt alive again.

Khadijah's unwavering loyalty belied her struggle to adjust to the concentration camp's primitive conditions. She had lived her entire life in comfort and luxury. Now she was being held in the unfamiliar desert and had to sleep in a makeshift tent. She was worse off than desert nomads. Yet Khadijah sacrificed her own comfort without complaint to help others. The empress of Mecca became a servant of the poor, sharing whatever food she had with impoverished families and assisting as a midwife. Watching his wife transform herself, Muhammad observed to 'Ali, "*Amir-ul-qawmi khadimuhum*" (True royalty are those who actively serve others).

Khadijah and Muhammad spent many hours strolling hand in hand about the camp. Though the situation was dire, 'Ali always saw them smile as they looked into each other's eyes. In a way, the boycott enabled Muhammad to refocus on his immediate family. No longer surrounded by dozens of followers, Muhammad could devote attention to his youngest daughter, twelve-year-old Fatimah. Father and daughter took many walks together inside the camp, and she soon became his protégée.

Without followers, however, Muhammad's revelations quickly dried up. During the entire period of the boycott, he experienced only one revelation of significance, a reminder to be patient:

> *La tuharrik bihi lisanaka lita'jala bih.*
> Don't hasten revelation by movements of your tongue, hoping it
>   will transpire.

> *Inna 'alaina jam'ahu wa Qur'anah.*
> We will reveal it when the time is ripe for wisdom to gather and
>   blossom forth.

If Muhammad desperately sought new revelations to help clarify the path forward, the passage reminded him that revelation cannot be forced. As the primary purpose of Muhammad's revelations was to help inspire others, being kept in confinement cut off the flow. Muhammad would have to wait years for a revelation to return.

Of course, no one expected the boycott to last long. The elders had anticipated the Hashemites would either abandon Muhammad or force him to recant within a week or two. The Hashemites, after all, were still pagans, including Muhammad's own uncle Abu Talib, the clan elder. Yet Abu Talib never forgot the oath he had sworn to his father as the old man lay dying. Unwilling to renounce that sacred pledge, Abu Talib protected his nephew even as conditions in the camp grew worse with each passing week.

Muhammad enjoyed additional support from the few followers from other clans who remained in Mecca, primarily Abu Bakr, Suhaib, 'Umar, and Al-Arqam. Though helpless to assist Muhammad publicly and aware that the elders had them under surveillance, the four men managed to meet in secret and devised a plan to smuggle food and water into the camp. Abu Bakr's cousin served as a guard outside the camp, and he agreed to be a clandestine conduit.

The smuggling network also proved useful when a fisherman from Jeddah arrived in Mecca with a letter from Ja'far. Abu Bakr ensured the epistle secretly made its way into the camp, where 'Ali read it aloud to Muhammad. Ja'far reported that Muhammad's followers had arrived safely in the Abyssinian capital, Axum. The letter relieved Muhammad's fears that his followers might have drowned or been captured. A smile returned to his face. His movement had made it to Africa and could live on even if he died in captivity.

The Meccans, meanwhile, had begun to notice the absence of Muhammad's followers, especially those from elite families. Fishermen from the coast selling salted fish in Mecca's market recounted stories of a large group of Meccans who had chartered a fishing vessel to Africa. The Meccan elders quickly dispatched horsemen to Jeddah to interrogate the fishermen who had transported the group. The investigation revealed that the attempt to quarantine Muhammad's message had failed. His followers might have fled Arabia, but they had received shelter among the Abyssinians, the only empire ever to besiege Mecca. If the Abyssinian king fell sway to their message, he might be tempted to return.

The public relations battle had taken an unexpected turn, and the Meccans resolved to eliminate the threat at once. The elders urgently dispatched Mecca's most eloquent emissary, a dapper young man named 'Amr ibn al-'As, to the Abyssinian capital of Axum. His retinue was laden with precious gifts, all designed to ease his mission. He was to bribe the Abyssinian ruling class to hand over Muhammad's followers, to be returned as captives to Mecca where they would join their leader in his internment camp.

❖ ❖ ❖

Aside from Ja'far's initial letter, Muhammad remained cut off from his followers in Abyssinia and completely unaware that the Meccan elders had dispatched a diplomat to bring them back in chains. Muhammad dictated to 'Ali a brief response to Ja'far, instructing the group to remain in Abyssinia until he sent further news. They were on their own.

Five hundred miles to the southwest, Muhammad's followers quickly adapted to their new life. For the first time, they could safely associate in public. After Ja'far and Barakah negotiated the rental of a housing compound in a middle-class neighborhood near the marketplace, the immigrants set about exploring the vast city. Abyssinian soldiers clad in armor decorated with exotic animal skins and carrying fine spears patrolled the streets, which were draped with bright textiles in red, yellow, orange, and aqua. Abyssinians wore beautifully embroidered garments of fine white cotton. The empire's clergy moved through the city in procession beneath colorful umbrellas, a sign of their respected status.

The capital was renowned for its churches carved out of solid rock and its massive obelisks, most standing nearly a hundred feet tall with intricate decorative carvings. When the Abyssinian Empire converted to Christianity several centuries earlier, they erected the obelisks as symbolic gateways to heaven, connecting mankind with the God of Abraham. At its raised base, each had a carved door, and stylized windows ascending toward a capstone representing the Divine Presence. At the city's Church of Our Lady Maryam of Zion, a special cadre of priests sworn to silence guarded a vault that supposedly contained the Ark of the Covenant.

Axum's roads were paved with large, elegantly interlocked stone slabs. Granite arches capped its thoroughfares. The arches' inscriptions, in ancient Sabaean script, proclaimed the empire's position as East Africa's dominant power. In fact, Abyssinia was the only African empire to mint its own coins, matching the other empiric powerhouses, the Byzantines and Sasanians. Each coin featured an image of the negus (king). The city's marketplace rivaled that of Damascus, with goods from Africa, South Asia, and even Europe.

To survive in the bustling metropolis, the Meccan immigrants followed Muhammad's earlier example and formed a cooperative, pooling their funds and dividing responsibilities. Bilal, whom Muhammad had designated to serve as *muhasib* (keeper of numbers), handled all accounting. 'Abdur-Rahman, 'Uthman, and Mus'ab set up shop in the central market to earn money to sustain the group. They left the city early in the morning to purchase goods wholesale from traders on their way to Axum and then sold the goods at retail prices at Axum's market. Ja'far and Barakah kept the group organized, while Lubainah and Bilal, the Abyssinians by birth, were tasked with community outreach to ensure a positive public opinion of the group.

After a month, Barakah turned one of the compound's halls into an educational facility where the group met daily to share knowledge and make decisions. Learning the local Ethiopic language became part of their daily ritual. In their study hall, the immigrants applied Muhammad's learning methodology to make their way in a new environment. The entire group voted on all decisions.

After two months, the fledgling Abyssinia experiment showed signs of success. Integrated into the local community, the refugees had organized well and even had begun to make money. Axum seemed to be a haven where Muhammad's followers could thrive.

Then the Meccan emissary 'Amr ibn al-'As arrived in the capital. Charming and witty, he had earned the nickname Dahiyah (cunning fox). A master diplomat skilled in the art of double-talk, 'Amr unpacked his high-quality leather, fur, and perfumes—gifts he soon showered on the negus's closest advisors. 'Amr took several weeks to build rapport with each of the king's top counselors, adeptly gaining their support. He hosted exquisite banquets in the beautiful mansion he rented.

Then he requested an audience with the negus, and soon he was introduced to the monarch. Respectfully addressing the king in flowery language, 'Amr warned of the danger posed by the Meccan refugees. "They insult Christ and Mary," he argued, hoping to spark the ire of the devout negus. The king's ministers echoed the concerns of their new friend from Mecca and urged the ruler to send the immigrants back with 'Amr.

The negus, however, sensed something was amiss. He refused to accept the fine gifts 'Amr brought for him and ordered his ministers to return the gifts they had received. He also refused to pass judgment on the Meccans before allowing them to plead their case.

A royal herald called the immigrants to the palace to stand trial and defend their right to remain in Abyssinia. Muhammad's followers, who had remained oblivious to 'Amr's presence in Axum, were shocked. Their relations with their new neighbors had been outstanding. The sudden news that the king himself was summoning them to defend their right to remain sent a ripple of fear through the community. The members voted to have Ja'far speak as their representative, with Barakah standing at his side to ensure accurate representation by the negus's court interpreter.

A small group of about a dozen of Muhammad's followers made their way to the palace for the trial. They gazed with awe at the citadel's massive stone walls draped with colored flags. Imposing soldiers stepped aside to grant them entry, as courtiers led them down a series of long hallways to the royal court. Entering the main room, they were stunned to see 'Amr standing at the center of the room by the throne, a vivid portrait of Mary and Christ painted on the wall behind him. The smirk on his face revealed in an instant why the group had been summoned.

After all the courtiers and ministers had assembled, the negus entered the throne room accompanied by his retinue of bishops and bodyguards. Everyone else bowed, but not Muhammad's followers, who had been taught that human beings prostrate themselves only to the Divine Creator.

The negus took his seat and asked, "Do you not bow to your prophet?" Ja'far replied, "No, we were taught to bow only to the Creator of the cosmos." The negus was struck by the man's principled stance and his courage.

Intrigued, he turned to 'Amr and instructed him to state his case. Like a smooth prosecutor, 'Amr enumerated a long list of accusations against Muhammad's followers. "They say women have souls and are our equals," he mocked. "What are women? We buy them and sell them in the market. How could they be our equals?!" Turning with a dramatic flair to the royal court, he added, "They even say animals have souls and rights!" The crowd laughed.

The negus, however, looked on with an air of boredom, unconvinced that any of these claims justified the Meccans' extradition. Noticing that his arguments had failed to move the one audience member who mattered, 'Amr made a last-ditch effort to shock the king, whose piety was clearly expressed in the large cross he grasped as a scepter. Pointing up at the Mary and Christ icon painted on the wall above him, 'Amr frantically asserted, "But worst of all, they curse Christ and Mary!"

The negus sat bolt upright with a look of astonishment on his face. He turned rapidly to Ja'far and with a voice of authority demanded, "What do you say of Christ?"

Ja'far instinctively turned to his training and leveraged the uniquely compelling content and style of Qur'anic revelation to win over the leader of East Africa's great empire. Without missing a beat, he replied, "I say what our prophet taught us in the Qur'an." Ja'far began to recite from the Qur'an's nineteenth chapter, named in honor of Mary herself.

Though the negus did not understand the Arabic words, the *surah's* rhythm and cadences captivated him. It echoed the iconic Christian chants dedicated to Mary, with the opening lines of each verse ending in a word that rhymed with Maria: *zakariyya, khafiyya, shaqiyya, waliyya,* and so on.

As his interpreter translated the lines, the negus listened intently to the *surah's* narrative. It recounted the remarkable story of a young woman named Maryam who chose to part with her society, living up to her name, which means "rebellious," by insisting on thinking for herself. "Remember the inspiring example of Mary, who chose to go into seclusion away from the comfort of her family to the wilderness, seeking a state of clarity." The verses then related how Maryam fled with her newborn son to save his life. In Ja'far's melodic recitation, the vignette evoked the immigrants' flight from persecution in Mecca—whose elders had even sent an emissary hundreds of miles in pursuit.

Ja'far continued to indirectly state his people's case by citing the example of Abraham, who also had to flee persecution from his own family. In response to threats of violence from his father, Abraham replied, "Peace be upon you! I forgive you and ask my Divine Mentor to watch over you with loving care and kindness." The refugees from Mecca, like the righteous before them, had dared to think differently, paid the price, and fled for their own safety, yet harbored no ill will. All they sought was a refuge to live in peace.

After Ja'far fell silent and the court interpreter completed his translation, the negus sat for a moment in pensive silence. He was surprised to hear of Abraham's magnanimous attitude in response to violent attacks, not to mention the verses that clearly held Mary in the highest regard, clearly disproving 'Amr's claim. After some time, the king stood up from his throne, descended the steps to the main floor, and slowly walked toward Ja'far. Raising his scepter, he drew a symbolic line on the floor and declared, "The difference between us and you is no wider than this line." To reinforce his message, he patted Ja'far on the right shoulder and announced, "You may remain in my land, personally protected by me, so long as you desire." Turning toward 'Amr with a look of deep annoyance, he grumbled, "Return to Mecca with your gifts—I would not surrender them to you for all the fine leather in the world!"

The immigrants had passed their toughest test yet.

That very week, Muhammad's followers celebrated their royally sanctioned asylum by breaking ground on land the negus gave them. They hired local builders to construct a mixed-use community center, Barakah's idea. Designed in the traditional Abyssinian style for a house of worship, though without religious symbols, the simple hall was painted white and green. The edifice, called a *masjid* (place of grounding), referenced a Qur'anic term for a location where people of all backgrounds could gather to find solace and exchange ideas. As the first mosque ever constructed, the Axum community center hosted both classes and individual meditation. Its focal point faced Jerusalem.

Muhammad's followers were grateful to the negus for his hospitality and wisdom, and they became his loyal supporters. When a rebellion erupted in Abyssinia, Ja'far led a delegation to the palace to offer military services to the king—even though Muhammad had insisted his followers remain nonviolent. The immigrants demonstrated that they did not blindly follow Muhammad's teachings, aside from his core admonition that they think for themselves and flexibly adapt to do the right thing in difficult circumstances. In other words, they had learned to apply his methodology practically rather than literally.

The negus thanked Ja'far for the generous offer, yet he feared that if he lost the battle, the refugees would be persecuted for supporting a deposed king. The entire group nonetheless ascended a hill overlooking the battlefield and prayed together for the negus's victory. Abyssinia had become their adopted land, and the Meccans insisted on being part of the society that had provided refuge in their hour of need. Many months later, when Muhammad finally received news of his followers' remarkable accomplishments and the negus's generosity, he declared Abyssinia a sacred land that his followers should never invade.

❖ ❖ ❖

'Amr ibn al-'As returned to Mecca empty-handed. The elders of Dar-un-Nadwah listened in disbelief as he recounted his failed mission and were furious to learn that, even from afar, Muhammad's revelations had managed to sway a great king. Meanwhile, in Mecca itself, the Hashemites refused to yield even as the boycott entered its eighth month.

Determined to clamp down even harder, the elders took aim at underground efforts to smuggle food into the camp. Abu Bakr had paid nomads to graze their flocks close to the camp and discretely throw parcels of food over the fence. In response, the elders declared a new ultimatum: if even a single member of a nomadic clan was caught assisting the Hashemites, the entire clan would be barred from trading in Mecca and denied access to sacred sites. A few brave bandits continued to smuggle food, but the situation inside the camp deteriorated.

The cold war heralded by the boycott dragged on for two more years. Muhammad endeavored to keep his mind fresh by teaching his daughter Fatimah and taking walks with his wife. As the Hashemite clan's resources dwindled, Muhammad and Khadijah funded much of the underground food network, though their wealth began to diminish. Even worse, Khadijah and Uncle Abu Talib began to show signs of malnutrition.

As news of seventy-year-old Abu Talib's weakening condition spread, the Meccan public grew increasingly agitated about the boycott. The standoff had achieved nothing aside from separating families and causing suffering to innocents; most of Muhammad's clan, after all, were not his followers. While elite families—in a clear rupture with Arabian custom—disowned sons simply for joining Muhammad, the pagan Abu Talib honorably stood by his nephew in accordance with Meccan tradition. The public began to grumble about double standards.

Five young men from Mecca sneaked into the camp to consult with Muhammad. While their fathers came from various clans, their mothers were all Hashemites, and they hated to see their cousins suffering. Under cover of darkness on a moonless night, the five dug under the barrier to gain an audience with Muhammad. Conscious of the ongoing public relations struggle, Muhammad counseled, "To end this boycott, you need to turn opinion against it. Call for an assembly around the Ka'bah, and disperse yourselves among the crowd."

The following Friday, after the elders' weekly meeting, the five young men headed to the Ka'bah as a crowd, including 'Amr ibn Hisham and other elders, gathered in the main square. One of the young men boldly strode up to the Ka'bah door and pointed to the nailed document that had begun to disintegrate after three years. "We did not approve of this innovation!" he declared. "It was done in our name yet without our consent."

At first the bewildered crowd remained silent, but then the four other men began shouting out from different parts of the crowd, echoing the call to end the boycott. Within minutes, the entire crowd began chanting as one against the "unjust" and "cowardly" boycott. The lead speaker then ripped the tattered boycott declaration to pieces as the crowd cheered—and 'Amr ibn Hisham's face turned red in embarrassment. His attempt to crush Muhammad had only fueled sympathy.

The crowd soon became a mob that set out for the concentration camp to burn the barrier fence and liberate the inmates. When they arrived, however, they found the camp silent. Most of the Hashemites had gathered, ashen-faced, outside Abu Talib's tent as the elder lay dying inside. The liberating mob carried Abu Talib on a stretcher back to his house, which had fallen into disrepair. To calm public rage, the elders visited Abu Talib and tried to make amends by helping the Hashemites restore their homes and reestablish their market stalls. But a few days later, Abu Talib died, surrounded by his wife and children.

Muhammad visited his uncle yet had to spend most of his time caring for his ailing wife. Returning home had not improved Khadijah's condition. One week after Abu Talib's death, Khadijah barely clung to life. Her relatives came to offer their final respects. The boycott had destroyed her.

Muhammad sat behind Khadijah, holding her close on the bed he had constructed for them years earlier. He supported her head on his chest as the family stood around her. Fatimah noticed tears flowing down her father's cheeks as he tried to sooth Khadijah. But nothing helped. As the sunlight waned, so did Khadijah's strength. Muhammad asked all present to leave the room. He remained on the bed, hugging his wife's lifeless corpse for several hours before finally leaving briefly to ask for water, clean linen clothes, camphor, and incense. He then ritually bathed her body and wrapped it in white linen.

Khadijah's family arrived in the morning to claim her body for burial in their plot. A debate ensued between her nephew Hakim ibn Hizam and Muhammad. The family had disowned Khadijah while she was alive, Muhammad argued, so they had no right to her when she was dead. Instead, he would bury her beside his grandfather. Muhammad's cousins dug the grave, and a small burial procession of only immediate family and Abu Bakr followed in the late afternoon. Khadijah's family did not attend. At the graveside, Muhammad embraced his daughters and then asked everyone to leave so he could say goodbye alone.

That evening, a delegation of elders, including 'Amr ibn Hisham, visited Muhammad's home to briefly offer condolences. Muhammad tried hard to remain composed, but 'Ali could see moments where Muhammad's pain nearly turned to anger. During these dark hours, 'Ali, Abu Bakr, and Zaid remained near Muhammad to provide comfort.

Khadijah's death was a devastating blow. "She was my place of serenity in an ocean of confusion," Muhammad recalled wistfully. "She believed in me when others shunned me. She brought out the best in me when others sought to obscure me. She supported me when others sought ways to impede me. She empowered me with her words, shared her wealth with me, and provided me with children."

With his core pillar of support suddenly gone, Muhammad gained even greater appreciation for the critical role Khadijah had played in his life: encouraging him to seize opportunities, developing his confidence, and comforting him in the face of stinging insults. She had repeatedly demonstrated foresight by seeing potential even when it was not obvious. She had patiently waited decades for his prophetic talent to blossom. Most important, she had a knack for seeing positive opportunities in seemingly negative situations. Vital elements of Muhammad's revelations, in fact, came naturally to her, and she provided an example for Muhammad as his greatest mentor and most devoted follower.

Now, after twenty-five years of marriage, Muhammad needed to develop a new support system to replace what Khadijah had naturally provided him. One week after her death, Muhammad convened his few remaining followers at Dar-ul-Arqam for the first time in years. They struggled to chart a path forward amid the wreckage. In one important step, they sent news of the end of the boycott to Abyssinia. When the message arrived, over seventy followers of Muhammad, including Barakah, prepared to return to Mecca, although Muhammad asked that Ja'far and two dozen others remain.

Two weeks after Khadijah's death, Muhammad at last experienced a new revelation, his first in nearly three years. It marked the ten-year anniversary of his first revelation atop Mount Hira. This time, out of Muhammad's mouth streamed the Qur'an's only complete and uninterrupted narrative: Surah Yusuf, a retelling of the biblical story of Joseph. Muhammad would later urge his followers to recite this *surah* whenever they felt helpless or anxious. The 111 verses possessed a special power to help restore confidence even in moments of despondence.

In the Qur'anic account of Joseph's life, Jacob, the young dreamer's father, warns that Joseph's unique prophetic talents are dangerous—although God has given him special wisdom to see deeper meanings behind the obvious, others will be jealous of his gift. Sure enough, the young man soon experiences a roller coaster of terrible setbacks and startling successes. Joseph's brothers sell him to a caravan of merchants, who take him to Egypt, where he is sold once again to a high official, before he is suddenly thrown into jail—and is just as suddenly summoned to interpret the dreams of the king. After his insightful analyses find him unexpectedly elevated to the second-most powerful position in Egypt, Joseph witnesses his life drama come full circle when his brothers descend on Egypt during a famine, seeking emergency food aid. Without recognizing Joseph, they prostrate themselves before him, making his childhood vision a reality.

A few verses revealed key insights gleaned from Joseph's saga:

> *Wa kathalika makkanna li-Yusufa fil-ardhi wa linu'allimahu min*
>   *ta'wilil-ahadithi wallahu ghalibun 'ala amrihi walakinna*
>   *aktharan-nasi la ya'lamun.* . . .
> It is in such mysterious ways that We arranged for Joseph to attain
>   a high position on earth, teaching him the interpretation of
>   the enigmatic. The Loving Divine is perpetually arranging
>   destinies, though most people are unaware. . . .

> *Wa ka'ayyim-min ayatin fis-samawati wal-ardhi yamurruna 'alaiha*
>   *wa hum 'anha mu'ridhun.* . . .
> Many are the wonders and signs in the cosmos and on earth, yet
>   most pass by them, oblivious to their great lessons. . . .

Hatta ithas-tay`asar-rusulu wa thannu annahum qad kuth-thibu
   ja`ahum nasruna.
When the messengers reach a nadir of despair and feel completely
   rejected without any hope, precisely then our assistance comes
   to relieve them.

Just as Joseph understood the divine message hidden in the king's
dream, the *surah* encouraged its audience to seek out messages of hope
hidden in plain sight—particularly in moments of despair. Had Joseph
not been enslaved, he would never have entered the home of a high
official. Had he not been imprisoned, he would never have met Egypt's
king. The brutal aggression of Joseph's brothers ultimately led him to
become the most powerful man in Egypt and thereby save the family
from starvation. Furthermore, despite the abuse he received at the hands
of his own siblings, Joseph eschewed revenge.

The chapter's message of hope, forgiveness, and steadfast confidence
in the Divine's long-term vision offered Muhammad a powerful source
of inspiration in a moment of deep sorrow. Regarding his own situation
through the prism of Surah Yusuf, Muhammad could appreciate that the
boycott had—like the death of his two sons decades earlier—challenged
him in unforeseeable ways and forced him to grow. The Meccans' aggression had compelled him to plant new seeds in Africa and in the
process test the universality of his message. Even the death of his wife
and uncle could be understood as having a deeper purpose: Muhammad
now had to push forward as a leader without a mentor or benefactor.

Though still grieving, Muhammad tried to channel the *surah*'s affirmative spirit by renewing his efforts in and around Mecca. Finally able
to move about unhindered, he took Zaid with him to the nearby town
of Ta`if, where the elites of Mecca maintained vacation homes. The local
elders received Muhammad as an important guest and politely listened
to his pitch. Yet after the meeting ended, they instructed children to
stone Muhammad as he exited the city gates—though only below the
waist so as not to mortally injure him. The children ambushed Muhammad and hurled pebbles at his legs as he passed, humiliating him with
the most demeaning sign of rejection in Semitic cultures.

For the first time, Muhammad had suffered physical attacks and been bloodied as he tried to share his ideas. Zaid began to rip his clothes to bandage Muhammad's wounds, while Muhammad looked toward the sky and moaned, "Lord God, I turn to you in my weakened condition, in a state of disorientation, scorned in the eyes of others. Oh Ultimate Comforter, who consoles in times of despair, you are the mentor of those who are alone and encumbered. You are my mentor, to whom else can I turn beside you? If I turn to those who do not know me, they regard me as strange. If I turn to antagonists who know me, they only further suppress me. I ask you to guide my path forward with your illuminating light, through which you cast away layers of darkness and rebalance the world's upheaval. I shall remain steadfast until you provide relief, as all resilience and understanding come from you."

Seeing the blood trickle down Muhammad's legs, Zaid's heart broke for his adopted father. In a fit of anger, he vowed, "I wish that the two mountains around the city would come together and crush its inhabitants for what they have done to you."

Muhammad gently replied, "I would not wish that, for I retain hope that the same youth who stoned me might one day carry my message to distant lands." Still, the pain of being assaulted while in mourning took its toll on Muhammad, who would refer to this period of his life as *'am al-huzn* (the year of heartache).

Muhammad and Zaid returned to Mecca after most residents had already gone to bed, since Muhammad wanted to avoid being seen in his bloodied state. He sent Zaid home alone and, while the city slept, made his way to the Ka'bah. He entered the Hijr Isma'il, the semicircular enclosure just outside the shrine—a sacred space reserved for the city's elders—and lay down upon the spot where his grandfather had sat five decades before. With his head symbolically on his grandfather's lap, Muhammad closed his eyes and contemplated the events of the worst day of his life.

Suddenly, in a liminal state he would later describe as "between being awake and asleep," Muhammad experienced a Divine response to his heartfelt prayer from that afternoon. In an epiphanic revelation, the prophet Moses appeared, embraced Muhammad, and said, "Feel at ease and compose yourself, my beloved brother." Moses then guided Muhammad on a spiritual night journey (*isra'*) to Jerusalem (city of wholeness). The setting offered a compelling thematic backdrop for Moses's message to Muhammad. Jerusalem had seen repeated destruction, only to be reconstructed from its ashes in even greater splendor. In fact, only a few weeks before Muhammad's night journey, Sasanian armies had devastated the city. Reports of the assault had reached Mecca, describing a once-great capital in shambles.

The Jerusalem that Moses presented to Muhammad, however, was a glittering jewel arrayed in full majesty. Awaiting Muhammad at a restored Temple Mount was an extraordinary assembly of biblical prophets. Moses introduced Muhammad one by one to the prophets, each of whom had persevered despite immense trials. Each prophet taught Muhammad a vital lesson and shared a piece of wisdom from his travails. Both the prophets and the dramatic setting provided Muhammad with inspiration to heal his brokenness and envision a better future.

In the epiphany's final phase, Muhammad heard a heavenly call instructing him and his followers to connect with the Divine fifty times per day. Moses, as Muhammad's mentor, advised, "Petition to decrease it—I am experienced and know that number is too much for any people to keep." After a lengthy back and forth, Muhammad ultimately succeeded in decreasing the directive to five times daily. Again, Moses counseled, "Petition to decrease it further—my people struggle to keep three." Too shy to petition any longer, Muhammad felt five times a day was doable, only to be roused from his epiphany by water dripping from the Ka'bah's waterspout onto his forehead.

As he awoke, Muhammad saw his wounds and the dried blood smeared along his legs and torn garments. Yet he felt completely rejuvenated by the nocturnal journey. He returned home to find 'Ali keeping a nervous night vigil in the front hall. 'Ali was shocked by the contrast of his cousin's haggard appearance and his smiling, buoyant face. Muhammad enthusiastically recounted the vision and its new insight: formal prayer needed a formal structure for people to reorient themselves throughout the day.

Muhammad had been praying ever since his first revelation atop Mount Hira, prostrating himself at various moments for a few minutes or even a few hours, but this had never become a formal ritual. The new prayer structure—called *salah* (connection) after the fragile rope bridges that connected people across chasms—would serve as a daily tool to help people reground and refocus.

That Friday morning, Muhammad taught 'Ali to wash his hands, face, arms, head, and feet in a symbolic gesture of purification, which Muhammad called *wudhu'* (illumination). Then, as the purple hue of early dawn spread across the landscape, the two climbed to the rooftop terrace. Muhammad showed 'Ali the set of prayers he learned during his night vision and instructed 'Ali to recite Surah Al-Fatihah and contemplate its meanings. As the first hint of light penetrated the sky over Mecca, the pair faced north toward Jerusalem and offered the first-ever structured Muslim prayer, as the sound of crickets echoed around them in the still morning air.

❖ ❖ ❖

As part of their ongoing public relations battle with Muhammad, the elders of Mecca ceased their attacks during the traditional forty-day mourning period for Khadijah. Once it concluded, however, 'Amr ibn Hisham orchestrated a new offensive: an aggressive smear campaign throughout Arabia. The elders contributed large sums of money to hire talented poets to compose cutting verse—called *hija* (stabbing barrage)—deriding Muhammad. The sardonic poets were sent throughout Arabia to recite their works slandering Muhammad as a vicious womanizer, thug, and lunatic. The elders understood that such attacks would not be tolerated in Mecca itself, but cunningly sought to discredit Muhammad throughout the region.

One daring poet trekked across the desert to the much-feared Ghifar clan, Arabia's most notorious marauders, to perform at the clan's market. The poet's shocking tales about a mysterious man in Mecca named Muhammad caught the attention of a young man named Jundub (grasshopper), a member of the clan's noblest family. Dissatisfied with his tribe's perpetual plundering, the young man noted their inconsistency in pillaging a passing caravan one moment and then generously donating some of the booty to poor nomads. He was averse to idolatry, which from a young age had also struck him as hypocritical. Jundub was so captivated by the poet's account of Muhammad that he set off on a three-week journey to Mecca to meet the man for himself.

On the surface, the savage Ghifar clan would have seemed like the last people in Arabia to welcome Muhammad's message. Yet Muhammad and Jundub immediately connected, and the young man decided to stay in Mecca to learn at the Dar-ul-Arqam academy for half a year. Muhammad was impressed with Jundub's determination to think for himself and chart a life of meaning. The young man was the first person who went out of his way to learn Muhammad's philosophy. All of Muhammad's previous recruits had been friends, relatives, or people who knew Muhammad and found him inspiring. For the first time, the mindset had been compelling on its own merit, even, ironically, via a smear campaign.

After six months of intense learning, Jundub packed a trunk full of Qur'anic chapter scrolls and prepared to return to his clan. Determined to change his people, the young man was undaunted by the seemingly impossible prospect of turning Arabia's most vicious nomads into progressive thinkers. Muhammad came to see him off and offered one last parting gift: a new name. Jundub was now Abu Tharr (far-reaching seed spreader). Moreover, leveraging the same grammatical composition his mother, Aminah, had used in her last words, Muhammad charged Jundub with a mission—*"Kun aba tharr!"* (Be a catalyst for positive change!)

Standing with 'Ali and Zaid at Mecca's northern pass, Muhammad watched Abu Tharr ride off alone into the distance. (The Ghifar were so feared that, unique among Arab clans, they traveled the desert without risk of being attacked.) The trio assumed they would not see the innocent young man again. But as they turned to walk home, Muhammad placed his hand on 'Ali's shoulder and observed, "The path of blossoming to a person's heart is like the path of water to the roots of a palm tree, which can take years to blossom and bear fruit—even seventy years in desolate and unfertile lands." Later that day, Muhammad experienced a new revelation:

In 'alaika illal-balagh.
Your task is merely to deliver the message eloquently.

A few days after Abu Tharr's departure, came a new revelation called Al-Inshirah or Ash-Sharh (The Consolation/Solace—literally, untying ropes tightly binding a harness to a camel), with a rhyming refrain:

Alam nashrah laka sadhrak
Did We not relieve the tightness compressing your chest

Wa wadha'na 'anka wizrak
And did We not cast off the mountain of burdens weighing you down

Al-lathi anqadha thahrak?
A feeling of hopelessness that had bent your back nearly to the
   breaking point?

Wa rafa'na laka thikrak?
And did We not raise you from obscurity, establishing your
   renown far and wide?

Fa inna ma'al 'usri yusra.
Then remember well, when the obstacle is defined, potential
   solutions flow with ease.

Inna ma'al 'usri yusra.
When the obstacle is defined, potential solutions flow without
   limit.

Fa itha faraghta fansab.
Therefore, once you refocus your perspective, stand up straight
   with confidence.

Wa ila rabbika farghab.
And remain unwavering in trusting your Cosmic Mentor's wise
   guidance.

The passage's key term was a new word in Qur'anic revelation: *yusra* (flow). The image conveyed by *yusra* is of water flowing around a rock in the middle of a stream. For eleven years, Muhammad had exhausted himself while trying to push against the rock of Mecca. In that time, he had attracted only 150 followers, just a dozen or so each year. It was time to stop pushing. Instead, he needed to flow around the rock.

A series of revelations reinforced the message. One noted that imposing the mindset is simply not possible:

> La ikraha fid-din.
> Do not in any way discomfort someone to try to force them onto
>   the path of success.

Another reminded Muhammad of the limits of prophetic accountability:

> Laysa 'alaika hudahum.
> It is not your responsibility to guide them if they do not choose
>   the sounder route.

Huda—direction provided by a hadi (expert guide)—showed wilderness travelers the safest route through difficult terrain. Like a hadi, Muhammad could guide only if invited and could not force people onto his preferred route or even stop them from following a destructive path. People possessed the inherent right to choose their direction. Forcing a plant to blossom only deformed its otherwise natural growth. People had to embrace the mindset freely.

Just as Muhammad gained these insights, a group of outsiders arrived in Mecca seeking his guidance. In his mother's native city of Yathrib, strife between rival clans had created a lingering tension. The city lacked a unified Dar-un-Nadwah assembly or chief elder, and competition among jealous elites shattered social cohesion. Though Muhammad had not visited his mother's hometown in several decades, some locals still remembered him. When the Meccans' smear campaign reached Yathrib, several of the city's elders sought to find out for themselves what Aminah's son had done to earn such scorn. Merchants from the coast who sold dried fish in Yathrib's markets provided an intriguing counternarrative: most of Muhammad's followers had fled to Africa and were thriving there as a community.

Despite the strife, Yathrib's elite longed for solutions. Unlike the Meccans, they actually wanted to improve their state of affairs—they merely lacked an effective path forward. A group of about seventy notables from across the city's clans decided to travel to Mecca during the pilgrimage season to seek Muhammad's advice. To avoid arousing the Meccans' suspicions, the notables traveled as merchants selling goods. They offhandedly inquired about the notorious Muhammad and gained an introduction to his uncle Al-'Abbas, one of the city's main moneylenders. When the Yathribites asked after his nephew, Al-'Abbas initially was protective, but when the visitors revealed their true interest in gaining Muhammad's assistance, he agreed to help broker a meeting.

Around midnight, twenty members of the Yathrib delegation arrived in a secluded valley on the outskirts of Mecca called Al-'Aqabah (the emancipation). Muhammad awaited them there, accompanied by Al-'Abbas, 'Ali, and Zaid. Muhammad listened quietly as the Yathribites described the breakdown of civic order in their city and the need for a stable system that could foster growth. They ended by appealing to Muhammad to come mediate in Yathrib. Muhammad responded by warning them of the dangers of adopting his ideas: doing so would surely attract the wrath of the Meccans, who had just spent three years wielding a devastating campaign against him. "Return to your people and make sure you take this step fully aware of the consequences and the benefits," he advised. "It is a decision only you can make, and once you do, there is no turning back."

The next day, the Yathribites debated the opportunity and finally decided as a group to take the risk. Two nights later, the entire delegation headed to Al-'Aqabah to meet Muhammad. Earlier that evening, Muhammad had sought out one of his top students, Mus'ab, with a special mission in mind. The young man from an elite Meccan family had been under virtual house arrest by his mother since returning from Abyssinia; he had been in the group that had left Mecca in the dead of night before the boycott started. His mother had frantically sought to convince him to stop following Muhammad—she even made a failed attempt at a hunger strike. Determined not to lose her son again, she had him locked in his room, tied to his bed. Muhammad's followers mounted a daring rescue mission and sneaked Mus'ab out of the house under the cover of darkness.

When Muhammad met with the Yathribites that night, he introduced them to Mus'ab. Rather than stagnate in his bedroom, the eloquent young man would return to Yathrib with the emissaries to test whether the locals were ready to receive Muhammad's message. The Yathribites agreed to this plan and smuggled Mus'ab out of the city in a large terra-cotta container. They also packed several Qur'anic scrolls provided by 'Ali, concealing them among their merchandise.

From among his many students, Muhammad had chosen Mus'ab because he belonged to the cultured elite and could diplomatically engage other elites in a divided city. Muhammad had learned from his negative experience in Mecca that if the city's elites felt threatened, his message of blossoming could not take hold. Indeed, the experiment in Abyssinia had succeeded because the king perceived no threat and in fact welcomed the revelations.

Mus'ab spent his first days in Yathrib gathering information about the city's complex social dynamics. Equipped with this intelligence, he began diplomatically navigating the local scene. He met influential leaders, who were impressed by his eloquence and refined manners. One by one, Mus'ab reasoned with them, often sitting for hours in the shade of lush palm trees. He then gathered small groups of elites who respected one another; if he could convince just one of them, the rest of the group would follow. The city's clashing factions slowly realized that they shared a common enthusiasm for Mus'ab's approach.

In less than a year, Mus'ab won over nearly all the city's elders. During the pilgrimage season, the original group of seventy again visited Muhammad in Mecca. Gathering in the same secret spot in the secluded valley, the Yathribites enthusiastically invited Muhammad to join them. In their eyes, he was a man with deep roots in Yathrib who at the same time transcended local political strife, an ideal insider-outsider who could arbitrate their tribal squabbles.

The request for Muhammad's assistance from outside Mecca reinforced the Qur'anic revelation's admonition to be patient and wait for receptive audiences. Nonetheless, Muhammad stalled for time, agreeing only to send some of his followers. He could not yet give up on Mecca.

❖ ❖ ❖

The day after his meeting with the Yathribites, Muhammad called together his top followers at the Dar-ul-Arqam academy to inform them of the agreement. Unlike Muhammad, none of them had roots in Yathrib. He was now asking them to turn their backs on their ancestral home and abandon their families to take up residence in a distant, unfamiliar city with an unfamiliar Arabic dialect. Still, many of these followers had had to flee the country overnight several years earlier. A more planned decamping to another city in Arabia seemed less daunting.

To prepare his followers for the transition, Muhammad described their move as a *hijrah* (migration)—literally, turning their back on the past to walk toward an unknown future. The word was commonly used to describe a husband and wife's decision to separate but not divorce, leaving open the possibility of reconciliation. Rather than continue to expend energy in Mecca on people not ready to change, his followers would shift their focus to a city eager for meaningful engagement. They would turn their backs on Mecca, but not permanently.

A new Qur'anic revelation explored the purpose of the *hijrah* through the analogy of bees. For years, Muhammad's followers heard him evoke the insects during sessions at Dar-ul-Arqam academy. *"Kun kan-nahlah!"* (Be like the bee!), he had encouraged. Seek the purest nectar from diverse sources, then process these sources to produce a healing honey with multiple benefits to the world. And even if the world eschews its benefits, the honey still sweetens and causes no harm.

Now came a revelation—called Surah An-Nahl (The Bees)—that drew inspiration from bees' ability to constantly seek out fresh flowers for their honey and establish new homes in the face of adversity. "Your Divine Mentor inspired bees to build their hives in mountains, trees, and vineyards" one verse declared, hailing the bees' ability to heed the divine call to adapt and rebuild. Invoking the concept of *hijrah*, the *surah* emphasized moving on in a positive spirit:

Wal-lathina hajaru fil-lahi mim-ba'di ma thulimu lanubaw-wi'an-
nahum fid-dunya hasanataw-wa la'jrul-akhirati akbaru law
kanu ya'lamun.

Those who have been wronged and abused yet muster the
courage—supported by the Loving Divine—to leave the past
behind will find a fertile and welcoming land, one that will
empower them to achieve successes and impact far greater than
they could have ever imagined.

After years of persecution, followers like 'Ammar, whose parents
had been murdered before his eyes, and Bilal, who had been dragged
across the scorching sand with a boulder on his chest, needed to find
a way to let go of any righteous anger or desire for vengeance. While
Muhammad and his followers had lost money, friendships, and even
loved ones, making the *hijrah* required a mental leap before embarking
on a physical transition. Letting go of the past meant more than just
forgiving. Muhammad's followers had to mature from a long-repressed
underground movement into responsible civic leaders for a city in
turmoil.

Such a dramatic transition also required an evolution in their relationship with the Divine from one of structured dependence to support-
ive independence. For years, Qur'anic revelations had primarily invoked
the Divine as *Rabb,* carefully nurturing the growth of a young plant. But
a maturing plant's thickening trunk eventually outgrows basic supports
and its deepening roots no longer benefit from small drops of water by
its base. Now that Muhammad's movement had at last outgrown Mecca,
the Qur'an increasingly invoked the Divine as Allah, a comforter who
provides emotional rather than structural support. The movement had
at last reached an adolescent phase, ready to experiment with independence while still buoyed by a loving guardian.

Another revelation introduced the prophet Lot, Abraham's nephew,
who had spent over a decade seeking to reform his people and was forced
to leave his home under cover of darkness to avoid an assassination plot.

Wa la yaltafit minkum ahad!
Let none of you look back!

Lot's wife had looked back and was consequently transformed into a pillar of salt, signifying preservation and stagnation. Salt was the ultimate preserver; Lot's wife had sought to preserve an unhealthy self-destructive state. Physically leaving Mecca would not suffice. The followers had to leave behind any thoughts of victimization to focus on a future they could shape in their own way.

The first to leave on *hijrah* was 'Umar, who had maintained a low profile while immersed in his studies. Before he departed, 'Umar stood before the Ka'bah and bellowed: "Oh people of Mecca, I am leaving for Yathrib. Anyone desiring to leave behind a mourning mother and a weeping widow with orphans, let him try to stop me." The astonished crowd parted as the giant walked to his horse and rode out of the city to the north.

Over the next six months, Muhammad's family (except for his eldest daughter, Zainab, who remained at Mecca with her pagan husband) and his followers gradually departed in small groups. Unlike 'Umar, they slipped out in the middle of the night, fearing their families would prevent them from leaving. Indeed, when Meccan leaders received word of a recently departed *hijrah* participant, they often sent out horsemen to forcibly return them. One search party, for example, found Suhaib, the former mentee of Ibn Jud'an and a close follower of Muhammad, resting in a desert cave at midday. The Meccan warriors eyed his pouch of gold coins and made him an offer he could not refuse: "You came to us poor, and now you walk away enriched with our money—which will remain at Mecca either with you or without you."

Forced to part with his life savings, Suhaib nonetheless remained optimistic about the future. "That was the best investment I had ever made," he later recalled.

Hamzah managed to leave Mecca unharmed, accompanied by Muhammad's daughters Fatimah and Um Kulthum. But Muhammad's daughter Ruqayyah, who was eight months pregnant, was less fortunate. While leaving Mecca with her husband, 'Uthman, two of his cousins attacked her, hurling her off her camel. She fell unconscious in a pool of blood and miscarried.

As more of Muhammad's followers disappeared from Mecca, the elders convened an emergency meeting in June 622, seeking measures to stem the tide. The elders were further concerned to learn about Muhammad's growing popularity in Yathrib. Should Muhammad himself decamp for Yathrib, he might mobilize a force to impede the Meccan caravans. The elders could not allow him to leave town, yet they lacked a justification to detain him under Arabia's tribal code.

At the Dar-un-Nadwah emergency session, 'Amr ibn Hisham once again stepped forward with a solution: they could arrange to have Muhammad stabbed to death by a group of twenty-one young men from diverse clans all at the same time. The participation of so many would divide the guilt, making it impossible for the Hashemites to seek a vendetta. They would instead have to accept the restitution offered by the clans. When Muhammad's uncle 'Abdul-'Uzza agreed to accept blood money on the family's behalf (despite having resigned from the Hashemite clan at the start of the boycott), the elders consented. At last they had a permanent solution to the Muhammad problem.

One of the enslaved workers at the assembly hall leaked news of the assassination plot to Muhammad. Waraqah's prophecy—"they will try to kill you . . . and force you out"—was about to be realized. Muhammad, who had long refused to abandon Mecca, finally relented. He and Abu Bakr planned their escape. That evening after prayer, Muhammad looked out his bedroom window and noticed men in the shadows below. Their swords unsheathed, the twenty-one young men in the alley waited for him to leave at dawn. 'Amr ibn Hisham, though eager to finish off his nemesis, had refused to allow the assassins to enter Muhammad's home and kill him in his sleep. The public would have seen such an extreme act as cowardly and dishonorable.

In the thick of night, Muhammad slipped out through a window the assassins could not see and made his way to Abu Bakr's home. The men then crept to a secluded spot where a pagan *hadi*, 'Abdullah ibn Uraiqit, was quietly waiting with camels packed for the journey. While assassins crouched by Muhammad's door, the trio headed south to a cave on the slope of Mount Thawr (Taurus) where they hoped to hide until the Meccans gave up the chase. The Meccans, however, hired expert trackers who managed to trace them to the mouth of the cave. But when the Meccans saw a spider's web undisturbed across the cave's entrance, the Meccans assumed it was empty. From inside the hollow, Abu Bakr watched terrified as 'Amr ibn Hisham's form appeared against the bright desert. Abu Bakr later recalled, "Had he not been distracted by the spider's web, he would surely have discovered us."

On the eve of the third day, the trio moved south toward the Red Sea coast before turning north along an unchartered path. The Meccans had placed a large bounty on Muhammad's head, and cutthroats eager for the prize money began a relentless pursuit. One bounty hunter, Suraqah ibn Malik, a nomadic guide himself, correctly surmised that Muhammad had chosen an unusual path and tracked down the escapees near the coast. As Suraqah approached, Abu Bakr leapt between him and Muhammad. Muhammad, however, asked to speak with the bounty hunter alone. The two conversed, and then, remarkably, the tracker rode away. Muhammad had convinced Suraqah that a reward better than the Meccans' bounty awaited.

After several more nerve-racking days traversing the open expanse to Yathrib, Muhammad and Abu Bakr at last arrived at Qiba, a suburb on the city's outskirts. Now within the jurisdiction of Yathrib and thus safe from bounty hunters, the men awaited the imminent arrival of 'Ali, whom Muhammad had left behind to ensure all the goods stored in his safety depository were properly returned to Mecca's elites. Simply by extending protection to Muhammad, the Yathribites paid a price: they lost access to Mecca's markets, and the Meccan caravan to Damascus would no longer stop in Yathrib.

The new challenge facing Muhammad was whether he could offer the Yathribites something valuable enough to offset their immediate economic and social loss. The main asset he had brought with him from Mecca was not wealth but a mindset he had formed into a philosophy through years of thoughtful reflection. The mindset combined a sense of transcendent purpose, a distinctive positive attitude, and practical techniques for effective implementation. Its essence:

Transcendent Purpose
- Material success does not bring fulfillment; it can be a helpful tool but is never the goal.
- All people are inherently equal and filled with potential.
- Merit trumps status and wealth, so focus on what an individual can and is able to achieve.

✧ The lifelong challenge for all human beings is to allow themselves to blossom: to unleash their dormant yet never fully maximized potential.

✧ There are many paths to blossoming, and this diversity is essential for a healthy society.

✧ Gather knowledge from a variety of diverse sources and then analyze the information to produce something new that can benefit others.

Positive Attitude

✧ Accept that blossoming is not easy, as it forces you outside your natural comfort zone.

✧ The blossoming mindset cannot be forced. People must desire to adopt it.

✧ Divine wisdom exists throughout the universe, able to inspire those ready to recognize it.

✧ Embrace imperfection: brokenness can be beautiful and an opportunity for growth.

✧ Do not trap yourself in past pain: grudges lead to stagnation, forgiveness to liberation.

✧ See yourself and the world around you as filled with creative potential, since maintaining a positive outlook increases your chances of success.

Practical Techniques

✧ Persevere by remaining flexible and flowing around obstacles.

✧ Work to transform setbacks into opportunities.

✧ Individuals cannot easily blossom alone, so embrace mentors for regular positive affirmation and encouragement.

✧ Blossoming requires constant refocusing, ideally achieved by reconnecting every day with the Divine, oneself, and others.

✧ Focus on the long-term (*akhirah*), athough one may not realize the beneficial results in one's lifetime.

⬥ Constantly rebalance between a focus on the future with action-based hope (*taqwa*) and on the past by learning from the wisdom of previous generations without stagnating.

As he prepared to enter Yathrib, Muhammad had a fully articulated methodology. His mother's hometown offered an unprecedented chance to apply it in practical ways, to transform a socially fractured desert outpost into an oasis of civic blossoming. Yathrib would be a critical test.

PART III

✧

APPLYING
THE MINDSET

7

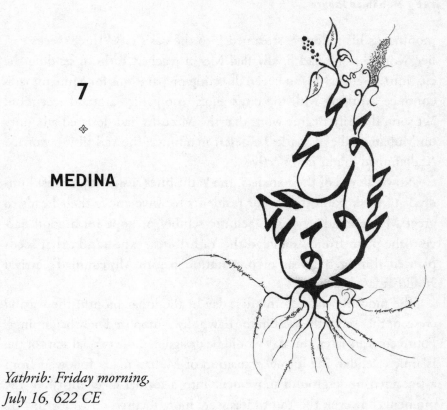

MEDINA

Yathrib: Friday morning,
July 16, 622 CE

Nearly all of Yathrib stared intently toward the horizon, scanning the shimmering desert sands. People climbed onto the roofs of their homes and scaled palm trees to gain a better vantage point. Thousands more crammed onto the two hills known as Thaniyat Al-Wada' that straddled the city's northern entrance, the same spot where the city commemorated the destruction of the Temple in Jerusalem with the annual Tish'ah B'Av day of mourning. With that somber fast just nine days away, residents had already begun the usual premourning preparation, eschewing meat except on the Sabbath.

For over a thousand years, the Yathribites had stood on their city's northern hills and gazed longingly toward Jerusalem. But instead of the usual mood of lamentation, on this morning the air crackled with barely contained jubilation. A messenger on horseback had arrived the previous evening with news that Muhammad had reached nearby Qiba and would be entering Yathrib in the morning.

Muhammad had been the talk of the town for the previous two

months, as his followers streamed into the oasis city. Three weeks earlier, word that he had finally fled Mecca reached Yathrib, sending the city into a frenzy. Mus'ab began directing preparations for Muhammad's entrance, working with the city's elites to organize a grand reception. Yet soon thereafter came word that the Meccans had declared a bounty on Muhammad and sparked a desert manhunt. The Yathribites worried Muhammad might never arrive.

Now relieved of their anxiety, the Yathribites rushed to harvest hundreds of fresh palm fronds for residents to wave above their heads to greet Muhammad. A classic Semitic symbol of hope for a good harvest, the palm fronds signaled the Yathribites' expectation that seeds planted during the year of preparation before Muhammad's arrival would at last bear fruit.

The morning marked the first day of the lunar month; the waxing crescent that set to the west in the dawn sky symbolized new beginnings. Fourteen years later, this day would be designated the official start of the Islamic calendar, the formal transition of Muhammad's followers from a fractured underground movement into a formal civic entity. In the moment, however, the Yathribites were more focused on Muhammad's anticipated homecoming.

In that expectant spirit, Yathribites who were normally at odds had put their differences aside to prepare a special musical reception for Muhammad. A poet from the Banu Najjar clan whose name is lost to history composed a brief celebratory song with an upbeat melody, a sharp break from the typical melancholy motifs of Semitic music. An impromptu city chorus of hundreds of men, women, and children had spent days rehearsing.

Yathrib's residents treated the occasion of Muhammad's arrival like a wedding reception, the herald of hope and rejuvenation. People dressed in their finest clothes, and many women carried hand drums. A hush fell over the crowd as the morning sun ascended, signaling the grand moment was at hand.

The first to glimpse Muhammad was a rabbi named Mukhairiq (deep-piercing knowledge). With a black turban and black tunic featuring knotted white and blue fringes proclaiming his position as a respected Jewish elder of the Banu Quraithah tribe, Rabbi Mukhairiq pointed dramatically toward a blotch on the horizon. People surged down off the hills, all seeking to be the first to welcome Muhammad.

Soon the outline of three riders came into focus, the bright morning sun blazing behind them. To the Yathribites, the scene unfolded like the fulfillment of an ancient prophecy. Like the three kings from the East proclaiming the nativity of Jesus, these riders seemed to herald the birth of a new civic order.

Muhammad, Abu Bakr, and 'Ali traversed Yathrib's northern pass surrounded by the throngs and headed toward the Jewish neighborhood of Banu Nadhir. As Muhammad entered the city, residents laid palm fronds on the path before his camel, a Semitic sign of deep respect that echoed the Jerusalemites' welcome of Jesus on his visit from Galilee. With great fervor, the Yathribite civic chorus burst into the song it had carefully prepared:

> *Tala'al badru 'alaina min thaniyyatil-wada'i.*
> The full moon has ascended to illuminate and redeem us as we
>   stand on the hills of mourning.

> *Wajabash-shukru 'alaina ma da'a lillahi da'i.*
> Our hearts overflow with grateful hope in anticipation of the
>   redemptive guide inspired by the Loving Divine.

> *Ayyuhal-mab'uthu fina ji`ta bil-amril-muta'i.*
> Oh one who has been raised from among us, you uplift us with an
>   enlightening message.

> *Ji`ta sharraftal-Madinah marhabay-ya khaira da'i!*
> You have come to elevate the prestige of Medina (our renewed
>   state), welcome, oh most inspiring of redemptive guides!

The song twice referred to Muhammad as a *da'i*, a person who rescues travelers unable to find a way out of a labyrinthine valley. Such a redeemer could transform hills long associated with mourning into symbols of uplifting hope—and transform a city named Yathrib into Medina. The term the songwriter used was not a common Arabic term but rather a northern Semitic concept expressed in Hebrew and Aramaic for a province or community built on established foundations reconsecrated with fresh purpose.

Muhammad looked out at the throng of Yathribites—now Medinians—crowded around his camel. Thousands of people awaited his direction in intense anticipation. As he prepared to descend from his mount and set foot in the city for the first time in over twenty years, the Yathribites placed palm fronds before him so he would not step on bare ground. Muhammad had started his movement with only a few dozen followers in a secret classroom, found himself confined in a concentration camp with armed guards, escaped a massive manhunt by a spider's thread, and been chased like a fugitive across the desert. Now he was received like a king.

But rather than bask in the glory, Muhammad was concerned. He had done little to earn their adulation, and the citywide celebration seemed premature.

The challenge before Muhammad was to inspire his new community to channel its fervent hopes into practical action without deifying him, to redirect their outward enthusiasm inward. He also had to determine the true state of affairs in Medina.

Muhammad had become the leader his grandfather had envisioned when choosing his grandson's name. But it was not clear that the people of Medina had the fortitude to live up to their city's new name, to carry out the hard work necessary to rededicate themselves and their community.

❖ ❖ ❖

As the chorus finished its performance, Muhammad addressed the crowd from atop his camel. *"Hathihi Tabah!"* (This is Tabah!), he responded with a warm smile. In the song, the Yathribites had renamed their city Medina, and Muhammad responded in kind with his own new name. *Tabah* was a term widely known among the Yathribites (its Hebrew equivalent, *tovah*, means pleasant or good) to refer to a soothing ointment and bandages placed on a deep wound to numb pain and initiate healing. While the locals' song emphasized the goal of a remade city, Muhammad had suggested a name that emphasized that they were only at the first stage of a long journey.

Then Muhammad raised his arms, extending them to either side in a sweeping gesture encompassing the entire crowd. *"Antum-ul-Ansar"* (You are the loyal supporters—literally, You are people who provide fertile land ready for planting), he said. If the palm fronds signified the Medinians' expectation for a quick solution to their problems, Muhammad politely reminded them that they had not yet sown the seeds for that harvest, yet they possessed enormous potential for greatness.

The city's elders surrounded his camel, each trying to grab its reins to lead him to his house to obtain the great honor of hosting Muhammad. To win his favor, each elder brought with him an enslaved servant or two and publicly emancipated them beside the camel. Muhammad looked upon the strange scene from the saddle on his she-camel, a well-bred animal known for her speed and elegance that he had purchased for an enormous sum. Muhammad treated her like a beloved pet and had named her Al-Qaswa (the liberated).

After a few minutes of deliberation, Muhammad unexpectedly descended from the saddle. The crowd murmured, surprised that he had dismounted in the middle of the road rather than at the home of his preferred host. Turning to the crowd, he announced, "I will allow Al-Qaswa to decide where we stay." He removed his camel's bridle, motioned for people to step back, and let her loose. Muhammad, the elders, and the bemused crowd all followed her through the winding roads of Medina.

The camel wandered for almost an hour, meandering south through the city until she reached the lands of the Banu Najjar clan, Muhammad's maternal relatives. At last she stopped at the southernmost tip of the city, on the outskirts of town, and sat down in front of a ramshackle date-drying facility that had been abandoned for years. Muhammad asked to whom this building belonged and learned that two orphans of the Banu Najjar clan—Sahl (easygoing) and Suhail (mild-tempered)—had inherited the factory from their late father.

Muhammad looked around and smiled. The property, surrounded by large swaths of open land, was the perfect place to begin his new urban construction project. After thanking the Medinians for their warm welcome, he politely asked to be excused so he could rest from his long journey.

Adjacent to the factory stood the home of Abu Ayyub (Job) and his wife, who by default became Muhammad's hosts. Abu Ayyub was a Jewish scribe and carpenter and one of Banu Najjar's elders—likely a distant cousin of Muhammad's. His fine house had two stories with a rooftop terrace. As he admired Abu Ayyub's intricate carpentry, Muhammad noted, "Banu Najjar are the most entrepreneurial clan among the people of Yathrib."

The next day, the elders of Medina's various clans descended on Abu Ayyub's home to pay their respects to Muhammad. Before they arrived, each sent their relatives to Abu Ayyub to ask when other elders were planning to come—so they could avoid visiting at the same time as their rivals. Muhammad learned about this from his host, offering a first glimpse of the civic dysfunction beneath the arrival ceremony's united front. In his conversations with visiting elders, Muhammad further gleaned that they had grandiose dreams yet remained oblivious to the hard work ahead of them. They assumed Muhammad would miraculously transform their city.

Muhammad had never seen anything like this problem before. In Mecca, he had struggled to find even a few dozen followers; once he did, they intuitively understood that they needed to work hard in order to progress. The often timid Sumayyah had come out of her shell to boldly proclaim the message in public. The often explosive 'Umar had restrained himself for years in quiet study and self-reflection. Evidently, Mus'ab had not emphasized that message of personal development during the past year. He had concentrated more on promoting Muhammad the prophet than discussing the complex process of change, no doubt a safer and less intimidating sell.

A few days after his arrival, Muhammad had his first revelation in Medina while sitting in his guest room at Abu Ayyub's home. The passage marked the beginning of an outpouring of revelations, ultimately comprising more than half of the Qur'an. It offered a candid message to the people of Medina:

Inna-llaha la yughayyiru ma bi qawmin hatta yughayyiru ma bi anfusihim.

The Loving Divine will surely not change the state of a people
until and unless they change their inner attitude and
perspective.

Muhammad then recited to audiences in Medina a *surah* that had been revealed shortly before his flight from Mecca. The Qur'anic chapter—Surah Bani Isra'il (The Children of Israel)—recounted the story of the exile of the Israelites from Jerusalem after the destruction of the First Temple and their subsequent return and exile again after the Second Temple's destruction. The chapter opened with a quick account of Muhammad's nocturnal journey to the Temple in Jerusalem—called al-Masjid al-Aqsa (the ultimate place of grounding)—then evolved into a narrative of Moses's struggle to prepare the enslaved Israelites for liberation.

The *surah* highlighted the Israelites' reluctance to change their status as exiles, instead constantly seeking quick and easy solutions to their plight. Even as they yearned for "the land promised by God," they berated Moses: "You and your God go fight [the Amalekites]—once you win, then we will enter the land." The Qur'an promised the children of Israel that just as they had once been exiled and redeemed, their current state of exile would end with redemption—but only if they changed their mindset and put in the significant effort required:

Fa `itha ja`a wa'dul-akhirati ji`na bikum lafifa.

Only once you have invested your full effort will We gather you
from far and wide.

The verse invoked *akhirah*, an agricultural term used to describe the phase when farmers wait to harvest the fruit of their labor after doing all the hard work to nurture a plant. The Qur'an used the same term to describe the concept of an afterlife: as the return on investments made in this lifetime, which may not be realized until years later. To achieve the *akhirah* phase of harvest and deliverance, one first had to invest enormous effort. In describing the promised assemblage of exiles, the revelation invoked *lafifa*, a cloth that is wrapped around itself, layer upon layer, to make a turban—uniting a disordered throng into a coherent entity.

Muhammad also shared a new revelation that highlighted Medina's positive characteristics: "The people who opened their homes and lovingly provided sanctuary to those who sought refuge hold in their hearts no ill feelings, instead graciously sacrificing for others even if it caused discomfort. Truly, those who step outside their comfort zone will surely succeed." In a reference to the scores of homes across Medina that were hosting Meccan refugees, the passage deftly cited such generosity as evidence that the people of Medina were capable of doing the hard work necessary to blossom.

The passages provided a path forward. An unprecedented outpouring of a dozen new names for the Divine in two verses further articulated that formula for success:

+ Al-Malik—the Reenergizer (used figuratively for *king*)
+ Al-Quddus—the Elevator of the assiduous (used figuratively for *holy*)
+ As-Salam—the Restorer of wholeness/Source of Solace (literally, repairer of cracks)
+ Al-Mu`min—the Provider of security (literally, builder of strong defensive walls)
+ Al-Muhaimin—the Clarifier of the obscure
+ Al-'Aziz—the Builder of strength (literally, trainer/coach)
+ Al-Jabbar—the Healer of fractures (literally, cast maker)
+ Al-Mutakabbir—the Compounder (literally, constructer of high levels)
+ Al-Khaliq—the Creator/Initiator (literally, fashioner of unique forms)
+ Al-Bari—the Refashioner/Architect (literally, transformer of discarded elements)
+ Al-Musawwir—the Ingenious Designer (literally, sculptor/artist)
+ Al-Hakim—The Wise/Prudent (literally, fuser of weak fragments to make strong ropes)

The torrent of names demonstrated the numerous ways the people of Medina could make progress. They needed to recognize that success comes from taking action and embracing their deficiencies as a challenge to improve. They needed to recognize that broken patterns must be reset in order to open up a space for original ideas and creativity. Thinking big meant seeing opportunities everywhere: turning raw materials into beautiful refined products, transforming once-rejected elements into fresh creations, daring to design new visions, and reconstituting shattered elements of their society.

Of course, names alone could not undo decades of self-destructive tendencies. After he finished meeting the city's elite, Muhammad made a point of asking to meet its ordinary citizens, who soon revealed a social dynamic of damaging double standards and hypocrisy.

The first commoners to visit were elderly women from various clans. They stood at the door of Abu Ayyub's main hall and trembled in awe at the opportunity for an audience with the celebrated prophet. Muhammad saw their nervousness and came to greet them with a smile. "I am a mere mortal," he humbly reassured them. He invoked his own Yathribite mother: "I am the son of a simple woman who sat on the bare ground and ate the porridge of the poor." Then he gently offered them seats beside him.

Just then Nu'aiman, a local Banu Najjar carpenter, burst in. A joker with a natural sense of comic timing, he had quickly endeared himself to Muhammad. "I brought a gift of quality honey," Nu'aiman jovially announced and presented the jar along with the honey vendor himself. Muhammad seized the opportunity to share the bounty with his guests.

"How did you like it?" Nu'aiman asked.

"Delicious!" replied Muhammad.

"Great! Please, pay the man!" Nu'aiman blurted with a laugh.

Muhammad cracked up. "I thought you brought the honey as a gift."

"It was a gift from you to me," said Nu'aiman. "The honey looked good, but I didn't have money to buy it." Muhammad laughed and motioned to 'Ali to give the merchant a pouch of silver coins.

The comic interlude amused the women, who finally relaxed and revealed the purpose of their visit. They had come to inform him that behind the smiling faces of nobles and clergy was a network of corruption. Many clerics accepted bribes to resolve disputes favorably for those with money, and most people in the city were too timid to challenge people in positions of authority.

The women were relieved when Muhammad listened sympathetically. He nodded his head in understanding and shared a dramatic new
Qur'anic revelation: "Do not blindly rely upon the judgment of Jewish
and Christian scholars and clergy in all matters, for they can allow themselves to be unjust even unto their own people. If you do so, then know
that your state will be akin to theirs. The Loving Divine does not bestow
serenity upon those who choose to remain in darkness."

The verses reassured the women that speaking out against corruption
was commendable. If Medina was to live up to its new name, such a
transformation had to start with honestly assessing societal ills and addressing them with practical solutions.

❖ ❖ ❖

The corruption that the elderly women had revealed soon fractured the
facade of civility. Members of two different clans started fighting over a
shared well in an orchard, and the minor disagreement quickly led to a
formal declaration of war and the invocation of ancient vendettas. "Let
us avenge the Battle of Bu'ath!" yelled one clan, citing a battle fought
more than a half century earlier. In no time, the city's clans took sides,
and their warriors gathered in preparation for battle at Medina's northern entrance—the very place they had stood less than two weeks earlier
to welcome Muhammad in a spectacular show of brotherhood.

Muhammad rushed out on his camel to intervene. He listened to
each side separately and then spoke to them together, reminding them
how they had recently overlooked their differences to celebrate his arrival. Surely, they had the ability to recapture that same spirit to avoid
bloodshed. Ashamed of their rash behavior, clan leaders shook hands
and even embraced in relief. Muhammad invited them for a communal
dinner at the abandoned date-drying facility.

After dinner, Muhammad discussed his concerns with Abu Bakr. He
might have calmed the tensions momentarily, but Medina needed a more
lasting solution to its social strife. The next morning, he invited Rabbi
Mukhairiq and Rabbi 'Abdullah ibn Salam (a prominent young scholar
who would become one of Muhammad's closest disciples and advisors)
to breakfast. As the men sat on the floor of Abu Ayyub's home eating
lentil soup, Muhammad recalled his experience as a teenage shepherd

sharing a communal well with other herders. An *ummah* (commune) agreement had governed how various shepherds peacefully shared the common resource, overseen by a *warid* (water manager) who sat by the well and kept the peace.

Muhammad proposed a similar arrangement to unite Medina's residents. Inspired, Rabbi Mukhairiq volunteered his home for a conference of the city's elders. Abu Ayyub, a trained scribe, volunteered to record the hoped-for agreement. After this meeting, a new revelation soon arrived that referred to these righteous Israelites:

> *Wa min qawmi Musa ummatuy-yahduna bil-haqqi wa bihi ya'dilun.*
>
> From among the people of Moses are communal guides of genuine sincerity and honesty who do their utmost to justly rebalance society.

The following day, Muhammad tasked Mus'ab with inviting all the clan elders to the conference. While some leaders were skeptical that any progress was possible, Mus'ab diplomatically persuaded them that it was in their best interest to cooperate. Each clan began to prepare for the conference, which was set for the following month on the day after the holiday of Rosh Hashanah, the Jewish New Year—a symbolic fresh start for Medina.

A few days before the conference, Muhammad was sitting on the outskirts of the Banu Najjar groves, watching his camel, Al-Qaswa, graze in the distance. The Banu Najjar men in his company ran to her, calling her to come. Yet the more they called, the farther away she moved. 'Ali was sitting beside Muhammad and observed the smile on his face. Muhammad slowly stood and motioned the men to leave the camel alone. He gradually advanced toward her, speaking gently. Raising his hand, he offered her fresh dates. She stood still and then advanced toward Muhammad. She lowered her head to eat the dates, as he gently took hold of her reins. As the scene unfolded Muhammad shared a new revelation:

> *Ud'u ila sabili rabbika bil-hikmati wal-maw'ithat-il-hasanati wa jadilhum billati hiya ahsan.*

Tenderly guide others to the verdant path of your Cosmic Mentor
by using judicious wisdom and calm poise, always engaging in
an appealing manner.

Running after Al-Qaswa only drove the camel away. Similarly, progress could not be forced and had to be advocated in a way that engaged the target audience without causing alarm. Muhammad's insight revealed that he had refined his approach since his first public discourse over a decade earlier at Abu Qubais, where he had astounded and driven away his audience by insisting that Meccans had become so complacent they were dull.

Shortly after sunrise on Thursday, September 16, 622, seventy of Medina's elders arrived at Rabbi Mukhairiq's home dressed in their finest garb. Mukhairiq and Rabbi Ibn Salam sat flanking Muhammad in the main courtyard. Muhammad asked those assembled to outline what they considered to be sources of disunity in their city. One by one the delegates representing each subclan presented their people's concerns without taking any responsibility. As they spoke, Abu Ayyub and 'Ali wrote a summary of what each person said. After all had finished, Muhammad repeated their concerns while also incorporating the grievances that ordinary citizens had confided to him.

Muhammad ended by crystallizing the common goal all Medinians desired: "Equal opportunity, equity in dealings and judgments, and fair access to communal resources." The assembly murmured in agreement, inspired to hear their complaints reiterated as a positive vision. Given these principles, Muhammad proposed a formal agreement to unify Medina. He invoked an agricultural term to describe the agreement: *mithaq* (covenant—literally, plaiting soft blades of diverse grasses into one strong braid). Bringing together isolated—and therefore weak—elements into a blend far stronger than its constituent parts, the agreement would unite isolated clans, joining men, women, young, old, and the enslaved in a strong civic entity.

As Muhammad outlined the articles of the new constitution of Medina, Abu Ayyub transcribed them on a long scroll he had specially prepared for the occasion. In its first sentence, Muhammad defined the collective of Medinians as an *ummah*, drawing on a traditional civic

agreement for a contemporary and forward-thinking purpose. The constitution's first three articles made clear that the model applied to shepherds sharing a well could be applied to a collective society comprised
of peoples from various clans with different religions and social status.

> *Innahum ummatuw-wahidatum-min dunin-nas,*
> They are one cooperative community drawn from many unique
> people,

> *'Ala rub'atihim,*
> Leveraging time-honored wisdom for a new purpose,

> *Yata'aqaluna ma'aqilahum.*
> Respecting tradition and upholding past commitments.

The constitution's opening reassured the city's Jewish elders that the
new order would not threaten their ancient heritage. The constitution
also balanced respect for individual identity and societal cohesion, declaring that while each person in Medina was unique, they also formed
a collective. The constitution continued by naming each of Medina's
clans and major subclans, painstakingly repeating the same language for
each and specifically noted that the agreement protected the enslaved of
each clan.

The constitution enumerated these essential elements in order:

1. One union out of many diverse groups and individuals.
2. All groups maintain their unique identity, preserving best practices while discarding unjust traditions.
3. All people possess equal rights, with no single group superior to
   others.
4. All enslaved have equal rights to dignity and opportunity. [Mu-
   hammad sought to modify enslavement in gradual steps to a
   form of employment that would allow the enslaved to earn
   money to eventually purchase their freedom.]
5. In the face of external aggression, all groups must unite as "one
   hand" to protect one another.

6. The agreement does not annul any preexisting commitments, including loans and debts.

7. All acts of treachery will be the responsibility of the individual, not their clan.

8. All people in Medina have the right not to join the union and will not be penalized so long as they remain neutral.

9. Justice is granted for all, including women, children, and the enslaved.

10. All groups are to contribute financially to the overall good of the union.

Two decades earlier, Muhammad had helped Meccan elders avert civil war while replacing the Ka'bah's cornerstone. With the constitution of Medina, he channeled that same spirit into concrete principles that provided a structure to help diverse clans overcome differences in a constructive manner. The constitution ensured, at least in theory, that each clan and subclan of Medina had an equal voice in the new system.

The word *Muslim* appeared nowhere in the constitution. Muhammad instead purposely chose the term *mu'minun* (those who are protected) to describe the document's signatories as under divine protection (*thimmah*). The constitution mentioned Muhammad only once, at the very end of the document, as final arbitrator if a dispute arose among the member tribes. Rather than serve as a ruler, Muhammad functioned as mediator and chief justice. The Medinians had initially asked that he become Medina's king—he refused and instead reserved the Arabic term for king (*Al-Malik*) for the Divine. God was king, and human beings needed to work out their social challenges themselves.

Gathered in Rabbi Mukhairiq's courtyard were dozens of people who had been bitter rivals until the conference. Yet, one by one, all signed the constitution, each as a representative of his clan or subclan. After signing, the participants agreed to meet as an assembly every three months to ensure smooth implementation of the new order. Several days after the signing ceremony, a new revelation came to Muhammad:

*Inna hathihi ummatukum ummataw-wahidataw-wa-ana rabbukum
  fat-taqun.*
This is your union, a unique collective, and I am your Divine
  Mentor who watches over you—so remain filled with action-
  based hope.

By invoking the Divine as a *Rabb*, the passage reminded Medinians
that their fledgling *ummah* needed careful stewardship to succeed, particularly in its nascent phase.

Muhammad sent a herald to announce the constitution in the main
square of each clan's neighborhood. He insisted that the herald read
every word aloud so ordinary people could know what their representative had agreed to and understand their new rights and responsibilities.
Commoners like the elderly women who had dared to share their concerns with Muhammad smiled, feeling a sense of pride that they had
contributed to their city's new constitution.

Meanwhile, several traveling merchants passing through Medina
heard the constitution read aloud in public squares. They carried the
news to Dar-un-Nadwah, where Mecca's elders once again felt threatened by Muhammad's growing popularity. Three months had passed
since their failed assassination attempt, and Muhammad had not only
been welcomed like royalty but had begun the process of uniting Yathrib's previously warring clans.

❖ ❖ ❖

To assure the city's inhabitants that the constitution addressed their
concerns, Muhammad wanted to enact the constitution "before the ink
dried," in the words of an Arabic idiom. He realized the city needed
a new community center where all residents could feel comfortable, a
gathering place with no history of some people entering only as someone else's guest. Barakah had recently returned from Abyssinia with reports of how well the *masjid* community center in Axum had managed
to bind the Meccan refugee community.

The morning after the constitution's signing, Muhammad gathered
two dozen of his leading followers—both veterans from Mecca and new

recruits like Abu Ayyub—at the abandoned date facility. A few months earlier, Muhammad had used the site as a neutral setting to host his reconciliation dinner. Abandoned for over a decade, the facility had begun to decay. Its mud walls were crumbling from lack of upkeep, as were the fire pits once used to boil date juice into molasses. Old date pits lay scattered about, and a few palm trees had sprouted in the desolate courtyard.

Muhammad asked his followers to partake in his vision. Here, the people of the city would together construct a new multipurpose building, a civic nexus and place of grounding: Arabia's first *masjid* (mosque—literally, place of grounding). With his walking staff, Muhammad began to draw the building's floor plan in the dirt. There would be three primary entrances, all without doors so anyone could enter, as well as a small tower from which to summon people to assemble. The building would also house a shelter and soup kitchen to serve those in need and out-of-town visitors. The main courtyard would have areas dedicated to learning, an open public version of the Dar-ul-Arqam academy.

Muhammad initially wanted to purchase the factory with his own money but ultimately agreed to split the cost with Abu Ayyub. Nonetheless, the community center would belong to everyone, the building and its land considered a public trust. In Arabia, all buildings—even synagogues and churches—belonged to an individual or a community group. This *masjid* would have no owner. Muhammad explained the concept to his followers using the term *waqf* (to stand immovable). The building would be open to all and permanently dedicated to God: *waqf-ul-lillah*.

In a sense, Muhammad was emulating his ancestor Qusai, who had built the Dar-un-Nadwah assembly—though that building continued to be privately owned. As a site belonging to all, the *masjid* recalled the original state of the Ka'bah. As the Qur'an declared, Abraham had built it "as the first public building established for all people of the world." Over the previous one thousand years, the Quraish tribe of Mecca had effectively made the shrine its private property, determining who could and could not enter. At the new *masjid* in Medina, no one would be a guest or visitor.

As Muhammad's followers eagerly shared ideas for the new center, they realized the building needed a special system to call people to congregate. Abu Ayyub suggested using a shofar, but others argued it would confuse Medina's Jews, who blew it only on special occasions. 'Abdur-Rahman suggested using bells, but others rejected them as too church-like. Hamzah suggested drums, but those traditionally called people into battle. After several hours of discussion, Muhammad suggested they revisit the topic the following day.

The next morning, when the group reassembled at the date facility, 'Umar suddenly spoke up to reveal a peculiar dream he'd had the night before that had featured a man calling out in a melodious voice. 'Abdullah Ibn Zaid—a Medinian elder who had been among the delegation at 'Aqabah—disclosed that he too had a similar dream. 'Umar suggested that having a person call people together would humanize the community gathering. Medina had unleashed 'Umar's creativity, as he enjoyed a fresh start in a new city where people did not immediately dismiss him as a boorish thug. He revealed to the group a composition for the caller to use:

Allahu akbar.
The Loving Divine is the most empowering source of all creation.

Ash-hadu al-la ilaha illallah.
I bear witness that the Loving Divine (Allah) is one and unique.

Ash-hadu anna Muhammadar-rasulullah.
I bear witness that Muhammad is a channeling guide (*rasul*) on
    the path toward the Loving Divine.

Hayya 'alas-Salah!
Hasten with a focused mind to reestablish broken connections!

Hayya 'alal-falah!
Hasten with a mind focused on the tools for success!

Allahu akbar.
The Loving Divine is the most empowering source of all creation.

La Ilaha Illallah.
The Loving Divine is one and unique.

'Umar's call to action captivated the group and would become known as the *athan* (proclamation—literally, that which perks up the ears). It called on people to improve themselves and be present to maximize the moment.

The *athan* referred to Muhammad's function as a *rasul* (messenger—literally, irrigation channel). He could do more than simply arbitrate in emergencies; he could channel energy into action, pushing the people of Medina to strive for greatness. 'Umar knew firsthand the value of such coaching: Muhammad had been the only person to see potential in him. Appropriately, the *athan* would go on to become a staple of Muslim societies.

Although several men, including 'Ali, volunteered for the position of *mu'athin* (proclaimer), Muhammad tapped Bilal, who was known for his melodious and resonant voice. The choice met with resistance; Bilal had a thick Abyssinian accent and could not pronounce Arabic correctly. When several of Muhammad's disciples protested that Bilal "massacred the language," Muhammad insisted, "None but Bilal will have this honor!" Elevating a foreign formerly enslaved man with poor Arabic pronunciation to the esteemed position of community announcer reinforced the egalitarian ethos of Medina's new social order by example.

Over the next month, people from all the city's clans helped erect the building, with many working together for the first time. Everyone volunteered their time, and all materials were donated.

The *masjid* quickly began to take shape. They built the roof from wooden beams made of palm trunks; at the rear was a raised platform (*suffah*) covered with a palm-leaf portico that housed the shelter and soup kitchen. Every day volunteers would prepare porridge to serve to the hungry. The building had no separate women's entrance or section, and women circulated freely throughout the building. The structure's lack of doors meant that even dogs, cats, and goats often wandered in. The Banu Najjar built Muhammad a pulpit to stand on when he addressed the people, with three steps rising up to a small square platform and carved motifs evoking Qur'anic imagery of blossoming vines, stars, the moon, and sun.

After the *masjid* was completed, Muhammad revealed a new Qur'anic passage to honor the occasion:

> *Lamasjidun ussisa 'alat-taqwa min awwali yawmin ahaqqu an taquma fih.*
>
> Certainly, a place of grounding (*masjid*) rooted from the first day in action-filled hope is a most worthy base upon which you can establish an effective society.

The Medinians' cooperation had led to the creation of a special new home. The passage evoked *asas*, a plant's deep foundational roots, as well as *taqwa*, the rope pulled to draw water from a well. To achieve their goals of a unified and redeemed community, the people of Medina needed to ground their hope in action.

The *masjid* moved the nucleus of Yathrib to the city's old southern limits. Muhammad, who had continued to refer to the city as Yathrib—even using that term in the text of the constitution—began to refer to the area around the community center as al-Medina (the new town). And he had big plans for it. In old Yathrib, each clan had operated its own neighborhood market with its own tariffs. In the new Medina, Muhammad invited local merchants from all the clans and social classes to set up their stalls and build permanent shops around the *masjid*, including along the building's outer wall. No one needed elite connections to open a stall. Soon, he hoped, people would build homes around the bustling central market, living together, rather than in enclaves, for the first time.

To encourage cooperation, Muhammad took his followers out to the surrounding fields to meet with the farmers by the well that had nearly started a civil war five months earlier. Medina, Muhammad had observed, lacked a system to ensure farmers received equal access to water for their fields. At his instruction, wooden channels—*rusl* (like his role of *rasul*)—were built to guide water to each grove, with one main channel from the central well feeding canals that ran to each field. The farmers would raise small gated dikes blocking each side channel for specific and consistent periods of time, feeding an equal amount of water to each orchard and field. (Some of Muhammad's canals in Medina's suburbs remain in operation today and can still be seen at Wadi Al-Khanaq.)

Next, he focused on sanitation: *At-tahuru shatrul-iman* (cleanliness/purity is half of security/faith). Just as Muhammad stressed to his followers the importance of proper hygiene, he insisted that a city needed to be clean in order to prosper. His first public efforts began when several butchers sought to open stalls at the new central market beside the *masjid*. Muhammad insisted that the market not lead to blood flowing through the streets and instead designated a special zone for butchers outside the market and away from nearby plants and trees, as he did not want fruiting trees contaminated by blood. Once the meat dried, the butchers were welcome to sell it at the market. The butchers' precinct marked the first designated zoning in Arabia.

Keeping Medina clean, Muhammad argued, was the responsibility of all citizens. He declared, "Removing waste from the path is an act of charity." Every time he walked through the market, he stopped to pick up garbage, setting an example that residents began to emulate. In the old Yathrib order, people would throw their refuse onto the street, signaling a lack of investment in public spaces. Muhammad's mindset, in contrast, emphasized respecting the community and the rights of others. Whatever values one applied at home one should apply throughout Medina's urban environment.

People from across Medinian society came to study in the *masjid*, where Muhammad liked to remind students: "Don't be an *imma'ah*," coining a new word.

"What is an *imma'ah*?" people asked.

He explained the word as a contraction of *anna ma'ak* (I'll do whatever you do.) It represented an attitude of blindly copying other people's behavior rather than thinking for oneself and adhering to one's own principles. "Ground yourselves!" he counseled, playing on the concept of the *masjid* as a place of grounding. "Even if other people choose to be irresponsible, be responsible yourself."

Muhammad's message not only improved Medina's sanitation and public health infrastructure, it also prepared the people of Medina for the future, when they would need to stick to their principles in the face of enormous challenges.

❖ ❖ ❖

As Medina's arbitrator, inspirational speaker, and sole prophet, Muhammad accumulated a vast amount of power. While he called on the people of Medina to uphold principles, he, too, guarded himself against corruption, vanity, and rash judgment. To ground himself, Muhammad made it a habit to sweep the *masjid* every morning. He also donated his entire wardrobe of exquisite robes, keeping one white tunic—a gift from Khadijah—that began to fray with constant use. Abu Bakr and several others offered Muhammad new garments to wear, but he insisted on patching his tattering tunic.

Once, while walking in the new market, he came upon his friend Nu'aiman, who was flirting with a group of young women. "These women are helping me find my missing camel," Nu'aiman explained. Muhammad laughed and continued his stroll.

The next day, he asked Nu'aiman, "Did you find your missing camel?"

Sheepishly, Nu'aiman admitted, "I never had a camel. I just felt ashamed because I try to be a good person when I am around you but feel hypocritical when I cannot remain consistent in your absence." Muhammad tenderly patted Nu'aiman's shoulder and smiled sympathetically.

Shortly after, as Muhammad sat teaching at the *masjid*, a pagan nomad wandered into the main courtyard and began urinating. Angry students rushed at him, yet Muhammad intervened, saying, "Let him finish." After the nomad had relieved himself, Muhammad instructed his students to wash away the urine. He took the man aside and said, "My dear friend, this is a public place used for prayer and assembly. It is not the proper place for what you have done."

Another time, just as Muhammad finished one of his public lectures, a single young woman stood up and begged him, "Marry me!" Muhammad quickly glanced away and asked the assembled crowd, "Is there anyone here willing to marry this young woman?" A man stood up to volunteer. Then Muhammad asked the woman, "Would you marry this young man?" She agreed, and Muhammad officiated their marriage on the spot. Muhammad wanted to send a clear signal that he had no interest in abusing his power or personally benefiting from adoration.

To balance his esteemed position in society, Muhammad made sure to mingle with common people by spending time in the new market outside the walls of the *masjid*. For the first time, products once sold in disparate parts of the city could be purchased in one place. Buyers appreciated the convenience and the savings that came with more competitive pricing. Merchants and artisans from across clans exchanged goods, creating momentum for a thriving economy.

Yet Muhammad began to realize that wealthy elites monopolized even this more unified and diverse marketplace. While market stalls were equally divided plots and apportioned on a first-come, first-served basis, the beneficiaries were primarily established merchants. Poorer people lacked basic opportunities because they lacked capital to buy materials or inventory. Newcomers like Suhaib, whose entire wealth had been confiscated as he fled Mecca, had skills but no capital. Many locals shared their concerns that wealthy merchants dominated the market. The market needed a structural solution. Muhammad glanced at scaffolding being used to repair cracks in the *masjid*'s wall and had a vision.

Late one afternoon, farmers working their fields heard Bilal chanting from the *masjid*'s tower, calling people to congregate for an assembly that did not match the usual prayer times. As people entered the *masjid*, they saw Muhammad standing patiently on his pulpit. Once the room filled, he chanted a new revelation:

> *Was-sama`a rafa`aha wa wadha`al-mizan,*
> The universe was established upon a system of balance,

> *Al-la tatghaw fil-mizan.*
> So remain vigilant and do not corrupt the system of balance.

> *Wa aqimul-wazna bil-qist wa la tukhsirul-mizan.*
> Make a conscious effort to set up systems to maintain that
>   equilibrium and beware of upsetting the natural balance.

After he finished chanting, Muhammad explained the significance of the revelation in his own words: "Just as the universe is established upon a system of balance, the wealthy possess extra funds that can help uplift the underprivileged." The people themselves had to carry out God's will to rebalance society, with everyone of means giving part of their extra funds to assist those less fortunate improve their economic situation. Muhammad redefined poverty as an inaccessibility of opportunity.

After the sermon, a man stood up in the *masjid* courtyard and declared, "I am poor—am I eligible to receive assistance?"

Muhammad sized up the man before replying, "You seem fit and healthy. Do you have an axe to cut down deadwood in the forest to sell in the market?" When the man replied in the affirmative, Muhammad said, "Then you are not poor."

Another man stood up and said, "I'm not strong and I cannot chop wood to sell."

Muhammad asked, "Do you have family and friends who can loan you money to buy cheese to sell in the market?" When the man replied in the affirmative, Muhammad said, "Then you are not poor."

People capable of using their talents and network to lift themselves up would not receive financing. To put his abstract policy into practice, Muhammad appointed Bilal treasurer of a new fund. Bilal walked through the crowd with his tunic raised to form a pocket to accept contributions. The men in the courtyard held back, less than eager to part with their coins. A crowd of women saw the men's hesitance and surged forward to donate their jewelry. Thus a group of spirited women made possible Medina's first public fund. A brick cabinet built in the center of the *masjid* courtyard stored the funds awaiting distribution.

The people of Medina needed a new term for this unprecedented approach to investing. While building the *masjid's* walls and roofs, they had used scaffolding to reach higher levels. These omnipresent raised platforms, known as *zakah*, became a powerful metaphor to describe Muhammad's plan to enhance market opportunity. A new *surah*, Al-Baqarah (The Magnificent Impact), the Qur'an's longest chapter, introduced the concept:

> *Wa atuz-Zakata wa ma tuqaddimu li'anfusikum min khairin*
> *tajiduhu 'indallah.*
> Establish systems of equal opportunity and remember that
>   whatever you institute to empower others will be enriched and
>   blessed by the Loving Divine.

Zakah described a complex process of helping people of lesser means achieve equality. The Qur'anic verse pointedly used the verb *to exchange* (*ita*) rather than *to give* (*i'ta*). An exchange of funds was not charity but rather an investment with benefit to the provider, the receiver, and society as a whole.

In a subsequent revelation—later added to Surah At-Tawbah (The Restoration)—the Qur'an outlined eight categories of people among whom *zakah* funds should be equally divided:

- ❖ *Al-fuqara*: the poor who had less than they needed to survive day to day
- ❖ *Al-masakin*: the disadvantaged who had enough day to day but not week to week
- ❖ *Al-'amilina 'alaiha*: the administrators collecting and distributing the *zakah* funds
- ❖ *Al-mu'allafati qulubuhum*: those suffering from trauma
- ❖ *Fir-riqab*: the enslaved and prisoners of war (for their liberation and support)
- ❖ *Al-gharimina*: those weighed down by overwhelming debt
- ❖ *Fi sabilillah*: any civic project that improves society
- ❖ *Ibnis-sabil*: travelers and refugees

In short, the beneficiaries of *zakah* were people most at risk of becoming enslaved: those lacking funds might have to sell themselves or relatives into bondage. Abductors often preyed upon vulnerable individuals without powerful families to protect them.

Under Bilal's direction, the process of gathering *zakah* funds was institutionalized, with a group of volunteers from diverse clans who routinely canvassed the city in pairs. Muhammad set clear guidelines for *zakah* to ensure that no contributions to the fund disadvantaged the investors. He outlined a suggested contribution level of only 2.5 percent (described with the fraction "1 in 40") of a household's extra savings, money that had been set aside for at least one lunar year (a period known as *hawalan-ul-hawl*). In addition, long-term savings that did not reach a minimum level (*nisab*) were exempt from *zakah*. *Zakah* was voluntary. In keeping with Muhammad's mindset, a person had to choose to invest.

Shortly after Medina instituted *zakah*, a wealthy merchant on his deathbed called for Muhammad. "I want you to be the trustee of my wealth, which I will donate in its entirety," he revealed.

Muhammad smiled at the gesture but declined the opportunity, suggesting instead that he bequeath the bulk of his estate to his children. "It is far better that you leave your children comfortable than for them to be left poor and a burden on society," he explained. When the man insisted on donating half of his wealth, Muhammad only partially relented, agreeing to accept a charitable contribution of one-third—establishing a principle in Islamic law that limits charitable donations to a maximum of one-third of an estate.

The underlying objective of *zakah* was to encourage wealth to circulate and fuel the economy rather than stagnate in the vaults of the affluent. In keeping with the Qur'an's emphasis on *yusr* (societal flow), new investment funds helped drive market activity. The wealthy helped the poor become self-sufficient, and they in turn supported the wealthy as empowered new consumers. *Zakah* effectively created the first middle class in Arabia.

To help emphasize the importance of employment, Muhammad encouraged business owners to create new jobs, even if they were not vital. "Commission the digging of a ditch, then the resealing of that same hole, if only to provide employment," he advised. Unemployment, in Muhammad's understanding, was a key economic gauge, with public works as a quick way to jump-start the process of raising people from idleness into a state of activity.

Ironically, women, who in Arabian society were required to remain at home, were some of the first to fully grasp this revolutionary concept (as demonstrated by their initial enthusiasm for donating to the *zakah* funds). Like the enslaved and other minorities, women suffered greatly from biases and unequal access. Women without a male provider, such as widows and orphans, were blocked from economic opportunities, and many fell into prostitution, one of the few options available. But Muhammad had heard stories of his unusual great-grandmother Salma, who, despite being a widow, carried out legendary business deals in Yathrib's markets. Surely, he thought, the women of Medina could follow in her footsteps.

Zakah funds therefore were used to teach at-risk women professional skills, like carpet weaving, sewing, carpentry, and even mercantile essentials. Once they had received basic training, the women had access to capital for starting their businesses and reserved spots in Medina's new market. Muhammad managed to eliminate prostitution in Medina by reintegrating these women into society. He also helped them find husbands to begin their own families.

With the wheels of the open market lubricated by *zakah*, Medina began to live up to its name as a place of flowing change—with benefits far exceeding mere financial progress.

❖ ❖ ❖

Mecca reacted with horror at Medina's success. After receiving news of Medina's new constitution, the elders sought to hinder Muhammad's civic project. 'Amr ibn Hisham suggested that the Meccans adopt a policy of harassment rather than an open declaration of war. They wanted to make the Yathribites reconsider their support of Muhammad without provoking the wrath of a much larger city.

The Meccans decided to hire small bands of nomadic raiders to harass shepherds and farmers on the outskirts of Medina. Realizing, once again, that he could not take his or his followers' safety for granted, Muhammad set up a network of scouts to sound the alarm about any approaching marauders.

Secure and prosperous, residents inside Medina celebrated Muhammad's first year as leader with a bountiful harvest. Heavier than average rainfall had left the city flush with extra produce, water, and wealth. Yet Muhammad's experience in Damascus had taught him that crops can fail overnight, with swarms of locusts wiping out entire fields in hours. He also often recited Surah Yusuf, with its reminder of how Joseph had planned ahead during years of plenty in preparation for an extended drought. At Muhammad's direction, Medina constructed five new cisterns to capture and store excess rainwater. Residents built new communal granaries as a reserve for the entire city, positioning them strategically amid the orchards so that the trees could block the sun and keep the contents cool. The city also stored dried dates and fruits for emergency use.

Now that Medina had political, economic, and security systems in place, people increasingly focused on social issues. The Qur'an reflects the stream of questions directed at Muhammad on diverse personal and communal topics during this period. The phrase *yas'alunak* (They ask you) began many verses, before declaring the iconic *Qul* (Respond to them). Issues included:

❖ Women's rights—*Yas'alunaka 'anin-nisa* (They ask you about the rights of women)

❖ Women's bodies—*Yas'alunaka 'anil-mahidh* (They ask you about menstruation)

❖ Inheritance—*Yas'alunaka 'anil-kalalah* (They ask you about inheritance)

❖ Social issues—*Yas'alunaka 'anil-yatama* (They ask you about the rights of orphans)

❖ Religious interpretation—*Yas'alunaka 'anir-Ruh* (They ask you about the Spirit)

❖ Tracking time—*Yas'alunaka 'anil-ahillah* (They ask you about the new moons)

Rampant gambling and intoxication were of growing concern to the community. People imbibed wine, an integral part of Arabian culture, throughout the day, and only a few nonconformists like Muhammad and Abu Bakr abstained. Excessive drinking led to many social ills, including domestic violence, squandering one's wealth, and public indecency. The Qur'an responded to popular concerns, primarily expressed by Medina's women:

Yas'lunaka 'anil khamri wal-maysiri.
They ask you about wine and gambling.

> *Qul fihima ithmun kabiruw-wa manafi'u lin-nas wa ithmuhuma*
> *akbaru min naf'ihima.*
> Inform them that these are both very harmful and beneficial, yet
> their harm far outweighs their benefit.

In response to people wobbling into the *masjid* in a drunken state, the Qur'an reemphasized the point: "Don't come to prayers and community meetings drunk; wait until you sober up and know what you are saying." As more residents began to limit their drinking late in the evening in order to awake sober for morning prayers, drinking became less socially acceptable as a recreational activity.

After a gradual detox process that lasted over a year, the Qur'an further revised its guidance for a receptive community: "Truly, intoxicants and gambling degrade and constrain your abilities, so avoid them in order to succeed!" Many Medinians, particularly women, poured their household's excess wine into the streets in a gesture of communal rehabilitation. The Jews of Medina, who had maintained their own religious traditions, continued to drink wine for religious ceremonies, yet even they saw drinking recede as an accepted social pastime. The ever-jolly Nu'aiman, however, could not kick the habit. When 'Umar berated him for frequent drinking, Muhammad defended his companion: "Don't curse him, for he loves God and is beloved to God."

A great drought devastated Arabia. No rain fell for an entire year, with an extended heat wave drying up the residue of the previous year's plentiful rains. Famine broke out across the region as harvests failed, and animals began to weaken from a lack of food. Mecca, set in one of the hottest parts of Arabia, with no resources of its own, was hit hard. As months went by without rain, farmers began hoarding their reserve produce rather than selling it. Wealth was useless as the market dried up.

The earth grew parched and dust storms descended on Mecca, coating the city with a red, hazy film. Famished residents wandered about in a daze, with some scavenging whatever seemed edible. In a twist of fate, the Meccans became like the Hashemites during the boycott, barely scraping by. Even the wealthy of Mecca suffered.

Medina, in contrast, had reserves of grains, dates, and water. The city thrived despite the drought, which only enhanced Muhammad's reputation as an outstanding leader. Employing a form of *zakah*, Muhammad organized the people of Medina to donate emergency relief for Mecca. He sent 'Uthman with a caravan of two hundred camels packed with grains and dried dates to help ease the Meccans' suffering. When 'Uthman's caravan arrived near the Ka'bah, the Meccans looked upon it like a mirage. The Banu Umayyah greeted their relative, who had specific instructions from Muhammad to grant the elders the honor of distributing the food aid. Muhammad hoped the elders would accept the supplies as a peace offering. The Dar-un-Nadwah assembly, however, was furious about having to accept the vital supplies, perceiving it as a public relations stunt to undermine the council.

One month after the provisions reached Mecca, the rains returned with a vengeance. The Meccans, liberated from months of suffering, responded with excessive feasting. Back in Medina, however, Muhammad urged residents to remain modest and take nothing for granted. At this time, a new Qur'anic revelation reminded the Medinians: "Eat and drink, but do not waste." Residents were encouraged to direct their celebratory energies toward improving society, not simply feasting.

The impetus toward community service came, in part, from the plight of one of Muhammad's top students in Medina, an enslaved Persian named Rozbeh (fortunate). Born to a noble family, he became a Zoroastrian priest at sixteen, only to be captured during battle by Byzantine soldiers and sold in the slave market of Damascus. There the archbishop purchased him and, impressed by the young man's potential, freed him to become a Christian monk. While on a missionary journey in northern Arabia, poor Rozbeh was captured yet again, this time by the notorious Ghifar marauders (Abu Thar's clan). Sold into slavery at Yathrib, Rozbeh became fascinated by his new master's Jewish faith and began studying in his free time with Rabbi Mukhairiq.

Muhammad met the young man in Mukhairiq's home and marveled at Rozbeh's dynamism. He assigned 'Ali to mentor him and renamed him Salman (one who seeks to complete himself). Eventually Muhammad brought up the question of Salman's ongoing servitude. "Why not discuss emancipation with your master?" he suggested. Salman did, and his master agreed to free him in exchange for planting an entire orchard of date palms as payment—on the stipulation Salman would do this during his time off. Inspired, Muhammad gathered his followers to help plant the orchard in just one day, thus securing Salman's liberation in a fraction of the time it would otherwise have taken.

The project illustrated the value of people donating a bit of their free time to work for the public good. Shortly thereafter, a new revelation came to codify the concept of setting aside time for service, linking it to setting aside time from eating and drinking:

> Kutiba 'alaikumus-siyam kama kutiba 'alallathina min qablikum la'allakum tattaqun.
> Fasting while sharing your time in the service of others is
>   recommended just as it was prescribed for those before you in
>   order to achieve a state of action-filled hope.

The verse introduced a new concept called *siyam*, which was derived from the word *sawm* (dividing a loaf of bread), used by Jews and Christians to refer to fasting. The Qur'an took the ancient tradition and introduced a new practice: taking action while fasting to benefit society. Muhammad instructed Medinians, who had just survived a great famine and shared resources with sworn enemies, to engage in a communal fast from dawn until dusk and reallocate time otherwise used for preparing meals to share their talents with others. *Sawm* taught Medinians how to conserve both food and time.

While an individual could practice *sawm* at any time, the Qur'an set aside a specific month for its application on a communal level. To mark the fifteenth anniversary of the Qur'an's first revelation, Muhammad designated the lunar month of Ramadhan (scorching heat) as a time for service and fasting: "The month of Ramadhan is when the Qur'an was first revealed as a guiding source providing all people with direction and purpose."

One week before Ramadhan started, Muhammad enjoyed a special family celebration: the marriage of his youngest daughter, Fatimah, to 'Ali. After Fatimah turned eighteen, Abu Bakr, as Muhammad's oldest friend, had offered to marry the young woman—a traditional sign of affection between close friends in Arabian culture. After Muhammad demurred that his daughter was still too young, 'Umar made the same offer and got the same response. The moment Fatimah turned nineteen, Muhammad announced her betrothal to 'Ali. The two had grown up together in the same home, and Muhammad knew that they had long been in love. He stipulated, however, that their marriage contract include a clause that 'Ali remain monogamous—although polygamy was common across Arabia.

Back in Mecca the elders were scheming. They felt humiliated at having to accept Muhammad's food aid and sought to end "the Muhammad problem" once and for all. The elders needed an excuse to rally people against Muhammad and instigate a direct military confrontation. In classic form, 'Amr ibn Hisham suggested a solution: relaunch the smear campaign, this time directed at what Meccans valued most.

"Muhammad is planning to attack the great caravan en route to Damascus," the elders announced outside the Ka'bah—ironically accusing Muhammad of what they themselves had perpetrated against Medina for two years. Fearing their fortunes were at risk, the city's inhabitants forgot Muhammad's kindness of just a few months earlier and quickly prepared for battle with cries of *"U'lu Hubal!"* (Rise up and show your greatness, oh Hubal!). The chant invoked Mecca's chief deity and marked a public declaration that the Meccans were now waging a religious war against Muhammad as an apostate who dared challenge the authority of the gods.

Hundreds of warriors from allied clans began converging on Mecca. As Medina had no army, the Meccan elders anticipated a quick and easy victory. Their plan was to besiege Medina and issue an ultimatum to the city's elders: hand over Muhammad, along with his Meccan followers, or face invasion. The Meccans assumed the Medinians would not risk pillage to protect a foreigner. For many of Mecca's elite families, the siege was also a chance to reclaim their wayward sons.

Muhammad's uncle Al-'Abbas, a pagan who had never left Mecca, was conscripted into the army. Just as the soldiers departed Mecca to march toward Medina, Al-'Abbas secretly dispatched a desert guide to deliver an urgent message to his nephew with a warning about the impending invasion. After Abu Talib's death, Al-'Abbas had assumed responsibility for their father's dying request to safeguard Muhammad. The warning was all Al-'Abbas could do to help as the situation rapidly escalated.

Unaware of the warriors charging toward their city, the people of Me-

roads, improving the irrigation system, and patching the houses of im-

exempt from participating in the fast. At sunset, residents gathered for

communal break fasts celebrating a day of hard work for mutual benefit.

The people of Medina had been celebrating for seven days when a

lone horseman raced into the city. As Bilal called the people for evening

prayer, the messenger arrived at the *masjid*, dismounted in a panic, and

ran into the courtyard, pushing people aside to reach Muhammad. Mu-

hammad had just eaten a date after twelve hours of fasting and commu-

nity service. The smile of contentment on his face quickly faded as the

want to upset the crowd around him, so he regained his composure and

As the Medinians enjoyed their dinner, Muhammad turned over the

news in his mind. A large Meccan army was fewer than ten days away.

Both his life and the lives of all the people around him were at risk. But

what could he do? Muhammad had spent the past fifteen years preach-

ing principled nonviolence, and he had no military experience. Yet, if he

8

THE ULTIMATE TEST

The Wells of Badr: 4:00 p.m., Monday, March 12, 624 CE

The elderly nomad and his sons hurriedly watered their flocks at the wells. An army from Mecca was heading north toward Medina and could be passing through the sleepy village of Badr at any moment. The nomads worried that the fighters might commandeer their sheep. Scanning the horizon for any signs of trouble, the old man suddenly tensed as two dark figures with covered faces approached on camelback.

As the riders drew closer, the elder noted their fine black tunics, embroidered with silver thread, and their unusual black headdresses. The nomads, who had never seen such exotic garb, were both bewildered by the strangers and relieved the riders were not Meccan military scouts. The mysterious men dismounted to allow their camels to drink.

Unveiling their faces, the middle-aged men approached the nomads. When the elder inquired from whence they came, the strangers responded in an odd Arabic dialect, "We are from Ma`!" The Ma` were an ancient Arabian clan in Mesopotamia. The riders' fine garb and silver jewelry indicated they were merchants on their way to Mecca—hardly a threat.

Wells in Arabia functioned as both literal and figurative watering holes: a place to quench thirst and exchange information. The taller of the two strangers began to make small talk, asking for directions to Yemen and then inquiring about the nomads' breeds of sheep and goats. "I was a shepherd in my youth," he revealed.

Proud that the stranger appreciated the quality of his flock, the elder further let down his guard. So, when the stranger mentioned rumors of a looming clash in the area, the elder offered him a bit of news. "Yes," he confirmed. "You refer to the Meccans and Muhammad."

"Who is this Muhammad?" the stranger inquired. He asked the elder about the location and size of the forces, so that he might stay out of their way.

The shepherd responded, "I cannot say for certain, but if the one who told me was correct, then the Meccans should be due south at the village of Al-Abwa, and Muhammad should be at Qiba."

In response to the news, the two strangers noted they should hurry on. Thanking the elder, they mounted their camels and soon disappeared around the mountain that loomed over the wells. On the other side of the mountain, the two riders encountered a small army of 312 men. A muscular figure clad in armor rode toward them. With an anxious look, he asked, "What news, oh Muhammad?"

The two men from Ma` were in fact Muhammad and Abu Bakr—and the armored knight was Muhammad's uncle Hamzah. The pair had sought vital intelligence on the arrival of the Meccan forces and had no way to obtain that information without giving away their own location. Muhammad did not want to lie and instead turned to subterfuge. A clan named Ma` (water) indeed lived in Mesopotamia. Telling the elder nomad *"Nahnu mim-Ma`"* (We are from water) was technically true, as humans, according to the Qur`an, are created from water.

"The Meccans will arrive before dusk," said Muhammad, using his years of experience on the caravans to calculate how quickly the attackers were closing in. "We must move fast and block their access to the wells."

Muhammad's undercover reconnaissance mission had also yielded the valuable intelligence that his own force's movements remained un-detected. The locals assumed he was still farther north, in the village of Qiba outside Medina. Instead, he had used the cover of night to lead his ragtag band of men to the outskirts of Badr, a small oasis along the caravan route.

While Muhammad strategized, the Meccans' tactic was straightforward. They knew many of Medina's men were away on caravan business, leaving the city largely unprotected. The Meccans would besiege Medina and deliver an ultimatum: turn over Muhammad or else. Ever conscious of appearances in the greater Arabian society, the Meccans did not want to come off as aggressors but rather as peacemakers demanding justice. Muhammad, according to the propaganda devised by the Meccan elders, had threatened their caravans. They had no quarrel with the Medinians.

The impending assault from Mecca had forced Muhammad to the ultimate test. For much of his life, he had taken months and even years to gather information, and carefully analyze it, taking action only after measured contemplation. The looming attack, however, meant Muhammad had just a few days to determine how to respond to a new challenge.

To defend his people, he had to make painful compromises on some of his most cherished principles. Subterfuge was not a noble form of human conduct—nor was violence. But in this crisis, both could help save lives and prevent greater devastation.

To offset his significant numeric disadvantage, Muhammad resolved to do the opposite of whatever the Meccans anticipated. While his small band of farmers and merchants lacked the weaponry and experience of the Meccan warriors, his troops had the element of surprise on their side. The Meccans would not expect an ambush by the wells of Badr. Even as the vastly superior Meccan army appeared on the horizon—the setting sun illuminating their long lances amid a massive dust cloud—Muhammad calmed his concerned followers. Turning to Hamzah, he observed, *"Al-harbu khidaj"* (War is won with strategy).

❖ ❖ ❖

Several days earlier, Muhammad had begun to prepare his followers for the fight of their lives. When the messenger from Al-'Abbas had interrupted the Ramadhan break fast to warn of an impending Meccan attack, Muhammad had initially kept the news to himself so that his followers might sleep peacefully. But the following morning, as he and his followers sat in a circle enjoying a predawn breakfast of dates and fresh milk, Muhammad shared a new revelation:

> *Uthina lillathina yuqataluna bi`annahum qad thulimu.*
> Permission is granted to those who are attacked, because they have
>   been greatly oppressed.

His followers were shocked. Ever since Muhammad's prophetic mission began fifteen years earlier, he had consistently maintained a philosophy of nonviolence, even forbidding self-defense. This new revelation reflected more nuanced thinking: while the Divine did not condone violence, in extreme cases self-defense was permissible. Even then, the verse did not include the implied words *to defend themselves*.

Muhammad then shared with his followers what the messenger had reported the previous evening: the Meccans were heading toward Medina to annihilate them. Muhammad sought advice about how to address the threat. Several people suggested taking shelter in Medina's small storage forts to defend the city guerrilla-style. But Muhammad refused to endanger the city's civilians and insisted on facing death in the open, in keeping with Arabian customs of valor.

But Muhammad explained that he did not want to press his followers to fight, as it was his head the Meccans were after. One by one, his followers placed their hands on his right shoulder and swore an oath: "We would sacrifice ourselves in your stead!" Abu Bakr added: "Go and fight under the protection of God. We will be there ahead of you!"

Bolstered by their resolve, Muhammad appointed his uncle Hamzah to head the fighting force. A valiant hunter known for wrestling lions, Hamzah had the most fighting experience. Though many of Medina's men were away on the caravan trip to Damascus, Hamzah managed to recruit a force of 314 for the defensive expedition, supported by twenty female nurses headed by Barakah. The group pooled their money to purchase weapons and quickly forge new arms.

Muhammad's one relevant skill was archery, which he had learned as a teenage shepherd to ward off eagles swooping down to seize defenseless lambs. He had never shot an arrow at humans or fought in battle, yet he began an emergency training program for the recruits. Joined by a group of Banu Najjar carpenters, Muhammad and Abu Ayyub quickly shaped bows and arrows. A local Jewish blacksmith forged a suit of armor for Muhammad. After three days of preparation and training, the army headed out on foot with sacks of food that many of Medina's families had donated. A cavalry of two horsemen accompanied the motley crew.

The army set out after nightfall, first making its way to Qiba. Muhammad kept their destination a secret except for a small group of core followers.

Two days later, the Medinian army reached the wells of Badr at dawn, before the shepherds arrived to water their flocks. The army hid behind a ridge on the opposite side of the mountain. Muhammad knew from his caravan days that the Meccans would stop at Badr to replenish their water supplies before the final push to Medina. He would surprise them there, choosing advantageous topography a safe distance from Medina.

During strategy sessions, Salman had shared a Persian military technique of dragging objects behind horses and camels to raise extra dust and give the illusion of a large force.

As Muhammad's army of 314 volunteers sped toward Badr's wells, they kicked up a large cloud of dust. Local nomads assumed Muhammad's army was in the thousands and rushed off to spread the news that Muhammad's massive force had seemingly flown from Qiba [eighty-five miles away] in a matter of hours! Muhammad understood that his only path to victory was using a psychological stratagem.

Muhammad's army quickly secured the higher terrain and set up their defensive line in front of the wells. From his tent set near the mountaintop Muhammad surveyed the terrain. The echo of enemy drums and singing thundered from the distance. Soon the Meccan army appeared on the horizon, silhouetted by the setting sun. Their lances carried the symbols of tribal deities and were adorned with the feathers of eagles, falcons, and ostriches.

The Meccans set up camp for the night and sent their young cooks ahead to search for water in the darkness. 'Umar captured one adolescent cook during a patrol and brought him back to the Medinian camp for interrogation. 'Umar grew impatient as the terrified boy struggled to provide an accurate head count for the Meccan army. When 'Umar began to slap him, Muhammad quickly intervened. He gently asked, "How many camels do you butcher and roast each day?"

"Ten," the boy responded. Muhammad turned to 'Umar. "They are about a thousand men." He knew that each camel typically fed about one hundred men. (In fact, there were 1,070 soldiers in the Meccan army.) Despite 'Umar's protests, Muhammad ordered the boy released and allowed to return to the Meccan camp, explaining that the cook was a noncombatant who could not be treated as an enemy.

That evening, after praying together, Muhammad's followers looked out at the Meccans' many fires and listened to the strains of music and laughter. As if on a hunting party, the Meccans had brought along musicians, dancers, and prostitutes. Indeed, they intended to return home with the heads of Muhammad and his top followers as trophies to be hung over Mecca's main gateway.

During the night, heavy rainfall caused flash floods that sent mudslides down toward the Meccan camp. As dawn broke, the hungover Meccans awoke to an eerie sound. The call to prayer and resonating chants of Muhammad's followers echoed like phantoms across the mountains. Though it was the seventeenth day of Ramadhan, Muhammad insisted that his followers refrain from fasting and eat a light meal of dates and vegetables. The fighters assembled to the rhythm of pounding drums.

The morning fell on the fifteenth anniversary of Muhammad's first revelation atop Mount Hira. This was hardly the way he intended to celebrate the occasion. He wore a black turban, symbolizing mourning over the impending confrontation, and stood between two flag bearers hoisting black-and-white banners, symbols of balance. Aggression and war were an imbalance in the natural order, and Muhammad signaled that he fought only because the Medinians had no other option.

While the Medinians stood at attention, waiting for the Meccans to line up for battle, Muhammad reminded them that they were fighting to defend themselves and not to seek vengeance. To kill when furious, he explained, was murder. He then divided his small force into five groups of sixty and instructed the flanks to rotate when they heard beating drums. This method allowed them to take breaks from the front line and make the Meccans think reinforcements were constantly emerging. A group of three hundred fighters would appear five times larger, seemingly outnumbering the Meccans.

Muhammad also instructed his men not to speak during the battle, breaking with the Arabian tradition of screaming to terrify opponents. After assuring his troops that they were in the right and would be victorious, he returned to his elevated vantage point, surrounded by fourteen men chosen for their speed who would convey his commands to the army below. When the Meccans finally assembled, they were struck by the still, organized lines of Muhammad's army standing in complete silence.

The top elder of Mecca and head of the army, 'Utbah, walked out accompanied by his son Al-Walid and brother Shaibah. In the Arabian martial tradition, these three challenged their opponents to an opening duel. Three Medinian men stepped forward to meet them. 'Utbah dismissed them, saying, "These are not our social equals! Send out our equals from our people!" Muhammad instructed his uncle Hamzah and cousins 'Ali and 'Ubaidah to step forward.

During this initial duel, 'Utbah and his son died, and Shaibah was injured. The death of Mecca's chief elder was a bad omen for the superstitious Meccans.

In the sudden leadership void, 'Amr ibn Hisham declared himself chief elder and stirred the army to attack en masse. With no clear strategy, the Meccans struggled to move forward, because the mud slicks beneath their feet were impeding them. Muhammad gave the order for his archers to release their arrows, sending the Meccans into a panic and breaking their ranks. As the Meccans surged forward in chaos, Muhammad instructed his army to maintain a defensive position.

The elders of Dar-un-Nadwah led the Meccan cavalry. Most would be killed, including the great poet Al-Walid ibn Al-Mughirah; Al-'As ibn Wa'il, the man who first called Muhammad an *abtar* (a metaphorically castrated man); and Umayyah ibn Khalaf, the slave owner who had dragged Bilal across the burning sands. Two twelve-year-old boys from

Banu Najjar felled Muhammad's archnemesis, 'Amr ibn Hisham. Muhammad had forbidden children to join his force, so the boys stealthily followed the army from a distance, then hid behind rocks as the battle unfolded. Using a slingshot, they stunned 'Amr before advancing and killing him with his own sword. The Meccans, seeing their elders fall around them and Muhammad's army seemingly reinforced as the flanks rotated, broke ranks and fled in panic.

As the two-hour battle subsided, Muhammad's face showed no joy. Seventy Meccans and fourteen Medinians lay dead. Seventy Meccans were the Medinians' prisoners. Refusing to savor a remarkable victory, Muhammad solemnly ordered his men to dig two large graves. He buried his dead in one and the Meccans in another. 'Umar objected, noting that the Meccans would have mutilated the Medinians' corpses and left them to rot had they won. He also wanted to kill all the prisoners of war. Muhammad refused and asked for the prisoners not to be bound and to be given water. A new Qur'anic revelation reminded the victors to humanize their foes:

> *In kuntum ta`lamuna fa innahum ya`lamuna kama ta`lamun.*
> Remember that in the same way that you feel pain, they also feel
>   pain, so be compassionate.

The Qur'an further urged calm even though the antagonism from Mecca had turned deadly:

> *Idfa` bil-lati hiya ahsan.*
> Push away aggression with kindness and understanding.

> *Fa ithal-lathi baynaka wa baynahu `adawatun ka`annahu waliyyun*
>   *hamim.*
> If you do, a seeming antagonist can be transformed into the
>   dearest and most loyal of friends.

> *Wa ma yulaqqaha illal-lathina sabaru*
> Yet be aware that only those with maturity and foresight can
>   transform animosity into friendship

Wa ma yulaqqaha illa thu hath-thin 'athim.
And know that anyone who can achieve such a difficult task is
truly fortunate and successful.

Muhammad informed the Meccan prisoners that they could earn their freedom by teaching ten of his followers to read and write. The prisoners would stay in Medinian households that he would instruct to "dress them as you clothe your families and feed them as you feed your families." Prisoners would eat at the same table and join the Medinians when they attended classes and prayers, so they might witness the mindset in action. Muhammad devised a new code of war ethics:

✦ Remember that those who stand to fight you have families like yours; they love and are loved.
✦ Be aware that what pains you also pains them. Therefore, do not mutilate or torture an opponent.
✦ Do not kill a woman or a child or an elderly person.
✦ Do not kill someone fleeing the battlefield.
✦ If your opponent yields to peace, then accept their call to peace, for life is sacred, and the salvation of one life is like the salvation of all humanity.

The military code that Muhammad established at Badr would later include additional specific restrictions:

✦ Do not cut down fruiting trees.
✦ Do not poison waterways.
✦ Do not burn crops and grazing fields.
✦ Do not disturb noncombatant civilians and those devoted to religious worship.
✦ Do not break down the doors of civilian homes.
✦ Treat conquered people with such an unexpected standard of good character that you win their respect and loyalty.

One of Muhammad's followers asked to marry a prostitute named 'Inaq (embrace), whom the Medinians had captured from the abandoned

Meccan camp, but Muhammad refused to force the woman to marry. Instead, he released her as a civilian, with instructions to return to Mecca and inform the elders that they would have safe passage in Medina to ransom their relatives. Muhammad hoped that the woman might also report the respectful burial of Mecca's dead and the humane treatment of prisoners, which might avert the Meccans' desire for vengeance. Though the Medinians could have easily chased the defeated Meccan army, Muhammad reminded his troops that true victory lay in avoiding conflict altogether.

✵ ✵ ✵

The people of Medina waited anxiously for news of the battle, fearing the worst. Residents gathered at the city's northern pass, as they had twenty months earlier, to witness Muhammad's safe arrival.

After hours of nervous anticipation, they saw 'Ali arrive on horseback, heralding news of their victory. The rest of the volunteers followed soon after. The Medinians welcomed them with the same greeting song they had debuted twenty months earlier and once again waved palm fronds.

Amid the celebrations, an orphaned five-year-old girl approached Muhammad from the crowd and took him by the hand. Several adults tried to shoo her away, but Muhammad motioned to them not to offend her. As the pair strolled through the alleyways of Medina with the girl leading the way, the curious crowd trailed behind them. The child took Muhammad to a courtyard, where she proudly presented him with her doll. When he saw the surprise on the elders' faces, Muhammad declared, "A truly victorious community respects its elders and encourages its youth." True victory, in other words, came not on the battlefield but in meaningful encounters like this one. (Though Muhammad could not know it, his validating attitude empowered the girl; she became a scholar, and her son, Sa'id ibn al-Musayyib, would be hailed as one of Islam's greatest sages—a member of the eminent *al-fuqaha as-sab'*, the seven cardinal jurists of Medina.)

Muhammad explained to the girl that one of his daughters was ill. He asked for permission to take his leave so he might go visit her. He quickly made his way to see Ruqayyah, who was bedridden and being nursed by her husband, 'Uthman. Ruqayyah had been yanked off her camel while fleeing Mecca, causing her to miscarry. She had lost an abundance of blood and remained in decline ever since. That evening, Muhammad brought her a basket of fresh fruits and prepared a bone broth soup for her. Before departing, he placed his hand on her forehead and prayed for her, then kissed her forehead. Ruqayyah struggled to smile at her father.

Early the next morning, one of Medina's old women went to the *masjid* to sweep, as was her daily ritual. She was surprised to hear sweeping sounds from within, as it was very early and the building should have been empty. Inside, she saw Muhammad holding a broom. He did not see her, but she looked on in amazement as the victor of Badr—dressed in tattered rags, barefoot, and head lowered in contemplation—swept the floors, with dust swirling around him in the cool breeze. Then a horse and rider galloped to a stop. Turning, she watched as 'Ali quickly dismounted and ran to Muhammad. The old lady could not make out the conversation, but she saw tears roll down Muhammad's face, as he slowly dropped the broom and walked out.

Ruqayyah was dead. The blow that the Meccans had struck against her had finally proved to be fatal. She was the first daughter Muhammad had lost and the third child he would have to bury with his own hands, another sad reminder of the fragility of his bloodline.

Muhammad's eldest daughter, Zainab, had chosen to remain in Mecca with her pagan husband rather than join the *hijrah* to Yathrib. Her husband, in fact, had joined the Meccan army at Badr and been captured in battle. As the Meccans began to ransom their prisoners, Zainab sent a payment of her own to Medina: a precious necklace that had once belonged to Khadijah. When he saw the jewelry, Muhammad began to cry uncontrollably, recalling the dearly departed love of his life.

The Medinians soon released Zainab's husband along with the necklace. Muhammad's son-in-law was greatly impressed by his treatment and decided to move his family to Medina. The Meccans were too busy mourning their dead to notice when the family fled. In fact, of the seventy Meccan fighters captured in battle, twenty chose to return to join Muhammad—which he took as a success far greater than winning on the battlefield.

With all his daughters now in Medina and all married, Muhammad's close friend Abu Bakr pressed him to marry again. A man in

Muhammad's position, Abu Bakr argued, needed a strong woman by his side. In fact, according to Arabian custom, leaders needed multiple wives to help solidify tribal alliances. The Meccans would be back, Abu Bakr reminded Muhammad, and they would be relentless. With so much at stake, Muhammad needed to reassure the people of Medina by acting like a wartime tribal leader by forging alliances through marriage.

The necklace Zainab had sent had sparked deep pangs of longing for Muhammad's one true love, Khadijah. She had proposed to him, igniting a romance only after the two had proved the resilience of their business partnership. Muhammad had remained monogamous for twenty-five years. In the five years since his wife's death, he had made a point of remaining single while his daughter Fatimah still lived with him.

Moreover, he had recently shared a Qur'anic revelation that underscored the value of monogamy, a practice that was not widespread in Arabia. "If you know you cannot be equally just among them, then marry only one," declared the Qur'an. It would ultimately limit polygamy to four marriages, as Abraham had four wives. The Qur'an further insisted on equality for the wives. "You will never be able to be equal in your treatment of wives even if you try," it revealed. "The Loving Divine has not made two hearts in the chest of a man," another verse acknowledged.

Muhammad sensed that the people of Medina were uneasy about the future. He had to reassure them that he was building solid alliances. It was once again time, Muhammad realized, to compromise on a cherished value. To seal key alliances, he would remarry.

Abu Bakr was delighted. His daughter 'Aishah was twenty-nine. Her independent personality had rendered her unmarriageable in Arabian society, and potential suitors had already broken two engagements. 'Aishah held an intense love for Muhammad, and Abu Bakr eagerly offered her hand in marriage. Muhammad agreed.

While 'Aishah loved her husband—she described him as a "very affectionate" lover "who slept cuddling in one garment" and a romantic who "would take the cup and bring it to my lips to drink, then would turn the cup around and place his lips where my lips had been"—the two frequently clashed. 'Aishah was strong-willed, prone to raising her voice and issuing demands. On several occasions, Muhammad had to stand between 'Aishah and Abu Bakr when her father wanted to discipline her for her treatment of Muhammad. When Abu Bakr went home, Muhammad would kiss her forehead and comment, "See how I defended you from your father?"

Despite their contrasting natures, Muhammad held 'Aishah in great regard, giving her the nickname Razaan (wisely grounded in reason).

The turbulence only increased when 'Umar proposed that Muhammad marry his widowed daughter, Hafsah, whose husband had died at Badr. Perhaps in recognition that his followers wanted him to act like a traditional tribal chief or perhaps out of sympathy for Hafsah, Muhammad assented to the marriage. By this point, Muhammad had secured permanent alliances with two of his closest followers, Abu Bakr and 'Umar, as well as with two of his other close followers, 'Ali and 'Uthman, who were married to his daughters. In doing so, he showed the people of Medina that he was planning for the city's future security and stability.

Because his second and third marriages were meant, at least in part, to consolidate tribal power and help bolster the confidence of his followers, Muhammad realized he also needed to show the value of marriages that brought no strategic alliances or personal gain. Within a year, Muhammad also married Um Salamah, a soft-spoken widow with five young children, the kind of woman who typically struggled to find a new husband. Another wife, Zainab, was divorced from a formerly enslaved man. By marrying women who were typically excluded as undesirables, Muhammad demonstrated that individuals seemingly broken in the eyes of Arabian society still had value in his eyes. If no one else wanted to marry them, he would—and in the process inspire other men to do the same.

Before his marriages, Muhammad had lived as a guest of Abu Ayyub, far removed from the luxury he had enjoyed in Mecca. But as the number of wives grew, he accepted that his family needed more space. At the suggestion of his followers, he had several small chambers built, one for each wife (and her children from previous marriages), along the eastern wall of the *masjid*. Each room had two doors, one opening into the courtyard and the other opening to the market outside. Though each wife had her own home, Muhammad technically remained homeless, rotating among wives. He would sweep the floors, collect firewood, and prepare meals while helping to care for their children. (None of the women Muhammad married during this period bore him offspring.)

Followers who knew Muhammad well saw his growing unhappiness with his polygamous state, as he had recently used the word *dharr* (harm) to coin a new term, *dharrah*, for women in a polygamous marriage (literally, a woman who is harmed and harms another).

Despite his clear preference for monogamy, he considered polygamy a necessity in the ongoing struggle to preserve Medina during precarious times. In a sermon he delivered during Friday prayers, Muhammad referred to *aqalludh-dhararayn*—"the lesser of the two harms."

Muhammad's remaining joy seemed to be his daughter Fatimah, who had become pregnant shortly after the battle of Badr. Muhammad regularly visited her and 'Ali to help the young couple prepare for a new life as parents. On Tuesday, December 11, 624, he visited their home with a basket of fresh pomegranates from the market and heard the cries of a newborn. Barakah, who had assisted the delivery, ran out to greet Muhammad with exciting news: "You have been comforted with a beautiful grandson!"

Overjoyed, Muhammad dashed in to see his daughter and 'Ali, who was at her side holding her hand. Muhammad kissed Fatimah's forehead, as he always did. Then, taking the infant from the midwife, he performed the *tahnik* ceremony. Holding the boy, Muhammad named him Al-Hasan (possessor of internal and external beauty). Barakah watched Muhammad with tears of joy in her eyes. She had witnessed his birth, the birth of his children, and now the birth of his grandchild.

Muhammad rejoiced in a rare moment of familial harmony. But there would be little time to celebrate the onset of a new generation. In early March 625, a horseman rode into Medina on a secret mission. Muhammad's uncle Al-'Abbas had sent him to warn that the Meccans had amassed a large army to avenge their dead at Badr. Three thousand men, accompanied by two hundred well-trained horsemen, were en route to Medina.

The Meccans had quickly paid the ransom for their prisoners of war, biding their time while secretly hatching a plan to annihilate Muhammad and Medina once and for all. The Meccans were organized this time, his uncle warned, having learned their lesson from the sloppy initial encounter at Badr. They had placed their hands in blood and sworn to take vengeance.

As he held his new grandson close, Muhammad, now fifty-five, had fewer than ten days to prepare for the fight of his life.

❖ ❖ ❖

After the old guard of Mecca's elders were killed at Badr, leadership passed to a refined middle-aged merchant named Abu Sufyan, son-in-law of the previous chief elder and a cousin of 'Uthman. Abu Sufyan did not care for fighting and had declined to join the original expedition. His wife, Hind, on the other hand, was a fierce woman who took the initiative to avenge the death of her father, brother, and son. Hamzah, 'Ali, and 'Ubaidah had killed her relatives at Badr. Concerned that her husband might be too reluctant to carry out the family vendetta, she masterminded Mecca's plan for revenge. Lest anyone doubt her zeal, she promised to emancipate a brawny Abyssinian enslaved fighter called Wahshi (savage) if he struck Hamzah down in battle, and she swore an oath to eat Hamzah's liver in vengeance.

Hind personally recruited the great warrior Khalid to lead the special force of two hundred well-trained cavalry that augmented the three thousand regular fighters. In a break with *Jahiliyyah* tradition, Hind decided to colead the Meccan army while accompanied by several hundred of the warriors' wives. The women would ensure no carousing took place before the battle—and that their husbands would not dare flee the front lines like cowards. Meccan women who had placed cotton in their children's ears to avoid listening to Muhammad were, ironically, beginning to empower themselves for the first time, though at Muhammad's expense. In a cunning move, Hind also insisted the Meccans engage Muhammad in battle on a Saturday to ensure that the Jews of Medina could not join him because it was their Sabbath day of rest.

While the Meccans had spent a year plotting their revenge, Muhammad had just over a week to prepare for their assault. He called an emergency meeting, during which the majority expressed a preference to remain in Medina and engage the Meccans in urban combat. But Muhammad was deeply concerned about the risk to the city's inhabitants and infrastructure. After several days of discussion, he finally managed to persuade his followers to take an alternate course of action.

A band of five hundred hastily recruited men marched out of Medina on Friday afternoon, trailed by Barakah and a cohort of nurses. The force managed to cut off the Meccan advance at Uhud, a mountain northeast of Medina's main entrance—and just five miles from the *masjid*.

Learning of the imminent danger, Rabbi Mukhairiq interrupted his synagogue's Friday evening prayer services marking the start of the Sabbath. "The Sabbath is not a barrier to doing one's duty!" he declared, announcing that he would join Muhammad at the front lines and urging others to follow his lead. Before he left the synagogue, the rabbi made a public declaration of his last will and testament. If he died in battle, his seven orchards would become a charitable trust administered by Muhammad to support widows and orphans. About two hundred congregants marched out with Rabbi Mukhairiq. The contingent arrived at Uhud before dawn, providing a great morale boost to Muhammad and his men.

Atop Mount Uhud, Muhammad surveyed the battlefield below alongside Abu Bakr, Hamzah, 'Ali, and Rabbi Mukhairiq. Unlike the raucous hunting party at Badr, a chilling sobriety hung over the Meccan camp. Seeking a way to limit casualties, Muhammad asked Rabbi Mukhairiq (who was familiar with the region) to identify the Medinians' weakest point. The rabbi pointed out that the Meccan cavalry could easily loop around the mountain and encircle the defenders. Muhammad quickly instructed his uncle to place fifty of their best archers on a rocky hill to the side of Mount Uhud as a way to dissuade the Meccan horsemen from mounting an attack from the rear.

Before combat began, Hind addressed the Meccan army and reminded the troops of their solemn duty to avenge their elders and reclaim Mecca's honor. In a poem she had composed for the occasion, she warned the men that if "you flee, we will divorce you!" Then, the thirty-two hundred fighters shouted a thunderous battle cry in unison: *"U'lu Hubal!"* (Rise up and show your greatness, oh Hubal!), once again invoking Mecca's chief deity. After the humiliating loss at Badr, the Meccans needed to recast themselves as martyrs for Arabian identity and crusaders against an infidel who dared defile the sanctity of their gods.

Muhammad waited patiently as a sea of several thousand inflamed fanatics bore down on his small band of men. On the front lines by Hamzah's side stood Rabbi Mukhairiq, surrounded by his two hundred men, their swords raised in defensive positions. Muhammad wanted the elderly rabbi to move to relative safety at the rear, but Mukhairiq insisted on making a statement to the Meccans that the Jews stood by Muhammad, even on the Sabbath.

As the Meccan horde drew near, Muhammad finally gave the order for his archers to release their barrage. Hundreds of arrows rained down on the Meccans, who panicked and turned to flee—only to be turned back by their women, who formed a line and urged their husbands to press forward. Taking advantage of the Meccans' confusion, Muhammad used the same strategy he had implemented at Badr. While his fighters rotated positions, camels at their rear dragged timber through the sand to create a dusty illusion of reinforcements.

In less than thirty minutes, the Meccan army fled in panic, pushing their wives aside. Pressing their advantage, hundreds of Medinian fighters dashed toward the Meccan camp to collect spoils, ignoring Muhammad's warning that the battle had not ended. Most of the archers posted on the side hill to defend the force's rear flank deserted their position, despite Muhammad's strict instructions: "Do not move from your posts unless I personally tell you otherwise, even if you see our bodies scattered across the field and vultures tearing our flesh apart!"

Amid the Medinians' premature victory celebrations, Khalid strategically regrouped the cavalry. The riders charged around Mount Uhud—just as Rabbi Mukhairiq had feared—and encircled Muhammad's army. Seventy-five Medinian men were killed and hundreds injured. In the turmoil, Wahshi carried out his mission, hurling a spear into Hamzah's heart. Rumors soon spread that Muhammad himself had been killed, prompting Medinian troops, including 'Uthman, to flee up the mountain for shelter.

Though still alive, Muhammad suddenly found himself abandoned at the back of his lines. Meccan fighters began hurling stones at him, breaking two of his teeth. He might well have died had Barakah not rushed into battle with her cohort of nurses. The women grabbed the weapons of fleeing Medinian fighters, as Barakah screamed, "Take the spindle and needle and give us women the swords and spears—we'll teach you what true bravery is!" The nurses surrounded Muhammad and led him to safety.

Abu Sufyan ordered the Meccan forces to push toward Medina and destroy the city. But Muhammad managed to rally his bloodied troops to block their path. When he saw Muhammad's fighters regroup so quickly after a massive defeat, Abu Sufyan decided not to gamble any further and ordered his forces to retreat. The battle ended in a semivictory for both sides: the Meccans had avenged their dead at Badr, while Muhammad had saved Medina.

Once the Meccans departed, Muhammad surveyed the battlefield. Rabbi Mukhairiq lay dead, a casualty of the onslaught. Hamzah's body lay mutilated, his liver chewed up and spat out in pieces on the ground. Hind had fulfilled her vendetta.

Though the Meccans had left their thirty-two dead to rot on the field, Muhammad had the bodies respectfully buried. Then he began burying his men. Rabbi Mukhairiq, whom Muhammad dubbed *khayrul-Yahud* (most outstanding among the Jews), was buried next to Hamzah. After the burial, several Jewish men informed Muhammad of Mukhairiq's last will and testament. The late rabbi's orchards became a charitable trust (*waqf*) that would remain in operation into the twenty-first century.

In remembrance of Rabbi Mukhairiq and his great sacrifice at Uhud, the Qur'an stated:

> *Wa ka'ayyim-min nabiyyin qatala ma'ahu ribbiyyuna kathirun fa ma wahanu lima asabahum fi sabil-illahi wa ma dha'ufu wa mas-takanu.*
> Remember the many rabbis who fought and died alongside prophets; they neither wavered in the face of overwhelming odds on the path toward the Divine nor showed signs of weakness nor allowed themselves to feel victimized.

The passage used the term *ribbiyyun* (plural of *ribbiyy*, the Arabic word for *rabbi*), as Rabbi Mukhairiq was only one of several rabbis to support Muhammad. The passage cited three cardinal characteristics of these learned men who understood the spirit of revelation.

Shortly after the battle at Uhud, Muhammad faced another devastating loss. His daughter Zainab died. Muhammad had to bury yet another of his children.

❖ ❖ ❖

As Muhammad grieved in Medina, back in Mecca Abu Sufyan was stewing over his decision to retreat at the battle of Uhud. His wife, Hind, had avenged her father's death, yet her husband had failed to prove himself a worthy elder. He needed to restore Mecca's prestige as well as his own. He had to demonstrate that he could rally many more men than his wife and end the business competition from Medina's thriving market.

For the next two years, Abu Sufyan devoted his energies to rallying tribes across Arabia to unite with Mecca in a common crusade against the infidels. He spread a rumor that Muhammad had assassinated a Jewish elder in Medina to annex his wealth. The tale served as a warning to tribal elders that Muhammad might send assassins after them, too, as part of a hostile takeover of their trade. Abu Sufyan's persuasive skills proved formidable, as a force of twelve thousand men began to assemble for a grand assault on Medina.

Once again, Muhammad's uncle Al-'Abbas leaked the news to his nephew by messenger. Muhammad had fewer than two months to prepare his still-recovering brethren to repel the massive army. He gathered his followers for yet another emergency discussion. The threat was greater than ever. Rotating flanks and sand-cloud illusions could not stop this throng. As Muhammad struggled to devise a more suitable response, Salman suddenly recalled another classic Persian military technique: digging a trench. Because Medina was surrounded by lava flows on three sides, the Meccan army could attack only from the north. A ditch along the entire northern pass would block their access.

Muhammad declared the idea ingenious and with a broad smile patted Salman on the shoulder. That evening, he and Salman mapped out the location, depth, and width of the trench for maximum efficiency. Over the following weeks, thousands of the city's inhabitants spread out along a three-and-a-half-mile stretch to hollow out a trench more than thirty feet wide and fifteen feet deep. Using primitive farming shovels, men dug while women and children carried away debris and prepared communal meals. In the last week, shifts worked around the clock and completed the trench just three days before the Meccan army arrived.

While Medina's men switched from digging to battle preparation, the women, children, and elderly took shelter in the city's strongest fortification. Muhammad appointed a woman named Safiyyah as mayor of Medina. She and several women, including Muhammad's wives 'Aishah and Hafsah, dressed in men's armor and stood as sentries atop the fort's battlements. Their outfits were designed to trick Meccan military scouts into reporting that male warriors defended the fort.

The Meccans had selected Friday, March 13, 627—the third anniversary of the battle of Badr—as the date for their final assault on Muhammad. As the sun rose that morning, drums thundered while twelve thousand men appeared on the horizon, again chanting *"U'lu Hubal!,"* their banners raised high above a cloud of dust. Abu Sufyan ordered his troops to spare none of the city's inhabitants, insisting that a complete massacre was needed to quash Muhammad. Abu Sufyan also promised to divide the city's fertile lands among the troops, along with large sums of money. They would sever and divide Muhammad's body as trophies for the allied clans, with Mecca getting the prize: his head.

But as thousands of warriors converged on Medina's entrance, they had to suddenly halt their invasion because of the massive trench. Standing at its precipice, the warriors realized they could not easily traverse the thirty-foot-wide ditch. Muhammad's archers on the other side greeted them with a hail of arrows. The confederate forces retreated out of range. What could have been an epic massacre soon turned into a tedious stalemate.

Because of the civic infrastructure Muhammad had established in Medina before the great famine, the city had sufficient stores to withstand a lengthy siege. For several weeks, the armies engaged in a protracted standoff. Only one formidable Meccan horseman—'Amr Ibn 'Abdi Wud—managed to get across the trench, but 'Ali killed him in a duel. It was the battle's sole instance of hand-to-hand combat.

As the armies exchanged arrows and javelins, several of Muhammad's men fell to the ground with injuries. To treat the wounded, Muhammad set up a large tent, which he called Dar-ush-Shifa (the abode of healing). The makeshift hospital was behind the front lines near the *masjid* and run by female nurses supervised by Barakah; they assessed the injured and assigned them to a hospital quarter based on the severity of their wounds. The tent's efficient assessments significantly reduced mortalities.

As the siege dragged on, Muhammad realized he needed to end it so Medina's market could reopen and restart the local economy. To quickly demoralize the besieging forces, Muhammad employed psychological warfare. He formed an elite corps of undercover spies, whom he dressed in the outfits of particular enemy clans and trained them to speak those clans' distinctive dialects. At night, using a temporary bridge, the men slipped over to the Meccan side and began to sow discord in the camp by spreading rumors that allied clans were giving up and heading home. The spies had strict instructions not to kill anyone—even though several had the chance to assassinate Abu Sufyan himself.

One by one, demoralized clans began to sneak away from the Meccan camp in the middle of the night, too ashamed to flee by daylight. The Meccans would awaken each morning to find yet another group had disappeared. Several sandstorms further reduced morale. Forty days after he had arrived jubilantly on the outskirts of Medina, Abu Sufyan found himself suddenly outnumbered by the Medinians. After two years of preparation and the investment of large sums of money, the Meccan crusade was a failure. The Meccan chief elder, humiliated, took his men and slunk home.

As the last of the allied forces disappeared over the horizon, Muhammad and his followers surveyed their abandoned camp. Remnants of tents fluttered in the wind, and embers from hundreds of extinguished fires still smoked. The Battle of the Trench had ended with a whimper. Fifteen thousand men had faced off on the battlefield, but only eight died (three Medinians and five Meccan allies). It was a dramatic victory for Muhammad's distinctive military philosophy: avoiding violence whenever possible and preserving human life at all cost.

When Muhammad first arrived in Medina five years earlier, he had cautioned the inhabitants that their celebration was premature. He had a similarly restrained response after the victory at Badr and the ragged stalemate at Uhud. But the Battle of the Trench had demonstrated that the Medinians could cooperate respectfully under enormous pressure, maintain disciplined self-defense, and refrain from causing unnecessary loss of life. Three times the Meccans had come to annihilate Medina, each time with greater force. Yet the people of Medina had held their ground, physically and spiritually. They had at last earned the right to rejoice.

Muhammad named the victory celebration 'Id al-Adh-ha (literally, the commemoration of shining through). The Arabic *'id* signified a celebration that returns year after year. *Adh-ha* derived from the term *dhuha* (first rays of the morning sun). For Semites, the concept of a day began at sunset, so sunrise signified a halfway point. The Medinians, Muhammad signaled, had endured an initial period of darkness. With the most difficult obstacles overcome, the path forward would be brighter.

Everyone in Medina was invited to attend the festival. Everyone dressed in their finest garments, and the aroma of roasted meat and freshly baked bread spread throughout the city. The *masjid* could not hold the thousands of celebrants, so Muhammad created an ad hoc jamboree in the wilderness area outside Medina that he named Masjid-ul-'Id (festive place of grounding). Muhammad introduced a new prayer of Divine thanksgiving: *"Wa hazamal-ahzaba wahdah!"* (And the Divine alone routed the confederate forces determined to annihilate us!).

With the Meccan military threat ended, Muhammad arranged for construction of temporary rope bridges so people could traverse the trench. Muhammad worked alongside the Banu Najjar to build a separate wood bridge for camels and livestock so the city's merchants would not miss the annual caravan to Damascus. He also organized a group of volunteers to maintain the trench in case of emergency.

The medical tent became a permanent clinic providing care, free of charge, its services supported by *zakah* funds and *waqf* endowments. Muhammad tasked Abu Bakr with hiring traditional nomadic doctors from across Arabia to work at Dar-ush-Shifa. A corps of volunteers led by Muhammad's wife 'Aishah attended women in labor. Muhammad had latticed openings woven into the tents' sides to allow the air to circulate while maintaining privacy. He recommended regularly bathing patients to maintain hygiene and burning incense to aid relaxation in an effort to enhance healing.

All these public health advances, however, could not save his daughter Um Kulthum. After months of illness, she died a few weeks after the victory celebrations. Once again Muhammad walked to the cemetery to bury one of his children.

Back in Mecca, Abu Sufyan and the elders struggled to restore their bruised reputation and recoup the extensive funds they had wasted on smear campaigns, mercenaries, and three failed battles. Muhammad recognized that the Meccans needed a way to save face in order to accept a peace treaty with a man they had denounced as an infidel.

One morning, several months after Um Kulthum's death, Muhammad spoke to his followers after dawn prayers about a vision he had the previous night. "I had a dream of us unarmed, dressed in white, and marching on Mecca." A peaceful march on Mecca might force the Meccans to sue for peace. According to Arabian custom, no fighting could take place during the holy months of the pilgrimage season. To respect this custom, the Medinian marchers would be unarmed. Several followers strongly objected, fearing the Meccans would massacre them in the desert.

When Muhammad explained his plan to the broader population of Medina, most shared the fear that this was a fatal mistake; only fourteen hundred men, women, and children volunteered to join the march.

Muhammad's wives drew lots to determine who would accompany him on his journey out of Medina. Um Salamah, the widow with five children, drew the short straw. Along with Barakah, the quiet and contemplative Um Salamah would serve as Muhammad's confidential advisors on the mission.

Muhammad did not reveal his broader objective: that the march would function as a declaration to the people of Arabia that he had never meant any harm and that the Meccans had provoked, persecuted, and initiated war. The marchers, all dressed in white, traveled in broad daylight. Nomads along the route were shocked to see the group passing through the desert—and began placing bets on whether the Medinians would be massacred or enslaved.

Muhammad's peaceful march placed the Meccans in an impossible position. If they massacred him and his defenseless followers, they would be regarded as cowardly, while Muhammad would be hailed as a brave warrior, facing death without flinching. If, on the other hand, the Meccans allowed him to enter, they would be regarded as weak and likewise lose face among the tribes. Either way, Muhammad won.

After two weeks of marching, Muhammad's group drew close to Mecca, forcing the Meccan elders to make a decision. To stall for time, Abu Sufyan decided to send out the cavalry under Khalid's leadership to block the marchers. As Muhammad and his group rested at the wells of Hudaibiyyah, not six miles from Mecca, Khalid's forces encircled them, though with strict instructions not to attack.

Muhammad had quietly prepared for such a stalemate. After consulting with Barakah and Um Salamah, he asked 'Uthman to serve as his emissary to Mecca, with clear instructions to use diplomacy to convince the Meccans to sue for peace as their only way out of their dilemma. 'Uthman was Abu Sufyan's first cousin and part of the ruling Umayyad clan. When 'Uthman approached the Meccan siege force, they opened up their lines and allowed him to walk to Mecca, where Abu Sufyan received him with kind hospitality.

Three days later, the elders invited 'Uthman to address them at Dar-un-Nadwah during the Friday assembly. 'Uthman spoke eloquently, reminding them that he was well respected by both sides, as both Muhammad's son-in-law and the cousin of Mecca's chief elder. 'Uthman presented an idea that Muhammad had suggested to him before he left the Hudaibiyyah wells: the Meccans should propose a peace treaty on their own terms and present it to Muhammad, who would have to accept its disadvantageous terms or risk appearing as an aggressor in the ongoing image war. That would shift the dilemma to Muhammad. Mecca could then rebuild its economic empire and regain its position as Arabia's leading city.

'Uthman's brilliant solution amazed the elders and they voted unanimously to sue for peace. They chose Suhail ibn 'Amr, a cunning negotiator and senior elder, to engage Muhammad. Two days later, on March 13, 628—the fourth anniversary of Badr and eighteen years since Muhammad's initial revelation—Suhail arrived at Hudaibiyyah accompanied by 'Uthman. Both sides met for the negotiations in a special tent, and 'Ali was chosen to transcribe the agreement. After several hours of formalities, which began with Suhail sitting at the same level as Muhammad and holding Muhammad's beard as he spoke (a typical Arabian custom when discussing an important matter), they consolidated the agreement over a meal of roasted meat.

Capturing the proposed terms, 'Ali began: "This is a treaty between Muhammad *rasulullah* and—" Suhail immediately objected to *rasulullah* (messenger of God—literally, the channeling guide of Divine wisdom), insisting that it unfairly honored Muhammad. Assenting to the objection, Muhammad asked 'Ali to remove it, yet the scribe refused. The unlettered Muhammad asked 'Ali to show him where the word appeared on the page and with his right thumb wiped it away. He then asked 'Ali to write "Muhammad ibn 'Abdullah," instead. Muhammad added, "It is always more noble to compromise one's honor in the pursuit of peace."

Muhammad did not simply compromise his honor, however; he capitulated on most of the treaty's terms, which were set to last for ten years. Muhammad and his group would return to Medina at once without entering Mecca. Muhammad's followers could defect to Mecca, yet no Meccan could join Muhammad, who would be obliged to return any defector to Mecca. Meccans could trade in Medina, yet Medinians could not trade in Mecca. Clans, though, were free to enter into allegiance with either side, and two Meccan clans—the Banu Khuza'ah and the Jewish Banul Harith, both ancient allies of Muhammad's grandfather—allied with Muhammad.

Years earlier, the elders at Dar-un-Nadwah had offered Muhammad almost everything to cease his teaching. At Hudaibiyyah, they had forced him to give up almost everything for the sake of peace. As Muhammad compromised on point after point, annoyance and deep concern registered on the faces of his followers, to the delight of Suhail. 'Umar objected particularly strongly, yet Muhammad quietly leaned on the counsel of Barakah and Um Salamah, who remained composed. Muhammad had entrusted his master plan to only these two women.

As they departed Hudaibiyyah, Muhammad's followers felt humiliated. Why should they compromise after they had repelled the much-larger armies of Mecca in three campaigns? Muhammad maintained silence through all their grumbling. He trusted that they would never intentionally undermine him. Yet he feared they might inadvertently betray his true intentions if they knew the strategy in advance—just as the teenage Meccan cook had unintentionally revealed the size of the Meccan army before Badr.

Moreover, Muhammad needed his followers to be upset so that news of their dismay would allow the Meccans to rejoice in their victory—just as his followers had celebrated prematurely at Uhud, only to be encircled by Khalid's cavalry. Muhammad had realized that the Meccan retreat at Uhud had been a secret strategy devised by Khalid to make Muhammad's followers feel overconfident and celebrate their victory so he could easily encircle them. For Muhammad, who made a point of learning from his adversaries, accepting the humiliating terms of the Hudaibiyyah Treaty would ultimately allow him to do the same: to encircle *Jahiliyyah*, in order to end it once and for all.

❖ ❖ ❖

As he returned to Medina, Muhammad set about replicating the strategy of his ancestor Hashim. Over a century earlier, when the Meccan elders had effectively cut Hashim out of their sphere of influence, he established his own diplomatic relations with the surrounding realms of Byzantium, Persia, Yemen, and Abyssinia. This granted him exclusive and lucrative business access that the Meccans lacked. Feeling surrounded and isolated, the Meccan elders ultimately capitulated and invited Hashim to return home to serve as Mecca's chief elder.

Muhammad planned to follow his ancestor's example by sending letters to the rulers of the empires surrounding Arabia that invited them to accept the message of blossoming. He had shared the idea during a private meeting with Abu Bakr, 'Ali, Salman, and several elders. Salman, who had grown up in a noble Persian family, cautioned, "No ruler will receive a letter unless it has a seal."

Inspired, Muhammad went to Medina's best silversmith, a Jew from the Banu Nadhir clan, and asked him to fashion a silver ring to fit on his right pinkie. Atop the ring the smith set a round stone of Abyssinian red agate carved with the Arabic words:

Allah
Rasul
Muhammad

Muhammad asked the smith to place his name at the bottom of the impression. Above his name came the word for his function: *rasul*—"the one who guides balanced flow." Above the job title came his mentor: Allah—the embracing Divine who served as the ultimate role model and the true destination of life's wilderness journey. Muhammad wore his signet ring with the red stone facing downward.

With 'Ali, 'Uthman, and Abu Ayyub serving as scribes, Muhammad composed letters to more than thirty rulers. Though lost to history, each letter appealed in unique ways, asking permission to trade and teach in their land, Abu Ayyub and Mus'ab recalled. Muhammad chose as messengers his most well-groomed and eloquent followers, knowing that attractive presentation could help the rulers be positively disposed toward his appeal.

Dihya al-Kalbi—deputized as a messenger—was renowned for his stunning looks, engaging personality, and refined manner. Dihya had flawless light skin and captivating hazel eyes; he hailed from a Christian clan in northern Arabia and spoke Greek fluently. Muhammad had him deliver the letter to Heraclius while the emperor was in Jerusalem for a special celebration commemorating the return of the True Cross. Heraclius took a liking to Diyha and was curious to learn more about the mysterious Muhammad.

As it turned out, Abu Sufyan was also in Jerusalem, along with a group of Meccan merchants, as their entourage had detoured from the route to Damascus to attend the Byzantine festivities. Heraclius called for an audience with the Meccans to ask their chief elder about Muhammad's character. "Had you ever accused Muhammad of lying before he made his prophetic proclamations?" inquired Heraclius.

To the astonishment of his fellow Meccans, Abu Sufyan replied honestly: "No, he was known as As-Saqid [the truthful] among us." The Meccan chief elder considered it dishonorable to lie before his peers, and his candid response led Heraclius to conclude that Muhammad posed no threat (though the emperor never bothered to send a reply).

Muhammad also dispatched messengers to eastern Arabia. The ruler of Bahrain, Al-Munthir ibn Sawa, received his letter with enthusiasm and asked Muhammad to send followers to teach and trade in his kingdom. Christian communities in eastern Arabia resonated with the message of one God who inspired human beings to unlock dormant potential. Regarded as heretics by the Byzantine Church, they welcomed Muhammad's community in a nod toward solidarity—a sentiment shared by some Jewish sects in eastern Arabia that were largely cut off from mainstream Judaism.

To the southwest, Muhammad's followers already had warm relations with the head of Abyssinia. Muhammad's letter to the negus asked the ruler to represent Muhammad in officiating his marriage to Ramlah, an early follower of Muhammad's who had fled Mecca with Barakah right before the boycott and remained in Abyssinia. Ramlah's husband—also an early follower of Muhammad's—had converted to Christianity in Abyssinia, even as the couple remained married. He had recently died of alcohol poisoning, leaving Ramlah widowed with two children. Muhammad's offer of marriage helped a widow in need and solidified a family connection to—of all people—Abu Sufyan, her father and Mecca's chief elder.

The negus agreed and sent Ramlah to Medina accompanied by a delegation of Abyssinians. Muhammad hosted the Christian delegation at his *masjid* and prepared a great feast in their honor. During the reception, the Abyssinians preformed a traditional dance accompanied by musical instruments. A week later, in response to another of his letters, a delegation of Christian clergy from Najran visited Medina. On the Sunday of their visit, Muhammad offered the *masjid* for Sunday worship services. Crucifixes, saint icons, bells, and incense filled the *masjid* for several hours. As a community center, the *masjid* welcomed all.

Muhammad's letter to the Sasanian emperor Khosrow II was not as warmly received. The emperor tore up the epistle and killed Muhammad's messenger, enraged that "this filthy goatherd dare address Khosrow as his equal." He demanded that Batham, his governor in Yemen, send assassins to bring him Muhammad's head. Two hardened killers arrived in Medina disguised as merchants and soon found Muhammad asleep and unguarded in an orchard.

As the assassins pointed their swords at Muhammad's neck, his eyes opened to see their masked faces glaring down at him. Muhammad smiled and closed his eyes. "Aren't you afraid to die?" they demanded, to which Muhammad calmly replied, "No." He slowly sat up and remarked, "There are those who pass through life like empty shadows, bending to the whims of others and never thinking for themselves. Even in life they are dead."

Amazed, the assassins desisted. They had killed many prominent men, all of whom had surrounded themselves with high defensive walls and fierce bodyguards. This leader, in contrast, dressed in rags, slept on the bare ground without crown or protection. If he posed a threat to the Sasanian Empire, something about him must be special. Like 'Umar before them, the two would-be assassins became instant followers.

Muhammad hosted them as his guests before sending them back to Yemen with a letter. Shocked by Muhammad's influence on two hardened killers—who now disavowed their old vocation—the governor Batham decided to invite Muhammad's followers to teach in his land and declared himself independent of Persia. Muhammad sent twenty-five-year-old Mu'ath ibn Jabal, a Medinian fluent in Hebrew and Aramaic, to engage with Yemen's large Jewish population.

Two other former adversaries accepted Muhammad's appeals: Khalid, the Meccan hero at the battle of Uhud, and 'Amr ibn al-'As, the Meccan emissary sent to Abyssinia to reclaim Muhammad's followers during the boycott. Both men, highly intelligent and independent minded, had overheard some of Muhammad's followers' teachings and were captivated. Their conversion defied the Hudaibiyyah Treaty and belied their status as the sons of elders killed at Badr. In fact, their conversion surprised Muhammad more than anyone else, as Khalid had been at the forefront of Mecca's military attacks—and 'Amr in the diplomatic ones—on his followers.

In Egypt, to the northwest, Muhammad's letter found favor with the patriarch of Alexandria, the Coptic pope Benjamin I. The Copts, persecuted by the Byzantines for over two centuries, were happy to ally themselves with Muhammad as an emerging regional leader. To seal their alliance, the patriarch sent his godchild Maria, as well as precious gifts of exquisite textiles and silver, to Muhammad (he added the latter to the *zakah* charitable funds).

Muhammad was smitten with Maria and took her as his wife. After their marriage, he made a public declaration: "*Inna lahum sihraw-wa rahima*" (When you enter Egypt, remember that its people are our in-laws and our maternal ancestors [via Ishamel's mother Hagar]). Because Maria came from a household of Egypt's elites, she was accustomed to living in luxury, and Muhammad gave her a home in a pleasant orchard, along with a maid.

Amid all this diplomatic activity, a surprise delegation descended on Medina in a massive cloud of dust. As he looked toward the horizon, Muhammad exclaimed, "*Kun aba Tharr!*" It was Abu Tharr, who had lived up to his new name and fulfilled Muhammad's confidence in his ability to transform others. Muhammad had not heard from his former student since the day he saw him off at Mecca's northern pass, yet after nearly a decade of preaching, Abu Tharr had managed to convert his entire clan of Ghifar as well as their neighboring clan of Aslam. Arabia's fiercest clans were now Muhammad's followers.

Just as Muhammad had anticipated, the Hudaibiyyah Treaty enabled him to engage previously unreachable audiences. In less than a year, his followers grew from a few thousand to over twenty thousand. Medina doubled in size, eclipsing Mecca's sphere of influence.

Recalling his followers' disappointment after the signing of the Hudaibiyyah Treaty, Muhammad reminded them of his philosophy's central concept of *yusr* (flowing around obstacles). In a famous declaration, he advised:

> *Innad-dina yusr wa lay-yushaddadina ahadun illa ghalabah,*
>   *fayassiru wa la tu'assiru.*
> Anyone who tries to be inflexible and constantly pushes against
>   obstacles with confrontation and conflict will be exhausted by
>   their persistent yet fruitless efforts. Therefore, always seek flow
>   and avoid unnecessary friction.

As Muhammad redirected ever more trade to Medina, the Meccans began to feel increasingly isolated. Each time they had tried to prune Muhammad's influence, he simply found a way to use their cuts to grow stronger. The manure they hurled at him became nourishing fertilizer. The Copts in Egypt, the Abyssinians, the east Arabians, and the Yemenites had all aligned with him and welcomed his followers as teachers. While adhering to the disadvantageous terms of the Hudai-biyyah Treaty, Muhammad had created a virtual encirclement of Mecca. The ultimate humiliation from the treaty was theirs, not his.

As the balance of power shifted, the Meccans dared not break the treaty. They would need to provoke Muhammad to rekindle the flames of war. Under Abu Sufyan's leadership, the Meccans surreptitiously urged their allies, the Banu Bakr clan, to raid and massacre Muhammad's pagan allies, the Banu Khuza'ah. The Meccans and the Banu Bakr clan orchestrated the attack in secret to avoid taking any public responsibility; they hoped Muhammad would retaliate in anger and appear to be one who violated the Hudaibiyyah Treaty. Only one man survived the massacre, by pretending to be dead. Bloodied, he made his way to Medina and reported to Muhammad how the Meccans had orchestrated the annihilation of his clan.

Muhammad had planned to defeat *Jahiliyyah* without violence, but many innocents had been murdered in defiance of a peace treaty. Against that deadly backdrop, the Qur'an's harshest passages were revealed. Called Surah At-Tawbah (The Reconciliation), the chapter is the only one in the Qur'an not to begin by invoking the name of God, indicating that though war might be unavoidable in certain situations, it remained a human failing that could never have divine blessing.

The chapter begins with an indirect proclamation of war against Mecca for its treachery. The verses refer positively to Muhammad's pagan allies as *mu`min* (protected) under *thimmah* (Divine sanctuary)—and alerts those who "had broken the treaty" that they have "four months to prepare." But the revelation remains open-ended, with no next move specified. In the spirit of constantly seeking to avoid bloodshed, the passage ends with this reminder:

> *Wa in janahu lis-salmi fajnah laha*
> And if they even show the slightest signs of suing for peace, then
> hasten to it.

News of Mecca's deceit spread throughout Arabia. The Meccans' "secret provocation" had backfired. Yet Muhammad's intentions remained murky, leaving the Meccans in suspense. Desperate to ascertain what lay ahead, Abu Sufyan himself traveled to Medina for an audience with his son-in-law. Muhammad accepted him yet sat silently throughout the visit. Abu Sufyan then went to his daughter Ramlah, whom he had not seen in years, to beg her for information. She insisted, "I would not betray my husband's trust even to you, Father!"

Only Barakah, Um Salamah, and four of Muhammad's closest followers—'Ali, Abu Bakr, 'Umar, and 'Uthman—knew Muhammad's plans. He intended to once again march on Mecca, only this time with an overwhelming force of thousands of fighters. The slaughter of the Banu Khuza'ah had convinced him that the era of *Jahiliyyah* had reached its end.

As with all his military strategies, Muhammad made a point of cloaking his tactics. He led his army out from Medina in a northward direction. He leaked their ostensible mission as being to ward off a potential Byzantine threat so that the Meccans might let down their guard. Meanwhile, Muhammad hired trusted desert guides to lead the Medinian forces along little-known routes that Meccan scouts did not surveil. The unusual desert pathways were also unknown to his own soldiers, lest any of them accidentally betray their mission. As Muhammad declared to his closest followers, "*Ista'inu 'ala qadha`i hawa`ijikum bil-kitman*" (Pursue your goals by maintaining the utmost secrecy).

For the first time in his life, Muhammad set out to initiate an offensive military maneuver.

9

✧

TRIUMPH

Establishing Arabia's New Meritocratic Order

Wadi Marr Ath-Thahran:
8:30 p.m., Thursday,
January 18, 630 CE

On a moonless winter evening, two men on horseback rode out of Mecca, their path through the city's outskirts slowed by the inky darkness.

Leading the way was Muhammad's uncle Al-'Abbas. His wife, Luba-bah, had been Khadijah's best friend and one of Muhammad's first followers. Because Al-'Abbas remained a pagan, the couple had never left Mecca, instead serving as Muhammad's eyes and ears in the city. To maintain his cover, Muhammad's uncle had joined all the Meccan assaults on Medina—but only after sending advance warnings to his nephew. This evening he had one last mission.

Riding alongside him was Abu Sufyan, Mecca's chief elder. A few hours earlier, Al-'Abbas had burst into Abu Sufyan's house with a shocking revelation. Undetected by Mecca's scouts, Muhammad had arrived outside the city and had camped with thousands of warriors by the nearby wells of Wadi Marr Ath-Thahran (valley of backbreaking bitterness).

A breathless Al-'Abbas explained that he had begged his nephew not to act rashly, and Muhammad reluctantly agreed to meet Abu Sufyan that evening before giving the order to overrun Mecca.

The news shocked Abu Sufyan. Yet Al-'Abbas persuaded the chief elder that it might not be too late to dissuade Muhammad from attacking. As the two rode out to the wells a few hours after sunset, the planet Jupiter was in ascendance. A quintessential man of *Jahiliyyah*, Abu Sufyan interpreted the bright planet's rise as an auspicious omen—its Arabic name, Al-Mushtari, meant "the one who persists uninterrupted." Suddenly optimistic for the fate of his city, the elder smiled.

As the riders climbed the hill above the valley of Marr Ath-Thahran, a warm glow shimmered over the summit, illuminating the night sky. Abu Sufyan grew wide-eyed as he reached the hilltop and stared down into a valley lit with ten thousand campfires. Traveling Arabian armies and caravans were always five men to a fire, so this meant that Muhammad's force comprised fifty thousand men. In an instant, any thoughts of resistance vanished from Abu Sufyan's mind. The chief elder knew he had to compromise at all costs to save Mecca.

Al-'Abbas led Abu Sufyan down into the valley toward Muhammad's tent, which was pitched at the edge of the camp closest to Mecca. Muscular, well-equipped guards surrounded it. As Abu Sufyan stared at the soldiers, Al-'Abbas said, "If these men look terrifying, you should see the rest of his army." The chief elder blanched.

Inside the tent, Muhammad received Abu Sufyan without saying a word. Anxious and uneasy, the elder finally broke the silence and began to beg for peace. No matter what he offered, Muhammad remained unmoved. Finally, Muhammad quietly yet firmly declared, "Clear Mecca of all arms and tell everyone to remain at home. I declare all homes a place of sanctuary, the Ka'bah a place of sanctuary, and Abu Sufyan's house a place of sanctuary. We enter in the morning!" With that, Muhammad stood up and exited the tent. A stunned Abu Sufyan staggered home. He had just surrendered Mecca to Muhammad.

Unbeknown to the chief elder, Muhammad did not have fifty thousand men in his camp, nor were most of his men fierce warriors. Rather, he had pulled off an epic bluff. Men from Medina, along with various Christian and pagan allies, had joined the stealthy march to Mecca, where they rendezvoused with men from the Banu Hilal tribe, a semi-nomadic Arab clan living north of Mecca that had adopted Jewish practices. Months earlier, Muhammad had married a Banu Hilal woman named Maimunah, solidifying a key strategic alliance that instantly increased the manpower available to him.

Each of the ten thousand men now under Muhammad's command had received instructions to light his own campfire to give Abu Sufyan the illusion of an army of fifty thousand. Muhammad had placed his tent on the edge of the camp so Abu Sufyan would not have the opportunity to pass through the main encampment and see the ruse. The tent's guards wore the few superior suits of armor and weapons available, and the artifice had worked.

Of course, no one knew what would happen next. Abu Sufyan quickly returned to Mecca to fulfill the conditions of surrender. Heralds proclaimed Muhammad's words throughout the city, with express orders to reverse the conditions in order to heighten the prestige of the chief elder: "Anyone who enters the house of Abu Sufyan has sanctuary, anyone who enters the Ka'bah has sanctuary, and anyone who remains in their home has sanctuary."

Mecca did not sleep that night. Muhammad had accepted the city's surrender yet revealed nothing about its fate. The Meccans had boycotted Muhammad; caused the death of his uncle, wife, and daughters; launched a vicious smear campaign maligning his character; placed a bounty on his head; thrice assaulted his adopted home of Medina; and then betrayed a peace treaty by massacring his allies. Any normal man would surely avenge such grave injustices.

❖ ❖ ❖

As dawn broke, an eerie silence hovered over Mecca, interrupted only by the occasional rooster's crow. No shepherds dared depart with their flocks for grazing that morning. No one lit the city's ovens, and no aroma of baking bread wafted through the deserted streets. The shutters and doors of every home remained bolted tight. Per Muhammad's instructions, the Ka'bah's priests had dispersed, leaving the shrine's door open. Meccans braced for the worst.

The distant sound of thundering drums broke the stillness. Thousands of Muhammad's men—Abu Sufyan had reported tens of thousands!—began their march. Amid hundreds of beating drums came a chorus of rising voices, their chant reverberating across the mountains surrounding Mecca and echoing through the city's abandoned streets.

Muhammad intended to enter Mecca without spilling a drop of blood. To do so, he had to dissuade the Meccans from even the slightest impulse to resist. Ironically, the elders' years-long propaganda campaign against him helped intensify the city's fear, and the booming drums and roaring chant ensured the local population was paralyzed into surrendering peacefully. Muhammad's army converged on Mecca from all four sides, further reinforcing the impression that a massive flood of men was overrunning the city.

As the men drew closer, their chant became intelligible. In contrast to the Meccan army's war chant calling on their city's chief idol—"Oh Hubal, elevate yourself!"—Muhammad's forces sang about God elevating all creation to new heights. Their song heralded the end of the era of *Jahiliyyah* and suggested that relinquishing willful stagnation could actually uplift the Meccans.

This song was the first and only time Muhammad associated God's name with soldiers—not at Badr, Uhud, or at the trench had he ever evoked God's name. The circumstances were different now. The city had already surrendered peacefully. The Meccans had made their fight into a holy war. Yet Muhammad had sought a holy peace. Only when the fighting was over could he evoke God's name.

Muhammad had composed the canticle himself, pointedly assigning all praise to the Divine. He had instructed each army division to memorize the words and practice chanting its melody. The hymn's message to the Meccan public belied the typical boasts of conquering armies.

While lacking the eloquence of Qur'anic revelation, Muhammad's canticle conveyed a direct message to the people of Mecca. He had not returned to his hometown to subdue or avenge but rather to help empower and restore equilibrium. Indeed, the composition mentioned Allah twelve times, a number that in Semitic cultures symbolized a state of wholeness. Just as the twelve months of the year together created a state of balance, the new system dawning over Mecca would embrace diversity while establishing a strong foundation for both communal and personal growth.

The canticle also made clear that the new system would reinstate the monotheism of Meccas, founding father, Abraham. In that spirit, Muhammad referred to his forces' entrance into Mecca as *fathu-Makkah* (the unlocking of Mecca), and the Qur'an called the epic moment *fathan-'athima* (the great unlocking). The city's potential, restrained for centuries under a system of willful stagnation, could at last be unleashed.

The moment appropriately coincided with the end of Ramadhan, which culminated in the 'Id-ul-Fitr festival. *Fitr* referred to the moment a new plant first pokes out of the soil into the world of sunshine, a delicate new beginning. The term also had a second meaning: baking bread quickly without yeast so the dough has no chance to rise, which reflected Muhammad's strategy of swiftly taking Mecca before the city could regain any disposition to rise up and fight back.

As the song's unusual lyrics began to sink in, Mecca's inhabitants cautiously peered out from their latticed windows and rooftop hiding spots. In astonishment, they beheld a mosaic of thousands of men from diverse backgrounds, religions, and ethnicities flowing into their city—as if the entire world, except for Meccans, was with Muhammad. The army stayed in formation, chanting in unison but damaging no property. During a break in the conquerors' song, the head of each of the four brigades called out, "No doors will be forced open, no houses will be sacked and pillaged, and anyone who remains in their home shall be safe!"

The multitudes cascaded toward the Ka'bah. Once the four division heads reached the shrine, they ordered a halt. Khalid was assigned to lead one of the main battalions entering the city. Muhammad wanted the Meccans to see how his fiercest enemies were now aligned with him, signaling that they, too, could gain acceptance and rise to new heights, if they so chose.

Muhammad did not lead the procession. Instead he entered Mecca via its northern pass and stopped first at the Mu'alla cemetery on the city's outskirts. Banned from his hometown for over eight years, he had not been able to visit the graves of his beloved family members. 'Ali noticed that as Muhammad approached the cemetery, his face changed, reflecting a rare mix of excitement and sadness. Tears formed in his eyes as he stood before the graves of his grandfather, his uncle, Khadijah, and his two sons. Muhammad knelt before their graves, sobbing silently. 'Ali and Abu Bakr stood at his side, their hands on his shoulders.

Muhammad remained kneeling for close to an hour. His grandfather had been the first to see potential in him and give him a name to live up to. His uncle had protected him and lost his life as a result. His wife had nurtured the potential in him and understood his calling, even when he did not. Without them, he could never have reached this moment— when he needed to channel their faith in him one more time. He would soon appear before the very people responsible for the deaths of two of those buried here and for causing him so much heartbreak.

As Muhammad knelt, a horseman raced into the cemetery, his horse snorting from the gallop. The rider approached Abu Bakr to deliver the news: Mecca was theirs. The city had surrendered without bloodshed, and all its inhabitants awaited the conqueror. Abu Bakr stooped beside Muhammad and gently said, "It is time."

Muhammad rose slowly. He turned to his men and instructed them to set his tent up near the grave of his grandfather. Though Mecca lay open before Muhammad, he would never spend another night in the city. He preferred instead to remain with his loved ones. Muhammad left his armor behind in the tent and mounted Al-Qaswa, the same loyal camel upon which he had fled Mecca eight years earlier. Then he rode toward the city.

As Muhammad approached, his army parted, opening a path for him. The Meccans peering out from their homes anticipated the grand entrance of a conqueror dressed in his finest with his head held high and surrounded by dignitaries. They were astonished to see a stooped man dressed in a simple white linen tunic and black turban—a far cry from the robust man who had first summoned the Meccans at Abu Qubais in his most exquisite garb.

Muhammad carried only the simple staff of a shepherd in his right hand. It signaled that he saw himself primarily as a shepherd, a role he had served as a teenager when various Meccan families had hired him to tend their sheep, guiding flocks to the best grazing grounds and protecting them from harm. "Rulers are shepherds over their people and are responsible for their upkeep," Muhammad often observed. His simple gesture spoke volumes to the Meccans: he would serve, not rule.

For more than eight years, Muhammad's former home in Mecca had sat abandoned. But as he rode into the city, he did not stop to reclaim it. The grand foyer where Khadijah had first received him, the rooftop bedroom that he had constructed with his own hands, and the large storeroom in which he had stowed the merchandise imported from Damascus—all those belonged to the past. 'Ali would stay in the manor during his time in Mecca, but for Muhammad the building was no longer home.

Nor did Muhammad stop at the Dar-un-Nadwah assembly, built by his ancestor Qusai. The council chambers had spawned all the machinations and smears directed at Muhammad. The base arena of politics had not brought out the best in Mecca's elders over the past two decades. Contemporary leaders had squandered whatever noble purpose Qusai had once envisioned for the hall. In any case, speaking to Mecca's elite was not Muhammad's objective.

Instead, Muhammad steadily approached the Ka'bah, his head bowed so low that his beard touched the back of his camel. As he drew near the sanctuary, his head slowly rose. Tears trickled down his cheeks as memories flooded over him. Here in the shade of the shrine he had sat on his grandfather's lap as 'Abdul-Muttalib led a private session of the city's Majlis ash-Shuyukh (congress of elders); as he did so, he occupied the honored chief elder's cushion beneath the Ka'bah's only drain spout. Though just a boy, Muhammad had internalized the elders' wisdom.

Here in the plaza in front of the shrine he had prostrated himself in prayer toward Jerusalem so many times, only to have the Meccan elders order animal intestines and manure heaved upon his head and back. While Muhammad had chosen to ignore their abuse, his teenage daughter Fatimah had removed the filth from his back with tears in her eyes. And yet here he was, back at last. This time, he could claim his grandfather's position as the ultimate elder of Mecca and all of Arabia.

As Muhammad's camel paused outside the Ka'bah, his men fell silent. For over two hours their voices had echoed across the mountains, their song reinforcing the themes of the new era's dawning. Their drumbeats at last stopped, and every soldier stood absolutely still. The formal changing of the guard had begun.

* * *

The streets were silent, as the people of Mecca began to emerge from their hiding spots, curious to observe the drama firsthand. Many rushed to their rooftops, looking down in amazement at the scene before them. A deluge of soldiers filled every street and trailed over the mountain passes as far as the eye could see. As the Meccans watched, Muhammad dismounted his camel and walked toward the Ka'bah's doors. He suddenly stopped, turned left, and approached the altar to two idols, where so many children had been sacrificed in pagan ceremonies to appease the gods.

The soldiers parted as Muhammad approached the altar. When Meccans returned from a long journey, they typically went straight to the altar to make a thanksgiving offering. Muhammad, however, stood defiantly in front of the two idols, the lovers named Isaf and Na'ilah. As he lowered his head in reflection, a tear rippled down his cheek. Then Muhammad reached out with his shepherd's staff and knocked over the male statue, which toppled onto its face with a loud thud, the clay form shattering into pieces across the plaza.

Breaking the tense silence—which had lasted nearly an hour—Muhammad began to chant a new revelation, his melodic voice resonating through the square:

> *Ja'al-haqqu wa zahaqal-batilu innal-batila kana zahuqa!*
> The era of liberating truth has ascended, while the age of deceptive delusions has vanished. Like a shadow, deception always fades away without leaving any lasting trace!

In this vivid metaphor, the Qur'an described the era of *Jahiliyyah* as a large shadow that casts darkness over everything yet disappears suddenly as the sun shifts and leaves no imprint, as if the shadow had never even existed.

The concept played on the Meccans' deep fear of not being remembered. They had clung to the system of *Jahiliyyah* for so long because they did not want to disappear like so many others. Yet that notion of longevity had been an illusion. *Jahiliyyah* had darkened Arabia for over a thousand years, and now it had vanished in an instant.

The image stood in sharp contrast to Muhammad's own role as a *rasul*, a guide of water flow. Unlike a shadow, water leaves a mark, reshaping landscapes long after it evaporates or seeps into the ground. By destroying the false sense of comfort provided by *Jahiliyyah*, Muhammad would help the people create a new system that would offer the Meccans a genuine and substantial legacy.

Even though the Qur'anic verse had only just been revealed spontaneously, Muhammad's soldiers picked up on the meter and melody and began chanting the words in unison. From their roofs and doorways, the Meccans listened intently.

With the declaration that the shadow of idolatry and willful stagnation had lifted with the dawn of monotheism and blossoming, it was time to physically remove the symbols of the old order. Among Muhammad's forces were representatives of most of Arabia's main clans, each of which had for centuries affixed a tribal idol to the walls of the Ka'bah representing their chief deities. As the soldiers continued chanting, a representative of each clan approached the Ka'bah. Using their swords and spears, the men began prying off the idols' lead fastenings.

Muhammad watched silently as the clans dismantled their own deities, signaling their decision to break free from the ways of the past. The action had to be the men's own. Genuine change had to come from an internal desire to improve and self-liberate.

For Meccans watching the scene, the destruction of the idols reflected the disintegration of the illusions to which they had long clung. For centuries they had lived in fear of these clay idols, yet no thunderbolt now descended from the sky to strike down the clan's representatives. The impotent gods had failed to defend themselves. Moreover, seeing the clans depose their own idols reinforced the notion that each person had the power to choose their own path.

Next, Muhammad silently ascended the Ka'bah's steps. It was on these steps that as a young orphan he had declared Barakah a free woman, his first act of liberation. Returning as a man in his sixties, he had a much larger mission: to help liberate the people of Arabia from the self-imposed servitude of *Jahiliyyah*.

Muhammad paused for a moment outside the shrine's open door, accompanied by twelve of his closest followers, including 'Ali, Abu Bakr, Bilal, and Salman. The last time Muhammad had been inside the Ka'bah was more than fifty years earlier, when his grandfather had used his esteemed position as chief elder to grant his young grandson access to a place that had been the exclusive realm of elite priests and elders. Muhammad had never forgotten the haunting interior, filled with idols, incense, priestly incantations, and blood sacrifices to the gods.

After pulling himself together, Muhammad motioned for the group of followers to join him inside. The formerly enslaved like Bilal and Salman, who never would have been permitted to enter, passed through the Ka'bah's door and struggled to adjust their eyes to the shrine's murky interior. In the gloomy haze, Muhammad kept his head bowed and his hands on his staff. After such sudden success, he had to think carefully about what to do next. Every word uttered over the next hour would indelibly shape the course of Arabia's new era.

He motioned to his followers to begin clearing out the Ka'bah. They carried hundreds of idols outside one by one. In the plaza surrounding the shrine, Khalid and other sons of Meccan elders systematically smashed the clay statues. The Meccans watched as members of the city's elite led the purge. Meanwhile Muhammad remained out of sight, meditating inside the Ka'bah.

After about an hour, the shrine's interior was bare—save for one item on the northwest interior wall. Muhammad's followers began to remove the Byzantine painting of Mary holding a young Jesus. Fifty-four years earlier, when his grandfather took him inside the sanctuary, the icon had mesmerized the newly orphaned boy. The image of young Jesus touching his mother's cheek as she embraced him had evoked his own mother's deathbed a few weeks earlier. Once again, Mary stared at him, a reminder of the life mission Aminah had bestowed upon him as she died: be a world-changer.

Muhammad looked intently at the icon. Then he lifted his hand, signaling to his followers that they should leave the picture in place. Unlike pagan statues, the icon was not an idol to be worshipped but a tribute to

predecessor prophets of monotheism, figures revered in Qur'anic passages. (It would remain there until 683 CE, when the Ka'bah caught
fire.)

Now Muhammad motioned for his followers to leave. As they exited
through the thick tapestry over the door, they looked back to see the
prophet prostrate himself, facing north toward Jerusalem. Narrow bands
of light illuminated a dusty haze of incense. The sound of the last idols
being smashed in the plaza outside punctuated the interior quiet. For
the first time in over a thousand years, the Ka'bah was devoid of idols,
and Muhammad's prayers to the sole Creator of the universe reverber-
ated as they rose through the shrine.

Thirty minutes later, 'Ali pushed open the door to inform Muhammad that his followers had cleared all the idolatrous debris from the
Ka'bah's precinct. It was time for him to address the people of Mecca.
Ending his solitary reflection, Muhammad exited the shrine and stood
on its top step. Without saying a word, he signaled to his core followers to implement a prearranged plan to gather the elders of Dar-un-
Nadwah before him. They summoned each elder from his home and
escorted him through the streets to the Ka'bah plaza.

Soon Muhammad's fiercest opponents stood arrayed before him, at
his mercy. Muhammad gazed down at them. An uneasy silence hovered over the thousands assembled, the largest gathering the city had
ever witnessed. The sun's rays glittered, reflecting off the thousands of
pieces of armor and raised spears of Muhammad's men. As the Meccans
watched from their rooftops, they assumed the moment of reckoning
had come.

Finally, Muhammad spoke. "I am the son of 'Abdul-Muttalib!" he
declared, reminding his audience of his grandfather, the chief elder, who
on that same spot sixty years earlier had publicly declared Muhammad's
unique name. Muhammad then looked the city's elders in the eye, one
by one, and asked, "What do you think I should do with all of you?"

They understood that Muhammad was challenging them to search
their hearts and compare what they would have done to him had their
fates been reversed. Everyone knew the unspoken truth, that the elders would have happily massacred Muhammad and his followers. But
Muhammad was granting them the chance to decide their own fate, a

critical first step in emerging from the *Jahiliyyah* belief that everything was predestined. The elders considered the question before responding, "You are an honorable and kind brother and the son of a gracious brother."

Muhammad closed his eyes. All were silent. The elders anxiously awaited Muhammad's response. After several minutes, he opened his eyes. Again, he looked each elder in the eye, one by one, removing all expression from his face. Finally, he announced, "On this day, I revoke the tradition of vendetta! No more blood! Go! You are absolved of your aggression. You are forgiven and granted a fresh start."

A wave of relief surged through Mecca. There would be no massacre. Traditionally, an Arabian conqueror would seize such a moment to declare, *"Al-yawmu yawmul-malhamah!"* (Today is the day of slaughter!). But as he descended the Ka'bah steps, Muhammad switched one letter in his final declaration, which inverted its meaning. He announced, *"Al-yawmu, yawmul-marhamah!"* (Today is the day of amnesty!).

❖ ❖ ❖

According to Arabia's traditional tribal code, the inhabitants of a conquered city became slaves of their conqueror. While Muhammad had terrified the Meccans into abject surrender earlier in the morning, with his unexpected declaration of amnesty they suddenly felt emancipated to step outside their homes—and their old selves—without fear. By declining to seek vengeance, Muhammad made clear he refused to see himself as an aggrieved victim or shackled to the past. In so doing, he demonstrated to the Meccans how to move forward.

As word of Muhammad's declaration of amnesty spread through Mecca, the frenzied emotions evoked by the day's drama prompted an astonishing reaction. Hundreds of Meccans spontaneously emerged from their homes carrying personal idols—clay figures their ancestors had revered for centuries—and began smashing the statues in the streets. Of their own volition, the Meccans began to dismantle the system of idolatry that had frozen them for so long.

While Meccans destroyed their idols, Muhammad and his disciples began to cleanse the Ka'bah: removing altars, scrubbing away remnants of blood sacrifices, and anointing the interior with precious perfumes to eliminate the stench of burnt offerings. After several hours, the sanctuary and its surrounding plaza were purified, ready for the new era of blossoming.

Muhammad then turned to Bilal and asked him to ascend the Ka'bah. Bilal climbed up the side of the shrine, grasping hold of its external tapestries, and soon stood atop the highest building in Mecca. The Abyssinian had once been dragged across the sand with a massive stone on his chest as a punishment for daring to insist he was a unique individual. Yet there he stood, above everyone, on the roof of the city's holiest edifice, proclaiming the *athan* (Muslim call to prayer) in his melodious accented Arabic: "Hasten with a focused mind to reestablish broken connections! Hasten with a mind focused on the tools for success!"

Bilal's cry signified that Mecca was no longer a pagan city but rather a center of monotheism, with the Ka'bah restored to its original purpose of worshipping the Abrahamic God. It was also a call to action. To embrace real change, the Meccans needed to go beyond merely smashing idols. Everyone, regardless of past or clan, could choose to unleash themselves. A new era of meritocracy and equality had begun.

Mecca's elders stared in shocked disbelief as a formerly enslaved African called them to action from atop their ancestors' shrine. Though Muhammad had pardoned them, they had declined to join in the idol smashing and shrine cleansing. Instead, because the public had overrun the elders' customary meeting spot beside the Ka'bah, they assembled under the canopy beside the Zamzam Well and watched the old order they had so desperately sought to preserve crumble before their eyes. The sight of Bilal atop the Ka'bah disgusted many of them.

"A black crow desecrating the holy sanctuary," grumbled Abu Sufyan. "The elders who died at Badr were blessed not to have lived long enough to see this day." His son Mu'awiyah nodded in agreement. Suddenly powerless, the Umayyad clan elites nurtured their resentment and humiliation—yet they would have to bide their time before taking revenge.

The elders watched as the people of Mecca streamed into the plaza to congratulate the city's new chief elder, Muhammad. He sat by the Ka'bah door, which he insisted remain open to all regardless of wealth, tribal prestige, creed, or gender. Curious Meccans seized the first opportunity in their lives to explore the shrine's interior. They gathered in clusters, talking about their city's abrupt transformation.

Muhammad noticed a poor man sitting beside a rich Meccan, who promptly yanked his garments away from the other man's touch. "There is no basis for fearing social contamination or for superstitious scapegoating," Muhammad declared. Then he posed a rhetorical question to the affluent man: "Did you fear that his poverty would transfer to you or that your wealth would transfer to him?"

As the stars began to sparkle, Muhammad returned to his tent on the outskirts of the city. Many of his companions, including Abu Bakr, 'Umar, and 'Uthman, slept in their old homes for the first time in years, while 'Ali spent the night in Muhammad and Khadijah's long-abandoned mansion.

Early the next morning, Muhammad arrived at the Ka'bah to initiate dawn prayers, the first time he had ever publicly led prayers in Mecca. As the sun rose, the elders again gathered before Muhammad outside the Ka'bah. In contrast to his taciturn demeanor of the previous day, Muhammad was quite communicative.

His first declaration of the morning addressed the elders of the Dar-un-Nadwah assembly. The elders were welcome to retain their positions in the new system, Muhammad announced, but membership in the council would no longer be limited by age or gender. Worthy females and males of any age would gain appointment to the assembly based on their knowledge and expertise. To emphasize the point, Muhammad announced his choice for the first chief Imam (senior spiritual leader) of Mecca: a sixteen-year-old named 'Attab ibn Usayd, who would also serve on the Dar-un-Nadwah council. In fact, Muhammad soon named several other promising youths from various clans to join the council alongside veteran elders.

Known for his precociousness and wisdom, 'Attab would serve as Mecca's chief Imam for the next twelve years, leading the city through turbulent days with a steady hand. But at the moment, the elders struggled to accept someone so young in such a solemn position of authority. Somewhat tempering the elders' shock was that 'Attab was from the Umayyad clan and a relative of Abu Sufyan's, as well as the son-in-law of Muhammad's longtime nemesis, 'Amr ibn Hisham. Although he was related to Muhammad's two harshest persecutors, the young man had displayed great merit. His surprise selection underlined Muhammad's discarding of the old Arabian custom of discriminating against members of enemy clans and venerating age and bloodlines over excellence.

A Qur'anic revelation reinforced the imperative to judge individuals on their own merits:

> *Al-la taziru waziratuw-wizra ukhra,*
> No soul shall bear the burden of another's conduct,
>
> *wa al-laysa lil-insani il-la ma sa'a.*
> as humans are only responsible for their own actions.
>
> *Wa an-na sa'yahu sawfa yura.*
> So, let each person prove their worth by showing their potential.
>
> *Thumma yujzah-ul-jaza'al-awfa!*
> Then they shall be amply rewarded!

For a tribal society in which clan relations defined civic affairs and social interaction, such a declaration amounted to a revolution.

Nonetheless, Muhammad understood that the old guard needed reassurance that they, too, could thrive in the new order. The ruling merchants of Mecca had benefited financially from idolatry, earning vast sums of money from pilgrims to the Ka'bah who purchased clothing and devotional mementos.

One by one, Muhammad called his former adversaries to appear before him. Rather than demand reparations, he gave each elder lavish gifts, including camels and silks he had brought from Medina. Though several of Muhammad's followers, including 'Umar, disagreed with Muhammad's leniency toward the elders, he did not justify his actions. But the unusual gesture suggested he sought to both ease their concerns and demonstrate the kind of fresh start he expected them to accord him.

The following day, Muhammad's family arrived in Mecca. His daughter Fatimah, his grandchildren, and Barakah had trailed a few days behind the army, just in case the situation grew precarious. Entering Mecca, they beheld a city transformed. But Muhammad wanted to make sure they did not mistakenly conclude that they were new royalty with special privileges.

He gathered the Hashemites, including immediate family and cousins. Whatever he owned he would share with them, Muhammad explained, but whatever was in the public domain would remain sacred. If they wanted wealth, power, and prestige, they needed to earn it like everyone else. He would not run Arabia like a family business. Nepotism would violate the new era of equal opportunities. Muhammad addressed his relatives one by one to ensure everyone understood. He began with his only surviving daughter: "Oh Fatimah, ask me what you please from my personal wealth, but do not transgress the rights of others or expect special favors for being my daughter." He repeated the same message for his one surviving uncle, Al-'Abbas. Muhammad soon backed up his words with actions. When he noticed his young grandson taking a date from a basket intended as a donation to the poor, Muhammad rushed to remove it from his mouth and informed the toddler that the date belonged to the needy.

Meanwhile, the volunteers in Muhammad's ad hoc army began to dismantle their camps outside Mecca and return home. Accounts of Muhammad's remarkable conquest soon spread across Arabia, and Muhammad realized that he needed to clarify his intentions to the surrounding empires and clans, particularly religious groups that might take the wrong message from his cleansing of the Ka'bah.

Muhammad dictated over eighty letters to communities throughout Arabia, dispatching messengers on horseback to swiftly deliver the epistles. What happened at the Ka'bah was not an attack on religion or houses of worship, Muhammad took pains to explain, but rather restoring a monotheistic shrine to its original state. Religious communities and their leaders need not fear. The problematic aspects of paganism were its unjust cultural practices like female infanticide, human sacrifice, and inequality. As someone who had himself been persecuted for his distinctive beliefs and denounced as an infidel in a holy war, Muhammad insisted that freedom of conscience should remain paramount.

To the Christians of Najran, who had sent a delegation to Medina and even held services in the *masjid*, Muhammad wrote: "There shall be no interference with the practice of your religion or your sacred observances; there shall be no changes in your rights or privileges. Your Churches shall be protected and no restraints shall be placed upon your sacred spaces. You will neither oppress nor be oppressed. You will commit to forgive all vendettas and commit not to practice vendettas. There shall be neither tithes nor taxes levied upon you, nor shall you be required to furnish provisions for troops."

To the Magi of Arabia's Zoroastrians, he wrote: "This is my letter conferring the protection of God upon the Zoroastrians and any descendants they may have, so long as they may remain, regarding their lives and their properties, whether they be in the hills or the plains, maintaining their wells and pastures. They will neither oppress nor be oppressed. They shall not be impeded in the possession of their fire temples as well as the landed property attached to them. None shall restrict them in the performance of their burials or the rituals of their religion."

According to the constitution of Medina, Jews were effectively "one *ummah*" (community) with Muhammad's followers and thus did not require any extra assurances. The Jewish clan of Banul Harith would remain in Mecca for centuries.

All people in Arabia, in fact, were free to practice their own religions. Aside from forbidding human sacrifices and infanticide, Muhammad left pagans to their own devices. Some pagans remained in Mecca with their idols for generations, with no pressure to convert. The city remained open to all people, as did the Ka'bah shrine.

One old practice that Muhammad did stamp out in Mecca was slave trading. Muhammad never formally outlawed slavery, which was deeply engrained in Arabian culture, but he made clear that slavery was antithetical to the message of Islam. After his conquest of Mecca, many locals made a show of emancipating their enslaved servants in Muhammad's presence—just as Medinians had done when Muhammad entered their city eight years earlier.

When Mecca's markets reopened after Muhammad's conquest, the city's onetime slave market remained shuttered.

❖ ❖ ❖

As the seat of the Ka'bah and the center of trade routes, Mecca was the de facto capital of Arabia. By conquering the city, Muhammad became

Arabia's ruler. People across Arabia were eager to be part of the new meritocratic civic order of hope and progress. The news of Muhammad's bestowing lavish gifts on his former enemies assured Arabian elders elsewhere that their positions would be safe in a system of equality.

Now that Muhammad had established himself among the Arabs, he faced a new problem: being idolized himself. The day after he entered Mecca, the locals began to hail him as "king of the Arabs." Concerned by the impulse to glorify him, Muhammad demurred: "I am a simple guide to help channel Divine inspiration into the lives of others." Muhammad repeatedly insisted, "Do not glorify me! Do not exult me!" To emphasize the point to his new followers, he added, "Do not idolize me!"

Muhammad did not smash false gods to become godlike himself. He wanted the new order exalted, not a human being. When various tribal leaders from across the region sought to name him Arabia's king, he again refused. "I was offered kingship, abundant wealth, and power, but I chose the life of a servant."

Muhammad technically remained homeless for the rest of his life. He never reclaimed his old manor in Mecca and instead camped in the wilderness. He did not fashion a crown for himself or replace his simple garments with extravagant robes. He did not adorn himself with precious jewels or insist people bow before him. He continued to meet the simplest of people without appointment or audience. As he observed, "The dominion of power was offered to me, yet I chose to be a servant and a guide of the people."

After the conquest of Mecca, Muhammad never married again. Many Arabian tribal leaders offered him their kinswomen, as was customary in dealing with a great chieftain and ruler, yet he politely declined.

Rulers in tribal societies typically placed their relatives in key leadership positions in order to consolidate and safeguard their power. Yet Muhammad intentionally refrained from assigning his family members to positions of power, unless they were the most qualified candidates.

Remarkably, after the conquest of Mecca, Muhammad began to increasingly withdraw from managing the new system he had established. In a way, he was part of the old order, and the youth who helped usher in the new order had to manage it themselves. He did not see himself as a political or military leader but rather as a catalyst for change: a spiritual leader and mentor. His preferred title, after all, was *rasul*. The success of the new system, Muhammad understood, would come only if others could replicate and sustain it.

The tribal elders of Arabia assumed Muhammad would establish himself at Dar-un-Nadwah. The assembly served as the central seat of power in Arabia. Indeed, when his companions from Medina saw Muhammad's hometown welcome him, they feared he would not return with them to Medina. "You welcomed me when others turned me away, and you risked your lives to support my message," Muhammad gently reminded them. "Do you think that now I would turn my back on you? You are a part of me, and I am a part of you!"

Medina, the one community that had proved its commitment to him and his movement when no other did, would serve as the new capital of Arabia. The new order he had established at Medina would become the model for the rest of Arabia. Mecca may have enjoyed the prestige of tradition as seat of the Ka'bah, but that value was based on the past. Medina, in contrast, was a vibrant place of flowing change that focused on the future.

As Muhammad and his family rode out of Mecca, Abu Sufyan and his son Mu'awiyah saw an opening. They understood that his bold victory had captivated the people of Arabia, but they also suspected that Arabs would struggle to embrace Muhammad's ideas. No one could simply overturn a millennium of *Jahiliyyah* in a few weeks. With Muhammad gone, they had the freedom to strategize their return to power.

If Muhammad was aware of the Umayyad clan's plans, he said nothing. He was focusing on Medina, where he needed to resolve an issue that had lingered for over fifty years in relation to his mother. In the decades since the burial, Muhammad had never returned to her grave. He had passed near the cemetery many times yet never dared to approach. The moment to seal that open wound had at last arrived.

As he entered Medina in the early morning, the people came out to greet him with the song they had chanted upon his arrival eight years earlier. "The full moon has ascended to illuminate and redeem us," they sang. Yet this time they had redeemed themselves. Thanks to their steadfast commitment, a new moon had indeed risen over Arabia.

Though a returning victor, Muhammad did not host a raucous

celebration or make an epic speech. Rather, he remained quiet, brooding about what lay ahead. That evening, he headed for the cemetery, guided by locals of the Banu Najjar clan and accompanied by several of his closest followers, including Barakah, 'Ali, Zaid, and Abu Bakr. He had last walked in the cemetery at the age of six, escorted by Barakah as tears rolled down his cheeks.

As they approached the simple cemetery dotted with foot-high mounds of earth marking each grave, gusts of wind caused the dust to whirl. The Banu Najjar clansmen stopped before a low-lying mound over a simple grave that was weathered by time. They turned to Muhammad and pointed at the burial plot. Muhammad stood absolutely still, staring down at the mound; tears filled his eyes. Then Muhammad knelt at Aminah's grave. Sobbing, he repeated his mother's final words: "Oh Muhammad, be a world-changer!"

More than fifty-four years had passed since he stood stupefied at his mother's grave, and he had, in his own way, changed his world. The long-established social reality of *Jahiliyyah* he was born into no longer existed. Orphans, women, the enslaved, and the downtrodden finally had a voice. Parents no longer feared their children might be abducted and sold into slavery. The implementation of his public health ideas had directly helped curb diseases like the plague that had claimed his father's life. Moreover, he had lived up to his name: becoming a role model for tens of thousands of followers, far exceeding the influence of his grandfather and his ancestors Hashim and Qusai.

If Aminah's death had marked the beginning of Muhammad's journey, his return to Medina as Arabia's leader completed the circle. Overwhelmed by more than five decades of pent-up emotions, Muhammad could not hold back his feelings. 'Ali noted that "he cried with so much emotion that he made us all cry."

Barakah knelt beside Muhammad. She stroked his shoulder and gently observed, "Indeed, you have fulfilled!" She had known Aminah well and could with authority reassure Muhammad that his mother would have been proud of the man he had become and the positive legacy he had bequeathed to his people.

The most powerful man in Arabia sat in the dust, crying, once again a simple orphan, a devoted and vulnerable son.

When the sun began to set, Muhammad finally stopped crying and bowed his head in reflection. Eventually, he stood up and returned to Medina, surrounded by his family and friends.

The next morning, Muhammad rose before dawn to sweep the *masjid*. That afternoon he carried firewood to the soup kitchen at the back of the *masjid*. He kindled a fire and prepared a broth, which he then served to the shelter's clientele. Afterward, he ground barley grains and prepared a simple dinner for his family. After dinner, he cleaned up and assisted with other household chores typically reserved in Arabian society for the enslaved and women. The world-changer had indeed chosen the life of a servant.

Muhammad's visit to his mother's grave not only closed a personal emotional circle but also marked his semiretirement from civic leadership. He began delegating leadership responsibilities. He would no longer serve as director of the *masjid*, instead assigning Ash-Shifa bint 'Abdillah to serve as head educator. She was one of his early followers, a brilliant woman whom Muhammad had previously hired to tutor his wives. Ash-Shifa was also an excellent scholar who had grown up in Mecca but had family roots in Medina. She would oversee all instruction in the *masjid* and in schools throughout Medina.

Appointing women to senior educational and clerical positions was another major break with *Jahiliyyah* custom and reflected Muhammad's strong commitment to merit-based leadership. For one of Medina's suburbs, Muhammad appointed as Imam a woman named Um Waraqah bint 'Abdillah ibn al-Harith. Middle-aged, she had displayed a mastery of the Qur'an, memorizing its passages and chanting them with mellifluous eloquence. She led the people of her neighborhood—both men and women—in prayer. Muhammad called her Ash-Shahidah (the expert witness) in a nod to her profound wisdom. He often visited her and counseled his closest followers to learn from her. She soon became a trusted advisor to top political leaders.

In addition to relinquishing his formal teaching duties, Muhammad turned over responsibility for Arabia's armed forces to a young prodigy named Usamah. Many of his followers protested the appointment of a sixteen-year-old to such an important post, but Muhammad saw that Usamah had an excellent ability to strategize. At Muhammad's direction, the force that conquered Mecca had disbanded, and Arabia thus maintained no standing army. Usamah would have to quickly marshal forces if the need arose.

Though Arabia under Muhammad's rule had no formal military or law enforcement, for the first time in its history people were free to travel without fear of attack or kidnapping. The strength of Muhammad's reputation among the tribes, and the new quasi-libertarian order he had established, provided for the safe flow of goods and people. Taking advantage of the newfound security, people from across the budding empire descended on Medina to meet the man who had ended *Jahiliyyah*.

When Muhammad received these visitors at the *masjid*, he wore his ragged tunic and eschewed any accessories except his signet ring, which he used to seal letters. He donated all the visitors' exquisite gifts to the community charitable trust to benefit those in need. When one delegation of dignitaries from eastern Arabia arrived at the *masjid*, they were confused to find a discussion group of simply dressed individuals sitting on the ground. Arabia's ultimate ruler surely had a throne, they assumed, and regal robes. They asked, "Who among you is Muhammad?"

❖ ❖ ❖

In the spirit of the job description etched in his signet ring, Muhammad had chosen to be a guide, not a ruler. In a way, the role of *rasul* meant returning to his days teaching at Dar-ul-Arqam, except now he could openly receive students from across Arabia. Acting as a *rasul* allowed him to live up to the name his grandfather had given him at birth: serving as an inspirational example of behavior that others might emulate.

Muhammad understood that he had an unprecedented opportunity to channel the divine message of personal growth and healing, but he also realized that, from the morning he entered Mecca, people would consider his every move and every utterance portentous. His brief private time inside the Ka'bah that day had been his last chance to be truly alone. Retreating to Medina, relinquishing leadership roles to the young, former slaves, and women, and dressing in simple linens were strategic choices.

As a *rasul*, Muhammad aimed to demonstrate how to implement ideas. With thousands of fervent new converts, he recognized their penchant for puritanism. To counter this impulse among his many new visitors, Muhammad insisted that his example not be frozen like a *Jahiliyyah* idol (*sanam*, the Arabic word for *idol*, literally meant frozen in time).

In his early days of prophethood, Muhammad had already given a name to his inspirational sayings: *Hadith*. The ancient Arabic word connoted footprints, specifically the footprints of others who had trod before to chart a new path. The art of Hadith had evolved over the centuries, and by Muhammad's time it signified a meaningful conversation that prompts reconsidering longstanding ideas in new ways. Muhammad called his sayings Hadith to distinguish them from the divinely inspired Qur'anic revelations.

More than 90 percent of historically credible Hadith come from the period following the conquest of Mecca. Muhammad's followers had swelled from just 150 when he fled Mecca eight years earlier to over 150,000 after his bloodless victory. Tens of thousands of these new followers peppered the prophet with questions and observed his actions—and Muhammad made a point of cultivating their curiosity. Although he had forbidden his followers to write about his life, he gave 'Ali and other select pupils permission to write down his most significant sayings. His teachings, rather than his biography, mattered.

The vast body of Hadith from the postconquest period show how Muhammad's style of speech and pedagogy evolved. No longer persecuted or on the defensive, he speaks with the confidence of an established prophet who had already turned sixty. His tone is that of a contemplative mystic engrossed in a quest for inner fulfillment. To reflect this spiritual search, Muhammad began teaching largely outdoors: on the sides of roads, in fields, and beside wells. Muhammad preferred to be out among people. He taught in an orchard, for instance, so that farmers could listen without having to interrupt their work.

A month after his return from Mecca, Muhammad sat with his students beside an orchard in Medina as a Jewish funeral procession passed. When he saw the bier approach, Muhammad paused the group's discussion so he could stand respectfully and asked his disciples to help carry the bier. Several new followers who had come from across Arabia were quizzical. "But that is a Jewish funeral?!"

Muhammad responded, "Is it not a soul, worthy of dignity and respect?" Though some zealous new followers wanted to view themselves as superior and separate, Muhammad urged them to look beyond social divisions. After the funeral passed, he added, "A true person of faith is someone who safeguards others from the harm caused by his tongue and his hand."

Muhammad made a point of pushing back against overzealous impulses. A few days after the Jewish funeral, Muhammad found a man sitting inside the *masjid* who proudly declared that he had decided to dedicate himself to worshipping God. He bragged that he was so committed to his new mission that he had left behind his wife and children, entrusting them to his brother's care. Muhammad tersely responded, "Your brother's actions are more righteous than yours. The hand that gives is better than the hand that takes." Muhammad did not want followers to misunderstand his example. He had retreated to meditate on Mount Hira only after ensuring his family's financial security—and he had never neglected familial duties, spending most of the week with Khadijah and their children.

Muhammad drove the point home a few weeks later when he encountered three men in the *masjid*, each trying to top the other with bold pledges of piety. "I will remain celibate," declared the first. "I will fast every day," vowed the second. "I will spend all nights in prayer," swore the third.

Muhammad stood at the pulpit and admonished them. "I am married, I don't fast every day, and I don't spend all my nights in prayer. I choose an approach of balance. This is my example (*sunnah*)!" A farmer who witnessed the exchange approached Muhammad to shake his hand. Feeling the roughness of the man's palm, Muhammad remarked, "I respect the working hand!" Though monks like Bahira and Waraqah had shared valuable insights, Muhammad insisted that hard-earned labor was more impactful than monastic seclusion and abstinence.

While Muhammad praised manual labor and entrepreneurial industry, he abhorred exploitative tycoons. As a young man in Mecca, he had established the Hilf-ul-Fudhul pact to protect vulnerable vendors from abusive Meccan elders and to ensure honest financial dealings. In fact, his intervention on behalf of a visiting Yemenite merchant had initially sparked the ire of 'Amr ibn Hisham. After the conquest of Mecca, Muhammad made a point of declaring to the local merchants, "I continue to uphold the pact that I swore during the era of *Jahiliyyah*, the Hilf-ul-Fudhul initiative to support the [economic] rights of all."

Meccan elders like 'Amr ibn Hisham were notorious for loaning money at exorbitant rates in order to trap impoverished people in debt bondage. Corrupt financial schemes like these deeply troubled Muhammad. While he had made small reforms to the practice during his early years in Medina, conquering Mecca enabled him to implement more significant chages by resetting the commercial terms of Arabia's markets. Qur'anic revelations forbade usury (*riba*) as a major societal injustice, describing someone "who exploits others" by "devouring usury" as "mentally ill" and declaring that the "one who devours through usury is in active war against the Divine." To clarify matters, the Qur'an observed, "The Loving Divine has blessed commerce and condemned usury."

As the *rasul* shaping Arabia's new order, Muhammad could implement systemic change across all of Arabia's clans. Extensive Qur'anic passages, guaranteeing the right of women to inherit, were revealed. The new inheritance laws were quite intricate, as they aimed to divide an estate fairly among diverse family members. These prompted scholars to develop new formulas to calculate an estate's division correctly—ultimately sparking new fields in mathematics.

When a plague broke out in Arabia about six months after the conquest of Mecca, Muhammad responded to the public health crisis by stressing the importance of taking responsible action to limit the disease's spread. He declared, "Every disease has a cure; therefore, seek healing." The prophet used his keen sense of observation to identify the concept of contamination and exposure—and deduced that isolating people stricken with disease was an effective way to exterminate contagious diseases.

He taught that individuals in a town hit by an epidemic outbreak should remain in place rather than fleeing: "If an infectious disease breaks out in a land, then do not enter it and, if you are present, do not leave it." Though he was not a physician or public health expert, Muhammad pioneered quarantine techniques, observing, "Keep the distance of one lance [two meters] to two lances [four meters] between you and the infected."

The effective implementation of quarantine techniques prevented the plague from spreading to Medina even as delegations of visitors continued to pour in from all over the Arabian Peninsula. The dedication of these new students and their hunger to learn impressed Muhammad. Upon receiving a delegation from Bahrain that had traveled over eight hundred miles to study, he observed, "Wisdom and knowledge are the greatest objective. Wherever and with whomever they may be found, they should be sought. Seeking knowledge is an essential duty of every person. Seek knowledge from the cradle to the grave"—even travel as far as China if necessary.

One day he walked into the *masjid* and saw a large class gathered around Medina's chief educator, Ash-Shifa—both the instructor and the majority of the students were female. "Oh, how wonderful are the women of Medina," he marveled. "Their modesty did not prevent them from competing with men in the pursuit of knowledge." Then he added, "To educate a man is to inform an individual, yet to educate a woman is to empower an entire nation!" Of his eight thousand top students, more than two thousand were women, many of whom surpassed their male counterparts. In addition, many of his top students were adolescents, as Muhammad enjoyed mentoring young protégés and quickly elevating outstanding ones to positions of authority so the public might benefit from their talent.

Muhammad's passion for young students extended to his own grandchildren. One elder who came to visit him was shocked to see the *rasul* on his hands and knees with his grandsons Hasan and Husain riding on his back. Muhammad asked him, "Why do you look so surprised? Have you never played with your children or shown them affection?"

The man said, "I have ten children grown into adulthood, and I have never hugged or kissed any of them!"

To which Muhammad replied, "The one who cannot be compassionate with his own children cannot be expected to be compassionate to others."

Muhammad's grandsons accompanied him to most of his public addresses. He often delivered sermons from the *masjid*'s pulpit with the two little boys in his arms, and on occasion he even interrupted sermons to attend to their needs. When he was prostrate in prayer, they would often playfully hop on his back like horsemen, shrilling in delight. Muhammad's public acknowledgment of children impacted the demographics of public assemblies, and parents felt free to come to the *masjid* accompanied by their children. A man once attended with his son and daughter—placing the daughter on the ground beside him and the son on his lap. Muhammad admonished him, "Treat your children equally!"

The *rasul*'s emphasis on children dovetailed with a remarkable development in his own life. Shortly after returning from the conquest of Mecca, Muhammad's wife Maria gave birth to a son. The boy was born on a moonless night, delivered into the capable hands of Barakah. In a moving ceremony, Muhammad named his son Abraham in honor of the great patriarch. With Abraham's arrival, Muhammad once again became a family man, spending much of his time attending to his young son. Filled with nostalgia, Muhammad also began visiting Khadijah's friends often and making food donations to the needy in her memory.

For the first time in decades, Muhammad was safe from danger and enjoying the sanctuary of family life. And, unlike his earlier blissful period with Khadijah and their young children, he had also now achieved the spiritual fulfillment that had so long remained elusive—not to mention living up to the expectations of his grandfather and mother. In a sense, this was the pleasant autumn of Muhammad's life, a time for him to enjoy the fruits of decades of suffering and perseverance—and it was further enhanced by the stimulation of brilliant students from all over Arabia as they engaged in open discussion about his teachings.

The tranquil days would not last long. On the morning of August 3, 631, Muhammad approached Abraham's bed to rouse his son. The boy was cold. Muhammad had twice before encountered this horror. Abraham had died in his sleep.

In yet another heartbreaking ceremony, Muhammad buried the infant in the same cemetery where his daughters were interred. Against the remarkable backdrop of a full solar eclipse, Muhammad placed Abraham's body in the grave, as tears streaked down his face. Superstitious Arabian society traditionally associated eclipses with bad events, as a black veil that covered the sun's face in a sign of mourning. "The heavens are saddened by your sorrow," his followers cried, as they watched the burial. Muhammad appreciated their sympathy but insisted that celestial events bore no relation to human activities. He softly responded, "The sun, the moon, and all the workings of the universe are set to a cosmic order and do not revolve around human affairs."

The death of Abraham revived that distinctive pattern of Muhammad's life: achieving noteworthy accomplishments, then retreating into family life to enjoy the fruits of his success—only to have a devastatingly tragic loss spark a new restless quest for fulfillment. Muhammad had yet again suffered a terrible loss and would have to dig deep to turn his pain into one more act of greatness. With a rapidly growing number of followers, the final task of his mission would be to make sure his belief system was robust enough to live on in perpetuity.

10

※

ISLAM

Preserving Core Ideals
for Posterity

Qiba: 5:00 p.m., Wednesday, October 16, 631 CE

With his back to an ancient palm tree, Muhammad sat on the ground in a circle of twelve scribes. Amid a sonata of chirping birds and running water from nearby irrigation channels, Muhammad coordinated his ensemble of assistants through a complex editing process of the Qur`an. Though reliant on the secretaries surrounding him to transcribe and rearrange passages in written form, Muhammad directed the entire operation from memory. Every passage revealed over the past twenty years existed as a distinct data point in his mind, and he guided his scribes to organize each word with precision.

Sitting to Muhammad's right was twenty-one-year-old Zaid ibn Thabit, a Medinian whom Muhammad had groomed to be a leading expert on the Qur`an; Zaid would ultimately consolidate a definitive version of the scripture. Zaid later recalled how the scribes had sat around a heap of texts arranged on a large straw mat, checking passages jotted down over the years on all manner of materials. "We compiled the Qur`an from many sheets into one," Zaid explained. "We assembled the volume from palm fronds, white stone slabs, parchments, camel saddles, camel ribs, and sheep shoulder bones."

When a divine revelation had suddenly emerged from Muhammad's lips, scribes rushed to capture it in writing. Sometimes the lack of writing materials forced them to scratch notes on camel saddles as the group rode through the desert or to use leaves pulled from nearby trees. From these diverse fragments of transcribed revelations—6,236 passages in total—Muhammad now labored to forge one coherent work.

Qur`anic revelations were not a linear narrative but rather comprised an extended series of reflections from distinct moments in Muhammad's life over the past twenty years. He therefore aimed to assemble a product that could resonate with audiences who were not present when each verse was originally revealed.

Periodically, he shut his eyes and fell silent, swaying in quiet contemplation for several minutes. Then his eyes slowly opened, and in a clear voice he directed his scribes to arrange passages and even entire chapters in a new order.

The scribes often struggled to keep up with the maestro's intense pace. In a flurry, Muhammad directed that they consolidate an isolated passage into an existing chapter, then called for them to shift another passage from its original chapter to a different one. Whenever he added something, he insisted the scribes read it back to him to ensure correct transcription. Despite being unlettered, he occasionally requested spelling revisions to certain words (because Arabic was written as it sounded, an illiterate person could spot mistakes) or gave special new names to important passages (for instance, dubbing the Qur`an's longest passage *Ayat-ud-Dayn*—Guide to Business Transactions). To help relax his team during the arduous sessions and inspire his creative flow, Muhammad preferred to sit outside in the cool breeze near running water.

Though he did not say so directly to his troop of secretaries, Muhammad was in a race against time. Blessed with his grandfather's genes and bolstered by a healthy lifestyle, he had fewer than twenty grey hairs (according to his valet Anas ibn Malik), and his wrinkle-free skin belied his sixty-one stress-filled years. Nonetheless, Muhammad could sense he did not have long to live, and his son Abraham's sudden death had shocked him into action to solidify a lasting legacy.

Ego was not Muhammad's driving motivation, which was the realization that his life's mission was incomplete. Muhammad had only changed his world, not the entire world. Ending *Jahiliyyah* and establishing a new meritocratic system were not enough. To truly become a world-changer, he must leave behind something that could continue to motivate people long after his death. The inspiring example that had roused the people of Arabia from willful stagnation to a state of dynamic blossoming needed to be preserved for future generations and audiences far beyond Mecca and Medina.

The recognition of his own mortality forced Muhammad into one last burst of creative inspiration. His followers needed a vivid description of the Divine Mentor to help replace the hundreds of shattered idols. They needed a coherent manual to help spark their blossoming. And they needed a practical methodology to help guide their lives toward real-world results.

With little time to wrap up his earthly work, Muhammad was forced to triage. He had named his mindset *Islam* (striving toward completion) and once again applied that attitude to his final days. He understood that many of his own grand dreams would remain unfulfilled. Lacking both the time and resources to turn his vision into reality, Muhammad settled on the next-best alternative. He would lay the foundation for others to build upon, expressing his teachings in the clearest possible terms so future generations could pursue their own blossoming and create their own world-changing ideas.

❖ ❖ ❖

The conquest of Mecca had sparked the removal of 360 idols from the Ka‘bah. Yet Muhammad recognized the innate human desire to understand reality through a tangible framework, which the idols had given them. While he taught that "the Divine is beyond the comprehension of mortal senses," the people of Arabia needed ways to relate to the unseen God of their ancestor Abraham. As someone whose own life had been shaped by the name given to him by his grandfather, Muhammad embarked on an unprecedented naming spree to help empower people to develop their own relationship with the Divine.

After sunset prayer one evening, as Venus sparkled brightly in the darkening sky, Muhammad sat with his disciples around a fire, relaxing after a long day of Qur'anic editing on the outskirts of Medina. Strong winds gusted around the group, causing the flames of their campfire to lash at the edges of the fire pit. Nearby, a Bedouin woman stood clutching her two-year-old son beside her family's own campfire. Each time the flames surged in their direction, she spun the boy behind her, shielding him from the flares. The scene enthralled Muhammad's disciples.

"Do you think that this mother would ever cast her son into the fire?" Muhammad suddenly asked.

His perplexed followers responded, "Never! She would rather die."

To which Muhammad mused: "Then know that the Loving Divine (Allah) is more affectionate and compassionate toward the creation than that mother is toward her son."

By using the vivid image of a mother shielding her vulnerable child, Muhammad evoked the original Semitic meaning of the term *Allah*: a mother unconditionally embracing her crying child. The Semites had originally understood the Divine as a feminine force providing sympathetic maternal love. Only when patriarchal structures replaced Arabia's ancient matriarchal system did the concept of God evolve to a powerful warrior defending his people. The word *Allah* had nonetheless retained its original feminine ending in Arabic, even as it was declined like a masculine noun.

The next day the call to assemble resounded from the *masjid* in the late afternoon, outside the usual prayer times. The people of Medina looked up, confused: Was there an emergency? When they entered the *masjid*, they found a smiling Muhammad standing at the pulpit. Once the courtyard filled, Muhammad looked around the crowd, as if to address each member personally, and declared, "The Divine has ninety-nine cardinal names, each essential to success. Anyone who truly understands and embodies them shall achieve lasting fulfillment." He then reminded his audience of the divine proclamation: "I am to my creation as they perceive me to be." If the Divine reflected human perspectives, Muhammad urged people in turn to aspire to live out godly attributes: "Emulate the characteristics of the Divine in your own lives."

The reference to 99 was not literal but rather an Arabic idiom to convey infinity. The Qur'an alone provides 120 names, while Muhammad employed an additional 400 names in Hadith teachings.

As a child watching his grandfather lead the elders' council, Muhammad had learned how to deftly deploy language to paint images with words. This deluge of Divine epithets thus replaced the Ka'bah's destroyed idols with a vibrant and multidimensional God constantly in motion who provided inspiration for people no matter their state of being. Each name described a relatable context that in turn evoked a metaphoric and beneficial function that the Divine provided.

Embedded in every moniker was a vignette of action and interaction. In fact, many names came in response to the specific challenges people who sought out Muhammad in Medina were facing in the final months of his life. On Friday mornings, Muhammad often sat beside the *masjid* pulpit to receive visitors, providing them with mediation and counseling. One day, a woman approached to complain about her husband and insisted on her right to get a divorce—a right the Qur'an had recently granted in a break with Arabian tradition. When Muhammad inquired why she insisted on a divorce, the woman explained, "My husband is physically unappealing, always disheveled and filthy." Muhammad asked that his followers find and clean up the vagabond husband.

An hour later, the once malodorous husband arrived at the *masjid* completely transformed: handsome, dressed in a fine tunic, and anointed in fragrant perfumes. Muhammad motioned for the man to sit beside his wife, who did not recognize him. When he reached out to touch his wife's hand, she objected, "Sir, I am a married woman!"

Muhammad smiled and informed her, "This is your husband! Do you still want to divorce him?"

Blushing, the wife replied, "No, I'll keep him."

In the moment of reconciliation, Muhammad announced, "The Divine embodies all beauty and loves to see beauty manifest everywhere and in everything." Thus was born a new Divine name: Al-Jamil (the beautifier, or source of all beauty).

In person, Muhammad could serve as a *rasul*, channeling divine inspiration to his followers and mediating their disputes. But for his mindset to live on, God had to remain an accessible mentor without Muhammad's personal intercession. The people of Arabia already believed that Abraham's God was the Creator, yet He remained a distant deity. For generations, idols had served as intermediaries. Without relying on graven images, people needed both intellectual and emotional ways to relate to God. Muhammad's many names finally made Abraham's God accessible and relatable. By providing hundreds of names, Muhammad gave individuals extensive opportunities to find the attributes of God that resonated with them.

To help people build their own direct relationship with the Divine, Muhammad drew on three key aspects of the relationships that had sustained his own life's journey: mentoring guidance, visionary inspiration, and sensitive healing.

The Divine could be experienced in many forms, including

❖ Ar-Raqib—the Gentle Shepherd who cares for the injured
❖ Ar-Ra`uf—the Empathetic Soother
❖ Ash-Shafi—the Healer who guides recovery that emerges from within
❖ At-Tayyib—the Applier of Ointment to wounds
❖ Al-Sami'—the Attentive Listener who does not judge

Muhammad bequeathed to future generations essential qualities that could help them succeed. They might not have a *rasul* physically present in their lives, but they would always have direct access to the dynamic Divine Mentor.

Taken together, the hundreds of names of God painted a multidimensional portrait of an unseen Divine force. More than twelve centuries before modernist art movements like Cubism tried to simultaneously present multiple perspectives on a single subject, Muhammad had fashioned hundreds of fragments of Divine attributes into an unprecedented and intricate depiction of God.

❖ ❖ ❖

Once inspired to emulate the Divine, people needed a guide to the art of blossoming. In the final months of his life, Muhammad faced the challenge of not only organizing thousands of scattered fragments of Qur`anic revelation into a coherent whole but also capturing the intensity of the moments of revelation so mass audiences could share them. While the editing process with his scribes involved organizing words, phrases, and entire chapters—as well as adding new ones—Muhammad was not bequeathing a scripture so much as an experience.

The term for the divinely inspired manual—*Qur`an*—actually described a process: blossoming. The Semitic roots *Q-R-A* signified a literal blossom and figurative chanted wisdom; the blossom is followed by fruits, wisdom by actions. In the ancient Semitic conception, the phenomenon of blossoming bridges awareness and action, consciousness translated into deeds. The Qur`an is not letters on a parchment or recited words but rather the reaction of readers and listeners who are choosing to change their behavior. In other words, the Qur`an is not an inanimate object but an interactive encounter that achieves success only if it sparks action.

The Qur`an therefore sought to captivate its audiences by offering a refreshingly novel experience. One striking aspect was its self-reflective tone, with revealed passages often commenting on their own purpose. "We systematically structured this Qur`an to inspire visionary thinking in stagnating people," it declared. Beyond articulating its own goals, the Qur`an clearly instructed its audience how to make the most of it:

> *Fa itha quri`al-Qur`anu fastami'u lahu wa ansitu la'allakum tuflihun.*
>
> When the Qur`an is chanted, listen carefully to its message and contemplate its methods in silent reflection so that you can be inspired toward the attainment of success.

Given Arabia's widespread illiteracy, Muhammad knew that the Qur`an as written scripture alone would not disseminate Islam to the masses. Rather, it had to be chanted, with written text serving as the score for a public recital that would engage diverse audiences.

Upon hearing the Qur`an, audiences in Arabia could not classify it according to any existing categories. It rhymed like Arabic poetry but did not adhere to strict meter. It echoed some of the undulating timbres of traditional incantation but with its own distinctive style. It recounted vignettes but lacked the formal structures of Arabic narrative storytelling. Every time its subject matter changed, so did the rhyme and rhythm of the passages—a completely new lyrical model. Moreover, it referenced biblical content but focused primarily on analyzing stories rather than recounting them. Part manifesto, part memoir, part meditation, part melodic presentation, the Qur`an resisted categorization to exist sui generis, fusing past models into an entirely new genre.

In keeping with its self-aware tone, the Qur'an offered instructions on how to recite it: *Wa rattil-il-Qur'ana tartila*—"Chant the Qur'an with clear elocution and rhythm for maximum impact." *Tartil* (eloquence), the term for the specific delivery style, described the careful hand motions used to raise a well bucket without spilling water. Recitation of the Qur'an required equivalent precision with the tongue and vocal cords. To train his followers to achieve *tartil*, Muhammad developed an entirely new field of elocution called *tajwid* (beautification). The term originally described how nomads tamed wild Arabian stallions, a kind of dressage Muhammad had observed as a child when he lived with the Banu Sa'd clan in the desert. Years of hard work and repetitive training ultimately paid off, creating prized stallions—or, in the case of the Qur'an, master reciters.

Muhammad had introduced the concept of *tajwid* early in his prophethood but formalized its rules of elocution only in the final months of his life. Previously, he had focused primarily on the ideas revealed in Qur'anic passages, but as he sat with his scribes Muhammad codified not just the correct order of the passages but also their vocalization. He instructed his followers in how to shape their lips to make the precise sound, identified when to elongate the intonation of certain vowels, and even altered the pronunciation of certain words.

In effect, Muhammad in his final months was creating a new language, replacing the old *Jahiliyyah* Arabic with Qur'anic Arabic. To express new ideas for an awakening after centuries of stagnation, the Qur'an's groundbreaking vocabulary drew on ancient root words to express fresh concepts. Muhammad even insisted on altering the spelling of certain key words. The transformed pronunciation, revised spellings, and distinctive melodic elocution together signified a new identity for the people of Arabia. The Arabic of the Qur'an—in content, style, and delivery—marked a new beginning.

Tajwid's emphasis on precise chanting also helped preserve aspects of the aura of revelation, with fluctuating tones and extended syllables evoking moments when passages first flowed from Muhammad's mouth and were then repeated for his followers. Muhammad recognized that people would soon be unable to hear him recite the Qur'an. By systematizing the rules of *tajwid* and creating a formal training program to teach them, he established the foundation for replicating revelations and launched an academic field whose graduates preserved standards to be passed down for generations.

The fastidious rules of *tajwid* contrasted with the free-form flow of the Qur`an, which proclaimed itself part of an active dialogue with listeners. The Qur`an sought to accompany people on their life journeys, offering an evolving experience rather than rigid routine. Just as the hundreds of Divine names provided many access points to God, the Qur`an aimed to make itself accessible to diverse audiences in various life circumstances. It sought to appeal to people's needs without dismissing their fears and concerns, offering a revolutionary approach to pursuing a fulfilling life.

The Qur`an initially positioned itself as *huda* (direction and guidance), helping travelers navigate toward their desired destination. Specifically, Muhammad evoked night navigation, with each chapter dubbed a *surah* (constellation of stars) and each passage an *ayah* (brightest star in a constellation). Yet in the final months of his life, Muhammad focused on how to apportion the Qur`an practically for recitation and study purposes. To enable audiences to review the entire corpus within a month, he instructed his followers to apportion the full text into 30 *ajza* (stems), each consumed in a day. For slower study, he specified 60 *ahzab* (branches) for two months' review and 120 *maqari* (buds) for four months' review.

The dueling metaphors of stars and plants captured the Qur`an's dual purposes: as a celestial guide to sustain focus on grand visions but also as a rooted growth to keep people grounded. To help audiences find ingenious ways out of willful stagnation, Muhammad structured a productive tension of vision and action, sublime and mundane. In fact, the Qur`an expressed a worry that it might be seen as too rarified for popular engagement, just as the Ka`bah had for centuries lost its original purpose as an open gathering spot for all people to instead become an exclusive shrine for elites:

> *Wa qalar-rasulu ya rabbi inna qawmit-takhathu hathal-Qur`ana mahjura.*
>
> And the *rasul* said, "Oh my Cosmic Mentor, my people have forsaken the Qur`an, instead preserving it like a hallowed yet hollow site."

In his final months, Muhammad seemed particularly focused on the Qur`an's practical applications. He sought to ensure that it remained accessible—beyond its lofty and at times abstract ideas—with easy entrance points for ordinary people to engage with its content.

As Muhammad compiled thousands of diverse revelations into a unified text, he was creating the first-ever Arabic book, a bound volume collecting physical pages for readers to pore over. The very existence of an Arabic book marked a definitive break with *Jahiliyyah* and began a new era of publishing and scholarship. Yet because most of Arabia was illiterate, the Qur`an could not be propagated on a mass scale as a tome. Thus *tajwid* instruction not only preserved a replica of Qur`anic revelation but created a training program that produced hundreds of talented reciters who could literally spread the word.

To reach audiences across Arabia, Muhammad sent out his most proficient followers in delegations that ranged from three to forty people to recite passages in far-flung towns. Upon arriving in a community, one member of the group would ascend the town's central platform used for civic announcements and entertainment. As one follower recited Qur`anic passages, the others would scout the crowd for captivated audience members to invite for study sessions. This propagation and recruiting process had begun relatively informally during the period of the Hudaibiyyah Treaty. In the final months of his life, Muhammad worked to equip his traveling delegations with a standardized volume of the Qur`an and clear recitation rules—hoping a consistent curriculum would help establish common ground among dispersed followers.

In the last few weeks of his life, Muhammad finally succeeded in fashioning this organized volume of the Qur`an, even as he continued through his final days to rearrange passages and add new ones. Producing a formal physical book, however, was hardly the end goal. The Qur`an offered a parable about a donkey carrying great books of wisdom on its back without benefiting in any way from the tomes. If the Qur`an failed to inspire change in its audience, it would become no more valuable than heavy books to a donkey.

Muhammad therefore placed great emphasis on having audiences understand and process the Qur`an's words rather than just memorize them. The chanted coordinates of *ayat* (plural *of ayah*) and *suwar* (plural of *surah*), he hoped, would evoke both rational reflection and spiritual awakening. The Qur'an was not ink on parchment nor sounds emerging from someone's mouth nor ears listening to chanting—but rather that precious moment when inspired listeners found the courage to blossom out of stagnation, unfurling their once-closed petals to reveal potential long hidden inside.

More than a millennium before the invention of the phonograph and radio broadcast, Muhammad created a unique style of oral recording, dynamic performance, and transmission. In the final months of his life, he remixed thousands of isolated snippets of intense revelation into a masterful magnum opus—capturing the verses' original expressive power in a compelling package for distribution across Arabia and beyond. The *rasul* was indeed a conductor, not only of sound and ideas but of energy.

❖ ❖ ❖

If the names of God and the Qur'an fulfilled their purpose, people might dare to blossom—but even then they would still need ways to direct that bold impulse into a sustained, lifelong commitment. Just as the *ayat* and *suwar* were distant guides in the night sky that helped people navigate the wilderness, more immediate markers would help human beings to ground their life journeys.

On his first trip to Damascus at age ten, Muhammad had watched the *hadi* guide the caravan at night by the light of a burning beacon in the distance. Local communities lit the flames atop watchtowers as a signal to passing travelers that an outpost of civilization was nearby, ready to welcome visitors and help reenergize them for the path ahead. Watchtowers were traditional Arabian desert markers, and their multilevels were known as *arkan* and their capstone beacons as *hajj* (lanterns). Spotting a distant beacon atop the *arkan* ignited a warm flicker of hope in caravan members, signaling a safe harbor in the desolate desert sea.

As new followers from across Arabia hastened to Medina to meet with Muhammad in his final months, he sought to turn the experience of their journey through the desert to Medina into a teaching tool. Two decades earlier, circumstance had forced him to teach furtively. Now he could freely expound on his ideas to large groups of followers, thoroughly articulating mature concepts without the pressure of rushed secret lessons or the distraction of running civic affairs. Beneath the surface aspects of each ritual lay an inner dimension that Muhammad aimed to illuminate for his new disciples.

A group of visitors from Oman and Bahrain joined Muhammad one day on a walk through the outskirts of Medina and came upon a lone palm tree. Muhammad sat beside the tree and remarked that one's journey in life was like an 'abiri sabil (wanderer traversing the wilderness). Navigating the mostly barren Arabian wilderness, Muhammad reminded his new followers, was too hazardous to undertake alone. Travelers needed to harness the few available resources and cooperate by sharing supplies and knowledge with other voyagers.

During the first twenty years of his prophethood, Muhammad often returned to the metaphor of the *arkan* to help his followers understand core rituals that could elevate them like levels in a tower. Each layer of ritual built on those below it, gradually raising individuals to new heights and perspectives. The symbolism pulled its audience in two directions, as the tower both guided travels across the wilderness and lifted them to a higher spiritual level.

The foundation level of the *arkan* was *shahadah*—a declaration of the oneness of the Divine—developed in the first year of Muhammad's prophethood. The word's ancient root *shahd* meant honeycomb, representing the culmination of a bee's elaborate process of collecting pollen, processing it, and ultimately producing honey—what two-year-old Muhammad had witnessed while suspended over a ravine to collect honeycombs. To sincerely bear witness to the oneness of the Divine, Muhammad argued, one had to first be like a bee: head out into the world to collect wisdom from diverse sources, then pause to process that knowledge, and ultimately produce beneficial results to help others. As the base of the *arkan*, the *shahadah* embodied Muhammad's core approach to leading a meaningful life: constantly learning from others and transforming gathered wisdom into practical results.

It took Muhammad another decade to unveil the *arkan*'s second level: *salah*, therapeutic prayer sessions to help repair broken connections. The term referred to the process of maintaining the rope bridges young Muhammad had traversed with his aunt Fatimah on their walking excursions outside Mecca. Suspended over ravines, the bridges connected divided places and brought people together—and the bridges' fragile strands required constant maintenance (*iqam*). Dawn prayers provided a daily opportunity to reengage upward with the Divine, midday prayers served as respites to repair outward social connections, and evening prayers a chance to reconnect inward with oneself.

Thirteen years into his prophethood, Muhammad unveiled the third tier as part of his campaign to invigorate Medina: *zakah* investing raised the disadvantaged by providing equal opportunities. In his youth Muhammad had helped build *zakah* scaffolding that provided elevated platforms for workers building walls. To help ensure the flow of capital to all in a community, Muhammad designated "one part out of forty parts" (2.5 percent—Muhammad loved broken fractions) of annual savings as voluntary contributions toward a community charitable fund. *Zakah* resources paid disadvantaged people to work on civic infrastructure projects, provided them with skills training, or helped them start businesses. The idea was to spur an uplifting cycle in which *zakah* recipients eventually became donors.

Just before the Meccan army first descended on Medina, Muhammad had introduced a bold fourth layer: *sawm*, reallocating time otherwise used for preparing meals to instead share talents with others. Based on an ancient term for dividing a loaf of bread, *sawm* encouraged people to set aside time to directly engage with others and develop healthy new habits. Muhammad designated the ancient Arabian month of Natiq—renaming it Ramadhan—as a time of rejuvenating community service. After spending daylight hours helping needy individuals and assisting with civic improvement projects, people would spend the evenings as a time to reflect on the upcoming year. His followers would spend the first ten days of Ramadhan identifying ways to improve in the year ahead. They would devote the next ten days to implementing new habits and the concluding ten to establish a plan to continue the new habits throughout the year. "If Ramadhan does not transform a person, making them better than before, its purpose was not accomplished," Muhammad explained.

Muhammad enjoyed discussing these four levels of practical implementation with the many visitors descending on Medina to study with him. Each level was filled with dynamic motion: outward to the world, then inward for reflection, then returning outward with something new. The rituals encouraged people to share resources and skills in thoughtful ways by dividing wealth and time—and to use the experience of giving to others to help improve oneself. For individuals navigating the wilderness of life, the *arkan* provided a pragmatic new methodology inspired by ancient concepts and infused with profound spiritual meaning. Yet visitors must have noticed that Muhammad's four-tiered *arkan* still lacked one key element of the real-world desert watchtowers: there was no beacon at the top.

Several months before his death, Muhammad at last wrapped up his intense editing of the Qur'an. While a few small tweaks and a handful of short new revelations remained, most of the work was done. Though exhausted, Muhammad immediately pivoted to address the missing element in the *arkan*. He gathered his followers at the *masjid* and shared a new Qur'anic passage, one of the last ten to be revealed:

Wa ath-thin fin-Nasi bil-hajji,
And invite all people up to the hajj,

Ya`tuka rijalaw wa 'ala kulli dhamiriy;
that they should come, whether on foot or riding;

Ya`tina min kulli fajjin 'amiq.
Gathering from every distant land.

Muhammad then clarified: "The *arkan* of Islam are five." He began listing the existing four *arkan* levels and added *hajj* at the end. When people heard the term, they initially assumed Muhammad meant the usual pilgrimage, when several thousand people from across Arabia would descend on Mecca to circumambulate the Ka'bah. The Arabs believed that Abraham had established the ancient *hajj* tradition—in his trademark hospitality, he had invited people from all corners of the earth to visit the house of monotheistic worship he had constructed in Mecca to break bread together and exchange ideas.

The term *hajj* (a linguistic cousin of the Hebrew word *hag*, or festival) described a celebration bringing people together. The ancient root described the desert beacon that drew weary travelers, like moths to a flame, from different directions to come rest in one place. The attractive power of a fire flickering at night connected the desert beacon to a festival gathering. (The Jewish custom of beginning holidays by lighting candles evokes this ancient association.)

Initially a reflection of Abraham's welcoming spirit and connection to the Divine, the hajj had lost its original meaning in the era of *Jahiliyyah*. In fact, Meccan elites exploited pilgrims for financial gain. With no products of their own to export, the Meccans began living off the Ka'bah. They sold trinkets and amulets to tourists and instituted rites requiring pilgrims to wear expensive ceremonial garments that they could purchase only in Mecca. This forced poor people, who could not afford the colorful pilgrimage clothing, to go naked around the shrine. While only elites could enter the Ka'bah, the general population performed bizarre rituals, walking in circles around the sanctuary while clapping and whistling. Any observer of pilgrimage ceremonies could immediately see class differences and social stratification, as well as the rank commercialism of the ceremony.

Part of what drew pilgrims to Mecca was a long-standing tradition that travelers could move safely through the desert during the month of hajj. As it was considered highly dishonorable for marauders to accost any caravans during the hajj month, merchants (including Jews and Christians) from across Arabia seized the opportunity to bring merchandise to Mecca's market. Most visitors camped in tents on Mecca's outskirts, though elders hosted upper-class guests in their homes, and rich elites had the privilege of staying in Dar-un-Nadwah's guest rooms.

When Muhammad issued his call for a hajj from the *masjid* pulpit, he explained to his audience that the pilgrimage would serve its original purpose. First, the renewed hajj would be for all people (not just Arabs) and an event where everyone was equal. All men would have to dress in the same simple white loincloth, the garb of the poor. No symbols of social status would be allowed, including head coverings, jewelry, and perfume. "There will be no distinction between man and woman, Arab and non-Arab, rich and poor, black and white," Muhammad explained.

The pilgrimage would revert to the original Abrahamic convention for exchanging ideas inspired by the Divine. Speaking from the pulpit, Muhammad previewed the convention's itinerary and agenda. Pilgrims would arrive in Mecca and gather outside the Ka'bah. They would walk in an organized fashion around the shrine seven times (representing each day of the week), meditating quietly to prepare themselves to absorb new concepts and information.

The next morning, the group would head outside the city to a desert mountain, which Muhammad renamed 'Arafah (networking to develop mutual understanding). Muhammad's new name for this mountain derived from a word in a recent Qur'anic revelation that explained why the Divine had not made humans monolithic:

> *Wa ja'alnakum shu'ubaw wa qaba'ila li-ta'arafu.*
> And We have fashioned you into distinct cultures and diverse
>   tribes so you might learn from and respect one another both
>   because of and in spite of your differences.

The full day spent at Mount 'Arafah provided time for networking among hajj participants. In the late afternoon, Muhammad noted, he would deliver a brief sermon, which would provide the initial stimulus for people to begin the process of analyzing and sharing ideas. At sunset, the group would move to the open space of Muzdalifah (gathering close), a valley where no tents were allowed. Everyone would have to sleep as equals on the bare ground, looking up at the night stars while reflecting on what had been taught during the day.

The next day, after dawn prayers and reflection, the group would decamp yet again, this time to the valley of 'Aqabah (emancipation), where Muhammad had years earlier first met the Yathribite delegation that had come to recruit him to their city. Muhammad gave the valley a new name: Mina (place of analysis—literally, dissect to evaluate each part on its own). There, participants would spend three entire days engaged in communal discussion, sharing insights and brainstorming new ideas.

The scene at Mina would be like bees forming a honeycomb. It was the *shahadah* come to life on a grand scale. Unlike *zakah* and *sawm*, the results of the public interaction would not be on the level of just one local community but rather all of Arabia, if not farther. The connections established during the discussions would span thousands of miles, and the benefit produced would reverberate far beyond Mecca. Indeed, on the fifth day, the group would return to the Ka'bah, again making seven circles around the shrine—only this time with participants reflecting on the novel ideas and renewed mission they had gained. Muhammad dubbed the hajj's culminating ceremony Tawaf-ul-Wada' (the new beginning—literally, leaving the past behind), dispersing people home filled with energy to share what they had learned and jump-start new projects.

Muhammad had crafted an ambitious capstone to the *arkan*. While each level had been designed to help people translate Divine inspiration into practical action, the hajj was by far the most logistically complex level—and he expected it to have the broadest influence. Muhammad clearly hoped it would round out the methodology to ensure that the tools for blossoming would remain accessible long after his death.

As he sent out hundreds of horsemen to all corners of Arabia to invite people to attend the hajj in Mecca six weeks later, Muhammad anticipated a substantial crowd. He and his followers hoped to attract several times the usual hajj numbers, a maximum of twenty thousand people. But a torrent of humanity would soon descend on Mecca, beckoned by the shining beacon atop the *arkan*.

❖ ❖ ❖

With the call to hajj, Muhammad at last had the opportunity to deliver his pitch (*'ardh*) to a receptive crowd. Due to his celebrity status, people from all over Arabia leapt at the invitation to catch a glimpse of the *rasul* in person and participate in this unprecedented outdoor convention.

Just as the hajj was set to begin, 114,000 of Muhammad's followers converged upon Mecca from all over Arabia. Joined by curious pagan, Christian, and Jewish spectators, the total crowd grew to over 120,000 people. The Arabs could not remember a time when so many people had gathered in one place.

Muhammad had dubbed the gathering Al-Hajj-ul-Akbar (the great convention), but no one was more surprised by the size of the assembled throng than he was. His wealthy son-in-law 'Uthman generously offered to provide food for the masses. His uncle Al-'Abbas, who had never left Mecca, took responsibility for organizing logistics, executing Muhammad's instructions with a team of volunteers who scrambled to manage the massive gathering. The multitudes needed meals, sacred areas had to remain clean, and the attendees required instructions for the five-day itinerary and program.

Late on Thursday evening, on the eve of the hajj's commencement, Muhammad arrived at Mecca with his family. They camped on the city's outskirts at Shiʻb Abu Talib, the same place his family had been confined during the two-year boycott. The choice of location was steeped in symbolism and a testament to the power of determined perseverance. The *rasul*, though, struggled to muster his strength, drained by the arduous Qur'an compilation. Spectators noted how he relied on a walking staff, his back bent, as he circumambulated the Kaʻbah seven times counterclockwise, formally declaring the beginning of the hajj. Scars and broken teeth from the Battle of Uhud marked his face. As he greeted participants, his voice was noticeably weak.

The next morning, on the plain of ʻArafah, people pitched their tents and organized the campsite in a massive, swarming multitude. In the late afternoon, shortly before sunset, the assembly followed instructions to collect around Mount ʻArafah, marked by an emerald-green flag fluttering atop a fifteen-foot pole. Al-ʻAbbas waited atop the mountain as the crowd parted for Muhammad, who rode on a camel led by ʻAli. With ʻAli's assistance, Muhammad ascended ʻArafah while grasping his staff for additional support.

When he reached the summit, Muhammad looked down at the throngs surrounding him in every direction. People from all walks of life and diverse tribes dressed in white had spread out as far as the eye could see—people who had chosen to open themselves up to a new experience and travel through the wilderness to Mecca to learn about how to blossom forth. Muhammad was the elevated beacon whose resonant energy had attracted them, and now he had one final and unique opportunity to share his mindset with a massive receptive audience.

Yet Muhammad's once robust voice had grown frail. To ensure his message reached hajj participants even at the far reaches of the crowd, Muhammad had devised an ingenious relay system. Hundreds of human conveyors stood at intervals throughout the crowd. Muhammad would utter a sentence, his uncle Al-ʻAbbas would repeat it in his booming voice, and the conveyors would in turn echo it in waves that rippled back through the crowd. The makeshift public address system managed to keep a multitude of 120,000 thoroughly engaged.

Muhammad called his speech a "Farewell Sermon" that he hoped would clarify his core message and provide guidance for the future. "It is possible I may not be here with you after this year," he announced. "Nonetheless, I expect you to be convening here again. I am handing you a bright torch and a guided path so that you can bring light to the world, liberating people from the darkness of ignorance and stagnation."

As he spoke, Muhammad kept turning to address different segments of the crowd. His main points emphasized equality by taking the principles he had established more than a decade earlier in the constitution of Medina and making them universal:

"Oh people, your blood, wealth, and individual hopes are all uniquely sacred—just like the uniqueness you witness today as we stand together united in this sacred space. All blood spilled before is forgiven. Let there be no more vendettas. Blood money due to us by whoever killed members of my clan is forgiven—as are the debts owed to us. So too does [my uncle] Al-'Abbas forgive all who are indebted to him. Do not transgress upon the rights of others or allow yourselves to suffer transgression.

"Oh people, women inherently enjoy the right to be supported on all levels, so uphold their rights. You have a duty to ensure their rights are upheld the same way that you have the right to expect their support. Elevate yourselves by empowering women!

"Oh people, do not revert after my death into discord, rivalry, and killing one another. I am leaving you with a sustainable system with the Qur'an, the Loving Divine as your exemplar, and the *sunnah* (formula) I have outlined for you in my teachings—a method that, if you uphold it, will safeguard you from falling into the ravines of confusion.

"Oh people, know that your God is one, unique, and the God of all people. Likewise, you all descend from one common ancestor and as such are equal before God.

"Oh people, you all emerged from a thin surface layer of earth, so remain grounded and remember who you are. You are all brothers and sisters before the Divine, emerging from the same source. None has an advantage over another through blood or lineage; neither does an Arab have privileges over a non-Arab. It is only by merit and accomplishments that you can rise one above the other. In a society of equal opportunity, the weakest among you is equal to the strongest. Seek your own elevation by empowering minorities among you, for they are protected by the sacred covenant of God. The most elevated among you before God are those with the purest spiritual core."

Then Muhammad paused to ask the crowd, "Have I articulated these points eloquently and clearly?"

The throng shouted back—*"Na'am!"* (Indeed!). One hundred twenty thousand voices echoed across the mountains in a roar.

Muhammad allowed the sound to reverberate before concluding with one last request: "Then let those present spread this message, precisely as they heard it, to those who were absent."

The multitude remained silent for several minutes, absorbing the words. This was the first time most of the participants had heard these concepts summarized in one place. Muhammad had just offered a précis of his life's work and a summary of the spirit of Islam.

As people broke out in conversation, a murmur spread through the crowd. That evening, everyone slept beneath the night sky at Muzdalifah with Muhammad's words echoing in their minds. They spent the next three days in extensive group discussions at Mina. With his thirteen-year-old protégé, 'Abdullah ibn 'Abbas, riding behind him, Muhammad waded through the crowd, greeting people and listening to the conversations. He would interject brief points and encourage them to keep going.

The hajj concluded with Al-'Abbas and his logistics volunteers directing waves of pilgrims back to the Ka'bah for the Tawaf-ul-Wada' closing ceremony, preparing participants to return to their communities with one final round of seven circumambulations around the shrine. For many participants, the experience had been exhilarating; for some, it was transformative. They burst out of Mecca in full blossom, on a mission to bring the spirit and message of the hajj convention to communities far beyond Arabia—some would venture as far as China. The five-day gathering had sparked a wellspring of energy in thousands of young people who would dedicate the rest of their lives to passing on what they had learned from the prophet leaning on his staff atop the mountain.

In honor of this great convention, Muhammad gave the Arabian month of Burak a new name: Thul-Hijjah (the great convention/

pilgrimage). In fact, after the hajj, Muhammad officially renamed all twelve Arabian months (arranging them in alternating twenty-nine and thirty-day lunar months) and also the days of the week. Burak, for instance, referred to camels resting during caravans bringing merchandise to Mecca in the pilgrimage season. The new name reclaimed the month's original purpose of exchanging ideas, not simply merchandise.

After a week in Mecca, with no fanfare or large delegation to see him off, Muhammad mounted his camel on a Monday morning and headed back toward Medina with Barakah, Fatimah, 'Ali, and his grandsons. He did not look back as he rode out of his hometown for the last time.

❖ ❖ ❖

When Muhammad's parents had died, he inherited nothing—aside from his mother's charge that he become a world-changer. Because that one sentence had proved more valuable than money, Muhammad determined to leave only ideas as his estate. Any formal estate risked exacerbating tension within his family. So in the final weeks of his life, Muhammad divested himself of all his wealth, giving away his assets to the needy (mostly orphans and widows), so he could focus on bequeathing values rather than property.

After returning to Medina from the hajj, Muhammad recuperated from the epic event by once again enjoying discussions with his closest disciples out in nature. One day, as the group relaxed on the edge of a well, Muhammad suddenly experienced his second-to-last Qur'anic revelation:

Yawma la yanfa'u maluw-wala banun.
On the day of judgment, neither wealth nor sons will be of any benefit.

Illa man ata-llaha bi-qalbin-salim.
Come instead before the Loving Divine with nothing more than a pure, complete heart.

Muhammad's mind was clearly focused on his ultimate legacy and what truly mattered during his lifetime of navigating the wilderness. To emphasize the passage's core message, Muhammad shared with the group a parable about two women. Her people considered the first woman righteous. She dressed modestly, remained chaste, and performed all the rituals. Yet in the privacy of her home she was viciously cruel to a cat, beating it and locking it up without food and water until it died a painful death. The second woman was the polar opposite of the first, a despised and ridiculed prostitute. Yet when she was walking through the wilderness and saw a dehydrated dog panting in exhaustion near a well, she tied her scarf to her tattered shoe and filled it with water to quench the dog's thirst. God was displeased with the first woman but pleased with the second and granted her eternal salvation for her sincere compassion.

Both the Qur'anic passage and its expository Hadith were Muhammad's last attempt to clarify for his followers—particularly zealous new ones—the ultimate goal of his mindset. He intended to shock his audience by holding up a prostitute as someone who could possess the ultimate pure heart. As an adolescent, other boys had tricked Muhammad into entering the Hanut, where he witnessed young women who had been forced into prostitution. The jarring encounter had left an impression: someone's being stuck in a lowly position in society did not mean they lacked the potential to make a beneficial contribution to the world. Muhammad pointedly used the word *salim* to describe the exemplar prostitute's "complete" heart, evoking the same S-L-M root as *Islam*, the lifelong attempt to achieve fullness. A reviled prostitute could serve as a model for success by finding her own way to become a world-changer.

After the discussion by the well, Muhammad went to the *masjid* and stopped in to visit his wives in their rooms off the building's central courtyard. He found they had no food. The most powerful man in Arabia took his armor—he lifted the heavy metal with some difficulty—to a Jewish merchant who lived nearby and pawned his last remaining possession for money to buy barley. (Muhammad could easily have acquired money from his many wealthy followers, yet he chose to do business with a Jewish man.)

Arab chieftains valued their armor as a cherished sign of honor, yet Muhammad made clear the physical item had no inherent value. Moreover, he had no need for warfare. Effectively penniless, Muhammad returned to his wives' quarters and crushed the barley to make bread for the women and his stepchildren.

The following morning, after dawn prayers, Muhammad received his final revelation:

> *Wat-taqu yawman turja'una fihi ila-llah.*
> Prepare yourself with action-filled hope for the day when you
> return to the Loving Divine.

> *Thumma tuwaffa kullu nafsim-ma kasabat,*
> Each soul will then receive full recompense for all it has earned,

> *Wa hum la yuthlamun.*
> And none will be treated unjustly.

When they heard the passage, Abu Bakr and 'Ali began to cry. They immediately recognized the verse as an enigmatic herald that Muhammad was dying. Looking back on his life while anticipating his legacy, Muhammad reiterated that the true value of a person's life was not wealth or blood lineage but the long-term effect of their actions.

Muhammad had entrusted the final full manuscript of the Qur'an to the custody of Hafsah, the most literate and best educated of his wives. The book was the only physical object he had left to bequeath—and he instructed that it belong to the community as a public resource. Because he lacked the strength to oversee a formal revision of the document, Muhammad asked that Hafsah place the final revelation "before *Ayat-ud-Dayn*" (a famous passage about debt and business transactions). Even in his final days, Muhammad was still revising the Qur'an.

That evening, Muhammad rode out of Medina with Abu Bakr, 'Ali, and Barakah to visit the cemetery for those killed at Uhud, including his uncle Hamzah and Rabbi Mukhairiq. On his return he passed Al-Baqi' cemetery, where his daughters and son Abraham were buried. As he sat by the graves, Muhammad cried and gently swayed in silent reflection. The next morning, he became ill and promptly withdrew from his remaining duties, including leading people in prayer. He suffered from a high fever and could not stomach solid foods. At his request, two men carried him to the doorway of 'Aishah's house so he could greet people at the *masjid*. Her bedroom door was closest to the pulpit and most easily accessible to visitors.

In the days that followed, hundreds of anxious people assembled at the *masjid*, anticipating news of Muhammad's recovery. After ten days, on Monday, April 20, 632—one day before his sixty-second birthday— Muhammad awoke feeling strong. His fever had subsided; he led the dawn prayers. When they saw he had apparently fully recovered, the Medinians were overjoyed. He assured them they should end their vigil and return to work. Relieved, his followers wished him well and began the workday.

Enjoying the quiet, Muhammad walked slowly from the pulpit to 'Aishah's room. When he entered, he was delighted to find that Fatimah, his only surviving child, had come to attend to him. Muhammad kissed her forehead, and her face brightened at the sight of her father walking again. After a simple breakfast of fresh camel milk, three dates, and a piece of bread—his first real meal in ten days—he lay on his simple mattress, resting his head against Fatimah's chest, just as Khadijah had rested on him in her final days.

After sunrise, 'Ali arrived to visit along with Hasan and Husain. Muhammad hugged and kissed his grandsons before telling 'Ali, "When I die, wash me, accompanied by men of my family. Do not remove my clothes. Bury me in the clothes I die in, in the place where I die." Muhammad then closed his eyes, and his breathing became more arduous.

Fatimah clasped her father tighter as tears rolled down her face and dripped on his head. "What a sad day this is, oh Father!" she lamented.

Muhammad softly replied, "No more sadness will befall your father after today." It was a heartbreaking reminder that Muhammad had led a life filled with setbacks, oppression, and trauma. He looked up to the palm branch ceiling as rays of sunlight filtered through the dried leaves to brighten the small room. He began to smile and with his last breaths declared, "*Bal-ir-rafiq-ul-a'la!*" (I long for the company of the Empowering Confidant!).

Muhammad the world-changer was dead.

Epilogue

THE ELUSIVE LEGACY OF MUHAMMAD'S MINDSET

Medina: 2 p.m., Monday, April 20, 632 CE

In the hours following Muhammad's death, Medina became a hub of confusion. Muhammad had left detailed burial instructions but no succession plan. The hajj "Farewell Sermon" served as his last will and testament. His inheritance was a mindset, not an empire with a clear political transition plan.

As Muhammad's body lay in 'Aishah's room off the *masjid*, Medina came to a standstill. Weeping punctuated the deathly silence. Some were in denial. "Muhammad is not dead!" insisted 'Umar. "Like Moses, he has merely gone into the wilderness to convene with the Creator and will return after forty days." Others argued, "No, he is in meditative sleep, seeking inspiration, and will soon awaken."

Seeing the confusion, Abu Bakr sought to calm the riled-up crowd by reminding them of the man's own teachings: "Muhammad was a mere mortal sent by God to help you find balance and unleash your greatest potential. If he were to die or be killed, would you then revert to your old ways and undo the great work that you have achieved? Let anyone who revered Muhammad know that he has died. But for those whose objective transcended Muhammad and sought out the Divine, know that the teachings and mindset inspired through him live on and can never die!"

Abu Bakr's declaration, though it temporarily assuaged the crowd, marked the beginning of a turbulent debate about Muhammad's legacy that has not ended. Muhammad had declined to dictate the terms of the order that would follow his death, a decision with momentous consequences. *Jahiliyyah* had surrendered only two years before Muhammad's death, hardly enough time to jettison its worst impulses—which would reemerge with a vengeance. Still, the *rasul* had insisted his followers should determine their own future.

Within a few years, the age of blossoming that Muhammad had established in Arabia would span thousands of miles and encompass millions of non-Arabs. Within a few years, his followers would also become embroiled in a protracted civil war. Assassins would kill three of Muhammad's first four successors, one of his widows would go to battle against his son-in-law, some followers would destroy the Ka'bah, and thousands would massacre one another. Those schisms have never healed and still shape international conflicts.

The raw energy Muhammad had unleashed during the hajj pulsated chaotically for decades, as his mindset rapidly evolved into a formal religion with a global reach in a kind of adolescent growth phase. One hundred and fifty years after Muhammad's death, however, a more mature Muslim civilization began to emerge, one that applied his mindset to set off a wave of innovation. In this period, brilliant Islamic scholars steeped in Muhammad's teachings developed algebra, algorithms, advanced medicine, complex mechanics, and even early flying machines. Their inventions became the basis of our modern world.

Muhammad's legacy thus remains open to interpretation. Some exploited and inverted it for power. Others chose to wield it as a powerful tool to improve the lives of all people. The moment Muhammad died, in other words, the fate of his teachings was out of his hands.

❖ ❖ ❖

While 'Ali prepared Muhammad's body for burial, Abu Bakr learned that local tribal elders had gathered nearby for an emergency discussion. These signatories to the constitution of Medina worried about the future of the *ummah*. Byzantine forces were gathering on the borders of Arabia, and the Sasanians had also begun to make hostile moves. Eager for a leader to organize a response, each tribal chief began angling to nominate a candidate from his own clan.

Abu Bakr watched, respecting Muhammad's decision to remain silent on succession. 'Umar, however, took immediate action. He grabbed Abu Bakr's right hand in an iron grip and flung it aloft, declaring, "I pledge allegiance to Abu Bakr as the *khalifah* [successor—literally, custodian or caretaker of Muhammad's mindset]." No one dared question the imposing man, not even the shocked Abu Bakr.

Meanwhile, people streamed into Medina to pay their final respects. As Muhammad's body lay wrapped in simple white linens, a procession of mourners shuffled past. "You have been a source of inspiration while alive," they testified. "May you continue to inspire after death."

By early evening, only Muhammad's closest family and followers remained, including Barakah, who had witnessed his birth sixty-two years earlier. At his request, they buried him in the ground beneath the bed. Al-'Abbas placed the linen-wrapped body in the burial niche, sealing the space with mud bricks. 'Ali then heaped three handfuls of soil into the grave, repeating Qur'anic passages with each scoop:

Minha khalaqnakum,
From the earth We created you,

Wa fiha nu'idukum,
And back into the earth We shall return you,

Wa minha nukhrijukum taratan ukhra.
Then from the earth We shall resurrect you once more.

While washing Muhammad's body several hours earlier, 'Ali had slipped off the *rasul*'s signet ring. He now presented it to Abu Bakr in a symbolic gesture. Abu Bakr wore the ring the next day as he addressed a crowd at his inauguration ceremony in the *masjid*. "I have been chosen to lead you, though I am not the worthiest among you. With the guidance of the Divine, I will do my utmost to be just. If I rule with integrity and benevolence, then assist me. However, should I become tyrannical and unjust, it is your responsibility to hold me accountable and block my transgression. So long as a community upholds justice and holds their leaders accountable, they will succeed. If they resign themselves to tyranny and abandon reason for blind obedience and corruption, they will surely succumb to failure."

For decades, Abu Bakr had been Muhammad's closest friend and a loyal confidant who provided vital support—but he had never led. His opening words suggested he appreciated both the power and precariousness of his position, a role he had not sought. In fact, Fatimah objected that he had been made successor without an election while her father's body was still warm. Along with her entire Hashemite clan, Fatimah refused to pledge allegiance to Abu Bakr. She died six months later, leaving 'Ali a widower.

Abu Bakr himself would not live long. He managed to repel Byzantine and Sasanian assaults on Arabia's border territories. But before he could leave any major mark, Abu Bakr died of a sudden illness less than two years into his role as *khalifah*, or caliph. Just before he passed away, he assigned a successor, returning the unwanted favor by naming 'Umar. Like Abu Bakr, 'Umar lacked any leadership experience. Yet in contrast to Abu Bakr's calm demeanor, 'Umar's manic outbursts made many concerned he might rule as a ruthless tyrant.

Becoming caliph, however, unleashed 'Umar's dormant potential. He gathered a team of brilliant advisors (including Barakah, Ash-Shifa, and Um Waraqah) and charted a strategic plan to apply Muhammad's mindset on a large scale. By emulating Muhammad's innovative military techniques, he devastated the Sasanian Empire, turning Byzantine attacks into dramatic victories and conquering Jerusalem and Damascus. Arab Christians, delighted to be freed from the yoke of oppressive Byzantine taxation, soon became the majority of 'Umar's soldiers. 'Umar, who was determined to establish an egalitarian society, insisted that his local governors live in ordinary houses without guards. He also established a special department to handle complaints against state officials and even ran a special intelligence service to monitor his administrators for corruption.

After conquering Jerusalem, 'Umar learned that the old site of Solomon's Temple (a building the Qur'an vividly describes) served as a rubbish dump. In an echo of the purifying of the Ka'bah, 'Umar himself organized the site's cleanup, laid the cornerstone for what would become the Al-Aqsa Mosque, and built a canopy over the former location of the holy of holies. On 'Umar's orders, Jews were permitted to return to the holy city after five hundred years of exile to pray once again on the Temple Mount. Before he departed, 'Umar wrote a constitution for Jerusalem (Mithaqu-Ilya) that mirrored the constitution of Medina, guaranteeing religious freedom in the city. In Damascus, 'Umar negotiated with the Christian Patriarch to rent part of the Cathedral of John the Baptist as a *masjid*. Muslims and Christians would continue to share the building for over eighty years. Just as Muhammad hosted Christian bishops for Sunday services in his *masjid*, several sacred spaces would be shared with Jews and Christians, including the shrine of the prophet Daniel.

Muhammad's waterworks in Medina also inspired 'Umar, who designed irrigation projects on a massive scale, even ordering a canal dug to connect the Nile to the Red Sea. He also assigned 'Ali to lead education efforts and tasked him with establishing two new university cities in southern Iraq: Kufah (abode of learning) and Basrah (abode of reason). These competing academic centers carried out Muhammad's urban-planning vision, with a *masjid* surrounded by academies, libraries, a hospital, and a vibrant market.

'Umar thrived in his leadership role, displaying unexpected genius as he applied Muhammad's mindset on a far grander scale than the *rasul* ever did. It was under 'Umar's governance that Muhammad's civic project grew into a global empire incorporating large non-Arab populations. But after he had been in power for a mere decade, a former Sasanian soldier assassinated 'Umar. As he lay dying, 'Umar nominated seven men as potential successors and insisted Medinians hold an open election to choose among them, with "girls as young as seven" permitted to vote. Barakah, by then ninety, died three days after casting her vote.

A week after 'Umar's death, Muhammad's son-in-law 'Uthman was elected caliph. Soft-spoken and introverted, 'Uthman was susceptible to the influence of his family, the Umayyad clan Muhammad had toppled from power in Mecca. The Umayyads yearned to reclaim power and convinced 'Uthman to assign his cousin Mu'awiyah (Abu Sufyan's son) as governor of the Levant (Ash-Sham). Other cousins, the sons of Dar-un-Nadwah's elders, gained prominent positions as well.

Though 'Uthman's rule saw even more rapid territorial expansion, many of 'Umar's good-governance reforms were slowly undermined, and the growing empire lacked a clear notion of what it stood for. Muhammad's core followers worried that the old *Jahiliyyah* order was slowly being reestablished. Most outspoken was Muhammad's former student Abu Tharr. He challenged Mu'awiyah's unscrupulous rule in Damascus and publicly denounced his distorted interpretations of the Qur'an. 'Uthman ultimately banished Abu Tharr to the desert, imposing a boycott on the dissident that ominously echoed the boycott of Muhammad.

Unrest only increased among the young, who felt the government had grown corrupt and nepotistic. Stress from the unrest made 'Uthman frail. One day, during the final months of his rule, 'Uthman sat at the well in Medina where Muhammad had received his last revelations. Suddenly, Muhammad's signet ring, which had passed down to each caliph, slipped from 'Uthman's finger and fell into the well, never to be recovered.

Thousands of protesters soon converged outside 'Uthman's home, yet he mostly ignored them and spent his time reciting the Qur'an—more preoccupied with reading the text than applying its teachings to address the protesters' concerns. After months of agitation to "revive the spirit of 'Arafah," several advocates (including Abu Bakr's youngest son) crept from the crowd into the house to meet the caliph. During the discussion, two radicals stabbed 'Uthman to death, and his blood gushed over the original Qur'an manuscript.

'Ali, who had been runner-up in the previous election, was unanimously declared caliph. Muhammad's son-in-law had spent twenty years establishing academies and refining scholarship standards while largely eschewing politics. But the Umayyad clan did not want to relinquish the political gains it had made under 'Uthman. They, along with Muhammad's widow 'Aishah, opened military assaults against 'Ali, demanding he carry out a vendetta against 'Uthman's killers. All-out civil war ensued. 'Ali was eventually assassinated, conceivably in a plot arranged by those who wished to see Mu'awiyah in power. 'Ali's son Hasan was certainly poisoned in a plot organized by Muʻawiyah and his son Yazid, whose forces tracked down Muhammad's other grandson, Husain, and slaughtered him, along with seventy relatives.

The strife marked the start of a schism between followers of Muhammad about who should inherit his mantle, a sectarian divide that remains unresolved many centuries later. The immediate outcome, however, was that Muʻawiyah managed to consolidate power as the next caliph and established the Umayyad Empire, headquartered in Damascus. The son and grandson of former Meccan chief elders (his father was Abu Sufyan), Muʻawiyah had been groomed for leadership. Highly ambitious and extremely intelligent, he knew how to operate diplomatically to reestablish his clan's dominance at all costs.

In a brilliant maneuver, the Umayyads decided to alter the image of Muhammad to influence the masses, most of whom had never met the *rasul*. They recast Muhammad as both a saintly messiah and a fierce conqueror. The empire hired pseudoscholars to concoct Hadiths that depicted Muhammad performing miracles and valiantly vanquishing new lands. The Umayyads appointed clerics and provided them with state-approved sermons that cursed ʻAli every Friday. Thousands of false traditions attributed to Muhammad emerged during this period, reflecting the Umayyads' expansionist policy and the increasing marginalization of non-Arabs.

Muhammad's original followers protested Umayyad rule, leading the Umayyads to besiege Medina and Mecca. When Umayyad forces used catapults to pelt the holy cities with scorching balls of resin, many precious documents burned, including early contemporary biographies of Muhammad and perhaps even the original Qurʼan manuscript, which disappeared during the siege. Even the Kaʻbah itself was destroyed, including the icon of Mary and Jesus. The Umayyads denounced dissidents as heretics, forcing Muhammad's original followers to disseminate his teachings in secret, a sad echo of the Dar-ul-Arqam sessions.

After nearly ninety years of domination, the Umayyads managed to institutionalize Islam as a dogmatic religion. What had begun as a liberating philosophy based on universal monotheistic concepts, the empire recast as a formal faith in contrast to Judaism and Christianity. When ʻUmar first entered Jerusalem, the local Christian leadership did not see him as representing a distinct new religion—and in fact wondered whether he might represent a new Jewish or Christian sect. Under Umayyad rule, however, clear restrictions delineated a divide between Muslims and non-Muslims—a far cry from the constitution of Medina or the spirit of the hajj.

Grassroots discontent with Umayyad rule ultimately brought a bloody revolution led by the sidelined descendants of Muhammad's uncle Al-'Abbas. The Abbasids massacred nearly thirty thousand Umayyads, and only one member of the clan managed to escape via the Damascus sewers. He fled to Spain to establish a new Umayyad caliphate—this time based on tolerance and merit. In the east, the Abbasids built a new capital city in Baghdad and instituted a meritocracy in which many non-Arabs and non-Muslims rose to prominent positions. Establishing a precedent for tolerance and free expression, the second Abbasid caliph, Al-Mansur, declared, "I will tolerate anything except challenges to my right to sit on this throne."

The adolescent phase of the post-Muhammad era had come to an end, giving way to a maturity that ushered in Islam's Golden Age. A peaceful rivalry between the Abbasid east and Umayyad west unleashed a competition for talent and accomplishment. Each of the two major arms of the Muslim world aimed to demonstrate on merit that they were Muhammad's true heirs.

❖ ❖ ❖

Shortly after the rise of the Abbasid Empire, a young child named Muhammad was born—not in Mecca but in a nameless Uzbek fishing village in the empire's remote backwater. The young Muhammad ibn Musa would later become known as Al-Khawarizmi, after his native region of Khwarazm. By the age of six, Muhammad had committed the entire Qur'an to memory. Recognized as a gifted student, Al-Khawarizmi was sent to Samarqand, where he studied classical Arabic and the oral traditions of Muhammad's life.

The young man was fascinated by Qur'anic passages that spoke of a mathematical code embedded in the creation of the universe, rendering numeric calculation as a reflection of the Divine. Al-Khawarizmi realized that Muslim scholars were struggling with an enigma as they tried to apply complex Islamic inheritance laws. How was it possible to divide an estate into many fractions, for example, if it allocated one-eighth to one person, one-quarter to another, and specified one-third, one-half, and one-sixth allotments to still others? Following the Hadith's parable of the bee, Al-Khawarizmi began exploring ancient works of mathematics from China, India, Greece, and Rome. He collected formulas from diverse sources and experimented for months as he tried to meld existing models into something new. At last he found a breakthrough solution: *al-jabr* (healing fractures), from which we get *algebra*—a method for turning broken numbers into whole ones.

Armed with his powerful invention, Al-Khawarizmi joined a camel caravan to Baghdad, a magnificent round metropolis with a great mosque at its center surrounded by a market. (The city would eventually become the largest in the world.) Al-Khawarizmi found Baghdad to be a hub of innovation, and he began studying with top Muslim scholars as well as rabbis, even becoming an expert on the Hebrew calendar. In fact, his treatise "Extraction of the Jewish Era" facilitated calculations of intervals between solar and lunar calendars that are still used today.

Al-Khawarizmi drew the attention of the caliph, who appointed him head librarian of Baghdad's leading intellectual corps, Bayt Al-Hikmah (the House of Wisdom). His treatises on algebra demonstrated how to use the new mathematical field to calculate the earth's circumference, efficiently allocate construction materials, design more accurate maps, make better financial projections, and more. Algebra's genius was finding value in broken numbers and showing how creative calculations could restore their wholeness. The innovation transformed the world, as the scribes of Bayt Al-Hikmah published many copies of Al-Khawarizmi's treatises, and the center's translators produced versions in Greek, Latin, Chinese, and more. Without algebra, the modern world would not exist—indeed the term *algorithm,* which underpins most cutting-edge technology, is simply the Latinization (Algorithmi) of the name Al-Khawarizmi.

Hundreds of other scholars mirrored the innovative genius of Al-Khawarizmi as they channeled Muhammad's mindset to produce groundbreaking inventions. Each visionary sought to emulate Muhammad by synthesizing existing knowledge to create new things—often with a result they could not appreciate in their own lifetimes. Some examples:

- ❖ Mariam al-Asturlabi followed Muhammad's emphasis on reading constellations (*suwar*) in the night sky to fuse the ancient Greek astrolabe with new algebraic calculations. In the process, she created an advanced navigation tool in the tenth century that remained in use into the mid-twentieth century.
- ❖ Ibn al-Haytham sought to help people with poor eyesight read the Qur'an. He became the father of modern optics, inventing glasses and constructing the first camera (from the Arabic *qumrah*—literally, small dark cabin).
- ❖ Zainab Ash-Shahdah, a pharmacist, was inspired by Muhammad's instruction to "seek healing because every disease has a cure." She created the first anti-inflammatory (from willow bark) to relieve migraines.
- ❖ Ibn Sina, known in the West as Avicenna, followed Qur'anic instructions on disease prevention, hygiene, and healing to become the father of modern medicine. European medical schools used his *Al-Qanunu-Fit-Tib* (Canon of Medicine) textbook into the early twentieth century.
- ❖ Al-Jazari sought ways to make ritual cleansing more efficient by using mechanical water pumps and became the father of modern engineering. Inspired by Muhammad's admonition not to waste water "even if you live beside a running stream," Al-Jazari built an iron robot in the form of a young maiden to dispense just the right amount of water necessary for handwashing.
- ❖ Ziryab emulated the Divine name Al-Jamil (the beautifier) by creating the fashion design and cosmetics industries, producing a wide array of wardrobes, developing the concept of a spa, and devising breakthrough recipes for hygienic products such as mouthwash, perfumes, lipstick, and toothpaste.
- ❖ Al-Farabi built on the constitution of Medina to create bold new concepts in political philosophy, and European intellectuals credit him as "the Second Master" for reviving Plato and Aristotle.

Al-Farabi argued for merit-based self-government with the maxim "You are your rulers."

The creation of universities that standardized systems of scholarship in part drove the outpouring of innovative thinking during the Golden Age of Muslim civilization. In 859, a wealthy businesswoman, Fatimah al-Fihri, established the first university, Al-Qarawiyyin, in Fez, Morocco. Her philanthropic commitment to education was inspired by the example of Ash-Shifa bint 'Abdillah, the brilliant female scholar appointed by Muhammad as head educator in Medina.

Drawing on the courtyard learning models Muhammad pioneered at Dar-ul-Arqam and the *masjid* in Medina, these early universities established formal models still in place over a millennium later. Department heads sat on an elevated *kursi* (chair) in particular corners of the courtyard; and teachers had professional credentials (*isnad*) and faculty affiliation (*kulliyyah*). Students worked toward diplomas (*ijazah*) and concluded their studies with a graduation ceremony featuring a tasseled fez and a gown evoking the *burdah* (cloak) Muhammad wore.

The university was open to students of all backgrounds, and instructors were chosen on merit. Pope Sylvester II studied at Al-Qarawiyyin University, and the Jewish philosopher Maimonides served on its faculty. Many women took advantage of these educational opportunities, and an astonishing 40 percent of the *'ulama* (eminent Islamic scholars) during the Golden Age were women. In Baghdad, a formerly enslaved Abyssinian named Thamal (herself an echo of Barakah) not only received an education but rose to become the first woman to serve as chief justice (Qadhi-al-Qudha).

As Europe suffered through the Dark Ages, Muslim civilization thrived—preserving and building upon classical wisdom, attracting top talent to its institutions, and implementing Muhammad's mindset on a magnificent scale. But after four centuries of flourishing, Muslim empires began to lose their entrepreneurial momentum. Internal complacency diminished the impulse to innovate, and external forces attacked from all sides: the Mongols in the Siege of Baghdad, Christians overthrew

Cordoba in the Reconquista (Christian Reconquest of Spain), and the Crusaders conquered Jerusalem.

The attacks destroyed the core of Islamic scholarship—libraries, universities, and intellectual guilds. The Mongols threw hundreds of thousands of books from Baghdad libraries into the Tigris River, destroying forever vital treatises on Arabic and early biographies of Muhammad. In a panic, Muslim scholars took desperate measures to preserve knowledge. They shifted the emphasis of education programs to memorization, because they regarded children's brains as virtual archives to preserve primary sources. Scholars streamlined hundreds of diverse interpretive traditions into just a handful and decreed a temporary freeze on new interpretations (*ijtihad*) to avoid abuse by nonexperts.

That temporary freeze, however, soon became permanent, as scholarship devolved into a system of stagnation. Academies concentrated on preserving the past, fearing any change might imperil their inheritance. Students learned about Muhammad's mindset, but teachers encouraged them to stay within the confines of established interpretations. Educational institutions, once independently supported by private community trusts (*awqaf*), became dependent on government largess and control. Trading their independence for stability, scholars quietly acquiesced to dictates from autocrats, adopting the maxim, "One thousand days of tyranny are better than one day of chaos."

The Qur'an, a work devoted to sparking people out of stagnation, instead became a rarified text that isolated scholars studied. These scholars were far closer to the cerebral example of Bahira the monk than Muhammad the *rasul*. A Qur'anic passage warned that such a reversion might happen, with the Qur'an becoming like a well-preserved yet empty historic house. Just as Muhammad had feared, once the Qur'an became a revered relic rather than a lived experience, torpor returned.

As the Golden Age waned, Europe's Renaissance began. Many Muslim scholars who remained determined to live out Muhammad's mindset decamped for Sicily, Venice, and even Russia. Whereas Muslims had for centuries served as custodians of classical Western thought, now the West became the inheritor and propagator of classic Muslim thought. European innovators devoured the books of classical Muslim scholars and began to apply Muhammad's methodology of gathering information from diverse sources to synthesize beneficial new advances.

In 1911, Muhammad 'Abduh, Egyptian mufti and senior cleric at Cairo's Al Azhar University, traveled to Europe and North America. Deeply impressed by the modern civic system and dynamic popular attitudes he observed, 'Abduh declared, "I went to the West and saw Islam, but no Muslims; I return to the East and see Muslims, but no Islam."

❖ ❖ ❖

As a Muslim who grew up in North America, I belong to a different generation from Muhammad 'Abduh. I spent my childhood not in the heart of the Muslim world but in a society where principles of freedom, accountability, equality, and merit were core parts of the culture. When I decided at age ten to start intensive Islamic studies to learn more about my namesake, I encountered Islam almost entirely within a theoretical scholarly framework.

As a teenager, I admired Muhammad. I wanted to know everything about his life because I desired to replicate him in every way I could. I tried to walk like him, eat like him, dress like him, even bathe like him. Because I often heard sermons about the splendors of the Muslim world, my dream was to go on hajj and have a transcendent spiritual experience at the Ka'bah. By the time I was twenty-one, I had saved enough money to join a group pilgrimage tour.

The reality of Mecca in 2002 shocked me. Pilgrims circumambulating the Ka'bah pushed and shoved one another to get close enough to the shrine to touch the black stone at its base. Others chatted on their mobile phones during the procession. I watched pickpockets snag pilgrims' wallets, shopkeepers rip off naïve shoppers, and others steal shoes at a mosque during prayers. The gap between my romantic expectations and the stark reality before my eyes was crushing.

For two days I moped around Mecca, annoyed and disillusioned. I had dedicated more than a decade of my life to studying Muhammad and his teachings. Had I wasted all those years? I finally decided to leave the commercialized downtown to walk in the wilderness. Those wanderings proved therapeutic, as I resolved to revive the spirit of Muhammad in a way I could relate to, one tied to ideas, not a place or person. I needed to think for myself, not just memorize.

In this new phase of my education, I became like the bee: intensely gathering information from as many sources as possible and analyzing the material to construct my own understanding of Muhammad's mindset. I analyzed every piece of data, scrutinizing it for accuracy. I sought to shorten as much as possible the chains of scholarly transmission that separated me from Muhammad. Approaching Muhammad with an open mind proved transformational: making my own sense of him forged a much more meaningful personal relationship with his legacy.

When I returned home from overseas, I began a third phase: producing curricula on classical Arabic and *tajwid* (elocution), opening an academy that trained both *tajwid* instructors and young students, and publishing textbooks that formalized my teaching approach for Western audiences. As I worked with young Muslims, I realized that many felt disconnected from their heritage. They struggled with identity crises exacerbated by toxic influences and asked probing questions about Islam and Muhammad's life. They expected me, as an educator, to provide answers, and I felt an obligation to offer thoughtful responses that might help resolve their doubts in healthy ways. To do that, I had to articulate my revised appreciation of Muhammad's genius.

Assembling a coherent portrait of Muhammad's life required piecing together scattered fragments and structuring them in an organized manner. What emerged from the reconstruction was the realization that Muhammad had endured terrible setbacks and traumatic suffering, only to turn his brokenness into an asset, unlocking latent abilities to improve the world around him. Moved by his own experience in overcoming challenges, Muhammad dedicated himself to inspiring others to see their imperfections as the very source of their potential. Despite all the pain, Muhammad refused to see himself as a victim. His nickname al-Badr Laylat At-Tamam (the fullest moon) referred to illumination of the darkness by his bright shining face.

Sadly, a shadow of darkness today hangs over many Muslim communities, which have stagnated in a kind of neo-*Jahiliyyah* for centuries. People can see the faded remnants of a civilization that once was the vanguard of modernity. They hear echoes of the accomplishments of the Golden Age yet remain cut off from the mindset that inspired them. Similarly, the *Jahiliyyah*-era Meccans still recalled Abraham and maintained his Ka'bah but had nonetheless lost touch with the core monotheistic values he brought to the world. Conscious of their squandered heritage, *Jahiliyyah* Meccans turned to scapegoating, blaming external forces for their setbacks.

As long as the mindsets of Abraham and Muhammad remain obscured, reviving the Golden Age will be difficult. Trying to return to a mythical past is not a solution, as I discovered as a teenager trying to mimic my hero Muhammad.

Jahiliyyah is not an epoch but a mindset—and willful stagnation can occur among any people. After stagnating in the Dark Ages for centuries, Europeans finally realized that the Muslims—long dismissed as heathens—had actually preserved classical European wisdom. Once the Europeans opened their minds to reclaim that heritage, they embarked on the Renaissance. Muslims can benefit from a similar perspective. Western knowledge is not heretical but rather has preserved and built upon Muhammad's core values.

Each time we use our cell phones, snap pictures with a camera, or use a search engine's algorithms, we benefit from the legacy of Muhammad's modern mindset. His mindset is not tied to Mecca or Medina, for as the Golden Age political philosopher Al-Farabi observed, "Medina is not a location but the manner in which a community comes together." Indeed, people of any culture or race can establish a "place of flowing change." As Muhammad declared in the final days of his life, "My progeny are those who uphold my legacy!"

On the day he was born, Muhammad was given a unique name—and with it a mission to model positive behavior to inspire others. The great inventors of the Golden Age sought to emulate his success by applying his mindset of blossoming to their own circumstances. Each manifested his methodology in trailblazing innovations that not only reflected their individuality but also transformed the world—precisely the lifetime goal Muhammad's mother had articulated for her son on her deathbed.

Indeed, Aminah's inspiring last words reverberate beyond six-year-old Muhammad to reach people of all backgrounds across the generations: strive to be a world-changer in your own unique way.

SOURCE
MATERIALS

❖

Classical Islamic scholarship
requires authors to write from
memory. The *'ulama* regarded books as secondary and supplementary
sources to knowledge learned literally sitting at the feet of the masters.
Their attitude is expressed in the maxim, "*Laysa bil-kutbi mithlana tasi-
ru falid-dajajati rishuw-walakil-la tatiru!*" (Do not think that by reading
books you will become a scholar, for a hen has feathers yet cannot fly!).

According to the *'ulama*, a work of scholarship is only a writer's own
intellectual property if he or she has: (1) learned from scholars with
chains of transmission back to the Prophet Muhammad, (2) memorized
and analyzed that information, and then (3) restructured the knowledge
to improve upon the work of previous generations. So strong is the traditional emphasis on memorization that my teachers viewed a sermon
delivered while reading from a piece of paper as inherently questionable.

Following *'ulama* standards, I authored this book from memory.
Only after the manuscript was complete did I consult the sources I
had previously learned (in many cases memorized). I provide some
information below so scholars and other curious readers can trace facts

presented, though a traditional work of Islamic scholarship would not normally include such detailed sourcing.

The bulk of the information included stems from the oral tradition passed down generation by generation. The *'ulama* consider the oral tradition purer than published books. Because publishing in the past was quite expensive (paying scribes and purchasing paper, binding, covers, etc.), producing a book almost always required patrons like government officials or well-connected merchants, whose sensitivities and prejudices the author needed to respect. Books therefore were ripe for being impacted by political agendas.

As explained in the introduction, this biography of Muhammad has been assembled from disparate fragments of information learned at the feet of eminent scholars, gathered from thousands of sources, and analyzed during decades of research. For example, the eyewitness testimony of Barakah is scattered throughout dozens of sources yet is invaluable. Imam Al-Halbi, in his *As-Sirat-ul-Halabiyyah,* notes that "Um Ayman [Barakah] was a crucial eyewitness"—a woman present throughout Muhammad's life, including the scenes of his birth and death. Her observations about Muhammad were recorded by numerous scholars in the years after his death. This biography fuses the various fragments of her testimony into a coherent form, buttressing her testimony with that from additional eyewitnesses.

Some descriptive material comes from historical studies published by academics based at universities in the West, particularly for descriptions of Byzantium, Abyssinia, and the regional geopolitics during Muhammad's time. The vast majority of content, however, is derived from original Arabic sources of traditional Islamic scholarship (most dating to over one thousand years ago).

The style of traditional citation by Muslim scholars is more narrative than standard Western footnote structure, citing sourcing as follows:

The Prophet Muhammad (peace be upon him)'s favorite fruit was watermelon, which he ate together with *rutab*, based on the Hadith narrated by Abu Dawud, via 'Aishah who said, "He was accustomed to eating watermelon with *rutab*, and would say, 'We balance the coolness of this with the warmth of this.'" And the Hadith narrated by Al-Majlisi via Husain ibn 'Ali who said, "He loved to eat *rutab* with watermelon."

Left unstated is that the sources in question are Imam Abu Dawud's book *Kitab-us-Sunan*, a universally known reference for Sunni audiences, and Al-'Allamah Al-Majlisi's *Bihar-ul-Anwar*, for a Shi'ah audience. Sunni and Shi'ah scholarship traditions do not always view sources in the same way, and sometimes their views even collide. As someone trained in both traditions, I do not favor one convention over the other. Whenever possible I have included facts from both Sunni and Shi'ah sources, and I have tried hard in most cases to include material that is agreed upon by both. In areas of dispute, I drew on techniques from diverse traditions to try to synthesize the most likely authentic account.

The science of determining the credibility of a Hadith is quite complex, revolving around two cardinal aspects:

⋄ the chain of transmission—called *isnad* (source) or *sanad* (support to lean on) and *silsilah* (chain)
⋄ the content—called *matn* (substance)

In the Sunni tradition, a Hadith is generally deemed credible (*sahih*) or not credible (*dha'if*) based on its *isnad* rather than its *matn*. Yet evaluating Hadith sources for accuracy requires open inquiry, even if a source is generally credible. Narrators, of course, were fallible human beings, each with their own inclinations. Knowing a narrator's personal story is essential. For example, Hisham ibn 'Urwah ('Aishah's great-nephew) was deemed a credible source because he heard traditions directly from his father, an eyewitness. However, after he became senile later in life, he began making odd declarations, including that Khadijah was forty and 'Aishah was nine when Muhammad married each of them. Both ages are off by more than a decade (one inflated, the other deflated)—resulting in grave misunderstandings of Muhammad that have persisted for centuries.

My due diligence process in evaluating each source cannot easily be replicated for the reader. Many data points and clues were considered over decades of research. Then, these thousands of specific individual deductions were in turn processed, analyzed, and refined into this book's narrative. For readability and practicality, every fact presented in this biography is not documented by a specific source.

Several traditional scholarly texts in classical Arabic serve as references and appear repeatedly in the sourcing: (Al-Bukhari) references *Sahih al-Bukhari*; (Muslim) *Sahih Muslim*; (Abu Dawud) *Sunan Abu Dawud*; (An-Nasa`i) *Sunan an-Nasa`i*; (Al-Bazzar) *Sunan al-Bazzar*; (As-Suhaili) *Ar-Rawdh-ul-Unuf*; (Al-Hakim) *Al-Mustadrak*; (Ibnu Hibban) *Sahih ibnu Hibban*; (Ad-Daraqutni) *Sunan ad-Daraqutni*; (Ahmad) *Al-Musnad*; (At-Tirmithi) *Al-Jami'-us-Sahih*; (Al-Halabi) *As-Sirat-ul-Halabiyyah*; (Ad-Darami) *Sunan-ad-Darami*; (Ibnu Kathir) *Al-Bidayatu wan-Nihayah*; (Ibnu Majah) *Sunan ibnu Majah*; (Ibnu Sa'd) *At-Tabaqat-ul-Kubra*; (Al-Hamawi) *Mu'jam-ul-Buldan*; (Abu Na'im) *Hilyat-ul-Awliya*; (Ibnul-Athir) *Al-Kamilu fit-Tarikh*; (Abu Ya'la) *Musnad abu Ya'la*; (Malik) *Al-Muwatta*; (At-Tabarani) *Mu'jam at-Tabarani*; (Al-Bayhaqi) *Sunan Al-Bayhaqi*; (Ibnu 'Asakir) *Tarikh Dimashq*; (Ibnu 'Abdil-Barr) *Al-Istithkar*; (Ath-Thahabi) *Siyar A'lam an-Nubala*; (Al-Qurtubi) *Tafsir Al-Qurtubi*; (Al-Waqidi) *Kitab at-Tarikh wal-Maghazi*; (Ibnu Hazm) *Al-Muhalla*; (Al-'Asqalani) *Fath-ul-Bari*.

These books are referenced below by citing the author's name along with volume/page or Hadith number in parentheses. Traditional scholars who collected Hadith created a standard order for them in their books, enabling specific Hadith to be referenced by an assigned number. For example, "Al-Bukhari (6830)" refers to Imam Al-Bukhari's *Sahih*, Hadith number 6830, while "Ibnu Kathir (5/215)" refers to page 215 of the fifth volume of Imam Ibnu Kathir's *Al-Bidayatu wan-Nihayah*.

Introduction

For details of Muhammad's physical appearance via many eyewitness accounts, including 'Ali, Ibnu 'Abbas, and Anas ibnu Malik, see: Al-Bukhari (3394, 3437, 3547, 3548, 5845); Muslim (168, 2330, 2338, 2347); Abu Dawud (4863); At-Tirmithi (1754, 3638, 3642); Ahmad (13381); 'Abdullah ibn Ahmad's Zawa`id-ul-Musnad, *Zawa`id-ul-Musnad* (944); Ibnu Hibban (6311); Abu Ya'la (369); At-Tabarani

(679); Al-Baghawi's Mishkat-ul-Masabih, *Mishkat-ul-Masabih* (5728); Al-Bayhaqi (1/386); As-Suhaili (2/199–200). Jabir ibn Samurah said, "I saw him on that day wear a red and white garment and he was more handsome than the moon in its fullness"; see At-Tirmithi (2811).

About Muhammad's request that his followers not write about him (other than the Qur`an) via eyewitness Abu Sa'id al-Khudri, see: Muslim (2004); An-Nasa`i (8008); Ahmad (11085, 11087, 11158, 11344, 11536); Ibnu Hibban (64). Muhammad's request "Do not glorify me" via eyewitness Ibnu 'Abbas and 'Umar, see: Al-Bukhari (6830); Muslim (1691); An-Nasa`i (7158); Ahmad (331); Ibnu Hibban (414); Al-Bazzar (1/299); Ibnu Kathir (5/215). Muhammad's quote "I am the son of a woman who ate *qadid*" (and in one variation "*tharid*") via several eyewitnesses, including Ibnu Mas'ud, Jabir ibnu 'Abdillah, and 'Uqbah ibnu 'Amr, see: Al-Muzzi (2/141); At-Tabari (2/64); Ibnu 'Asakir (4/82); Ibnu Majah (3312).

Translations of the Divine names, Qur`anic passages, and terminologies are based on numerous Arabic etymological and linguistic sources including *Tafsir Asma`il-lahil-Husna* by Az-Zajjaj; *Al-Asma`u was-Sifat* by Al-Bayhaqi; *Al-Maqsad-ul-Asna* by Al-Ghazali; *At-Tahbir Fit-Tathkir* by Al-Qushairi; *Al-Luma'u Fil-'Arabiyyah* by Ibn Junni; *Al-Bayan wat-Tabyin* by Al-Jahith; *Mabadi`-ul-Lughah* by Al-Iskafi; *Fawa`id fi Mushkili-Qur`an* by Al-'Izz ibn 'Abdis-Salam; *Dalil-ul-Ayati-Mutashabihatil-Alfath* by Siraj Salih Mala'ikah; *Mukhtar-us-Sihah* by Ar-Razi; *Al-Mu'Jam-ul-Kamil fi Lahjatil-Fusha* by Dawud Sallum, *Mu'jam Maqayis-il-Lughah* by Ar-Razi; *Al-Muyassar fi Takhrijil-Qira'atil-Mutawatirah* by Muhaisin; *Al-Buduruz-Zahir* by Al-Qadhi; *Al-Muzhir fi 'Ulumil-Lughah* by As-Suyuti; *Lisan-ul-'Arab* by Ibn Manthur; *Tahthib-ul-Lughah* by Al-Azhari; *Al-Mudhish* by Ibnul-Jawzi; *Al-Ajnas Min Kalamil-'Arab* by Al-Qasim ibnu Sallam; *Al-Kitab* by Sibawayh; *Al-'Ayn* by Al-Khalil ibn Ahmad; *Sharh-Al-Mu'allaqatis-Sab'* by Az-Zawzuni; *Taj-ul-'Arus* by Az-Zubaidi; *Mat-Tafaqa Lafthuhu Wakh-talafa Ma'nahu Fil-Qur`anil-Majid* by Al-Mubarrid; *I'rab Amma Ba'd* by Ibn Al-Amin Al-Jaza'iri; *Asas-ul-Balaghah* by Az-Zamakhshari; *Tarikh-ul-Adab-il-'Arabi* by Hanna al-Fakhuri; *Sharhu Milhatil-I'rab* by Al-Hariri; *Asrar-ul-Balaghah fi 'Ilmil-Bayan;* and *Dala`il-ul-i'jaz fi'ilmil-Ma'ani* by Al-Jurjani.

Chapter 1

Account of the birth, including time, date, and naming ceremony via eyewitness Al-'Abbas, see: As-Suhaili (1/278–89); Al-Halabi (1/69–73 and 78–124). Ibnu 'Abbas mentions Muhammad's birth and death both falling on a Monday; see Ahmad (2502).

For information on Muhammad's parents, Aminah and 'Abdullah, see As-Suhaili (1/210) and for background on 'Abdul-Muttalib's mother, Salma, and her Jewish Banu Najjar roots, see: As-Suhaili (1/206); Al-Halabi (1/48–68).

Descriptions of Bedouin selection process and details of Muhammad's early years were provided by Halimah and her children during first hajj. Their testimony was gathered by Ibnu 'Abbas, Ibnu 'Umar, and Ibnuz-Zubair; see: Ahmad (17196); As-Suhaili (1/283–294); Al-Halabi (1/24–153).

For description of Yathrib at time of Muhammad's visit, including narratives around his time there with Aminah who took "him to visit his maternal family [akhwaluh] from Banu Najjar" and learning how to "swim in the pond of Aris the Jew" (the same well where his signet ring would be lost over seventy years later); account of Aminah's death and famous quote "Oh Muhammad, be a world-changer," see: Al-Bukhari (5873); Muslim (2091); Sabil-ul-Huda war-Rashad by As-Salihi Al-Hashimi (2/120); Al-Halabi (1/74, 154–64); Ma'alimu Taybah by Majd Ad-Din Abadi; As-Suhaili (1/48–81, 2/372); Al-Hamawi (5/430–31); Ibnu Sa'd (1/116); Ibnu 'Abdil-Barr (1/30).

Chapter 2

Account of 'Abdul-Muttalib rediscovering Zamzam and near sacrifice of 'Abdullah, see: As-Suhaili (1/214–16, 257–73); Al-Hamawi (4/463–67); Al-Qurtubi (18/82); Al-Fakihi (1002, 1003, 1004, 1008); As-Suyuti (12/434); Ibnu Kathir (7/29); Al-Albani (26).

Ibnul-Athir provides valuable descriptions of Jahiliyyah, see Al-Kamil Fit-Tarikh (1/502–684), as well as 'Abdul-Muttalib's affinity for Jews (2/15) and account of Muhammad's ancestors Hashim and Qusai (2/16–23). For pagan rituals and Meccan idolatry, see Kitab-ul-Asnam by Al-Kalbi (pp. 22–78).

Account of 'Abdul-Muttalib's death and Muhammad's foster care at home of Abu Talib, see: As-Suhaili (1/300–13); Al-Halabi (1/164–71); At-Tabarani (8/252).

Chapter 3

Account of Bahira, see: As-Suhaili (1/313–18); Ibnul-Athir (2/37); Al-Halabi (1/171–77, 195); Ath-Thahabi (1/55); Ibnu Kathir (2/264); At-Tirmithi (3620); Al-Bazzar (3096); At-Tabari (11/80); Al-Waqidi (2/33).

Account of Muhammad's youth in Mecca, Ibnu Jud'an, and Hilf-ul-Fudhul, see: Ibnul-Athir (2/41–42); Al-Halabi (1/178–92); As-Suhaili (1/242–56); Ibnu Hisham (1/141–42); Ibnul-Mulqin (2/153); Al-'Asqalani (3/1097); Al-Bukhari (379); Muslim (214); Ibnu Hibban (330); Ibnul-Mulqin (7/325); Al-Haithami (8/89); Ibnu 'Adi (4/59); Ibnu Mundah (969); Abu Na'im (3/318); Ibnul-Qaisarani (3/1690); Ahmad (24892); Abu Ya'la (4672); At-Tirmithi (708); Ibnu Taymiyyah (8/540); An-Najjar (p. 100) Al-Khudhari (1/14); Al-Albani (72).

Chapter 4

Account of Khadijah, the proposal, marriage, Muhammad's love for her, and their family life, see: As-Suhaili (1/322–25); Al-Bukhari (3816, 3818, 3821); Muslim (2435, 2437); Ibnul-Athir (2/39–40); Ahmad (24310, 24864); Al-Halabi (1/193–204); At-Tabari (2/281); At-Tirmithi (2017, 3875); Ibnul-Jawzi (2/210); Ath-Thahabi (127); An-Nasa'i (8361); Ash-Shawkani (249); Ibnu Majah (1997); Al-Bazzar (4/249); Al-Haithami (6/223, 9/223–27); Ibnu Hibban (7006, 7008); Ibnu Kathir (2/293–94); Ibnu Sa'd (8/174). Scholars agree that Muhammad was married fifteen years, "qablal-bi'thah" (before his prophethood), and it is undisputed that he was forty at the time of his prophethood. Forty minus fifteen gives us twenty-five. This places Muhammad's marriage to Khadijah in 595 CE; see Ibnu Kathir (2/295).

To deduce Khadijah's age at the time of her marriage to Muhammad, I cite her own testimony to her best friend, Lubabah (who recounted it to her son Ibnu 'Abbas), that she was twelve years old when she saw the firasah reader in the market proclaim the future of Muhammad—who was nine at the time of the incident. Shaykh Bahauddin Al-'Amili mentions

Khadijah was twenty-eight years old at her marriage to Muhammad; see *As-Sahih min Sirat-in-Nabi* (2/114); Al-Hakim (3/200); Ad-Dulabi in *Ath-Thurriyyah At-Tahirah An-Nabawiyyah* (p. 52); *Tarikh-ul-Khamis* by Shaykh Husain ibn Muhammad Diyarbakri (1/264); Ibnu 'Asakir (1/303).

It is important to note that sources vary in describing Khadijah's age from twenty-five to thirty at the time of marriage. Her age being twenty-five at the time of marriage is related by Ibn Kathir (2/294), Al-Bayhaqi (2/72), and Baladhuri in *Ansab-ul-Ashraf* (1/98). A telling clue is the Qur'an's declaration (78:33) that the "ideal" in a union is for the couple to be *atrab* (of the same soil), meaning the "same generation"—that is, within five years or the "same year." At-Tabari says, "*Atrab* means they are of the same age" (*sin-iw-wahid*). As-Sa'di says, "*atrab* means *'ala sin-iw-wahidim-mutaqarib*" (close in age). Al-Baghawi says "*mustawiyatin-fis-sin*" (similar in age). Al-Qurtubi says—"*al-aqranu fis-sin*" (of the same generation). And Ibnu Kathir says, "*Atrab* means of the same age."

Account of mediating the elders' dispute and birth of Fatimah, see: As-Suhaili (1/336–47); Ibnul-Athir (2/42–45); Al-Halabi (1/204–65). The account provided by Al-Halabi inspired Al-Busairi to give his epic poem about Muhammad the title *Al-Burdah* (The Mantle).

Account of Muhammad's period of unhappiness leading to his treks to Hira, see: Al-Bukhari (4953); Al-Qurtubi (10/335–51); Ar-Razi (11/190–209); Ibnul-'Arabi (4/408–13); Az-Zamakhshari (4/770–77); Al-Baghawi (4/631–42); Ibnul-Athir (2/46–47); Al-Halabi (1/322–34).

Chapter 5

Account of first revelation and Muhammad's initial response is drawn from numerous sources, including Al-Bukhari (3, 4, 4953, 6982); Muslim (160, 161); As-Suhaili (1/396–411); Al-Qurtubi (10/358–62); Ar-Razi (11/215–19); Ibnu Hibban (33); Al-Haithami (8/259); At-Tabarani (6/287); Ibnul-'Arabi (4/418–23); Az-Zamakhshari (4/781–85); Al-Baghawi (4/647–50); Al-'Ukbari (392); Al-Ujhuri (785–86); Al-Halabi (1/334–75); Al-Maturidi (10/575–82); Abu Hayyan (10/309–40); Ibnul-Athir (2/48–50).

Account of Waraqah, see: As-Suhaili (1/330–35, 396–411); Ibnul-Athir (2/48–49); Al-Bukhari (4953); Al-Halabi (1/381–427); Ibn Man-thur (8/420–23).

Account of Sumayyah and repression after Abu Qubais speech, see: Ibnu Sa'd (4/101); Ibnu 'Abdil-Barr (4/1589, 1864); Ibnu Mindah (1/92); Al-Balathiri (1/157); Al-Majlisi (18/241); As-Suhaili (2/337); Ibnul-Athir (2/60–76).

Account of Al-Walid's attempted intervention, see: Al-Ujhuri (742); As-Suhaili (2/216).

Account of 'Umar's conversion, see: Ibnul-Athir (2/84–86); As-Suhaili (2/120–26); Ash-Shawkani (3/502); Ibnu Daqiq Al-'Id (2/424); Ath-Thahabi (3/375); Al-Hakim (6897); Al-Bayhaqi (420); Ad-Daraqutni (1/123); Al-'Asqalani (1/198); Al-Busairi (7/166); Ibnu Sa'd (3/267); Az-Zaila'i (1/199).

Discussion of letters at openings of Qur'anic chapters (like Taha), see As-Suhaili (2/308).

Account of Bilal and the elders' boycott discussion, see As-Suhaili (2/7–89).

Chapter 6

Account of migration to Abyssinia with all its details—including seeing the "Church of Mary of Zion," discussion at negus's court, and Muhammad's followers offering him support during a rebellion—via eyewitness Um Salamah, see: Al-Bukhari (434, 1341, 4230, 4232); Muslim (528, 2502, 2499); Ahmad (1740, 1742); Ibnu Hibban (3181); Al-Haithami (6/27); Abu Na'im (1/114–15); Ibnul-Athir (2/76–82); Al-Halabi (1/456–87); As-Suyuti (1/149); As-Suhaili (2/90–119); Ahmad (1740); Al-Wadi'i (96, 1672); *Takhriju Siyari A'lamin-Nubala'* by Shu'aib Al-Arna'ut (1/216, 429).

Account of popular uprising against the boycott, deaths of Abu Talib and Khadijah, and subsequent visit to Ta'if, see: Al-Halabi (1/488–512); As-Suhaili (2/223–34); Al-Bukhari (3884, 4772); Muslim (24); Ibnu Hibban (982); Al-Arna'ut (2486); Al-Albani (126); Ibnul-Athir (2/87).

Scholars debate whether the *isra'* (the night journey to Jerusalem) was an epiphanic vision or a physical journey. This discussion arises from the wording in the Qur'an to describe it as a *ru'ya* (a vision perceived in the soul's eye), rather than *ru'yah* (the physical act of seeing with the eyes). The main sources for it being a spiritual vision are 'Aishah and Huthaifah ibnul-Yaman, who said, "The prophet's body did not depart, rather the night journey was spiritual (*walakin usriya bi-ruhih*)." The same opinion is also transmitted via Al-Hasan Al-Basri, a prominent student of 'Ali. The distinction here is that it was a vision and not a dream—that is, of divine inspiration rather than a figment of the imagination. Nonetheless, most Sunni and Shi'ah theologians believe that the night journey was a physical one. See: Al-Qadhi 'Iyadh (1/147); Ibnu Hisham (2/46); At-Tabari (14/445); Al-Halabi (1/514–86); As-Suhaili (2/187–212); Ibnu 'Abdil-Barr (135).

Account of Jundub (aka Abu Tharr), see: Al-Bukhari (3522); Muslim (2473, 2474); Ibnu Hibban (7133); At-Tabarani (1/23, 3/150); Al-Bazzar (3888); Ahmad (1019, 21525); Ibnu 'Abd-Al-Barr (1/252–55); Al-Haithami (9/330); Ibnu Kathir (5/8); Ad-Dailami (4145); As-Suyuti (5627); Ath-Thahabi (2/49); Az-Zarkali (2/140); Al-'Asqalani (7/107).

Account of Yathribite delegation, see: As-Suhaili (2/245–52); Ahmad (15798); Ibnu Hibban (7011); At-Tabarani (174); Al-Haithami (6/45, 100).

Account of elders' assassination plot and Muhammad's subsequent escape, including leaving 'Ali to return possessions in the safety depository, see: As-Suhaili (2/306–29); Qur'an 8:30; Ibnu Kathir (3/177, 218–19); Al-Bukhari (3905, 3906, 5607, 5807, 6079); Muslim (2009); Ahmad (25626); At-Tahawi (4076); Ibnu Hibban (6277, 6280); Al-Haithami (6/56); Al-Baghawi (7/106); Al-Bayhaqi (12477); At-Tabari (2/372); Al-Hulli (123); Ibnu Taymiyyah (7/110); Al-Albani (5/384).

Chapter 7

Account of *hijrah* and arrival in Yathrib, see: Al-Bukhari (3906, 3911, 3925); Muslim (2381); At-Tabarani (611, 3605); Al-Bazzar (1746); Al-'Asqalani (7/307, 735); Al-'Iraqi (2/342, 7/239); As-Suhaili (2/187–212); Al-Bayhaqi (1/298); Ahmad (23061); At-Tirmithi (3690).

Account of Abu Ayyub and Muhammad's praise of Banu Najjar, see: Al-Bukhari (3807, 3789, 3790, 5300, 6053); Muslim (2511, 2512); Abu Na'im (6/391); Al-Busairi (7/319); Ahmad (16050, 16051, 16052); At-Tirmithi (3910); Ibnu Hibban (7286); An-Nasa'i (8340); At-Tabari (6/125); As-Suhaili (2/340–41); Ibnu Hibban (5110).

The original name of Surah 17 as "Surah Bani Israel" appears in numerous Hadith, including Al-Bukhari (4994) and At-Tirmithi (3402). In fact, Al-'Asqalani declared that "the *surah*'s name during the time of the prophet Muhammad, as well as that of the generations that came after him was Surah Bani Israel"—see *Fath-ul-Bari* (8/388). Ibnu 'Ashur said, "It was called Bani Israel, during the time of the followers of the prophet"—see *At-Tahriru wat-Tanwir* (5/15). Imam As-Sadiq, a prominent descendant of Muhammad, referred to the chapter as Surah Bani Israel, see *Nur-uth-Thaqalain* by Al-Juwaizi (4/115). Muhammad himself referred to it as Bani Israel—see Az-Zamakhshari (2/854) and *Ruh-ul-Ma'ani* by Al-Alusi (15/5).

Account of Nu'aiman, Rabbi Mukhairiq, and Rabbi ibn Salam, see: Ibnu Sa'd (3/371); Ath-Thahabi (5/331); Ibnu Hajar (6/351); Al-'Iraqi (3/154, 164); *Wafa`ul-Wafa* (1/170); Al-Bukhari (4330); As-Suhaili (2/373–76); *Ansab-ul-Ashraf* (pp. 74–76, 90); Al-Waqidi (164, 215).

Dating Constitution of Medina (including its text) to the day after Rosh Hashanah in 622 comes as follows: Muhammad entered Yathrib on Friday, July 16, 622. The constitution was signed two months after he entered the city, Thursday, September 16, corresponding to the third day of the month of Tishri in the year 4383 of the Jewish calendar. The two-day holiday Rosh Hashanah begins on the first of Tishri, see: Muslim (1538); As-Suhaili (2/346–50); Ibnu Kathir (3/222).

Account of abandoned date factory, 'Umar suggesting the *athan*, and Bilal assigned task of chanting it are covered in various Sunni sources, see: Al-Bukhari (604, 2774); Abu Dawud (498, 502, 503); As-Suhaili (2/335–60). The Shi'ah believe *athan* was revealed via Gabriel and not via 'Umar's dream.

Construction of *masjid*, its layout, and incident of urinating nomad via Anas ibnu Malik, see: Al-Bukhari (428, 446, 496); Muslim (285, 509); Abu Dawud (452); An-Nasa`i (702); Ibnu Majah (528, 529, 530, 744); As-Suhaili (2/336 and 339).

Establishment of *zakah* fund, see: Ibnu Qudamah (4/161–62); Abu Dawud (1568, 1604). The eight categories of *zakah* recipients are described in the Qur`an 9:60.

For Muhammad's progressing declarations on alcohol, see: Al-Halabi (2/375); *Al-'Aqd-ul-Farid* (6/381); Al-Ghazali (2/325); *Kanz-ul-'Ummal* (4/27). The Qur`an discusses the three stages of alcohol's eradication:

Passage 4:43 urges people not to attend public gatherings while intoxicated. Passage 2:219 states that there is both benefit and harm in wine, but the harm is greater. Passage 5:90 urges that alcohol be eschewed altogether. It should be noted that these prohibitions are informing rather than forceful.

Account of drought that beset Arabia, see: Al-Bukhari (8/573); Al-Baghawi (4/111–22).

Salman's youth, religious journey, redemption from slavery, and strategic ideas in battle via eyewitness Ibnu 'Abbas, see: Ahmad (23225, 23737); Al-Bazzar (2500); At-Tahawi (4772); Al-Hakim (4/784); Ibnu Hajar (3/118–20); Al-Wadi'i (84, 442); Al-'Asqalani (3/265); Al-Haithami (2/315, 8/43, 9/335); Ibnu Hazm (9/226); At-Tabarani (6058); Abu Na'im (1/201).

Account of 'Ali's marriage to Fatimah, see: *Maqatil-ut-Talibiyyin* by Abul-Faraj Al-Asfahani (59); *Ar-Rawdhah min Al-Kafi*, by Al-Kulaini (2/180–81); At-Tabari (2/410); Ibnu Sa'd (8/22–23); *Al-Amali* by Shaykh At-Tusi (1/93–99).

Chapter 8

Account of Badr, see: Al-Haithami (9/216); As-Suhaili (3/48, 79–89); Muslim (1763, 1779, 1901); Al-Bukhari (2301, 3141, 3950, 3956, 3958). Incident of the five-year-old taking Muhammad by the hand after his return from Badr is described in Al-Bukhari (5724).

Examples of Muhammad preaching principled nonviolence include, "In times of confusion, break your sword and remain at home. If an enemy enters upon you with intent to kill you, go into your storeroom and sit on your knees. If they follow you, say to them, 'If you kill me you will bear the guilt of my murder! I have broken my sword and will not kill you.'" See Al-Wa'idi (557).

Muhammad's admonition before battle not to harm civilians via Abu Bakr: "Do not harm/kill a woman, or a child, or an aged person, nor cut down fruit trees, nor destroy buildings, nor harm livestock—unless you are butchering it for food—nor flood palm groves, nor burn them! Never confiscate the property of civilians nor freeze their livelihood!" See *Takhrij Sharh as-Sunnah* by Shu'aib Al-Arnaut (2696); Malik (2/448); *Al-Madawwanat-ul-Kubra* (2/7); Ibnu Abi Shaibah (7/655); Ibnu Kathir

(2/320); Ibnu Hazm (7/297); Ash-Shawkani (8/74); Ar-Riba'i in *Fath-ul-Ghaffar* (4/1778); Ibnu 'Asakir (2/9); Ash-Shafi'i (5/594); Al-Bayhaqi (3/387).

Similar to the debate over Khadijah's age at the time of her marriage to Muhammad, there is confusion surrounding 'Aishah's age. The myth alleging she was nine years old at her time of marriage would place her birth in 615 CE. This is impossible given the established fact that Ibnu Hisham's narrative (via Ibnu Ishaq) lists 'Aishah among the first nineteen people to accept Muhammad's prophethood in 610 CE. Furthermore, 'Aishah's mother, Um Ruman, was widowed at age twenty-seven in the year 592; married Abu Bakr at the end of that year; and gave birth to 'Aishah three years later in 595. Moreover, Muhammad's youngest daughter, Fatimah, was ten years younger than 'Aishah—and Fatimah was nineteen in 624 when she married 'Ali. By this timeline, 'Aishah was age twenty-nine in 624 when she married Muhammad. The level of maturity 'Aishah displays in the Meccan period and her account of important events clearly reveal her as a mature woman, not a young child. Her being an adult (over nineteen) at the time of her marriage to Muhammad is supported by several sources, including *As-Sahih Minas-Siratin-Nabi* by Shaykh Al-'Amili (3/285–87); *Bihar-ul-Anwar* by Shaikh Al-Majlisi (23/291); Ibnu Hajar (8/232).

Account of Rabbi Mukhairiq's decision to interrupt Sabbath services, pledge his lands as a permanent trust, and martyrdom at Uhud, see: Ibnu Sa'd (1/502); Al-'Asqalani (3/373); Ibnu Rajab (2/485). Rabbi Mukhairiq's orchards still exist as a charitable trust in Medina, located just north of the Well of Salman.

Account of Barakah taking charge to save Muhammad's life with her admonishment "take the spindle and gives us [women] the sword!" see: Ibnu Sa'd (8/223–26); Ibnu Kathir (7/325); Ibnu 'Abdil-Barr (13/178); Al-Hakim (4/63).

Account of first 'Id al-Adh-ha via eyewitness Hafsah bint Sirin, see: Muslim (890); Al-Bukhari (971); Abu Dawud (1158); At-Tirmithi (530, 541); Ibnu Majah (1303).

Account of the treaty at Hudaibiyyah via eyewitnesses Anas ibnu Malik, Al-Bara` ibnu 'Azib, and Al-Maswar ibnu Makhramah, see: Al-Bukhari (1778, 2698, 2731, 4178); Muslim (1253, 1783); Abu Dawud

(2117, 2736, 2765); Ibnu Hibban (4872); Ahmad (15470); Al-Bayhaqi (4/99); Ibnu Daqiq Al-'Id (4/448); Ibnul-Mulqin (10/368); Ibnu Kathir (4/229); Al-Haythami (4/125); Al-'Asqalani (2/361).

Details of Muhammad's signet ring, including how 'Uthman later lost it at the well of Aris (about 1.8 miles south of the *masjid*) via several eyewitnesses, including Ibnu 'Umar, Ibnu Mas'ud, and Anas ibn Malik, see: Al-Bukhari (3106, 5868, 5874, 5878, 5979); Muslim (2091, 2092, 2094); Abu Dawud (4217, 4218); An-Nasa'i (5207, 5209, 5217, 5292, 5293, 5879); At-Tirmithi (1748); Ibnu Hibban (5499); At-Tabarani (6/371, 7/114); Al-Bayhaqi (5/2175); Al-Haithami (5/156).

Account of Heraclius incident in Jerusalem via eyewitness Abu Sufyan and Heraclius's Arab courtier "the Christian At-Tannukhi," see: Al-Bukhari (7, 4553, 6260, 7541); Muslim (1773); Ibnu Hibban (6555); Ahmad (15655); Abu Dawud (5136); Ibnu Janzawayh (961); At-Tabari (7831); Al-Haithami (8/237); Ibnu Kathir (4/266, 5/14); Al-'Asqalani (1/45).

Account of Abyssinian delegation permitted to perform and pray in the *masjid* via eyewitnesses 'Aishah, Anas ibnu Malik, and 'Ali, see: Al-Bukhari (907, 4894); Muslim (892, 1941, 1943, 1945, 1946); Ahmad (860, 12564).

Account of Sasanian emperor asking Batham to assassinate Muhammad, and Muhammad sending Mu'ath to engage Yemen's Jewish population, see: Al-Bukhari (1496); Muslim (19, 26); Ibnu 'Asakir (18/195); Ibnul-Jawzi (3/451); Al-Bayhaqi (11592); At-Tabarani (44); Abu Na'im (1/231); Al-Haithami (8/290).

Evidence that the Banu Quraithah were not massacred comes from several traditions dating to the later Medinian period where Muhammad was asked by members of the Jewish clan to mediate in matters of marriage and divorce. One incident involves a man named Rifa'ah al-Qurathi (of the Banu Quraithah) who divorced his wife—a friend of 'Aishah's. Al-Awza'i greatly objected to the myth of the massacre of the Banu Quraithah, stating, "As far as I know it is not a decree of the Divine to chastise the many for the fault of the few; rather to reprimand the few for the fault of the many." Ibnu Hajar al-'Asqalani called the legend a "deviant tale" in his *Tahthib-ut-Tahthib*, and At-Tabari called the fable an "unsubstantiated allegation"; see Al-Bukhari (2639, 5792, 5825); *Tafsir Al-Mizan* by Allamah At-Tabtaba`i (9/82); *Tahthib-ut-Tahthib* by Al-'Asqalani (9/40); *Tarikh Tahlil Al-Islam* by Dr. Shahidi (pp. 88–90); *'Uyun Al-Athar* by Ibn Sayyid An-Nas (1/17); *Al-Maghazi An-Nabawiyyah* by Ibn 'Uqbah (pp. 82–83).

Account of Maria, and her comfortable home in the lush "groves of 'Aliyah" in the "lands of the Jewish Banun-Nadhir" clan via 'Ali, Ibnu 'Abbas, and Ibnu 'Amr, see: Ibnu Kathir (7/74, 8/192); Ibnu Sa'd (8/171); At-Tabarani (3/13); Al-Bazzar (10/304); Al-Haithami (5/181, 7/129, 9/164); Al-'Asqalani (9/200); Al-Hamawi (5/138); Ibnu Sa'd (1/107); Ibnu 'Abdil-Barr (1/153); Ibnu 'Asakir (3/144).

Muhammad's declarations about *yusr* via Ibnu 'Abbas and Anas ibnu Malik, see: Al-Bukhari (39, 69, 6125); Muslim (1734, 2816); Al-Baghawi (2/470); Ibnu Hibban (351); An-Nasa`i (5049); Ash-Shawkani (6/3207); Al-Busairi (1/115); Abu Ya'la (6863); At-Tabarani (372); Abu Dawud (4946); Ahmad (2136, 2556); Al-Bazzar (4872); At-Tayalisi (2730); Ibnul-Qaysarani (5/2785); Ath-Thahabi (3/422); Al-Haythami (1/66); Al-'Asqalani (1/485); As-Suyuti (5462).

The Qur'an's severest passages revealed in Surah 9 concern the Banu Bakr clan, who broke the Treaty of Hudaibiyyah by massacring the Banu Khuza'ah. Important context on these verses and the incident that sparked them are provided by At-Tabari (11/351–53); *Al-Basit* by Al-Wahidi (10/301–3); *Al-'Athbun-Namir* by Ash-Shinqiti (5/285–86); Ibnu Kathir (4/114); Al-Qurtubi (8/78); Ibnul-Jawzi (2/238–39); Ibnu Abi Hatim (6/1758); and Ibnu 'Ashur (10/120–24). Ibnu 'Ashur comments that "the Qur'an sanctions the execution of the guilty from the Banu Bakr because they massacred the unarmed Banu Khuza'ah in cold blood and betrayed the peace treaty" (120–21), "yet the passage continues by stressing (*tawkid*) that pagans who kept the pledge are not to be harmed." See: Ibnu 'Ashur (10/123); Az-Zamakhshari (2/249); Abu As-Su'ud (4/45).

Muhammad's advice to "pursue your goals by maintaining the utmost secrecy," via Mu'ath ibnu Jabal, see: At-Tabari (1186); Abu Na'im (6/96); Al-Haithami (8/198); Ahmad (66); Ar-Rawyani (1449).

Chapter 9

Accounts of Muhammad's bloodless entrance into Mecca via eyewitnesses 'Ali, Ibnu 'Abbas, and 'Umar, see: Al-Bukhari (1846, 4274, 4276, 4280, 4287); Abu Dawud (3022, 4156); Muslim (1780); An-Nasa`i (4067); At-Tabarani (19/182). For account of Jewish troops in Muhammad's army, see At-Tirmithi (1558).

Muhammad's dramatic declaration, "Today is the day of amnesty," via eyewitnesses 'Ali and 'Urwah ibnuz-Zubair, see: Al-Bukhari (3944, 4280); Ibnu Abi Hadid (17/272). Muhammad's remark, "I am the son of 'Abdul-Muttalib!" see Al-Baghawi (2506). Muhammad's statements about not fearing contamination by the poor, see Al-Baghawi (2599, 3064).

Muhammad's attitude toward slavery is clear from the thousands of Hadith and over a hundred Qur`anic passages in which emancipation of the enslaved is highly encouraged, including as an expiation for many sins and portioning one-eighth of the *zakah* funds for the emancipation and support of the enslaved. The Qur`an 12:13 states: "Shall I not inform you of the path to success? It is to emancipate the enslaved!" The Qur`an 24:33 also encourages people to free the enslaved and to marry them. Muhammad declared that one of the worst sins is to sell a free person into slavery, encouraged his followers to emancipate the enslaved in a bid to completely end the institution, forbade beating the enslaved, and led by example when he emancipated the enslaved in Ta`if. This mass emancipation was described by numerous eyewitnesses, including Ibnu 'Umar, 'Ali, Anas ibnu Malik, and Ibnu 'Abbas. Muhammad's passion on the issue of slavery makes sense, given that he was nearly abducted into slavery as a toddler and later freed his own slave (Barakah) as a child. He sought to unlock the potential of every human being but via persuasion and encouragement rather than forced measures. He also recognized the complexities of mass liberation, as evidenced by the enormous difficulties Moses faced with the ancient Israelites' wandering forty years in the desert after fleeing from bondage in Egypt. While Muhammad never fully outlawed slavery, it should be noted that the Qur`an is the only religious book that envisions a future time "when no enslaved person can be found to emancipate" (5:89). See: Al-Bukhari (97, 2114, 2491, 2522, 2524, 4798, 5691, 6337, 6715); Muslim (1501, 1509, 1661, 1657, 2249); Abu Dawud (3940, 3966); At-Tahawi (5369); Ibnu Hib-ban (4308, 4316); Abu Na'im (6/333); An-Nasa`i (3142, 3144, 3145, 4874, 4878, 4947); At-Tirmithi (1541, 1635, 1638); Ahmad (3257, 9773, 17020, 18091, 19437, 19623); Abu Ya'la (5725); Ibnu Kathir (8/429); Al-Bazzar (14/362); Ibnu 'Adi (4/293); Ibnu 'Asakir (2/658); Ad-Dimyati (310); Ibnul-'Arabi (4/401); Al-Munthiri (2/249); Al-Ishbili (1635); At-Tabarani (3/285, 7/234, 8/131); Al-Wadi'i (353); Ibnu Majah (1625, 1984, 2812); Ibnu Hazm (9/35, 8/24); Al-Bayhaqi (4/203); Ibnu 'Abdil-Barr (6/319); Al-'Iraqi (6/194); Al-Bukhari's *Al-Adab Al-Mufrad* (181, 188); Al-Makki (2/180); Al-Haithami (4/245); Ash-Shafi'i (615).

Muhammad's quote "I was offered kingship, abundant wealth, and power, but I chose the life of a servant" and reassuring Medinians via Ibnu 'Abbas and Abu Sa'id Al-Khudri, see: Ash-Shawkani (9/44); At-Tabarani (10686); Ibnu Kathir (6/50, 8/674); Abu Ya'la (1092, 4920); Ibnu Sa'd (902); Al-Haithami (6/192, 10/32); At-Tirmithi (3904); Ah-mad (11730, 11842); Ibnu Abi Shaibah (33018).

While there is a common perception that women cannot hold posi-tions of Muslim religious leadership or scholarship, Muhammad himself provided two clear counterexamples: naming Um Waraqah Imam of her community and Ash-Shifa bint 'Abdillah as Medina's head educator. He named Um Waraqah as an Imam "because she had mastered the art of the Qur`an and memorized it" and assigned her a *mu`athin*. See: Ah-mad (26739); Ibnu Khuzaimah (1676); Abu Dawud (592); Ibnu Sa'd (8/457); *Irwa'-ul-Ghalil* by Al-Albani (2/225); *Tanqih-ut-Tahqiq* by Ibnu 'Abdil-Hadi (2/82).

Based on the example of Um Waraqah, eminent scholars such as At-Tabari, Ibnu Hazm, Ibnu Rushd (Averroes), Ibnu 'Abidin, and many others (including modern scholar Dr. Muhyi Hilal As-Sarhan in his book *Adabul-Qadha`* [1/202]) have declared that a woman can hold public office so long as she is qualified. See: *Al-Ahkam As-Sultaniyyah* by Al-Mawardi (65); *Al-Mughni* by Ibnu Qudamah (9/39); *Bidayat-ul-Mujtahid* by Ibnu Rushd (2/429); *Al-Muhalla* by Ibnu Hazm (9/429);

Ash-Shawkani (8/508); *Al-Hashiyah* by Ibnu 'Abidin (5/354); and *Sharh Adab Al-Qadhi* by Ibnu Muzzah (3/160).

The Hadith narrated by Ibnul-Qattan in *Al-Wahm Wal-Iham* (5/685) mentions "*Imamat Um Waraqah bi-qawmiha*," which is broader than her neighborhood and implies a larger district of many people (*qawm*). Acclaimed Shafi'ite scholar An-Nawawi stated, "Abu Thawr and Al-Muzni and Ibnu Jarir [At-Tabari] permitted that a woman lead men in prayer behind her, as transmitted from them by Al-Qadhi Abut-Tayyib, and Al-'Abdari." See *Al-Majmu' Sharh Al-Muhaththab* (4/223).

Ibnu Taymiyyah declared, "Ahmad [founder of the Hanbalite school] permitted a woman to lead men in prayer, when the need arises, in cases when she is an expert on the Qur'an, when they are not, so she can lead them in *tarawih* prayers, the same way that the prophet peace be upon him assigned Um Waraqah as an Imam for her neighborhood and assigned a *mu'athin* to her." See *Al-Qawa'id An-Nuraniyyah* (1/78). Ibnu Taymiyyah clearly reiterates: "I say, for men to be led by a woman who is an expert in the Qur'an during the night prayers of Ramadhan is permissible, based on the widely known (*Al-Mashhur*) from the opinion of Ahmad." See *Naqdu Maratibil-Ijma'* (290).

Muhammad establishing meritocracy, including appointing sixteen-year-olds 'Attab and Usamah, see: Al-Bukhari (2753, 4250, 4469, 7187); Muslim (206, 2426); Ibnu Hibban (7059); Al-Jami' (1416); Ibnul-Jawzi (3/453); Ibnu Kathir (5/111); Ibnu 'Abdil-Barr (3/635); *Athar Ad-Da'wah Al-Muhammadiyyah fil-Hurriyyati wal-Musawah* by Ibnu 'Ashur (study published in 1934).

Muhammad's comment "every disease has a cure" and his concept of health barrier via 'Ali, see: Ibnul-Qaisarani's *Takhriju Zadil-Ma'ad* (4/135); Ath-Thahabi's *Thakhirat-ul-Huffath* (4/1864); Muslim (2204); Ahmad (14597); An-Nasa'i (7556); Abu Dawud (3874); *Ad-Dirayah* by Ibnu Hajar al-'Asqalani (2/242); *Al-Adabush-Shar'iyyah* by Ibnu Muflih (2/336).

Muhammad's encouragement to seek knowledge (even "travel as far as China") and encouraging women's education via Ibnu 'Umar, Ibnu 'Abbas, and Hasain ibnu 'Ali, see: Muslim (332); Abu Dawud (316); Ibnu Majah (224, 531); At-Tabarani (10439); Al-Bazzar (6746); Ibnu 'Abdil-Barr

(17); Al-Qawqji (40); Al-'Ajluni (1/154); Ibnu 'Adi (4/118); Ad-Darami (335); Al-'Asqalani (3/321); Abu Na'im (8/361); Al-'Uqaili (2/230); Abu Ya'la (320, 2837); As-Suyuti (1105, 5246); Al-Bayhaqi (1/292); Ibnul-Qaysarani (1/416); Ibnul-Jawzi (1/347); Ath-Thahabi (22, 34).

Account of Muhammad playing with his grandchildren and bringing them to the *masjid* via 'Aishah, Jabir ibn 'Abdillah, and Ibnu 'Amr, see: Al-Bukhari (5997, 5998, 7376); Muslim (2318); Ahmad (6494); At-Tirmithi (1924); Abu Dawud (4941); Al-'Asqalani (1/62); Ibnu Daqiq Al-'Id (127). Visiting Khadijah's friends and sending them food in her memory, see Al-Bukhari (3818).

Burial of Abraham and its coinciding with a solar eclipse (helps pinpoint day and time and other related events) via eyewitnesses Ibnu Labid, Ibnu Mas'ud, and Ibnu 'Umar, see: Ahmad (6868, 23629); Ibnu Khuzaimah (1393); Ibnu Sa'd (327); Al-Haithami (2/210).

Muhammad standing out of respect for Jewish funeral and instructing his followers to help carry the bier, via eyewitnesses Jabir ibnu 'Abdillah and Anas ibn Malik, see: Al-Bukhari (1311); Muslim (960); Ahmad (14427, 14591, 14812); Abu Dawud (3174); An-Nasa`i (1922, 1928, 2049); Al-'Aini (7/278); Al-Baghawi (70, 1262); At-Tabarani (6/40).

Chapter 10

'Uthman ibnu Abil-'As and Ibnu 'Abbas recalled: "I was sitting with the prophet [Muhammad] when his eyes were closed. Then he opened his eyes with a keen look in them, and he informed me that he had just received the revelation of *Innal-laha Ya`muru Bil-'Adli Wal-Ihsan* and asked me to place it in Surah An-Nahl, the ninetieth passage." For an account of revelation and the writing process, see: At-Tabarani (315, 8322); Al-Bukhari (893); Ahmad (2922, 17918, 17947); Al-Haithami (7/51); Ibnu Kathir (4/516); Abu Hatim (13456); Ibnu Sa'd (410); Ash-Shawkani (3/267); Al-Baghawi (2077, 3456).

In total, Muhammad had forty-three primary scribes, of whom 'Ali and Zaid ibn Thabit wrote the most. Muhammad's main scribes at Mecca included Ibnul-Arqam, 'Ali, Fatimah bint Al-Khattab, Khadijah, Barakah, Sa'id ibn Al-'As, Khalid ibn Sa'id, Abban ibn Sa'id, Ibnu Abi Sarh, 'Umar, 'Uthman, and Abu Bakr. Muhammad's main scribes at

Medina included Ubayy ibn Ka'b, Zaid ibn Thabit, Thabit ibn Qays, Talhah ibn 'Ubaidillah, Sharahbil ibn Hasanah, Hanthalah ibn Ar-Rabi', Ibnu Rawahah, Sa'd ibn Abi Waqqas, Hudhaifah ibn Al-Yaman, Khalid, 'Amr ibn al-'As, Ibnu 'Abbas, and Ibnu 'Umar. See At-Tabarani (4748).

Zaid ibn Thabit remarked, "While with the Messenger of God, we compiled the Qur'an from many sheets into one." See: Ahmad (5/184); Al-Hakim (2/668); Ibnu Hibban (1/320); At-Tirmithi (5/734).

Zaid said, "I was a scribe of revelation . . . writing it on palm fronds," and later, "compiling [the Qur'an] into one volume from the lower cuttings of palm fronds [al-'usb], white stone slabs [al-likhaf], cloth and raw animal skin sheets [ar-riqa'], cured leather parchments [qita'-ul-adim], camel-saddles [al-aqtab], camel rib bones [al-adhla'], and shoulder bones of sheep and camels [al-aktaf]." See: Al-Bukhari (4986, 7191); Ahmad (76); Al-Haithami (8/260); At-Tirmithi (3103); Al-Marwazi (45); An-Nasa'i (7995).

'Uthman and Ibnu 'Abbas narrated how specific passages were compiled in the Qur'an, observing that some chapters would be revealed with a large number of passages, yet at other times only individual passages would be revealed. In those cases, Muhammad would say, "Place this passage in the *surah* that has such and such passages and place it between such and such passages." See: Ahmad (399, 499); An-Nasa'i (8007); Abu Dawud (786); Ibnu Hibban (6919); At-Tirmithi (3086); Ibnul-'Arabi (2/445); Al-'Asqalani (1/44).

Apportioning the Qur'an for regular study (monthly, weekly, etc.) via eyewitnesses Ibnu 'Umar and Ibnu 'Amr, see: Ibnu Hibban (756); At-Thahabi (3/84); Al-Qastalani (4/459); Al-'Asqalani (8/668); Ahmad (6516, 6873); An-Nasa'i (8064); Ibnu Majah (1114, 1346); Ibnu 'Ashur (19/20); Ath-Tha'labi (7/132); As-Sa'di (582); Ibnu 'Atiyyah (4/209); Ar-Razi (24/457). Concept of *tartil* derives from the Qur'an 73:4 and 25:32.

Account of mother shielding her child from flames via eyewitness 'Umar, see: Al-Bukhari (5999); Muslim (2754); At-Tabarani (3/232); Ibnu Kathir (2/197); Abu Na'im (3/264).

For Divine names, see: Al-Bukhari (365, 2736, 6410, 7392,); Muslim (2677); At-Tirmithi (3506, 3507, 3508); An-Nasa'i (7659); Ibnu Majah (3127, 3128, 3860); Ahmad (7502, 10532); Ibnu Hibban (807,

808); At-Tabarani (4/235); Abu Na'im (3/144); Al-Bayhaqi (56, 57); Al-Uqaili (3/15); Ibnu 'Adi (7/468).

Account of Divine name Al-Jamil via eyewitnesses Abu Sa'id Al-Khudri, Ibnu Mas'ud, and Abu Umamah al-Bahili, see: Muslim (91, 147, 1015); Al-Haithami (5/135); Ahmad (4/133); Al-Hakim (1/26); Ibnu Hibban (5466); At-Tabarani (5/60); Ahmad (3789); At-Tirmithi (1999).

Parable of *abiri sabil* (wilderness journey) via eyewitnesses 'Ali, Ibnu 'Umar, and Ibnu 'Abbas, see: Al-Haithami (248); Ibnu Daqiq Al-'Id (126); Al-Bukhari (425, 6416); An-Nawawi (40).

Though there were over one hundred thousand witnesses to the Hajj and the Farewell sermons, vivid testimony comes via eyewitnesses 'Ali, Ibnu 'Abbas, Ibnu 'Umar, and Jabir ibnu 'Abdillah. Jabir's account is especially extensive and detailed. See: Al-Bukhari (1739, 1742, 4406, 5550, 6043, 7078, 7447); Muslim (1218, 1679, 2224); Abu Dawud (1905); An-Nasa`i (656, 4092); At-Tirmithi (3087); Al-Wadi'i (1259); Ahmad (20419); Ibnul-'Arabi (6/179); Ibnu Hibban (1457, 3944); Al-'Ayni (14/517); Al-Haithami (3/268); Ibnu Majah (2512, 3074); Ibnu Qayyimil-Jawziyyah (5/171); At-Tabarani (6/70); Al-Baghawi (7/149); Ibnu Kathir (5/173); Ibnul-Qaysarani (3/1290); Al-Busairi (1/218).

Muhammad divesting himself of all possessions, including pawning his armor to a Jewish neighbor, via several eyewitnesses, including 'Aishah, Anas ibnu Malik, Asma, and Ibnu 'Abbas. 'Aishah and Juwairiyyah testified: "He neither left behind, at the time of his death, a single dinar or dirham . . . nor any possessions." See: Al-Bukhari (2739, 4461); Al-Hakim (573, 1568); Ibnu Majah (2436, 2437, 2438, 2439).

Parable of two women (both Himyarite Jews, "Bani Israel" from Yemen) one with a cat contrasted with one (prostitute) with a dog via several eyewitnesses, including Ibnu 'Amr, Asma, and Ibnu 'Abbas, see: Al-Bukhari (127, 538, 3318, 3321); Muslim (2245, 2619); Ibnu Majah (4256); Ibnu Hibban (7489); Al-Bazzar (15/257). Qur'an 26:89 refers to *Al-Qalb-us-Salim.*

Account of final month of Muhammad's life, see: As-Suhaili (4/380–437); Al-Bukhari (4435); Muslim (2444); Ibnu Majah (1620); Ahmad (26346); An-Nasa`i (7103); Ibnu Hibban (6617).

Epilogue

Account of events from Muhammad's death till the Abbasid period, see: Al-Bukhari (1242, 2704, 3670, 3700, 7207, 7217, 7219, 4454); Muslim (1759); As-Suhaili (4/438–61); Ibnu 'Asakir (67/98); Al-Bazzar (1/98, 193); Ibnu Hibban (6607, 6919); Ibnu Kathir (7/60–194); At-Tabarani (1628); *Tarikh-ul-Khulafa* by As-Suyuti (6–422).

INDEX

✧

.